Constructs of
Sociality and Individuality

Constructs of
Sociality and Individuality

Edited by

P. Stringer

Department of Psychology
University of Surrey
Guildford   Surrey
England

D. Bannister

High Royds Hospital
Menston   Ilkley
West Yorkshire
England

1979

ACADEMIC PRESS

London ● New York ● Toronto ● Sydney ● San Francisco

A Subsidiary of Harcourt Brace Jovanovich, Publishers

ACADEMIC PRESS INC. (LONDON) LTD.
24/28 Oval Road
London NW1

United States Edition published by
ACADEMIC PRESS INC.
111 Fifth Avenue
New York, New York 10003

British Library Cataloguing in Publication Data

Constructs of Sociality and Individuality
   1. Social psychology
   2. Personality
   I. Stringer, P. II. Bannister, Donald
   301.1   HM291   79–40872

   ISBN 0–12–673750–9

Typeset by Bishopsgate Press Ltd., London
Printed by Whitstable Litho Ltd, Whitstable, Kent.

Contributors

J. ADAMS-WEBBER, *Department of Psychology, Brock University, St Catherine's, Ontario L2S 3A1, Canada*

D. BANNISTER, *Department of Psychology, High Royds Hospital, Menston, Near Ilkley, West Yorkshire, LS29 6AQ, England*

HAN BONARIUS, *University of Utrecht, The Netherlands*

STEVE DUCK, *Department of Psychology, University of Lancaster, Fylde College, Bailrigg, Lancaster LA1 4YF, England*

FRED A. ELAND, *University of Utrecht, The Netherlands*

FRANZ R. EPTING, *University of Florida, Gainesville, USA*

C. P. HARGREAVES, *QSS Department, Rutherford College, University of Kent, Canterbury, Kent, England*

SHEILA HARRI-AUGSTEIN, *Centre for the Study of Human Learning, Wargrave Road, Henley on Thames, Oxfordshire, England*

†GEORGE A. KELLY

A. W. LANDFIELD, *Department of Psychology, 209 Burnett Hall, University of Nebraska, Lincoln, Nebraska 68588, USA*

MILLER MAIR, *Department of Psychological Science Services and Research, Crichton Royal Hospital, Dumfries, Scotland*

JAMES C. MANCUSO, *Department of Psychology, State University of New York at Albany, 1400 Washington Avenue, Albany, New York 12222, USA*

MILDRED McCOY, *Department of Psychology, University of Hong Kong, Hong Kong*

PETER DU PREEZ, *Department of Psychology, University of Cape Town, Rondebosch, South Africa 7700*

ALAN RADLEY, *Department of Social Sciences, Loughborough University of Technology, Loughborough, Leicestershire, England*

FRASER REID, *School of Behavioural and Social Science, Plymouth Polytechnic, Drake Circus, Plymouth, England*

A. J. ROSIE, *9 Swanley Road, Welling, Kent, England*

PHIL SALMON, *Institute of Education, University of London, England*

†Deceased.

PETER STRINGER, *Department of Psychology, University of Surrey, Guildford, Surrey, England*

LAURIE F. THOMAS, *Department of Psychology, Brunel University, Uxbridge, Middlesex, England*

Acknowledgements

The editors are grateful to Mrs Gladys Kelly for agreeing to the publication of the essay "Social Inheritance" by the late George Kelly.

The editors and the publisher also wish to thank the following for their kind permission to reproduce material from other volumes:

W. W. Norton & Co., for quotations from "The Psychology of Personal Constructs" by George A. Kelly; Avon Books for a quotation from "Jonathan Livingston Seagull" by Richard Bach; The Bodley Head and William Morrow for a quotation from "Zen and the Art of Motorcycle Maintenance" by R. Pirsig.

Contents

x *Contents*

Part II Method

**SELF-ORGANISED LEARNING AND THE RELATIVITY
OF KNOWING: TOWARDS A CONVERSATIONAL
METHODOLOGY**

Part III Substantive Contributions

Introduction

P. Stringer and D. Bannister

The origin of this volume lies in the Second International Congress on Personal Construct Theory held in Oxford in July, 1977. When the congress programme emerged it appeared to a number of us to represent several new directions in personal construct psychology (Kelly, 1955). One of the clearest was an explicit attention, in at least one-third of the papers presented, to concepts which have customarily been categorised as "social psychological". There were contributions, for example, on identity development, attraction, person perception, interpersonal prediction, social skills, social relationships, and social rules and norms, as well as on the other related topics which may be found in these pages. Several of these papers have been published in Fransella (1978).

To have made this observation says something equally about our perceptions of social psychology and of personal construct psychology. It presupposes a demarcation of social psychology as a subdivision of psychology, made up of familiar textbook topics. It assumes that a majority of the personal construct work prior to 1977 was not primarily concerned with anything that might be identifiable as social psychology. The observation would have been greeted with mixed feelings by George Kelly. He did not find it necessary or useful to divide up his psychology into clinical, cognitive, developmental, social psychologies. But if personal construct psychology had *had* to be identified with any of these subdivisions, social psychology could well have made the strongest claim.

Historically the association of personal construct theory with clinical psychology has been undeniable. Kelly himself and many of his students were clinical psychologists. The two first monographs to be based essentially on the theory (Landfield, 1971; Fransella, 1972) were on clinical topics. Introductory texts on the theory and on repertory grid technique were by authors working in clinical settings (Bannister and Mair, 1968; Bannister and Fransella, 1971; Fransella and Bannister, 1977; Ryle, 1975). Published papers reporting work which used the rep grid can be found with twice the frequency in the fields of psychopathology and psychotherapy as in all other substantive fields together (Fransella and Bannister, 1977; Slater, 1976). Significantly, there were few indications that clinical questions were being viewed in terms that would have seemed familiar to social psychologists. Although personal construct theory is an entirely suitable framework for the interpenetration of social and clinical concepts, it has only been achieved in limited ways — for example, through a common reference to person perception and implicit personality theories.

A good deal of clinical psychology, whether in its more medical or humanistic guises, is undoubtedly open to a charge of individualism. The charge has stuck on to personal construct psychology; and has been used to deny its relevance as a way of examining social psychological phenomena. It is aggravated by misconceptions about the meaning of "personal" and the peculiar contribution of repertory grid technique (cf. Stringer, this volume). Both have been interpreted in terms of a phenomenological stance, the justification of which is thought to lie in its attention to what is unique to the individual. But for Kelly, the person, which is all that his psychology deals with, was only constituted in relations with others; constructs were chiefly available through interaction with others and obtained their meaning in the context of that interaction as well as through their more general and socially determined presuppositions.

Despite the way in which the repertory grid technique has often been used, construct elicitation is not intended, in terms of the theory of personal constructs, simply as a means of access to what is private and unique to the individual. Nor should it be thought of as merely tapping into the templates or verbal labels that an individual uses. Language and construing are not separable. Construct elicitation is an act of communication which is made possible by its basis in a shared social reality. The sense which can be given to forms of construing (and these may equally be non-verbal as verbal) rests partly on general presuppositions which are understood by the communicating parties and partly on the meaning which is created within the particular relational context of the communication. Construing and listening to construing is a social psychological act both through its necessary reliance on widely shared understandings and through its power to modify relations. If users of the repertory grid have sometimes treated the interpretation of constructs as problematic ("what do his constructs really mean?"), it has been because they have failed to appreciate these points. One of the most important lessons of personal construct theory is that the relation between "psychologist" and "subject" is an essential part of what is achieved by psychological inquiry. To interpret the subject's constructs is in part to interpret that relation; to interpret the relation is to understand the constructs.

A key assumption held by Kelly was that man is forward-looking and proceeds in an anticipatory mode. Conversation (of which construct elicitation is a highly formalised example) can be considered as anticipatory talking and listening. An individual's contribution to the conversation is both in anticipation of the other's reaction to what has been said and in anticipation of what will thereby be revealed of the other's construct system. If each is mutually construing the other's construct system (Kelly's definition of social psychological process) the two forms of anticipation are interdependent. The succession of anticipations carries forward the evolving relation.

There has been a tendency to view personal construct psychology, if dealing with relations at all, as relevant only to dyadic interactions. The attention given to the therapist–client relation is partly responsible. In addition, the repertory grid has often been taken as providing information about a set of dyadic relations, viewed asymmetrically, between the person completing the grid and significant others. Although group processes have rarely been examined through personal constructs, there is in principle no reason why they should not be. Many groups could be considered as a semi-connected lattice of relations, constituted through the procedure outlined above (see Fransella and Joyston-Bechal, 1971). A collective or group construct system could be construed by an individual or a group in a manner analogous to the construing of one person by another. Equally, the process of construing would constitute the individual–group or inter-group relation.

Alongside language and discourse, and group processes, as perhaps the most pressing agenda items for a socially-oriented personal construct psychology lie a range of developmental questions. The way in which construct systems emerge, particularly in the very young, has scarcely been examined. One would be looking for an explanation of how the infant becomes a "person" and how self-hood is acquired (see Bannister and Agnew, 1977). It follows from our previous remarks that this would involve the examination of mutual construing, both verbal and non-verbal, within those relations which are available to the infant.

It has been suggested (Bannister and Fransella, 1971) that the integration of social psychology with other more individual areas of psychology might be achieved by thinking through the implications within personal construct theory of the concept "role". Kelly had this to say about role (quoted in Bannister and Fransella, 1971, pp. 49–50):

> Role can be understood in terms of what the person *himself* is doing rather than in terms of his circumstances. There are two traditional notions of role, one the very old notion that role is a course of action which is articulated with the actions of others, so that together you and the other person can produce something. The more recent notion proposed by sociologists and other theorists is that a role is a set of expectations held by others within which a man finds himself encompassed

and surrounded. Personal construct theory tries to put role within the context of something a person himself is doing and it springs from a notion that one may attempt to understand others in terms of their outlooks just as a personal construct theory psychologist tries to understand human beings in terms of their outlooks.

So anyone who attempts to understand others in terms of the outlooks they have, rather than their behaviours only, may indeed play a role. This isn't to say that he tries to conform to their outlooks, he may even try to stand them on their heads, but if he tries to understand others by putting on their spectacles and then does something, then that which he does could be considered as a role. So we have three notions of role here. The oldest notion, the notion of a course of activity articulated with the action of others, I suppose that notion could be tied up with the notion of man as the economic entity, "the economic man". The more recent notion of man surrounded by a set of expectations, I suppose you can say would be a notion that would undergird the society which had seen itself composed of "ideological men" conforming to ideas, ideologies. But if we follow the notion of role that comes out of construct theory, I wonder if we might not develop the notion of man as a society composed of "empathic man" or "inquiring man". Men who seem to understand and do it by active inquiry, using their own behaviour not as something to act out, but as a means of understanding their world.

Although this volume originated from the 1977 Oxford Congress, only five of the present contributions correspond at all directly to papers presented on that occasion and these have been re-written and expanded. The remainder are original material written especially for "Constructs of Sociality and Individuality".

The one exception is George Kelly's "Social Inheritance", written in about 1930. It has almost become the custom to include an unpublished essay by Kelly in edited volumes on personal construct theory (cf. Bannister, 1970, 1977; Fransella, 1978). "Social Inheritance" is included here for its appositeness rather than in obedience to custom.

The plan of the volume covers three main streams of Kellyan work, these being broadly meta-theoretical and theoretical argument, methodological considerations and substantive research. Within personal construct psychology such a division should be no more than a too convenient fiction. That we have used it reflects the dominance of habits of thought familiar in much of psychology generally. Fortunately, a number of the present authors roundly defeated any attempt to confine their thoughts within these neat bounds; but we keep to the scheme in the hope that readers will feel encouraged personally to re-structure the pattern of contributions, to suit their own requirements.

In the first of these three main sections, there is a movement from the personal to a more apparently detached view of social psychological significances in personal construct theory. The last chapter serves as a link to the second, methodological section in which the progression runs from a synoptic review to an account of a specific investigation. The final section of substantive material falls roughly into three subsections. Firstly there are two chapters which take a broad look at certain substantive aspects of personal constructs in a social context. They are followed by rather more specific reviews and analyses of work on social competence, reprimand and rule-violation and social relationships, from the viewpoint of personal construct theory. Finally, three particular studies are described, ending as we began, with political subject-matter.

References

Bannister, D. (Ed.) (1970). "Perspectives in Personal Construct Theory". Academic Press, London and New York.

Bannister, D. (Ed.) (1977a). "New Perspectives in Personal Construct Theory". Academic Press, London and New York.

Bannister, D. and Agnew, J. (1977). The child's construing of self. *In* "1976 Nebraska Symposium on Motivation" (Ed. A. W. Landfield). University of Nebraska Press, Nebraska.

Bannister, D. and Fransella, F. (1971). "Inquiring Man". Penquin, Harmondsworth.

Bannister, D. and Mair, J.M.M. (1968). "The Evaluation of Personal Constructs". Academic Press, London and New York.

Fransella, F. (1972). "Personal Change and Reconstruction". Academic Press, London and New York.

Fransella, F. (Ed.) (1978). "Personal Construct Psychology 1977". Academic Press, London and New York.

Fransella, F. and Bannister, D. (1977). "A Manual for Repertory Grid Technique". Academic Press, London and New York.

Fransella, F. and Joyston-Bechal, M.P. (1971). An investigation of conceptual process and pattern change in a psychotherapy group. *Br. J. Psychiat.* **119,** 199–206.

Kelly, G.A. (1955). "The Psychology of Personal Constructs", Vols I and II. Norton, New York.

Landfield, A.W. (1971). "Personal Construct Systems in Psychotherapy". Rand McNally, New York.

Ryle, A. (1975). "Frames and Cages". Sussex University Press, Brighton.

Slater, P. (Ed.) (1976). "Explorations of Intrapersonal Space". Wiley, London.

Foreword to "Social Inheritance"

D. Bannister

George Alexander Kelly was born on a farm near Perth, Kansas, on 28 April 1905. His education was a kind of mid-western jigsaw which as time went on was increasingly put together by Kelly himself. When he was four years old his father moved the family to Eastern Colorado to stake out a claim to some of the last free land offered to settlers in the West. There Kelly attended elementary school on the few occasions when his parents could spend a few weeks in town and for the rest, he studied at home under the tutorship of his father, a former Presbyterian minister. When the westward venture failed and the family moved back to Kansas he lived away from home in Wichita, attending four different high schools. At eighteen he went to university and took a degree in physics and mathematics intending to become a mechanical engineer. But a concern with social issues (partly aroused in intercollegiate debates) spurred him to enrol at the University of Kansas to study educational sociology. His masters thesis was a study of Kansas city workers' distribution of leisure time activities. He then taught for a while—speech, an Americanisation class for prospective citizens and sociology. After a sudden reversion to work as an aeronautical engineer back in Wichita, he went to Edinburgh on an exchange scholarship. There he received a Bachelor of Education degree in 1930, studying under Sir Godfrey Thompson and completed a thesis dealing with the prediction of teaching success. Back in America he finally entered psychology by completing a Ph.D. on stuttering at the State University of Iowa.

Some years after Kelly's death an American psychologist, William Perry, devoted part of a year of world travel to a visit to Scotland to try and locate Kelly's Edinburgh thesis. He never found the thesis but by dint of archeological shrewdness, perseverance and good fortune he found, beneath the dust piles of an Edinburgh library cellar, a paper by George Kelly clipped to a letter to Sir Godfrey Thompson asking him to draw the attention of Cyril Burt to the work. It is this paper, "Social Inheritance", which we publish here.

In his obituary a colleague depicted the course of George Kelly's life in terms of the metaphor of "pioneer" (Thompson, 1968). He wrote:

> For example, he is among the first to found a psychological clinic for service and training when the majority of American psychologists saw little future in this direction. He was a leader among that small group of psychologists who effectively demonstrated during World War II that clinical psychology could make a unique contribution to the maximum utilisation of human resources. He had the courage to propose a theoretical alternative to positivism and logical empiricism when the latter were clearly favoured by the majority of American psychologists. These and many other pioneering advances were usually initiated and carried forward with a minimum of physical resources. Like any successful pioneer he "made do" with whatever was available. He built his equipment with materials at hand; he often salvaged talented students from other collegiate programmes in which they had lost their way; he "constructed" his own theory of human behaviour in order to rationalise and systematise his views of a man's creative efforts to understand himself and his relationships with others.

This raises the question of whether this long lost and now rescued paper throws any light on Kelly the pioneer, whether it has value in presaging George Kelly's later invention of personal construct theory or whether it is merely a matter of biographical curiosity—a sample of Kelly the young man.

Certainly in its style the paper is unmistakably George Kelly. It exemplifies that relaxed irreverence which marked much of Kelly's writing. Consider the statement

> a cultured man was one whose mental faculties were scrubbed and burnished until they reflected without the distortion of originality all the abstractions of the day. A man so reflected is still considered by some to be a cultured man.

Equally it shows that long before the publication of construct theory Kelly knew well that he, like the rest of us, was in the interpretation business and he vigorously rejected the notion that we are truly designating "realities". Fifty years after Kelly wrote this paper we are still trammelled in the nonsense of the nature-nurture controversy, still turning our concepts into "variables", still capable of conducting solemn arguments about what percentage of "intelligence" is to be attributed to heredity and what to environment, still wandering in a ghostly land where, having operationally defined a concept as vague and politically loaded as "intelligence", we worship our operational definition. Kelly in 1930 could cheerfully and cogently dismiss the whole nonsense:

> although we may ardently attempt to prove the supremacy of nature over nurture, or vice versa, little graphite is wasted computing the relative importance of food and cook and few rural debating societies spend a Friday night haggling over the relative value of seed and soil. When it comes to the more practical situations we find that nature seems to demand constant nutrition and nurture is part of the natural order.

But perhaps the most significant aspect of this early essay is the argument running through it that education should be about personal meaning and that it is through the personal meaning which we give to our education and the personal way in which we live it out that we give back to our society that which we have created. Twenty-five years later George Kelly was to extend this argument far beyond education and to show how we could see life as a matter of personal meaning drawing from and giving to social meaning. It is an intriguing part of the cyclic quality of written "conversation" that Phillida Salmon and Anthony Rosie in their essays in this volume, have re-drawn from the later Kelly the theme which he ventured as a young man.

Reference

Thompson G. G. (1968). George Alexander Kelly (1905–1967). *J. Gen. Psychol.* **79,** 19–24.

Social Inheritance

George Kelly

The term, "Social Inheritance", is a new coinage in man's system of thought exchange. It is so-called because it is to be compared and contrasted with biological inheritance. Yet there have been many terms used which imply the same meaning. Herbert Spencer called it "the superorganic" inheritance; that inheritance which is dependent upon the existence of the organic, and yet, which is not transmitted organically. C. H. Judd calls it " . . . the accumulation of social capital or culture complexes . . . that not inherited by wild animals or plant life". "Culture" is a term which in its true meaning is synonymous with "Social Inheritance". The trouble with using "culture" is the fact that the term has a false connotation. Culture originally meant cultivatedness. A cultured man was one whose mental faculties were scrubbed and burnished until they reflected without the distortion of originality all the abstractions of the day. A man so afflicted is still considered by some to be a cultured man.

Then there is the rather popular idea that our social inheritance includes only the aristocracy of learning, that it is a sort of title conferred upon that knowledge of ancient and noble lineage. A mathematics professor once told us that he hoped none of us would ever find his course useful. He was decidedly successful in persuading me that I had no use for the stuff from then on. He had given his particular branch of study a crest and a coat-of-arms and had attempted to withdraw it from productive toil.

The Germans had a term, "kultur" which had a slightly different meaning. To them it meant the German mode of life, the sum-total of things German. With the exception of the provincialism which they read into the term, their conception was very close to the real meaning.

Human institutions, language, tools, methods, governments, schools, manners of living, are the elements which make up our social inheritance. All our folkways, mores, and fads are to be included in this classification. Without excluding any development of the human mind which is transmissable, culture becomes the sum and total of things human. This interpre-

4

tation of culture avoids the controversy as to which parts of our social inheritance merit the term "culture", and which do not. Here, knowledge of the steam engine becomes just as truly a part as are the meditations of Marcus Aurelius, and every bit as complex. Which of the two is the more valuable, is another question upon which we hope to throw some light later on. The important thing at this point is to recognise that both are contained in society's inheritance.

To Auguste Comte should be given credit for the first use of the term "Sociology" which is now become generally recognised as the study of the phenomena of social inheritance. In his "Positive Philosophy" published in 1839 the term first appears. The study represents the newest off-shoot from that study of the unknown and irrelevant which we call, "philosophy".

There are at least two problems in education, rather distinct problems, to which a study of the social inheritance is related. Educators want to know, in the first place, how much school achievement can ever be expected from a child who makes a certain score on an intelligence test. Can anything be done to increase that child's educability? Can the test score be raised? Will an alteration in the environment of early childhood help any? Are the differences in ability as we find them in our schools attributable to variations in the home environment or to variations in the biological heredity? These belong to the first type of questions which educators want answered.

The second problem is one of determining what the curriculum should contain. To be sure, the choice is not as great for the dull pupils as for the brighter ones, and, to that extent, the two problems over-lap. But the curricular content is not automatically determined, even by an IQ as low as 70. Dr Ogburn of Chicago University once told us that "It is at the activities required by culture and the activities occasioned by the original nature of man where the planes of the super-organic and the organic meet". Thus, to the educator, the problems present themselves in such a fashion as this: Should little Nancy Dugan from down on the High Street "whose father's a drunkard, whose mother is dead" be conscripted for service in Caesar's Gaelic Wars, armed only with a modest IQ to help her in the fray? Will her industry compensate for her lack of mental alertness? That is the first type of problem. Then, supposing she should enlist with Caesar and emerge with the flag of victory clutched in her eager fingers; what of it? Now, what is the value of that classic barbecue in her social sphere? Of course, little Nancy likes it. Her cheeks will glow with true Scottish pride when the eyes of her friends come to rest on the "D.P." now framed and hung above the kitchen grate. I'm assuming that "D.P." stands for "Discharge Papers" or whatever Caesar was in the habit of awarding his faithful legionnaires. Yes, and in his sober moments, even Old Man Dugan himself will be proud of Nancy's achievement. Well, to be sure, this is all hypothetical, because, as things are,

Nancy would have been tried in an Advanced Division and condemned to a technical school. There would be no Roman coat-of-arms above the Dugan's kitchen grate and on Saturday nights Old Dugan would still have difficulty in making the three flights of stairs under his own power. There seems magic in the fact that *"Omnia Gallia in partes tres divisit"* and the second problem for the educator is to discover the true secret of that magic.

Is Environment Principally Responsible for Variation in School Achievement?

The nature versus nurture problem is not so much a question of which is the more potent as one of discovering the spheres of influence which these two factors dominate. Although we may ardently attempt to prove the supremacy of nature over nurture, or vice versa, little graphite is wasted computing the relative importance of food and cook and few rural debating societies spend a Friday night haggling over the relative value of seed and soil. When it comes to the more practical situations we find that nature seems to demand constant nutrition and nurture is a part of the natural order.

It will do no harm at this point to refresh our minds on the classic arguments on this question. The following account is given by Starch in his "Educational Psychology", p. 77.

Similarities of Abilities Among Related Defective and Low Grade Persons

Quite a number of studies have been made in recent years concerning the frequency with which defective persons are either distantly or closely related. One of the first studies was that of the Jukes reported by R. G. Dugdale in 1877. Max Juke, born in 1720 was a shiftless truant, who married an equally worthless woman. Up to 1877 there had been five generations with approximately 1,200 descendants among whom have been traced the following types of persons: 310 paupers, 7 murderers, 60 habitual thieves, 50 prostitutes, 130 convicted of crime, 300 died in infancy, 440 physical wrecks from debauchery, only 20 learned a trade, and 10 of these learned it in prison. The estimated cost to the State of New York has been put at approximately $1,000 a person. In contrast with this lineage, a comparison has been suggested with the Jonathan Edwards family, which had approximately 1,400 descendants in the same period of time. Among them there have been 120 graduates of Yale alone, 14 college presidents, over 100 professors, 135 books of merit have been written by various members of the family, and 118 journals have been edited by them. Aaron Burr was the only black sheep among them and he can certainly not be classed as an intellectually defective person. (Winship '00).

Poellman of Bon (Guyer '16, p. 271) made a study of a family called the Zeros in which 800 descendants were traced through six generations back to a female drunkard. Among them were found 102 professional beggars, 107 illegitimate offspring, 181 prostitutes, 54 inmates of almshouses, 76 convicted of crime, and 7 murderers. The cost to the state was placed at $1,206,000.

More recently a very interesting study was conducted by Dr Goddard of the Training School of Vineland, New Jersey. Dr Goddard ('12) traced the ancestry of a young girl who had been brought to his institution. It was found that the lineage went back to a man, Martin Kallikak, a soldier in the Revolutionary War, who was the progenitor of two lines of descendants. (See Figure 31). He had an illegitimate son whose mother was feeble-minded. This was the establishment of a line - - A - - which had, down to the time of the study, 480 direct descendants among whom were found the following: 143 feeble-minded, 292 unknown, 36 illegitimates, 33 prostitutes, 24 alcoholics, 3 epileptics, 82 died in infancy, 3 criminals, 8 keepers of disreputable houses, and only 46 normal individuals. Apparently human nature does not gather grapes of thorns or figs or thistles. After his return from the war, Martin married a woman of normal intelligence and from this lineage - - B - - there had come during the same period of time 496 direct descendants, of whom all were normal individuals with the exception of five, one of whom was reported as mentally defective, two as alcoholics, one as sexually immoral, and one as a case of religious mania. There were no epileptics or criminals and only 15 died in infancy. The remainder were good citizens, including doctors, lawyers, educators, judges, and business men.

One thing seems to stand out very conspicuously from the numerous facts of family histories that have been unravelled in recent years, namely that much defective mentality, degeneracy, and crime is a matter of ancestry. General opinion among persons in charge of institutions for defectives is that two-thirds of all cases are due to heredity and one-third to environmental or unknown causes.

No one can listen to these accounts without being profoundly impressed with the potency of inheritance and yet it is only fair to point out that there was both biological and social inheritance operative. The hotel in which Martin Kallikak met the feeble-minded mother of the line A, was not a comparable environment to that established by Martin for the children of his line, B.

To continue with Starch's argument:

Pearson has shown that the resemblance in physical characteristics among brothers and sisters is approximately 0·50. He gives the following coefficients of correlation for various physical traits.

	Brother and Sister
Hair Colour	0·55
Cephalic index	0·49
Height	0·50
Eye Colour	0·52

Starch continues by showing similar correlations between mental abilities of brothers and sisters, from a study which he made himself:

Reading—speed		0·51
Reading—comprehension		0·64
Writing—speed		0·72
Writing—quality		0·46
Size of reading vocabulary		0·07
Spelling		0·05
Arithmetical reasoning		0·38
Addition—attempts		0·71
Addition—rights		0·44
Subtraction—attempts		0·43
Subtraction—rights		0·29
Multiplication—attempts		0·37
Multiplication—rights		0·25
Division—attempts		0·46
Division—rights		0·56
	Average	0·42

Memory		0·31
A-test		0·50
Geometrical form test		0·07
Tapping		0·65
	Average	0·38

Starch concludes from this, first, that "the resemblance of siblings is apparently no greater in those mental traits which are directly affected by school work than in those which are not so affected". And secondly, "the resemblance of siblings is approximately as great as in mental traits as in physical traits".

Odin, in his study of 5,233 noted French men of letters living during the period 1400 to 1830 inferred that if France as a whole had been as fertile as Paris in the production of genius there would approximately be 54,000 great men of letters instead of less than 6,000. But here again the complimentary aspect of biological and social heredity was not sufficiently taken into account to make the results conclusive.

At this point a few moments might well be taken to repeat Professor Thomson's citation of Miss Burk's paper on the variability of intelligence.

The general plan of inquiry was to correlate (1) true children with their true parents, and (2) foster-children with their foster-parents. Clearly if heredity is the main factor the former correlations should be high and the latter zero, whereas if environment is the main factor the correlations should be equal in the two cases. Both the true parents of the control group were white, non-Jewish, American, British, or North European born, and so also were the true parents of the foster-children, as far as this could be traced or inferred. The children were all legally adopted, and not merely in a less responsible relationship to the foster-parents. Great care was taken in equating the control-group and the foster-group in every relevant point that could be conceived of. The Stanford-Binet test was used in obtaining the mental ages of both the parents and the children, and various other measures and observations were recorded, including an assessment of the home conditions by means of the Whittier Scale, and of cultural conditions of the home, separately, by means of a special scale devised for the purpose, based on such matters as the speech of the parents, their education, the size of the home library, the artistic taste apparent in the home, and the like. Probably the following table best sums up the quantitive side of the work:

Correlations of Child's IQ with	Foster-Group		Control-Group	
	r	*N*	*r*	*N*
Father's M.A.	0·09	178	0·55	100
Mother's M.A.	0·23	204	0·57	105
Father's vocabulary	0·14	181	0·52	101
Mother's vocabulary	0·25	202	0·48	104
Whittier index	0·24	206	0·49	104
Culture index	0·29	186	0·49	101
Income	0·26	181	0·26	99

Heredity is shown to account for differences of as much as five times those accounted for by environment.

I cannot help but quote Starch's general conclusion at this point:

Nature predominates enormously over nurture only in the relative and not in the absolute sense. This distinction must always be borne in mind in studies of heredity. In fact, in the absolute sense, nurture predominates enormously over nature.

I don't think Starch himself quite understands what he has said but he apparently has realised in attempting to sum up his argument that there are two spheres which nature and nurture dominate respectively. Obviously, when one variable does not vary, it can scarcely be said to be the cause of variation in another: however, the non-varying factor may be a potential cause in that it may be necessary to the existence of the other. Starch's statement is at least a partial recognition of the fact that for a given culture level, nature is more significant, but for a given biological level, culture is more significant. In other words, when we limit our study to Edinburgh school children in the year 1930, we have chosen a very narrow range on the scale of culture, but the scale of biological inheritance has scarcely been shortened. Again, if we limit our study to, say, the great navigators of history, we shall find that their social inheritance has made all the difference in the world in determining their achievement, while we have good reason to believe that the quality of their biological inheritances remained approximately constant. Why, Angus McIntosh, with an IQ of 88 is obviously better off than Yon Yat Sun, whose father is a tribal leader on the northern slopes of the Himalayas. Angus, who has no hopes of entering the Royal High School, can do problems in mathematics that would have stumped Pythagorus and can solve domestic problems that would have driven Solomon into the regions beyond Jordan. What is the difference? There is little reason for believing that the biological inheritance has so favoured Angus. The reverse is more likely true. Yet Solomon was a king and Angus will be a plumber—the educators have told him so. Evidently, one's station in society is finally determined somewhat by the relative amount of culture at his command. This relative amount of culture wielded by an individual in a particular society seems to be a function of his intelligence.

From the data now available we are led to the tentative conclusion that the variation in school achievement as the educator finds it in his classroom is due principally to variation in the biological heredity of the pupils. But the educator wants to know more nearly the exact relative weights of heredity and environment. Although several authors have attempted to assign exact percentages to these weights, obviously, it is impossible to do so with any great degree of certainty, at least at the present time. The educator wants a working hypothesis, however, and in giving him that hypothesis it is better to make the errors come out on the conservative side. What is the conservative side? The teacher who has had considerable class-room experience will tell you that there are few things as exasperating as a dull pupil. "Try as I will", says Miss Tress at the Friday night teachers' whist drive, "I simply can't get Nancy to see the difference between a gerund and a gerundive". Now tell Miss Tress that Nancy's failure to register impressions is not due to any fault of her teacher but to an unfortunate array of genes. There will be a sigh of relief: but will you not have furnished that school mistress with a too convenient alibi? If environment is to be conceived as playing a minor role, why be so concerned about home conditions, kindergarten, and playgrounds? Although over-emphasis upon the potency of environment may lead educators to attempt the impossible, over-emphasis upon the potency of heredity may turn the school into a mere sorting machine. From the standpoint of the pupil the conservative estimate should favour the environment.

What Should the Curriculum Contain?

This is the second problem in education upon which a discussion of the social inheritance has a direct bearing.

The social inheritance is composed of innumerable elements which have been accruing since the day the grandson of the pithecanthropus taught his offspring that women could be temporarily brought to submission by means of a stick grasped near one end. The development of a method of making fire and the transmission of that institution from one generation to the next is an interesting illustration. Just how fire was first discovered, no one knows, nor is it known how the first firemakers plied their craft. We do know, however, that in some tribes a priesthood was established for the firemakers, so revered were they. Yet who of us, by rubbing sticks together as did those aboriginal clerics, can produce fire? In fact, the very skill of stoking a fire seems to have been lost to some of us. The point to be inferred is that not all our social inheritance need be transmitted to every member of society. Even those elements which are most important historically need not necessarily be included in the accoutrement of a classically educated man. If the end of education is to pass on selected elements of the social inheritance, then evidently, the selection is not entirely upon the basis of historical significance.

Again, there is the persistent belief that certain of the culture elements when studied are effective as mental discipline. In the light of recent investigation this contention becomes doubtful.

Then there is the argument that certain culture traits are to be selected because few people have the imagination, the muscular skill, or the sensory equipment to acquire them. Not so many years ago while I was sitting in a Philosophy of Education class, it occurred to me that few people could wiggle their ears. I also observed that there were occasions when the possessor of that highly specialised skill attained a certain degree of social recognition. Whereupon, I set apart that hour of the day for practice. Fortunately, the examination included no questions on ear-wiggling, else my grade might have been even more hazardous than it was.

Should selection be based upon the difficulty of mastery? Yes, say some. But then why do we study Latin instead of Chinese? Evidently difficulty is not the final criterion.

Then, there is the argument that certain elements are to be selected because of their broad applicability. An artist implants form and colour onto a strip of coarse cloth. We gaze at the dried paint and experience a new pattern of feelings. A musician touches our ears and fancy is set swinging across the whole range of human experience. A poet with the home-made tool of language carves the most delicate details of thought. A philosopher, a mathematician, a scientist, touches the length and breadth of human experiences, but with a sweeping gesture that takes little notice of the third dimension in which the different strata of society lie. It would be interesting to compute, if possible, the effect the steam engine has produced upon thought. Then it would be interesting to trace its development. What we would find would be that the steam engine, although important, is not a single invention but an accumulation of social capital to which three rather obscure men, working independently, in three different countries, added its final increment. For centuries men had wanted to fly. Great minds which were in possession of this broadly applicable culture had attacked the problem. Suddenly, two small-town bicycle mechanics with grease on their hands and dirty handkerchiefs in their pockets added the last increment to the accumulation of social capital. But they were none too quick, for simultaneously, others were doing the same thing. A knowledge of the details of bicycle making, as well as of a few of the general principles of aerodynamics was essential to the final production of the airplane. The point to be gotten is that progress demands the transmission of both broad and narrow principles. And on what basis should the selection be made? On the basis of applicability, not necessarily broad applicability, but on the basis of applicability to the creation of new culture elements! There are many unfinished accumulations of social capital needing only a few more small increments for completion. There are many half-finished accumulations and others scarcely started upon which each generation will cast its offering. Now, who is a cultured man? Not necessarily the one who has sopped up the most of his social inheritance, but the one who has partaken liberally of what he needs and sparingly of what he does not need in order to make his contribution.

I trust this hasty treatment of the criteria upon which culture elements are to be selected for transmission has not caused us to lose sight of Nancy, or of Angus McIntosh. It has a very direct relation to them, for it is very important that Nancy and Angus produce. You may say that what they produce is not of lasting value; can scarcely be dignified by the name of culture. Yet their very continuance in housework and plumbing under changing conditions compels them to make, along with others, new adjustments, new institutions, new culture. But we shall come back to this argument later.

How is culture formed? What are the related variables? Several theories have been suggested. There is the theory that civilisations go through a sort of cycle of definite changes. This is called the Successive Stages Theory. Then, there is the argument that biological factors are the causes of social change. Mutation, mixture, and selection, according to this argument, produce biological changes which, in turn, cause social change. It has often been suggested that changes in environment, such as climate, have produced physiological improvement. More recently it has been suggested that

Endocrinology can explain the growth of culture. Then too, there is the saying that necessity is the mother of invention.

To discuss thoroughly the possibilities of these suggested explanations would require considerable time and patience, neither of which we are fortunate enough to possess.

True, there seem to be periods of excitation and depression in the history of society. The Golden Age of Pericles was followed by a period of political chaos. Rome fell. The Dark Ages came, and so on. But at no point in history is there exact similarity with the situation in a previous age. The changes are somewhat cyclical, the path of progress would appear to follow a helix. If the Successive Stages Theory is to be interpreted as meaning that for a given stage the culture level is constant and that the social inheritance is parcelled out to us according to the stage we have reached, we must admit some truth in the theory. The difficulty, however, is that these stages have to be rather arbitrarily set off and that even within a particular stage the culture level varies steadily. Observe the rapid increase in culture during the last fifty years, especially in the newer sciences. Looking back we can observe that in a larger sense the social inheritance has been, not only increasing, but steadily accelerating. The lapses in the process have been momentary compared with the whole advance. As a final criticism it should be pointed out that the Successive Stages Theory is more a description of the rise of culture than an explanation of the related variables.

As regards mutations, mixtures and selection there is little reason to believe that they have influenced mental traits more than physiological traits. To be sure, physiological traits have been somewhat changed during the period of history. Armour used by Tenth Century warriors fits with uncomfortable snugness upon undersized men of today. But vastly more ill-fitting is the cultural accoutrement of those Tenth Century warriors. While physiological changes have been slight and uncertain, there has been nothing uncertain about the cultural changes which have taken place during the last thousand years. So we can scarcely consider these biological phenomena as causes if they have failed to influence physiological traits in any proportion to the changes undergone in the social inheritance.

Climate certainly has something to do with the way men live. Hottentots could scarcely be expected to devise the igloo nor could the Esquimaux be expected to invent the fly-swatter. On the other hand, the American Indians lived in an invigorating climate for many centuries without building a civilisation as great as that existing under this abominable Scotch mist. True, the Aztecs had a calendar that was nearly as perfect as our own, and the Incas had a system of compulsory labour for everyone under a highly organised scheme of regimentation, but we can scarcely give climate the whole credit for that.

The hormones secreted from the endocrin glands have a great deal of effect upon the emotional making-up of an individual but no one has been successful in showing a progressive change in these secretions that would sufficiently account for the social progress of the race.

"Necessity is the mother of invention", is a little metaphor which is used in the same careless way in which most metaphors are used. One can think of hundreds of instances when it was more necessitous that men should fly than that day when the Wright brothers drew lots to see which should be the first to pilot their new flying contraption. It is hard to conceive of a necessity for a motor car any greater now than a hundred years ago, unless it be the fact that our neighbour now has one makes it necessary. As far as the race is concerned, necessity seems to be pretty fairly constant. Of course, radical changes in the social adjustment such as war may direct progress into certain lines, but mostly to the exclusion of other lines, so that the rate of total production is increased comparatively little. A notable instance of the effect of necessity on invention is that of the German development of the glider. Just after the war the Germans were prohibited from constructing high-powered airplanes. Immediately, they turned to the construction of gliders, and it was not long before Germans were accomplishing feats such as staying aloft for hours in motorless planes while the inventors of other nations were scarcely getting their machines off the ground. While engineers in other countries were still installing 90 horsepower engines in two passenger training planes, German pilots were going aloft carrying four passengers behind a 35 horsepower, three cylinder engine. Gliders had taught them how to use a long slender tapering wing. But while German genius was being directed in these lines, British and American inventors were perfecting the welded steel fuselage and the radial aircooled motor. Apparently necessity steers rather than stimulates invention.

Ethnological classification of peoples is first made on the basis of language. The dividing line between the savage and the barbarian is the attainment of a written language and between the barbarian and the civilised man it is the possession of a phonetic alphabet. The tools of communication, both of language and transportation are the most accurate index of the height of culture attained by a society. The argument to be advanced at this point is that tools of communication not only help pass down the social inheritance but are essential in making acquisitions to it. If we should stop all communication today, I fancy it would have the same effect on the construction of culture as it did on the construction of the Tower of Babel. Only upon the interplay of ideas in new and changing situations can culture be built. Where there is ready and quick intercommunication which takes place as soon as ideas are crystalised, there is ready and quick selection and adoption of those ideas which are useful. Culture consists, in one sense, of adopted ideas, ideas which have been selected by a process of interplay. Once the selection is made and adopted it is retained until it is forgotten or replaced by a more desirable idea. The new idea will probably be an improvement upon the old and will include a more complex array of elements, some of which will have been carried over from before. On the other hand, if a culture trait is forgotten, that is, not transmitted to the succeeding generation, the selection must be made all over again. Thus the speed of accumulation of social capital is a function of both the culture base and the facilities for interplay. The latter, in turn is probably a function of the culture base. If this assumption is valid, then the increase of culture should follow an exponential curve and should be practically independent of individual genius. This is very nearly what we find. Genius seems to be fairly constant in society at all times and the rate of increase of culture appears to be in a state of acceleration. It has been suggested that the formula for compound interest $-- P_t = \phi_0 (1 + r)^n$ might hold. Some studies have been made along this line. An attempt was made in the University of Minnesota to follow up the inventions subsequent upon the adoption of the plow sulky. For a short period the exponential formula held true until the influence of the tractor and the re-adaptation of the disc plow either submerged or replaced the influence of the plow sulky invention. Another study in the same school was made of the adoption of the city-manager type of municipal government. The results showed an ogive curve. Adoptions of the system were infrequent at first, then gradually became more frequent only to drop off again, apparently as modifications of the mayoral system became more popular. What little study has been made on these phenomena tends to show that for a given culture trait both the improvement and scope of adoption follow the exponential curve until the influence is submerged by multiple modifications and selections.

If then we accept the contention that the function of education, in a broad sense, is to facilitate accretion of social capital both for the sake of the individual and of society, the task of the educator becomes more than just handing down the social heritage. Not only must the social heritage be passed down but the legatees must be taught how to manipulate it, how to use it, how to select from it, and how to build upon it. In short, they must be put into the great game of interplay and taught how to give, take, and select. Isolate them, and they hide their one talent till you return, while the men to whom were given five talents have with them made five more. What we arrive at is a doctrine of education closely resembling that of Dewey, but which I believe, was partially devised in America before Dewey's time.

One more point needs to be taken up before we return to Angus and Nancy. There is in America a new theory bearing on democratic education developed since Dewey wrote his "Democracy and Education". It is that a comparatively small amount of culture is actually contributed by the class of people who are termed "geniuses", the people whose name are in print. Leaders are leaders, only in the Rooseveltian sense, people who can observe which way the crowd is going and who run and get in front. Professor Walter Robinson Smith of the University of Kansas has taken the initiative in teaching this theory. His argument runs something like this: three things contribute to a great leader, a great occasion, a great personality, and a great following. The leader simply adds a large increment to an already massive structure in order to complete an invention, whether it be social or physical. The main structure is supplied by the average and mediocre people, each of whom brings his little contribution and throws it onto the pile.

Take Dewey, himself, and his doctrine of tentative ends in education and free interplay of ideas in the school-room. The American pioneer was like that, long before Dewey was born. It was the average American who discovered that he had to change his mind frequently if he was ever to build up his country. It was the average American schoolboy who would not be silenced when he wished to express his ideas in the school-room. A president of an older American university gets the credit for introducing the elective system now so widely used in America. But it was the students who had first conceived it, and not the brilliant ones at that. It was the ones of mediocre intelligence from the farms and small villages who were determined to get their money's worth from "that thar new state university place, that dad's tax money is goin' tew". Imagine young fellows like that, fellows of mediocre intelligence, to whom a lone fence on the prairie "clutters things all up", being told that what they want is an original knowledge of the Sanskrit to take back to the cows. It was useless to refuse them entrance because the university belonged to those fellows. It was through their self-sacrifice that a university was possible. Now the educational philosophers and leaders in the field are coming to the conclusion that a flexible curriculum and non-bookish education is alright.

Suppose we make the assumption that one's ability to contribute to culture varies in direct linear ratio to his intelligence. With a distribution seven sigmas in length and with 2% of the population in each of the outside compartments, 10% in each of the next, 23% in the next, and 30% in the middle compartment, let us assume that the upper 2% produce twenty-six units of culture. The number of units produced by each of the other groups runs as follows, 110 units, 221 units, 210 units, 115 units, 30 units and 2 units. The middle 76% of individuals have produced exactly 72% of the total culture. It remains to be proved by those who hold to this theory that the relationship between intelligence and the ability to produce culture is linear. It is not hard to imagine that the proof might be forthcoming.

Now, what is the magic of the fact that "Gaul, as a whole, is divided into three parts"? There are many culture-elements which Nancy can use in her selection process, but Latin is very probably not one of them. Give little Nancy the social inheritance which she needs for turning her talents into social capital. Divide it into three parts, if necessary, just like Gaul. Place psychoanalysis in her hands, if there's really anything to the stuff, and who knows but that Old Man Dugan may sober up yet. Give her home making, nursing, a practical kind of child psychology, but above all, give her a Roman coat-of-arms with all the status it implies to hang above the kitchen grate.

And as for Angus, already he knows something that most of the boys at the Royal High School have overlooked. He knows of the appalling need for bath tubs in Edinburgh. It would be worth while to spend years in putting Angus in possession of that part of his social inheritance which would enable him not merely to install bath tubs, but to sell bath tubs, to create a market for them, to create a demand for the most practical and inexpensive kind of bath tubs. He may have an IQ of 88 but from one viewpoint his period of schooling needs to be the longer for it.

There are many of those who will argue that this interpretation of human needs is narrow, low, and vulgar and who will point with admiration to the great souls of the age who live "not by bread alone" but who, I may venture to say, will grudgingly buy one of Angus's bath tubs and be the better soul for it. If psychological science has shown anything it has shown that the millions of humanity never will and never can be "great souls". The tide of mankind has advanced slowly and steadily while these sorts are like waves on the surface which have rushed hither and left you in the sunlight of the upper atmosphere. The ocean of humanity is not to be stirred by the same winds that splash its surface. The masses of men are continually with us and we gain nothing by ignoring them. The social inheritance should be a free store upon which all the little Nancy Dugans and Angus McIntoshes can draw, a store in which the small parcels are wrapped with care and presented without stigma.

Part I

Theory and Meta-Theory

Personal Construct Theory and Politics

D. Bannister

There is a particular though commonplace way in which political and psychological theories can be related to each other: namely by letting one form of theory entirely subsume the other so that the subsumed theory is both denigrated and explained away. It becomes a mere *datum* for the subsuming theory. Thus, if a psychological theory is viewed as pendant to a political theory, then the psychological theory becomes merely a sign of the times, a symptom of malaise or progress, a minor social manifestation of the way in which political power is structured. Conversely, if a political theory is viewed in purely psychological terms, then it can be reduced to a pathology, a social habit system, an example of more or less deviant mental processes. What Kelly called pre-emptive construing ("nothing but" construing) diminishes psychology (from a political standpoint) to a mere cultural epiphenomenon and politics (from a psychological standpoint) to the social excrescence of personal dynamics.

Psychology as a Subset of Politics

As an example of the pre-emptive political construing of a psychological theory consider the article "George Kelly: another nasty liberal" by Skelton-Robinson (1974). In this paper the author conducts a kind of Marxist analysis of personal construct theory. He concludes that construct theory is essentially "a weary piece of liberal ideology, propaganda for capitalism". Kelly is seen as denying "material reality" in order to enable us to ignore social injustice and deny the need for revolution. Skelton-Robinson asserts that:

> according to Kelly the starving aren't hungry, they just construe it that way. This way of thought is familiar to us from those liberals who argue that "the working class aren't really poor, they waste the money they earn", or "council housing estates aren't ugly and inadequate, they get like that from the way people treat them". Education is one of the liberal answers to social evils, or in Kelly's terms

21

new constructs which will make this actual wage a higher wage, this kind of housing better housing. To Kelly material circumstances don't exist, only ways of interpreting them, and all ways of seeing them are equally justified.

Personal construct theory is not regarded, in this context, as a system of thought to be explored for its potential psychological usefulness. It is examined in order that it can be identified as one of the tools which the ruling class might use to confuse and mislead the exploited. The theory, from this point of view, has no more intrinsic interest than red spots have, once they have served to diagnose measles. Skelton-Robinson goes on to argue;

> really Kelly's construct is man-the-master-of-nature, or man-the-pursuer-of-power. Men who seek to subdue nature, society, other men to their personal wills are set up as the ideal against which to measure all mankind.

That this is a travesty of construct theory is not important; that it is a devaluing of psychological modes of construction is.

Clearly, as part of a political argument, we can treat psychological theories as merely pieces of cultural power play. Just as we can politically argue that Russian painting is simply communist propoganda or rock music is merely a bourgeois opium for the masses. But when we do this we are construing pre-emptively, we are asserting that the psychological theory, the painting, the music are *nothing but* forms of political trickery: we are not seriously concerning ourselves with meanings they might have as psychological theory, as paintings, as music.

Politics as a Subset of Psychology

Just as we can reduce psychological theories to a kind of absurdity by analysing them in purely political terms we can trivialise political theories if we choose to consider them wholly within a psychological frame. Fiction provides us with a fine illustration of the latter strategy in the novel "Arrival and Departure" by Arthur Koestler (1943). A young Hungarian communist plays a role in the resistance to fascism at the beginning of the Second World War. He is caught, imprisoned, tortured and finally escapes to Portugal, intent on joining the British army in order to continue his fight against fascism. Before he can travel to England he suffers a total psychological collapse and is treated by a psychoanalyst. She seeks to demonstrate to him that his work in the anti-fascist resistance movement was simply his unconscious way of seeking punishment in order to expiate his guilt for accidentally killing an envied brother in childhood. The psychoanalyst further shows him that his political beliefs are only reflections of his childhood struggles with his parents. Viewed *purely* psychologically his treasured political commitments and *credo* are but the long shadows of his infantile pathology. The construing is pre-emptive and political theory is portrayed as *nothing but* a symptom of unresolved psychodynamic conflict.

Alternative Constructions

But there are ways of relating political and psychological theories without reducing either to the status of mere data for the other. If we avoid pre-emptive construing then we can consider what light might be cast on political issues by construing them psychologically and what light might be cast on psychological issues by construing them politically. We thereby take both modes of construction *seriously*. Our concern is with both.

For example, since political theories are acts of construction, then we can see what light is cast on them by looking at them from the point of view of the psychology of personal constructs.

Consider the political theorising that has been given its form, for well over a century, by the superordinate construction LEFT *versus* RIGHT. From a Kellyan viewpoint, in interpreting any construct subsystem, we must take particular note of the bipolarity of construction—that is particular note of what is being *contrasted* with what. Equally, we must note how the superordinate/subordinate lines of implication change if a regnant super-ordinate construct is altered in any way.

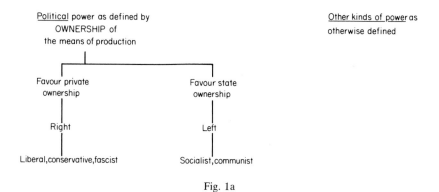

Fig. 1a

Figure 1a is an admittedly oversimplified and diagrammatic representation of the lines of hierarchical implication of the traditional LEFT *versus* RIGHT construct. The construct at the very top is extended from one pole only since it is a "political" construct subsystem that we are considering. If we had extended from its contrast pole "other kinds of power", we would have been looking at lines of implication for another kind of subsystem.

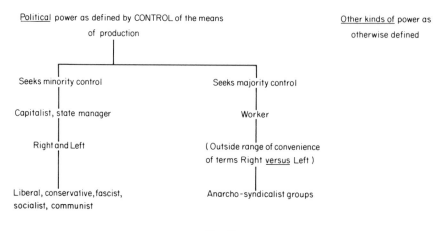

Fig. 1b

From then on the lines of implication run down from each pole, from the superordinate definition of the nature of power to the subordinate issue of particular political groupings.

Now consider Fig. 1b which examines an alternative construing of the same issues. In this case the construct of *ownership* has been replaced by the construct of *control* at the most superordinate level. In this (Fig. 1b) construction it has been assumed that *ownership* is simply the legal form which control took in capitalist society just as *tenure* was the legal form of control in feudal society or *organisation* is the legal form of control in a managerial society. This implies that "ownership" is itself subordinate to the construction of *control*, which must, by this logic, be used as the over arching superordinate. With *control* as the most superordinate construction, the lines of implication then link through various forms of control (including non-capitalist forms of class control) and thereby the alignment of political groupings is changed completely. *Right* and *Left* now appear on the same side of the bipolar construct and are contrasted with direct *workers' control* (of industry) groups at the opposite pole. It is a reflection of the fact that *workers' control* of industry is not currently a major political issue (while *ownership* is a major political issue) that the vast majority of all political groupings should appear on one side of the construct with only very small groupings on the other.

This analysis is not a novel creation of a construct theory way of viewing political beliefs. In essentials, it was set out as a political thesis many decades ago by Burnham (1942) in his book "The Managerial Revolution". What we might gain by an analysis which focuses on the bipolarity of construction and its superordinate/subordinate structure is not "new" political ideas as such but a clearer understanding of the contrasting implications of different political arguments.

A further exemplary psychological analysis of political construing is offered by Du Preez (1972) in his examination of the constructs used in South African parliamentary debate. He shows how, at the centre of the elaborate political debate in the South African parliament, three parties have used superordinate constructs which are *not directly relatable*. Thus the National Party centred its reaction to particular concerns and events around the construct *survival – non-survival* for the white race (in both a cultural and physical sense). The United Party was largely trying to make sense of policies and proposals in terms of a *cost/effectiveness* economic construct, while the Native representatives were talking in *moral/humanitarian* terms. Du Preez shows how "the facts" for each group were determined by their modes of construction. In addition to analysing change over a period of twenty years (e.g. the Nationalist change from a "racial" to a "national" mode of construction) he showed that there is a clash between these political groupings which *cannot be resolved* in a logical, debating sense. The very superordinate constructs of the debate (their constructs of the nature of identity) occupy different "universes of discourse".

Conversely, we can extend our understanding of psychological theories, particularly when they are given a social form, by construing them politically. A historical example of our failure to recognise the political implications of psychological undertakings is our development of the intelligence test. This can be viewed as a cycle of political cause and effect. From the beginning, intelligence tests were primarily validated in terms of their capacity to predict educational performance and the whole structure of education is, at one level, politically defined. Most notably since the middle of the nineteenth century, the ruling classes have used the provision of different sorts and levels of education as ways of cohering class groupings and ordering possibilities of employment, status and access to ideas. Our educational system reflects the political structure of our society. Thus, not only was our way of conceptualising "intelligence" socio-politically derived but the use of intelligence tests as selection criteria helped to strengthen further the system which had given them birth. It can be argued that all psychological theories which postulate a fixed nature for the individual (the notion of IQ constancy, trait theories in personality, the notion of psychological "genetics") inevitably help to define and sustain the social and political *status quo*. Had we, from the beginning, recognised the *political* implications of our scientific position, then our freedom to choose our logic and its consequences, rather than reflect social forces, would have been enhanced.

Although there is some current recognition of the political implications of work in the field of intelligence there is still a vast amount of writing and research in psychology which almost totally ignores the interface of psychological and political argument. Consider the paper by Flanagan (1977) reporting the development of a major American research project on "improving our quality of life". The research report begins with a definition of the quality of life of adults, segmenting it into areas covering physical, mental and material well-being; relationships with other people; social, community and civic activities; personality development and fulfilment and recreation. Large numbers of questionnaire responses were collected aimed at assessing the quality of life of various strata of American society. The research sought to establish the determinants of "quality of life" and generate a simulation model which could evaluate proposals for improving the quality of life.

The startling aspect of this very extensive project is the entire absence of discussion as to the way in which the very notion of "quality of life" is defined by political ideologies. There is a concomitant failure to recognise that proposing programmes for improving the quality of life, without reference to the nature of *conflict* within society, is an absurdity. The authors seem to feel that once views are given some kind of psychological research basis, they are intrinsically valid and politically unquestionable. Yet, up to this point in history, societies have been patterned around multiple and institutionalised forms of the master–servant relationship. This confronts us with questions concerning whether it is master or servant that is favouring what "quality of life" and for master or for servant: if change is envisaged then change controlled by whom and for whom. Finally, how does being master or servant itself define "quality of life".

There is an aprocryphal tale of a token economy programme in an American hospital which nicely illustrates the interplay of psychological and political construing. In this hospital, it is said, a token economy programme of the traditional Skinnerian type was initiated. The arrangements were standard so that any patient on the chronic back ward who did "good things" (such as buttoning up his flies or turning up for dinner on time or talking in a friendly manner to other patients) was rewarded with plastic tokens which could be exchanged for goodies such as cigarettes, parole and so on. Any patient who did "bad things" was negatively reinforced, i.e. received no tokens. Much to the surprise of the planners of the programme, it seemed to have little effect on the behaviour of the patients. None of them were at all interested in gaining tokens—well this is not quite true, there was one very enthusiastic patient who rapidly accumulated large quantities of tokens—but in general the programme was greeted by massive apathy. This was surprising since, although there can be much argument about the long-term value of token economies, in the short term they often produce noticeable changes in patient behaviour. A committee of inquiry was established to try and find out why the token economy programme was having so little success. Eventually the members of the committee fathomed the cause. Apparently the one patient who was behaving well and amassing large numbers of tokens was an entrepreneurial type of character who had his own private contract with his fellow patients. If any of them smashed a window or took the teeth out of a ward orderly he would instantly reward them by gifts of his tokens. Apparently the two token economy programmes nicely cancelled each other out.

Clearly we can make a kind of sense out of this situation by viewing it as a straight political conflict, with two forces competing for power—the fact that one force was official and the other unofficial is a political commonplace. Such a situation raises a fundamental psychological question. Is a psychological theory effective (that is to say does it provide means of prediction and control) over someone who understands the theory as well as (or even better than) the official proposers of the theory. It equally raises fundamental political/psychological issues to do with the nature of rebellion.

Politics as Context

The most immediate gain from considering psychological theorising in relation to political theorising is that it will oblige and enable us to consider the *context* of the people we are striving to understand. Kelly argued that a construct is meaningful only *within a context* and we can take this argument to imply that we can make sense of people only *within a context*.

There have been a number of writers who have explored the significance of particular, political contexts in their psychological analyses. For example, historically Karen Horney has postulated a relationship between the nature of capitalism and neurosis. Currently a number of writers in the Women's Movement cogently seek to show how psychological theorising (such as that of Freud) relates to the political oppression of women. However, established traditions in psychology encourage us to carry out experiments in a specially bleached and neutral environment and to seek generalisable results by avoiding particular contexts. We thereby create and explore situations which represent nothing in anyone's life. Equally our theorising as psychologists contains relatively little reference to the political context of their arguments and observations. This on the specious grounds that it guarantees that we are objective and our science is uncontaminated by "values".

Reflexivity

Kelly proposed, as a primary requirement for any psychological theory, that it be reflexive—that is to say that the theory account, among other things, for its own construction, since its construction is a psychological act.

This demand for reflexivity has to be met at many levels. It needs to be met by ensuring that we do not use one psychological language and set of assumptions in talking about our "subjects" and a different language and set of assumptions in talking about ourselves, "the scientists". Further, it requires us to regard our personal experience not as subjective, anecdotal nonsense, inadmissible in scientific discourse, but as a source of argument and a way of exploring the meaningfulness of the generalisations which we make. We ought not to proclaim publicly that which has no personal meaning for us.

As one form of response to the reflexivity requirement I will outline, in broad terms, the way in which I have experienced and managed the interplay between psychological and political construing. In doing this, I am extending an implicit invitation to you to consider the problem in the light of your own biography.

My interest in formal psychology developed in early adolescence. At that time I read Freud, Jung and a fair number of standard psychological texts, such as those of Brown and Woodworth. I doubt if I made much of them in any academic sense, but they were part of my exploration of my own nature and the nature of my relationships with other people. At that time I believed that a person's life entirely reflected their self moulded "character". I saw myself and other people as essentially "individuals" whose actions were wholly determined by their individual nature. My then hero was Paul Gaugin, a quintessential "individual". I regarded society as something to be rebelled against. In non-conformity lay freedom and I envisaged the possibilities of freedom as infinite. Thus, as I then interpreted it, psychology represented a commitment to the idea of the independent individual. It was a way into the mysteries of the autonomous inner man.

In late adolescence my personal concerns swung very much away from psychology and towards politics. Looking back, the swing seems to have been part of a change in my assumptions about what was important in life, what "explained" life. The change was away from the assumption that life could best be understood in terms of the nature of individuals and towards the notion that life could best be understood in terms of the nature of society. Some of the particular events on which this swing pivoted, I well remember. I was sixteen at the end of the Second World War and, like everyone around me, I was confronted with the full revelation of the then totally exposed concentration camps in Nazi Germany. The confrontation was visual in the form of newsreel film and documentary and detailed by the growing number of reports which tabulated the specifics of genocide. It seemed blasphemous to talk about the autonomy of individual character when contemplating the fate of concentration camp victims. Indeed, a concern with psychology in the sense I had cherished it suddenly seemed trivial. Increasingly, I felt that political systems were at the core of human life and political argument and political action were the most *significant* forms of argument and action. The superordinate construct remained the same, individual *versus* social, psychological *versus* political, but I had moved to the contrast pole of the dimension. So complete was the new commitment that for some years I became a political activist and a full-time, paid member of the staff of a political group.

In my mid-twenties I made a tentative move back to the "individual" pole of the construct, back to viewing life in primarily psychological terms. Again I enacted the reconstruing and gave it "behavioural" form, by becoming a professional psychologist. One of the experiences which informed this move was a period as a student, working in the chronic back wards of a psychiatric hospital. In terms of the inferences I drew this was the converse of being confronted with the existence of concentration camps. On the chronic back wards I was faced by people who had spent twenty or thirty years withdrawn into some alien personal state that did not permit them to engage with the world. Granted I could and did make social/political comments on their situation, yet it seemed clear that the institutional locking away of these people related to what had happened *within them* as particular individuals. They were, in a significant sense, self-imprisoned.

I say that my move back along the individual–social dimension was tentative because the bipolar construct of psychological–political, in its simple dichotomous form, was itself beginning to break up. I became increasingly concerned with the notion of *interplay* between persons and their world, though at first I was unable to find any kind of psychological framework which made much sense of "interplay". Traditional psychological theories seemed designed to force me back to the dichotomy in its original form. Thus behaviourism, however sophisticated, left me struggling with a stimulus–response paradigm which seemed to make the social *environment* the prime source of change. Other psychological frameworks, such as trait theory or various hydraulic models (e.g. psychoanalytic theory) while presenting largely *internal* explanations of a person's life disturbed me by depicting the person as essentially the victim of internal forces. Both kinds of theory depicted people as *victims*, either internally or externally determined.

For me, as for all of us, the choice between "psychology" and "politics" was a personal, and thereby a moral, dilemma. It was not simply an "intellectual" or "career" choice. At times I experienced my commitment to psychology as a kind of self indulgence, a failure to answer the call of duty embodied in politics. At other times political preoccupations seemed a kind of evasion of personal issues.

When I came to reflect on it, a particular value of personal construct theory was that it highlighted the possibility of seeing psychology and

politics, not as the two poles of a single construct, but as alternative constructions. The opposite of psychology became physiology and the opposite of a
political theory became any doctrine which saw man's active choices as being
made without reference to institutionalised power. I realised that I had
trapped myself by giving politics and psychology the status of *realities* rather
than seeing them as ways of construing reality.

This realisation was part of the general experience of finding that construct theory was personally relevant, personally usable. I had found
psychological theories, up to that time, more or less adequate as ways of
viewing "subjects" or "organisms" or "patients", but not pertinent to, or
even downright insulting about, my own situation and action. I found that I
could increasingly use the language of construct theory in commenting on
my own constructions, my own hostilities, my own superordinate dilemmas.

I began with increasing deliberation to explore the interplay between the
two modes of construction as I had practised them. As a consequence, I was
more at liberty to pursue political concerns in my psychological writing,
Bannister (1966, 1970, 1973) and Bannister and Bott (1973). I was equally
at liberty to attack political issues within psychology as a profession; issues
such as the advertising of private health services within the British
Psychological Society, South African employment requirements for professional psychologists and the evolution of a democratically structured
psychology department at the hospital within which I worked.

Conversely, I began to examine ways in which political arguments are
psychologically sustained. This is not so much a remarkable discovery but
more a matter of recognising the obvious. A clear case is the way in which the
adherents of the polar opposites of a political construct nourish each other.
The common belief of Left and Right is that all issues are to be seen as
subordinate implications of the construct private control *versus* state control
and each is thereby psychologically necessary to the other. They symbioti-
cally enhance each other's sense of identity and self-importance. *Alternative*
constructions are thus rendered psychologically uninhabitable and their
proponents experience their commitment as irrelevant to the "real" issues.

Superordination

Ultimately, if two modes of construing are to be related, they must be seen in
terms of a third mode. The import of Kelly's Fragmentation corollary is that
two subsystems can only be integrated by a third more superordinate system
which subsumes both. In the case of psychology and politics this may mean
that we have to climb the superordinate ladder to some such mode of
construction as philosophy or religion (one or other being the over arching
superordinates for most of us) in order to elaborate the relationship. At this

level we can compare all manner of theories in terms of the *values* assumed in each, the portrait of human kind painted by each.

If psychological and political theories are not merely intellectual postulates about people but are *stances towards them*, then we would be wise to try and extract from the massive detail of any particular theoretical approach the essential statements it is making about the nature of human kind and the nature of the human situation. In this way we can explore what it signifies (Bannister, 1970), that "essentially what Huxley portrayed as the ultimate horror in *Brave New World*, Skinner re-presented as a true Utopia in *Walden II*".

Construct Theory as a Statement of Values

If we wish to sketch out, in value terms, the ideology implied by personal construct theory we might well derive it directly from the philosophical assumptions underlying the theory, to which Kelly gave the name *constructive alternativism*. He formulated this doctrine in a number of ways but perhaps most simply in the words "we assume that all our present interpretations of the universe are subject to revision or replacement". Here Kelly is arguing that we cannot directly apprehend or determine reality, we can only place kinds of interpretations upon it which enable us to relate to it. Reality is not seen but visualised. Inevitably and properly our interpretations reflect our stance and serve our purposes and they are passed to and fro between us so that our realities are negotiated.

The effect of such an assumption is to make doubt and questioning central to human existence. Thus the values of personal construct theory are not consonant with the values of any political theory which prescribes the nature of reality or which makes truth, in any form, the particular possession of a group.

This brings personal construct theory into collision with many historical value systems. Politics is about power and to date political systems have usually worked on the basis of powerful minorities constraining the lives and directing the fate of relatively powerless majorities. By way of justification ideologies have been constructed around the belief that one group is intrinsically superior to another. Hence beliefs in the superiority of ruler over ruled, white over black, Gentile over Jew, man over woman, native over foreigner, the legitimate over the bastard, management over workers, baron over serf, the owner over the propertyless and so forth. Construct theory accepts the notion of difference, but not the notion of superiority. Every construct system (which is to say every person) is valid in its own right. To argue that one construct system is superior to another is to accept the terms, purposes and criteria of one system as valid and to deny the validity and point of the "inferior" system.

It is significant that Kelly proposed this as central to his psychological arguments a quarter of a century before he formulated it as the psychology of personal constructs. Consider any characteristically elitist statement: in this case one by Hugh MacDiarmid (1978).

> The key to my whole position is this. Since the dawn of history in all countries at all times all that has gone to build up what we call civilisation has been produced by an infinitesimally small element of the population. If that infinitesimally small element in the population were to be excised, all the remainder of mankind couldn't do anything at all to rebuild the elements constituting civilisation.

The whole tone and message of Kelly's 1930 essay "Social Inheritance", published in this volume, is exactly and diametrically opposed to this statement.

The issue is pursued further in the choice corollary of construct theory, which, if we examine it for its implied value, proposes that life is about choice and that choice is about the elaboration of the person—the growth, liberation, extension of grasp, of the person. Since construct theory is essentially egalitarian it follows that it cannot countenance the "extension" of one person or group at the cost of another. Tyrannies, small or large, domestic or institutional, personal or class, are intrinsically unacceptable. The constriction of people, even when, as often, they collude with it, is the prime evil. Kelly pointed to this in his (1962) essay "Europe's Matrix of Decision".

> Get some notion of what a person's system of channels is like and you have a rough sketch of the network within which he is prepared to exercise his human right to freedom. Observe the shrinkage of a man's system, and you find yourself a witness to a gradual human enslavement, enslavement without barbed wire or coercion. It is this enslavement by atrophy of ideas that we sometimes call institutionalised behaviour. We are usually thinking about mental hospitals, prisons and orphans' asylums when we use the term, but the same kind of enslavement can occur in societies and nations.

The doctrine of superiority, whatever form it takes, is a logical articulation of the governance of the powerful over the powerless. In contrast to it, an ideal and a purpose can be attributed to personal construct theory. In the simplest possible terms, the political and psychological intent of construct theory is the total diffusion of power. Thus, psychologists committing themselves to personal construct theory, are committing themselves to those traditional, though as yet largely unimplemented, political beliefs expressed in values such as liberty, equality and fraternity. Personal construct theory, like any psychological theory, can be seen as having, as one of its many characteristics, a human purpose: namely, that institutional power be diffused in order that personal, communicative power can be freely expressed.

References

Bannister, D. (1966). Psychology as an exercise in paradox. *Bull. Br. Psychol. Soc.* **19,** 63, 21–26.

Bannister, D. (1970). Psychological theories as ways of relating to people. *Brit. J. Med. Psychol.* **43,** 3, 241–244.

Bannister, D. (1973). The shaping of things to come. *Bull. Br. Psychol. Soc.* **26,** 293–295.

Bannister, D. and Bott, M. (1973). Evaluating the person. *In* "New Approaches in Psychological Measurement" (Ed. P. Kline). Wiley, London.

Burnham, James (1942). "The Managerial Revolution". Jonathan Cape, London.

du Preez, P. (1972). The construction of alternatives in parliamentary debate: psychological theory and political analysis. *S. Afric. J. Psychol.* 23–40.

Flanagan, John C. (1978). A research approach to improving our quality of life. *Am. Psychol.* **33,** 2, 138–147.

Kelly, G.A. (1962). Europe's matrix of decision. *In* "Nebraska Symposium on Motivation 10" (Ed. M. Jones). University of Nebraska Press, Lincoln.

Koestler, Arthur (1943). "Arrival and Departure". Jonathan Cape, London.

Skelton-Robinson, M. (1974). George Kelly: another nasty liberal. *In* "Rat, Myth and Magic", cyclostyled publication.

The Personal Venture

Miller Mair

There are some things too painful for me to know. There are places too frightening for me to go. There is knowing that is too burdensome for me to seek. There are joys that are too intense to enjoy. There are flames of living too hot for me to handle, too dangerous to dare. Partly living is a safer way to be. Stepping aside, looking the other way, going somewhere else, staying well away makes it easier to bear. To survive, I have to ignore what I cannot endure. This practice of ignorance limits the pain of experiencing and if the world would only stand still I could perhaps know only what I want to know.

The history of the world is as much a history of ignorance, of the practice and perfection of ignoring, as it is a history of knowing and coming to know ourselves, the world. Every way of knowing is of necessity and at the same time a way of ignore-ance. Every pattern of sensing we create in the course of our lives is a way of responding to some aspects of the world and remaining unresponsive towards others.

There is a widely shared myth at the present time, certainly in academic circles, that the pursuit of knowledge is a fine thing, and that ever so many of us are blandly engaged thereon. The assumption seems to be that a great many people *want* to know more and more. Not wanting to know, hiding from knowledge, is thereby a reprehensible sign of laziness, lack of motivation or stupidity. And yet I'm not sure how many of us really want to know much, if anything, beyond what we need to cope, to be acceptable to those others whose acceptance is needed if we are to get along reasonably painlessly.

While the pursuit of knowing is doubtless a widespread and enduring commitment of the human race, most of us, I suspect, do not want to know many things irrelevant to our ordinary lives and do not want to know if this will distress, disturb, destroy the securities of what and how we already know. And so you could see the vast outpouring of theses in Universities, for instance, as reflecting a few genuine questions posed more or less audibly towards the unknown, and many pretences at knowing, dutiful practice-runs

35

in the arts of socially sanctioned ignoring, personal investments in the social benefits of showing that you have come to know what to ignore, and have come to understand how to pose questions honed towards appropriate ignorance. Thereby you are unlikely to be troubled by knowledge coming in any forms other than those structured by our presently acceptable blindnesses.

I am not arguing here against the pursuit of knowledge. Rather I am trying to draw attention rather crudely to the necessary interweaving of our ways of coming to know and our ways of coming not to know. Any human activity can be pursued for purposes other than its apparent and expressed purpose. What appears to be the pursuit of knowledge may quite often be better seen as an equally assiduous and structured pursuit of ignorance. Whatever any person is doing is some part of a *personal* undertaking by that person in the context of his circumstances in time and place and society. Both extending and delimiting what we know and how we come to know are important and intimately related human activities. But in *personal* terms both knowing and not knowing are bought at a price, and the price is high, far higher than we have generally come to suppose. Neither coming to know or ignoring, which is anyway an aspect of knowing, are in themselves good or bad but can only be judged in the context of the human ventures in which they occur.

What I want to talk about here is *personal knowing*, what it is to *be personal* and *to know personally*. This will provide a general background against which to consider George Kelly's psychology of personal constructs and something of what might be involved in the struggle to create a *personal* psychology.

Kinds of Knowing

So far I have been using the word "knowing" in a very undiscriminating way. Some attention to kinds of knowing is needed. In what I have said so far I have been referring to knowing as something far more embracing than the meaning often given to the term. Intellectual knowing is but one aspect of knowing. Many of our academic conventions lead us to pay almost exclusive attention to this aspect of knowing and so draw attention away from other forms of knowing. I want to draw attention to four modes of knowing— knowing that . . . , knowing how . . . , knowing as living personal experiencing . . . , knowing people.

Knowing that such and such is the case or that this or that happened, is familiar enough to us. This form of knowing is concerned with identifying objects and things, with cutting up our experience into usable chunks which can be identified and assessed, examined and tested. Much of our vast accumulation of knowledge about the world is in the form of knowing that certain things are the case and that certain things are likely to happen under certain conditions. We could not get through any day of our lives without knowing that many things are reliably so. Much of science is to do with increasing our range in knowing that the world is reliably structured in particular ways.

Knowing how to make things work or how to achieve certain ends is related but different. Here we are concerned with knowing in practice how to make things happen the way we want them to happen rather than simply knowing that things happen in a certain way. We are here dealing with knowing how to make a difference to aspects of the world according to our wishes. The development of "know-how" or technology gives us practical control, power, the possibility of making things do what we want and turn out the way we decide. Again we could not survive without developing this kind of knowing of how to go about achieving particular ends we seek, rather than being the victim of circumstances which we might know about to some degree but not control.

I can, however, know that it is possible for people to fly with hang gliders and even know that this is so for very good aerodynamic reasons. I can know how to fix myself into the harness, how to use the controls to bank and turn, how to launch myself over the edge of the cliff towards the mercy of the wind. But knowing *personally* what it is to glide on the air, to commit your actual life to what you know, to those wings, to dare to step into nothing from this cliff, that's quite a different thing. Here you are involved with your own life, not in principle or at second hand. This is *knowing as living personal experiencing*. You are at risk if you dare to know personally. Sometimes it will be exhilarating, fun. Sometimes hard, even tragic and you may need courage to endure, to survive.

The focus of much academic knowing is on learning things which are of little or no direct relevance to the learners involved. Personal issues are involved for each of them, but they may be to do with not letting parents down, climbing the present academic hurdle in order to set oneself up socially and professionally, establishing a certain impression of yourself in the eyes of others, proving to yourself or others that you are able to accomplish what you have always feared you could not. So with a focus on the academic *topic*, the personal quest of coming to know may be obscured and missed. But in talking directly of knowing as lived personal experiencing I want to draw attention to the central personal involvement in this act of knowing. What is happening here is happening to me, in me, by me. In personal knowing we are attending to something of what the person is centrally engaged in in his life, at the frontier of his experience, where he is most alive. At this frontier of experience, even in everyday affairs, we are considering the person actively daring to know what matters to him and where he is vulnerable to change. The practice of ignorance is specially inviting here where, very often, no one else will see and where you are alone. We should not wonder that a few lives only penetrate at all deeply into the possibilities of the personal.

Knowing People

Knowing that and *knowing how* are both involved in knowing people as well as in knowing other kinds of events. Much of the impetus of psychology as a general discipline has been towards *knowing that* certain things can be claimed as true or likely to be true about people or about aspects of people. Similarly, much of applied psychology has been concerned with *knowing how* to help, shape, change, control, guide, persuade, modify, people's behaviour and experience in therapy, institutional arrangements, work training, classroom learning and such like. It is when our ideas about knowing people reach no further than *knowing that* and *knowing how* that we are likely to become bad psychologists and particularly dangerous people.

Knowing as living personal experiencing is also involved in knowing people. Daring to know, meet, feel for, be present to and with people, others and ourselves is analogous to being present in a living way in other circumstances of our lives. Much of what follows is an attempt to spell out a little of what seems to me to be involved in personal knowing. But first I want to draw attention to one feature of knowing people whose importance is, I think, often ignored or underestimated.

Being Known

One aspect of reflexivity not often stressed is that knowing other people involves *being known* or the possibility of being known. Being known is an intimate aspect of knowing and coming to know people. By this I mean more than the possibility that we will become known by others if we seek to know them. This itself has important implications, but more important is the possibility, which I will make as an assertion, that only and in so far as we are known by another or others do we become ourselves and inhabit our own lives. Only as we are known and live into the knowing of others do we more intimately come to know ourselves and therefore more of what we can come to know in others.

The importance attached by the scientist-psychologist to not being known while at the same time seeking to know *about* others and know *how* to influence their behaviour in predictable ways is highlighted in the traditional role of the experimenter in psychological studies. The experimenter is expected to be detached, anonymous, impersonal, bland, uninformative and in control. This is of course, in part, the psychologist's attempt to imitate his hero, the physical scientist, but it also seems to me, to be a major step into the used but largely unexplored meta-psychology of purposeful ignorance which characterises so much of what passes for the pursuit of knowledge in psychology. If we structure our means of inquiry such that massively important, though troubling, aspects of our legitimate subject matter are obscured and disregarded then we are engaged in the human venture of knowing what we want to know or what we feel we can handle. But in practising the necessary arts of ignorance we are here also belittling our subject matter to fit the Procrustian bed of our own competence.

Nor is it unreasonable that in everyday life as well as in the structure of the psychological experiment we should so often seek to avoid being known. Knowledge is power, greater knowledge is greater power. Things known about become subject to the will and intentions of those who know about them. So often in our social life, and this is again quite explicitly reflected and even highlighted in formal psychology, people are out to predict and control their circumstances as much as they can so that they may themselves survive and succeed. So much of our knowing is of the *knowing that* and *knowing how* kinds, and since these especially focus our attention on gaining the upper hand on our circumstances, it is not surprising once again in the human realm to find that much of our attention is devoted to finding how people's behaviour can be controlled and changed to fit the convenience or profit of others. In this kind of struggle for knowledge which gives power, the upper hand, it would not seem unreasonable to seek to know rather than be known. Where manipulation and abuse by others is anticipated it is reasonable to keep your own cards close to your chest while thinking of as many ways as possible of getting a peep at your opponent's hand or so shuffling the pack that, all unbeknowns, the odds have been shifted in your favour, for a time anyway.

Sometimes also, to be known is to see and sense your own behaviour in a different light. There is the threat in this that you will find that your ways of hiding truths from yourself as well as others are made apparent to you as well as others. One of the dreads in this is that you may be tricked, trapped or unarguably persuaded that you may be responsible for activities you had till then denied or ignored. You may find that you have been building and maintaining the prison bars and palace guards you have claimed were unfairly restricting your freedoms and limiting your achievements. You may find that in being known from a different perspective and in the understanding of another that your own carefully constructed angles of blindness towards yourself and your actions are bypassed. The afflictions you suffer as symptoms of some malady undermining your everyday life may come to be known as expressions of your own fearful avoiding of other and more painful pains you dare not experience. You may in all this begin to sense yourself as responsible for a wider realm than you had wished to know and being held responsible by others where previously you were in receipt of sympathy, pity and care.

Once again, coming to know personally through being known by another can be seen as something not always to be lightly allowed. You may find yourself being expected to stand where you are only prepared to crawl or walk where you had convinced yourself and others that you should be carried. Being known, and coming thereby to know otherwise than before plunges us into the very heart of personal and social life, into questions of power, control and responsibility. No wonder we like to draw attention away from our ways of limiting what we dare to know, and often struggle to seem to be only what we are yet able or willing to undertake.

Knowing Personally

It is easy at times anyway, to get the impression that knowledge is something separate from the knower, somehow out there and apart. Michael Polanyi (1958) has pointed out that we seem to attend *from* some mysterious and unidentified centre *to* that which holds our attention. That *to* which we attend claims us with its reality, while that *from* which we know remains invisible, unsubstantial, unrealisable. The realm of the personal includes the impersonal and is not antagonistic to it. The opposite of the personal is perhaps something like the unknowable, but the impersonal is only possible within the ambit of the personal. The impersonal is designated by persons.

To be personal is not therefore to be subjective since the act of objectifying is a personal act. To objectify that which is set over against the experiencing centre of self, to set at a distance, separate from, hold apart, to distinguish from the ever active self are all means of being, ways of coming to know oneself, the world. What happens so often, however, is that in separating self off from formed events, the living in-former is forgotten and the events so formed allowed to parade as independent reality from which the person is excluded. The *act* of objectifying is lost and the objects of attention allowed to lay claim to a separate reality. In this way the whole realm of the personal can be shrunk, lost and ignored. Objectifying, instead of a being a means towards a fuller understanding of the personal, can and often does become a way of ignoring, obscuring and denying the complex webs of our ways of being in and coming to know ourselves and the world.

Being Personal

It is one thing to suggest that all knowledge is basically personal. It is quite another thing to *be* personal. Much of the time we so organise our ways of living that we are scarcely involved in our own lives, we cut off or all but turn to objects of stone, large chunks of what might otherwise be living and often painful experiencing. We create and often get taken over by the masks we wear in so many situations. We have many modes of becoming impersonal, of impersonating what a person might be rather than *being* personal.

I have suggested elsewhere (Mair, 1977) that it is sometimes useful to think of a person as a community of selves rather than a single self, a single entity. The successful businessman, for instance, may act here as a ruthless perfectionist, there as the devious politician, somewhere else as the indulgent protector. All of these selves, so to speak, will reflect something of him personally. Yet none may reflect how, sometimes and fleetingly, he feels most intimately in the privacy protected by his public faces. There he may be a weeping child, scarcely known, unrecognised, by all these partial imperso-nations he offers as himself. The weeping child remains through the years, unapproachable by these competent, hard, successful adults who have grown up to protect and stand between the world and this vulnerable creature. In acting as they do, they allow the man to ignore and all but escape from this painful, needy, frightened, shameful little creature. It is as if the whole community of this man's selves grows from and is organised so as to protect the child from direct meetings in the world, to protect the man from ever having to become that little child again, to cope in such a way that the reality of such a child will scarcely be suspected by others. The man's life is lived through what he partially is, but scarcely if ever through where he is most sensitive.

All our impersonations, objectifications, separations, distancings, can be seen as aspects of our personal functioning. But to *be* personal is to live and know in and through those aspects of yourself which are on the exposed and fearful frontier between your most vulnerable sensibility and the world of your experiencing. To live always in relation to warnings and evasions may be to survive, control and prosper. Most of our lives are, and have always been, taken up with just this kind of surviving. Very seldom do people dare to live personally, on the frontier. The struggle towards understanding of what may be involved in being personal has engaged man for thousands of years. This struggle, sometimes explosively creative, often timid and partial is what I would call *the personal venture* of man. But in every single life in whatever place or time it is not a communal undertaking but always *a* personal venture. Each individual stands alone when he or she inhabits, dwells in and lives from his or her personal space. It is when you inhabit and live from your uniqueness, rather than semblances which meet more logi-cally the expectations of yourself or others, that you are being personal.

Personal Inquiry

In psychological research, the bowdlerisation of the pursuit of knowledge is often carried to exquisite lengths. Instead of encouraging the pursuit of questions of personal importance—that is, personal inquiry—research is often a mentally paralysed scramble to find something that has at least the form of a question so that something resembling an answer can be sought.

Pursuing personal concerns in psychological research, making your research a form of personally important action, is incredibly hard for most people. Anyone confronting his supervisor with personally important questions is likely to be told that their question is too big or meaningless or not amenable to scientific inquiry or would take too long to answer. They are then quickly encouraged to turn instead to more conventional, safe, already trodden paths and methods which are known to meet the approval of the department staff and the conservatism of the likely external examiner.

For the research student to battle on with what matters to him personally can and usually is a very lonely, often frightening and sometimes desperate business. If he refuses to accept other people's questions and ready made solutions then he is likely to have to work much harder than others even to begin to formulate whatever the issues really are for him. It is so much more convenient to take issues already shaped in someone else's terms from the literature. He is likely to have to struggle to find ways of separating himself sufficiently from the issues to begin to see what they are about. He will probably have to develop methods of his own to fit his concerns since standard off-the-supermarket-shelf approaches are unlikely to be adequate to his particular needs. He is likely to move quickly outside the area of concern, confidence and competence of his supervisors and many of his companions where he may feel lonely, abandoned and at times hopelessly lost and misguided. Through all this he is likely to sense more acutely than ever before the intense pressures being placed on him to take a more conventional line, to compromise, to be sensible. After all, he can always do "real" research afterwards when he is not so bounded by the requirements and fears of the academic world to meet thesis standards.

In this way personal inquiry is often stunted. What is involved in personal inquiry is again and again side-stepped.

This kind of issue in the context of research is of course repeated daily in ordinary life. Am I to compose my sufferings in the shape of other people's remedies or sing my own longings against the closed incomprehension of others? Am I to listen to the telling of your story and risk the destruction of my carefully formulated securities? How can I possibly trust the uncertain whispers of my own experiencing against the clearly articulated reasonableness of what so many others continuingly repeat?

The Cost of Being Personal

Often in everyday life, in mental hospitals, in psychotherapy, in psychology and psychological research I believe we grossly underestimate the *cost* of knowing personally, of personal inquiry. To undertake any personal venture is to start from and return to your own experiencing, your own ways of sensing, feeling, shaping. You are essentially alone in this, even though you may well want and need to make reference to the values and standards of others often and longingly. But the opinions of others cannot, however authoritative and impressive, be a final or crucial basis for judgement and choice in the realm of the personal. To venture personally is often lonely and unsupported, sometimes actively resisted by others. You are likely to lose your familiar contact with segments of the social reality which has served to keep you in some recognisable space in the social geography of others and yourself. To venture personally can be a demanding, painful, exciting, frightening thing to do. It can be so because on this frontier, everything is new, again and again, always new. You cannot shield or prepare yourself with the armaments of yesterday. When the next step is taken you are again naked, at the beginning, unsophisticated, on your own.

In knowing in the impersonal mode of the personal we are taught how to separate off parts of ourselves so that only a delegated contact is made with the issues which confront us. In coming to know through lived personal experiencing we are plunged into a much more complete involvement. Personal knowing takes all of you, all your sensibilities are relevant. Body as well as brain, feelings as well as intellect, reaction as well as reflection are involved. Knowing in this way calls on your life and not just a little corner labelled "research" or "education".

Knowing personally involves you in changing, in giving up something of who you were for who you may become. It means loss of old moorings and fixed boundaries and the repeated possibility of the loss of who you have taken yourself to be. It means sometimes the disruption of settled social relations and expectations. It means facing guilt in the struggle to determine for yourself in all honesty what is good and what evil now, for you here, at this time, rather than taking it for granted as given in labelled social packages. In all this you have to pay now, again and again. There is no postponement or buying your experiencing on tick or by credit card. Suffering as well as joy is involved. No wonder I certainly, and we generally, do very little of this kind of venturing. No wonder we search for ways of avoiding the issues and softening the blow, and hope to achieve control without pain and rewards without responsibility.

To venture personally, even in small measure, takes courage and requires persistence. It requires humility and readiness to give up the old forms that circumscribe your security for new shapes which may emerge in honest meeting with new circumstances. Often you will have to survive by some kind of thin line of trust sustained by whatever strength you can muster. Fear is the ever present enemy and the ever present terror that in stepping with your life into the unknown you may lose everything you have as well as everything you are.

All this may seem exaggerated and unlike everyday notions of knowing and change. My claim would be that this is because so seldom do we venture personally beyond the already plotted conventions of our place and time. We have come to asssociate inquiry with tedium, with the meeting of imposed expectations and regulations rather than personal danger.

A Personal Psychology

What, then, may be involved in developing a psychology of personal knowing? It is just such a question, I believe, that George Kelly tried to answer in his psychology of personal constructs (Kelly, 1955). I also believe that the kind of undertaking involved here is still largely beyond our understanding, partly because Kelly himself was not able to spell out the full scope of what he was trying to create. Whatever might be implied in talking of a personal construct *psychology* remains obscure and largely ignored. Yet, I suspect, Kelly's crucial contribution lies in preparing the ground and building some of the foundations for a personal psychology. He was, I think, struggling to put his fingers under what was and is generally accepted as psychology and quite literally shake the old foundations, suggest a different kind of discipline and ask a different level of question from those previously asked.

In suggesting that Kelly was attempting to create a psychology of personal knowing I want to suggest also that he got only so far along the road in doing this. His concern with knowing is apparent in his fundamental postulate and corollaries, in his central concern with procedures of personal experiencing, in his claim that his is a methodological theory and in his underlying metaphor of "man the scientist". However this metaphor, because of the way in which we presently conceive of science has resulted in the theory being labelled a "cognitive" theory. In this way it is recognised as being about knowing, but is conveniently shrunk into theory of thinking rather than of the whole man. Kelly was mainly concerned with the kind of knowing I have referred to as living personal experiencing, though also with knowing how and knowing that.

He clearly recognised the enormity of the issues involved for mankind as well as for particular men and women. In his essay on "Psychotherapy and the Nature of Man" (Kelly, 1969) he uses the story of Adam and Eve as a metaphor of the devastating and profound implications of seeking to live by understanding rather than obedience. In seeking to become like gods and grapple personally with the knowledge of good and evil our prototypic man and woman lost the comfortable protection of ignorance and gained access to the pains and uncertainties of the venture of knowing. In the myth too it is recognised that knowing involves undertaking guilt, labour, suffering and sweat as well as the fearful freedoms of choice. Kelly, in using this old story, indicates the continuity of man's struggle for personal responsibility in knowing, and suggests that human issues involved in personal knowing have been confronted over the centuries in different guises. While science at present is the focus of man's quest to know, for thousands of years this human venture has been grappled with under the heading of religion.

So what does any of this imply about central issues in a personal psychology? For me it suggests that a personal psychology will require involvement and reflection thereon. It will be equally concerned with our ways of knowing and our ways of not knowing. It will necessarily start from what matters to someone and be evaluated in relation to what it matters for. Important questions are something like, "What is involved in knowing or coming to know or in ignoring and coming to ignore?" or more simply, "*How* do we know?"

At present most of psychology is built on the assumption that we already know the right or best ways of coming to know, and these are enshrined in "the scientific method". But this is not adequate for a personal psychology. What is at issue is our ways of knowing and not knowing, how we formulate and pattern our engagements with events. The radical challenge which Kelly poses to psychology is in suggesting that its present reliance on acceptable, already given and handed down methods is the problem and not the solution. We do not explicitly know much about the means by which personal inquiry, personal ventures in knowing, are undertaken. The problem facing a personal psychology in detaching itself from general psychology is akin to that faced by the church during the Reformation. Instead of accepting the authority and rituals of authorised priests as knowing the only route to salvation, the reformers claimed each man as his own priest. The challenge posed by Kelly is all but spelled out in analogous terms when he claims each man as his own scientist. Each man has intimate, if inarticulate, experience of personal knowing and ignoring and if *man the knower* is to rise above *man the scientist* he needs to find ways of asking himself and others, "How do we know?", "How can we know?"

Knowing and Meeting

I am not sure that a personal psychology would look much like psychology as we know it now since it is pitched at a different level and questions the very ground we presently stand on. We have been through an objectifying phase of inquiry and many have now plunged into a subjective mode. But a personal psychology will be no more a subjective discipline than an objective one, it would be concerned with coming to know intimately as well as peripherally or formally, it would be as much concerned with creative description and formulation of experience as with drawing conclusions from the outcome of action, it would be as much an art as a science and concerned with coming seriously to know, by whatever means can be developed, something of the danger, pain and patterned procedures of personal knowing.

But personal knowing involves being known. In a personal psychology our ways of engaging with each other and ourselves are at issue. Part of the immediate problem of a personal approach to knowing is that we need to develop ways to address and listen to our own experiencing, as well as hear and understand what others are saying in their actions in relation to their circumstances. We need to learn to use and trust and value and explore a language of feeling and give voice and shape to our inarticulate knowings and engagements with each other.

A personal approach to knowing is therefore inevitably social, but goes beyond a concern with social roles and strategies to a deepening concern for persons in relation, their possibilities of meeting and coming to know each other centrally rather than at a distance. If we are to find ways of exploring further the nature of personal knowing and meeting then we are going to need alternative metaphors for guiding and sustaining our inquiries. It is here that Kelly seems to me to have stayed too close to the model of science which centres round the experiment as the pivotal experience. While wishing to retain this, I'd want to "kick the experiment upstairs", as Kelly did with the concept of "learning", and accept that personal knowing is necessarily experimental, necessarily about experience and lived into action.

In doing this I believe we need some further model of inquiry which will help us to penetrate more deeply into what lies between us, to help us to meet and come to know what is involved in being known. A personal psychology will need to formulate itself around some basic understanding of inquiry which, from the very beginning, accepts that we create our understanding in relationship, between us, rather than as separated scientist constructing an edifice of specialist knowledge in the terms accepted only by his own fraternity. We need some basic model of inquiry which includes involvement, recognition of equality of significance, personal meaning, exploration and progressive sharing of understanding and confusion, giving as well as receiving, knowing as well as being known.

Thus a personal psychology might well need to incorporate some modes of inquiry which stood in relation to more traditional psychology as "conversation" does to "interview" or even "interrogation" or as "loving intercourse" does to "casual prostitution" or even "rape". In this we will be involved across the boundaries which at present divide clinical from social psychologists or experimental from speculative, physiological from cultural. We are likely to be concerned with addressing and conversing with works of literature and art, religion and warfare, as well as with each other and ourselves. Such a discipline, whatever it turns out to be, will reach towards meeting without manipulation and will be founded on personal ventures in knowing. It should help us to respect our ways of ignoring as well as care for the possibilities of personal meeting and the kinds of change which are involved therein.

References

Kelly, G. A. (1955). "The Psychology of Personal Constructs", Vols 1 and 2. Norton, New York.

Kelly, G. A. (1969). Psychotherapy and the nature of man. *In* "Clinical Psychology and Personality" (Ed. B. Maher). Wiley, New York.

Mair, J. M. M. (1977). The community of self. *In* "New Perspectives in Personal Construct Theory" (Ed. D. Bannister). Academic Press, London and New York.

Polanyi, M. (1958). "Personal Knowledge". Routledge and Kegan Paul, London.

Construct, Reflect and Converse: The Conversational Reconstruction of Social Realities

Laurie F. Thomas

Introduction

George Kelly's original statement (Kelly, 1955) offered elegant form to a model of man (Shotter, 1975) which embodies the humanistic, person-centred approach in psychology (Bugental, 1967). Personal construct psychology identified individual constructions of experience as the source of a person's behaviour: and then re-construed behaviour as the test-bed for a person's constructions. Kelly fashioned his own experience including that as psychotherapist and teacher into a statement which was specific, coherent and comprehensive. He summarised his position in a fundamental postulate and ten corollaries. These warrant the description "scientific theory" as that term is used by the more rigorous exponents of the philosophy of science (Popper, 1972). This is uncommon in psychology where the term "theory" is applied to almost any attempt at explanation (Bannister and Fransella, 1971) and where the expression "scientific theory" has for too long been associated with physical instrumentation and with a non-phenomenological or anti-experiential interpretation of repeatability (Rogers and Coulson, 1968).

The form given by Kelly to his model of man is, by its very nature, contentless. It may be inhabited by any system of constructions which would constitute "a person". Indeed, as will be argued later, it may be animated by any system of constructions which would constitute "an organism".

The potency of Kelly's published system was that it offered not only a theory but also the beginnings of an integral and symbiotic methodology. To claim that Kelly's theory and repertory grid techniques mark a watershed in social science comparable to Copernicus and the telescope in natural science, may not appear historically so outrageous, as it now does to many contemporary psychologists. Together the theory and the methods contain the embryo of a new breed of aids for navigating the psyche, and for exploring and charting personal, interpersonal and social space. Most of these new psychological tools have yet to be invented but some basic design principles are beginning to emerge. As these are translated into practice they will help equip the workshops wherein vehicles for journeys into new worlds of human experience are being built (Castaneda, 1969). But as yet the theory is undeveloped (Mair, 1977; Radley, 1977) and the methodology only at a stage analogous to the technology which produced the rough-hewn lenses of the pre-Galilean era.

Awareness and the Focused Grid

How can the lens be ground more truly? The repertory grid displays elements of a person's experience and how he or she orders these as arrays along personal "constructs". These constructs are sections through the individual's system for attributing uniquely personal meaning to experience (Ogden and Richards, 1923). The elements and constructs are represented as the columns and rows in a matrix. They are normally recorded in the order in which they are elicited. A detailed description of the procedure and variations on it are to be found in the "Manual for Repertory Grid Technique" (Fransella and Bannister, 1977). But this table of results (i.e. the raw grid) offers participant explorers of their psyches only very fragmented, kaleidoscopic glimpses of their constructions of experience. Careful professionally guided talkback through the pattern of meaning hidden in this display, is required to enable the participating psyche explorer to interpret this data in significant and personally relevant terms (e.g. Fransella, 1972). The FOCUSED grid technique (Thomas, 1976) uses a two-way re-ordering procedure to enhance the quality of the grid display. Similarity matrices are calculated separately for elements and for constructs (Bannister and Mair, 1968). These are cluster analysed to reveal that unique re-ordering of the elements which produces minimum cumulative difference between adjacent columns, and that re-ordering of constructs which produces minimum difference between rows. In the SPACED FOCUSED grid display (Thomas, 1978) the distance between re-ordered rows and columns, is inversely related to their similarity. Figure 1 shows how this illuminates the constructions of experience employed by one individual manager in evaluating the people who work for him.

The earlier factor analytic methods for seeking patterns in grid data contain the danger of mystification. Having no appreciation of the mathematical manipulations that transform the grid into the display, the client must take the resulting graphical representation on trust. This is also

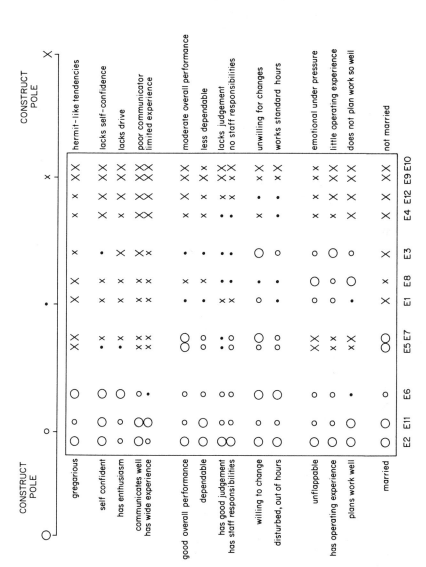

Fig. 1. A spaced focused grid.

true for many of the psychologists who use the INGRID analysis. In contrast to these factor analytic methods (Slater, 1976) the focused grid display preserves all the elicited data, only systematically reorganising it to clarify the experiential image. The path from raw grid to focused grid is crystal clear. By placing "like" along with "like" the pattern of construing is brought into focus revealing relationships which were implicit but not apparent in the raw grid. Talking a person back through the experience of eliciting a grid is greatly enriched by using the SPACED FOCUSED grid as the basis for discussion. The emphasis moves from the task of identifying the relationships between elements and constructs to an appreciation of the implications of the revealed patterns of meaning. The originator can more easily comprehend the pattern. The role of the professional guide, interpreter, intermediary or change agent is subtly transformed. Released from the need to seek for these patterns in the data, the guide is free to attend to the process whereby the constructions of experience are themselves construed.

The talkback conversation can be guided in several directions. It can be conducted in the Rogerian mode (Rogers, 1969) to enable the client to reflect on and reconstruct his or her own experience in his or her terms. Or the focused grid may serve as a starting point for intentionally directed change such as that involved in learning about statistics or management. As personal scientist, the individual may be exploring completely new ground or he or she may be investigating familiar public ground to make it their own; to use it for uniquely personal purposes. The quality, structure and control of the talkback or talk-on conversation may vary from Rogerian to Skinnerian. The form it takes emerges from the shared intentionality of the co-participant explorers, who may decide to reflect, to elaborate, to refine, to differentiate, to extrapolate and to reconstrue their constructions of experience in those ways best suited to their purposes. The SPACED FOCUSED grid provides one experiential "still photograph" as an aid to such exploration.

Two-way cluster analysis lends itself to real-time data processing. The speed of an online computer allows the grid to be focused at each stage of the elicitation procedure without disrupting the flow of the conversational process. The opportunity to reflect upon the focused part grid enhances the quality of subsequent elicitation. The elicitation procedure can also be programmed to become part of an online computer-aided conversation with oneself. The conversation is guided by the emerging patterns of meaning in the progressively focused grid. The DEMON program (Thomas, 1968) and its PEGASUS derivatives (Thomas and Shaw, 1977) provide such an online conversational facility which has the advantage of being completely confidential. The data file on the computer may be deleted at the end of the online session and all record of the conversation disappears.

Another less spectacular method of real-time data processing is a manual grid sorter specifically designed to facilitate the search for structure during the face-to-face elicitation conversation (Thomas, 1972). This recruits much of the advantage of the online interaction without the cost of computing and has the added advantage of remaining visible and completely under the control of the co-participants.

But such techniques are only the first crude attempts at experiential lens polishing. There is nothing sacrosanct about the tabular form of the grid. In fact Kelly himself saw construct systems as fragmented, partially permeable, hierarchical structures. There is almost infinite scope for the development of methods for eliciting and processing and displaying an individual's constructions of experience (Harri-Augstein, 1978) and for using these to generate powerful and relevant learning conversations in education, training and therapy. "Beyond the grid" technology is at the early developmental stage. It can be assumed at all subsequent points in this chapter that whenever repertory grids are mentioned as the basis for conversational techniques, "models of the psyche" techniques could eventually replace them.

Awareness of one's own constructions is the particular condition of man (Sherrington, 1952). Consciousness has been variously defined (Tompkins, 1963; Pask, 1973; Mair, 1977) but in essence all definitions relate to this ability to construe one's own constructions. The Sociality Corollary states that ability to construe another's constructions is a necessary prerequisite for entering into social process with that other (or to be more precise, the ability to construe the construction processes of another is a prerequisite condition). Perhaps personal construct psychology needs some additional corollaries, one of which would relate to consciousness or self-awareness, e.g. SELF-AWARENESS COROLLARY.

> To the extent that a person construes his own constructions of experience, he or she acquires consciousness. To the extent that a person construes his or her own *processes* of construction he or she acquires more complete awareness of themselves as a person.

Thus Kelly's reflexive use of the grid can be developed to encompass this process of meta-construing. Formal recognition of this possibility adds a new dimension to his theory. But for investigating and enhancing the quality of interpersonal and social processes, the individual grid and its derivatives are not sufficient.

The Two "Social" Corollaries

Kelly's theory contains two corollaries which may be construed as primarily relevant to social interaction.

THE COMMONALITY COROLLARY:

To the extent that one person employs a construction of experience which is similar to that employed by another, his processes are psychologically similar to those of the other person.

THE SOCIALITY COROLLARY:

To the extent that one person construes the construction process of another, he may play a role in a social process involving the other person.

It will be demonstrated that these are necessary but not sufficient for an adequate understanding of interpersonal and social process.

VERBAL OR OPERANT COMMONALITY?

Many studies in the literature treat repertory grids as a branch of psychometrics. The assignings of unfamiliar "offered" elements to the only partly-defined poles of "offered" constructs are rightly treated as questionnaire or semantic differential data. "Experientially-unlike" is equated with "unlike" and results crushed into a common mould using agricultural statistics. When data is collected and analysed in this way the designation "repertory grid" ceases to have any meaning. The offering of verbal labels does not necessarily tap similar elements of experience in each user, nor does the two-ended verbal description of a rating scale equate with the bipolar differentiations occurring naturally in each person's construing. When the results from such mass surveys are compounded into composite pictures of socialised man, i.e. a teacher, a manager, a schizophrenic or a psychiatrist, the model of man that emerges has little in common with Kelly's personal scientist. But let us not condemn such well-established practices. There is nothing inherently immoral about them. They are the social science equivalents of the astrologers' use of the telescope. Hopefully, speculations built from such studies will eventually find their proper place within the pool of human knowledge alongside Pythagoras's theological ruminations on the mystical properties of the square on the hypotenuse. They are interesting exercises in the use of human ingenuity which did in fact yield valuable, if unexpected, by-products. If commonality in Kelly's sense is not to be established by mass survey techniques, what remains? A more comprehending look at the theoretical issues is always a good empirical starting point.

An early study by Mendoza (Mendoza and Thomas, 1972) showed that people looking at an art object (an Indian miniature painting) each make their own visual differentiations. The components or elements out of which one person constructs his experience of the painting are not those through which another construes it. When one individual's personal elements are elicited and used to construct a repertory grid, the resulting constructs are also extremely personal and idiosyncratic. The words evoked as pole descriptors often convey only the most shadowy meaning to anyone other than their originator (Fig. 2).

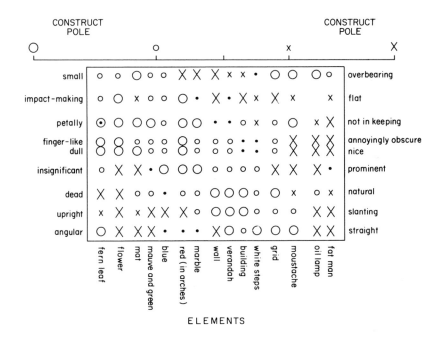

Fig. 2. Grid of perception of an Indian miniature.

This is because, for most of us, the experiencing of art objects is private and uncommunicated. We either have no language in which to express it, or only a very eccentric treatment of the resources in the public word pool. This is in contrast to areas of well established public usage, such as, for example, coins of the realm, where continual social validation creates a shared terminology which is mapped, in an apparently agreed manner, on to similar constructions of experience.

Between these two extremes lies a continuum of possibilities for commonality. For example, two similarly expert bicycle riders almost certainly have quite large areas of similarly constructed experience but they may have no agreed language in which to identify and exchange it. Polanyi (1967) has called this non-conscious understanding "tacit knowing". In contrast to the bicyclists, two students discussing their newly acquired understanding of personal construct theory may engage in sophisticated exchanges about emergent poles and constellatory constructs. Asked to elicit a grid, raise their own awareness, or to converse effectively together, however, their understanding is revealed as a free floating, merely verbal, system unrelated to any usable construction of concrete experience.

How then can the repertory grid be used to explore commonality? Among those studies which examine individual experience, Stewart (1976) and Duck (1973) have inferred commonality from similarity of elicited verbal labels. Among members of a freely communicating society talking about well established everyday matters, similarities in personal vocabulary may provide a good first approximation to similarities in constructions of experience. But even a superficial look at the ascent of man (Bronowski, 1965) reveals that his painstaking attempts to achieve significant shared new understanding often founder on the difficulties encountered in creating and maintaining an operationally common terminology. There is no basis for assuming that what a close-knit cultured or professional community find difficult to achieve in two or three generations should be any easier for an aggregate of only inadequately communicating individuals to achieve in a few committee meetings.

An alternative approach is to ignore the words people use to describe their constructions and to define an operational or operant commonality. What would this involve? If two people sort the same set of objects into the same two groupings, does it follow that they have some commonality of construing? Possibly. If they agree that certain additional objects would go into one or other grouping whilst certain other objects would not go into either, does commonality appear more like? Well perhaps. If one of them can take a random sample from a set of objects and operationally define his construing by physically ordering the objects in a row, could the other demonstrate his commonality by adding items from the remainder of the set to this ordering in positions which gain the complete agreement of the first? Well, even within the restricted confines of this experimental set-up that is not exactly what Kelly meant by commonality. He did not equate isolated behaviours with isolated experiences, but as the pattern emerges the similarity grows. Two people who had developed exactly the same total constructions of experience would act similarly, faced with the same events. Similarity of action is some indication of similarly constructed experiences. Confidence in commonality increases when people produce identical orderings of an array of elements.

The PAIRS analysis technique (Thomas *et al.*, 1976) for comparing two repertory grids, is based on this assumption. The technique requires that the two people involved share a pool of common experience. They negotiate a set of common elements of experience from this pool. One example might be a set of sculptures among a group of art students; another a set of faults that occur in the paint finishes on a quality car among a group of industrial visual inspectors; and a third might be a set of videotapes showing typical events that occur in the classroom among a group of teachers of ESN children (Pendleton, 1976). Given a shared set of common elements of experience, each of the two participants elicits a separate grid producing their own set of personal constructs. The elements are assigned to the poles of the construct (or rated, or ranked) in the usual way. The assignings of the elements on the first construct in one grid are in turn compared with the assignings of the elements on every construct in the other grid. The highest degree of match with any construct is taken as the degree of commonality of the first construct in the first grid with the construing represented in the other grid. Thus verbal labels are ignored and only operant commonality is noted. The procedure is repeated for each construct in the first grid. The pattern of matching scores indicates the nature of the operant commonality of the first grid with the second. A similar procedure is used to match the second grid onto the first. The two patterns of commonality are not necessarily symmetrical. A few constructs in one grid may fully subsume most of the constructs in the other, whereas the reverse relationship would show a number of constructs with little commonality.

This method has been used with some success by me and my collaborators to study perceptual phenomena and non-verbalised construing, analogous to the art object and bicycling examples. In a study of how visual inspectors construe the quality of ladies' underwear, the PAIRS method was used. Three inspectors produced repertory grids. The analysis showed similar patterns of ordering among a negotiated and shared list of garment faults. These three inspectors also exhibited similar search strategies, as revealed by an eye-movement camera. How well two of these grids related, irrespective of verbal descriptions, is shown in Fig. 3.

A fourth inspector, nominally doing exactly the same job, demonstrated quite a different search strategy and produced a grid which a PAIRS comparison showed to have little similarity with the other three (Thomas *et al.*, 1978).

Such studies are a healthy antidote to any tendency for social psychologists to rely solely on people's verbal descriptions of their constructions of experience. True commonality cannot be equated with either verbal agreement or identical ordering of arrays of elements. The repertory grid must be used to add rigour to a more comprehensive conversational methodology.

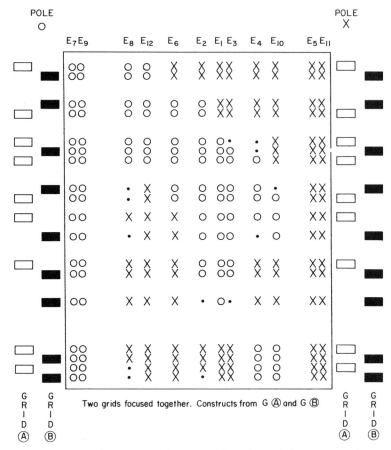

Fig. 3. Two grids prepared for pairs analysis.

A Conversational Methodology

The only valid test of whether two individuals have similar constructions of experience is for them to explore each other's constructions in detail and in depth and to agree what is shared. If a third observer independently attempts to make such a judgement he will almost inevitably construe the constructions in a selective and distorted way. Only by fully entering into the constructions of each, and by participating in the exchange conversations, can a third person hope to make a reasonable judgement about commonality between two others. The exchange grid technique (Thomas and Harri-Augstein, 1977) has been developed in a series of investigations as a tool for enhancing the quality of communication in a learning conversation. In its most elementary form the exchange grid is elicited as follows:

Two people identify an area of apparently common experience. Each elicits their own set of elements and uses these to construct a repertory grid by any of the usual methods (Fransella and Bannister, 1977). Having completed the grid, each now contributes their elements and their pairs of pole descriptions to a common pool of ideas, out of which each constructs a new grid.

A variety of exercises in conversational exchange are now possible:

(a) Comparison of the original two grids reveals the degree of unforced verbal commonality.

(b) Comparison of the two new grids reveals the degree to which the two are willing to create verbal commonality, i.e. use each other's elements and construct labels.

(c) The list of elements and constructs common to the two new grids can be used to extract two verbally common grids. Once completed, these can be examined for operant commonality. Two procedures for making such a comparison are available—the DIFF method merely subtracts one grid from the other and displays the pattern of differences; the CORE program (Thomas and Shaw, 1977) uses an alternating iterative process for progressively removing the least common elements and constructs until a shared common CORE GRID is revealed.

(d) Both new grids can be separately focused to examine how the participants each use the other's elements and constructs. Do the foreign Es and Cs form separate clusters or do they intermingle with the originator's Es and Cs?

Careful conversational exchanges on the basis of (a), (b), (c) and (d) reveal the degree of true commonality and serve to elaborate, refine and extend it.

A number of investigators using these techniques have reported the creation of apparent "ah-ha" experiences in which some personally significant perceptual, cognitive and affective organisation appears to be challenged as the participant attempts to enter the other's constructions. New constructions of familiar events then emerge and the participant finds himself thinking, feeling and perceiving things differently (Pope, 1978; Harri-Augstein, 1978).

The discussion so far, and a re-reading of Kelly's Experience Corollary, leads to the inevitable conclusion that a pure measurement of true commonality is, by reference to the Heisenberg principle, impossible. The process of measurement inevitably disturbs that being measured. The elicitation process triggers off its own reflective mechanisms and comparison of construings between people inevitably leads to further exchanges. The illusion of pure measurement is best relinquished in the full acceptance of the advantages of a truly conversational technology.

The SOCIO-GRID Technique

The techniques for mapping one grid on to another described in the previous sections can be extended to explore the constructions of experience among a group. Grid-based conversations are used to generate an array of shared elements that span the range of experience which is to form the content of the exploration. Each participant uses this array of elements to construct a repertory grid, producing individually elicited constructs. The PAIRS technique is used to operantly map grids one on to the other. This technique replicates within the SOCIO-GRID analysis (Thomas *et al.*, 1976, 1978). Each grid is mapped on to each other grid in the group and measures of operant commonality are obtained for each pair of grids. The matrix of operant commonality measures serves as the basis for generating a sociometric type of display showing who construes what most like whom (Fig. 4). The analysis also produces a listing of all the constructs from all the grids ordered to illustrate a continuum from those which are most operantly shared by the group to those which are least shared. A MODE GRID is composed from the shared elements and the fifteen most common constructs. The SOCIO-NET display, the commonality listing and the MODE

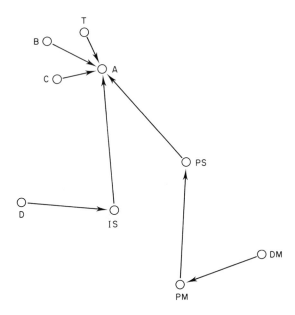

Fig. 4. A socio-net. Key: A, B, C, D = Inspectors; T = Trainee; IS = Inspection Supervisor; PS = Production Supervisor; PM = Production Manager; DM = Divisional Manager.

GRID may be used in conjunction with a verbal usage analysis to generate a conversation among group members which explores commonality both operantly and verbally to produce a shared construing of the similarities and differences among their constructions. Thus the technology enables the state described in the Sociality Corollary to be achieved. The basis for social interaction is improved.

Sociality and Social Process

The suggestion for a self-awareness corollary arose from analogy with the Sociality Corollary which states that the construing of another's processes of construction is a necessary prerequisite to entering into social interaction with them. The exchange grid technique offers the possibility for operationalising the study of social process within the paradigm of personal construct psychology.

The exercises described on p. 59 can be taken further. If two people, Sid and Fred, produce grids relating to a shared area of interest, it is possible for them to use these to explore how they construe each other's constructions. One method is for each to produce a copy of their grid sheet showing the verbal labels of their elements and constructs but omitting the assignings of the elements on the constructs. Sid is then asked to complete Fred's grid and Fred completes Sid's grid. If they attempt to reproduce the assignings as they believe the other originally elicited them, a comparison of the "other's grid" with the original grid (using DIFF or CORE) reveals the extent to which Sid can enter Fred's, and vice versa, constructions. Let us call this *understanding*. If the grid is completed as the participant feels the other should have originally completed it, then the comparison reveals the patterns of *agreement* or disagreement. Mutual comparisons reveal the potential for productive conversation. But Kelly's conception of construing of the other's processes of construction is not properly explored with this methodology. A new grid is required in which Sid construes Fred's processes of construction. An approximation to this is for Sid to participate in an exercise in which Fred's constructs become the elements in a grid for Sid. Sid then explores how he thinks and feels about Fred's constructs and by implication about Fred's processes of construing.

Thus a reconsideration of Kelly's original intentions provokes extensions of the conversational methodology. But this in turn raises questions about the theory. Is the Sociality Corollary sufficient to allow a complete exploration of social process? It is not. When linked with the suggested self-awareness corollary, many social processes are illuminated. A person who construes another's constructions but does not construe his own, will generate a different form of social process from someone who construes his own constructions in addition to the other's. Pask (1975) has proposed a theory of conversation in which he introduces the concepts of object-language and meta-language. These are closely analogous to constructions and construing of constructions. Pask's minimal conditions for conversation are the existence of two participants (P-individuals) each using both an object language and a meta-language. Avoiding, until later, a consideration of other logically possible cases (i.e. object language only on each side or object language on one side and object and meta-language on the other), what does Pask's definition of conversation imply for Kelly's theory? Social process requires self-awareness and sociality, i.e. construing of one's own as well as the other's constructions. But is this sufficient? Reference to the inter-personal analysis methods of Laing (1970) would lead us into their apparently infinite regress. Sid construes Fred's construing of Sid's constructions and his own. This is treacherous ground; co-counselling, encounter group, transactional analysis (Berne, 1972), or social skills training, would suggest that one of the areas which yields the most idiosyncratic forms of construing is where individuals construct their experience of social interaction. By standing on Kelly's shoulders we recognise the need for a contentless model of social process. Each would animate it with their own constructions of social experience. Perhaps a *SOCIAL AWARENESS* corollary is required:

> The forms in which a person construes his or her constructions of social interactional processes will condition their ability to consciously influence their processes of interaction with others.

A grid methodology is required to make this operational. The elements of experience are interpersonal events. Work with this form of grid has shown successful results in the training of industrial and commercial managers. The grids were used both to raise their awareness of their own processes of man-management and to trace out the changes in their construing of such interpersonal events before, during and three months after, the training course (Harri-Augstein, 1978).

But what of the "social" processes that accrue in the absence of self-awareness and/or social awareness. The study of social processes among animals (Ardrey, 1972) has been very successfully extended by modern ethologists who appear to use concepts analogous to Kelly's. At the insect level the conception is analogous to an object—object language interation in Pask's terms. Higher up the phylogenetic scale there is some evidence of embryo sociality beginning to emerge. In the human area it is interesting to realise that the data from which much of traditional psychology has been invented derives from situations which do not contain these conditions for social awareness.

Operant Conditioning, Ethology and Personal Construct Psychology

Bannister quotes Kelly (1970) as arguing that behaviour therapy has been misinterpreted even by Skinner (1957, 1971), its inventor. He claimed that it is the patient who is the true experimenter and that the behaviourist-experimenter is merely a technical assistant in the exploration. Tolman (1932) can be seen as making similar observations about Hull's rats (Hull, 1932). Acting as if the patient was unaware of his condition the behaviourist identifies some substance (e.g. food or money) as reinforcing. This reinforcement is then used as the only coinage in a pay-off game. The genius of Skinner's methodology is that because he originally worked with animals he necessarily had to invent a simple form of non-verbal language in which to conduct the learning conversation. Thus the audio tone used in teaching a pigeon to play ping-pong is reconstrued as sign language in which the behaviourist communicates with the real experimenter, the pigeon. The pigeon explores his artificially organised environment, reconstructing his experience of replicated events, to obtain food. Thus Skinner's move towards operant conditioning produced an alternate construction of the position Kelly was advocating. The animal's existing behaviour and therefore its reconstruction of experience was taken as the starting point for the learning conversation. By observing not the behaviour but the meaning of the behaviour within his own intentional system, Skinner is able to conduct the learning conversation in simple non-verbal terms. Schedules of reinforcement and the carefully designed space–time relationships of the Skinner box mechanisms constitute the syntax of a very operational non-verbal language. The delivery of food pellets or tones was carefully designed into the organism–technology system to provide exactly the validation of the construing which personal construct psychology would require. The signals enabled the animal to differentiate and elaborate its constructions of the experience which Skinner was so carefully replicating for it.

The ethologists (Tinbergen, 1953; Lorenz, 1977) were developing an essentially similar conversational technology but they had the situation in clearer perspective. Rather than invent an impoverished language in which to intervene, they learnt the language of the animals, and rather than impose their own purposes as Skinner does, the ethologists observed the emergence of the animals' own intentionality. The animal experimented to discover viable constructions of experience and man intervened to construe the constructions. The ethologists' conversational methodology meets some of the requirements for social interaction which are being developed in this chapter. In their identification of innate releaser mechanisms and in their experimental interactions using these mechanisms, the ethologists are construing the endowed constructions of the other and thus fulfilling the requirements for sociality. In "Man meets Dog" Lorenz shows self-awareness and social awareness but most people would consider this awareness to remain one sided. Some animal lovers such as Gerald Durrell, Joy Adamson or Gavin Maxwell might contest just how one sided the interaction really was.

There is a generation of Ph.Ds to be acquired by carefully translating the methodology and findings of behaviourism and ethology into the paradigm of personal construct psychology. It would be worth doing so. Personal construct psychology would gain much from the rich methodologies of behaviourism and ethology. Those disciplines would be transformed by the creation of one philosophical and methodological continuum in animal and human psychology. There are numerous dissertations I would dearly love to supervise. "The personal construct system of the laboratory rat", "Reinforcement construed as validation of constructions of experience", "The man-animal relationship reviewed", "I construed a mountain, did it construe me?", "Interaction, transaction, manipulation and service as examples of mutually self validating construing", are some of my fantasy titles. Perhaps this reconstruing of psychology might help to disperse the nature–nurture issue.

The ethologists' findings imply that construing the replication of events is not the only source of anticipation. Perhaps one ought to argue for a set of ENDOWMENT COROLLARIES:

(i) Organisms are born with a set of constructions of experience (e.g. innate releaser mechanisms); and
(ii) organisms are more likely to acquire certain constructions at certain critical times (e.g. imprinting).

Social Psychological Experiments as Learning Conversations within a PCP Paradigm

Once we acknowledge that all psychological experiments may be more usefully reconstrued as learning conversations, the mystery of much of the shifting "factual" sand on which psychology is built, disperses. Currently accepted experimental "facts" are the outcomes of some very peculiar restrictions on conversation. The technical assistant to the participant-explorer deliberately attempts to enter an alien system of constructions. As pseudo-scientist he or she assumes some very bizarre conceptual and perceptual blindnesses and may, in using standard forms of experimental instruction, restrict their vocabulary to a non-negotiable fixed sequence of sentences.

But no human can fully role-play this alien. His or her own system of constructions obtrude and the learning conversation is therefore conducted from within a different framework from that preplanned system within which the "results" are collected, interpreted and reported. It is the lack of commonality between the participant-explorers and their technical assistants which contributes most to the variability of psychological data. That and the participant explorer's inability to construe the constructions of the technical assistant as pseudo-scientist. Rosenthal's (1966) original observations and all the subsequent work on the social psychology of the psychological experiment are most easily interpreted from within personal construct psychology.

Much of what now passes for data in social psychology can, thus, be reconstrued as no more than the ephemeral chit-chat generated within conversations in which one conversant role-plays an alien and the other is unable to construe his constructions: not, in Kelly's terms, a very social process.

The Hawthorne experiment has long stood as a grotesque monument to a very explicit attempt to play out the pseudo-scientific paradigm. The production figures of the relay assembly and bank wiring rooms are the "data" generated in a bizarre almost non-verbal conversation. Lighting and tea-breaks varied, and silent observers sat in corners all day totally immersed in what was going on. Elton Mayo and his co-workers had a difficult time preserving their alien role. The Hawthorne plant workers would not or could not maintain the official version of the conversational game. They warmly appreciated the interest being shown in their activities and worked accordingly. It was this construction of the lighting and tea-breaks and not the events themselves that produced the continuing increases in output. Evidence in social psychology must always be construed in such experiential (and not experimental) contexts if we are to understand social process more adequately. The hard repeatable data is not to be found in the behaviour of people; but in the consistent relationships between their behaviour and their constructions of experience. The repertory grid and the video-recorder may together reveal more stable insights than either can reveal alone. Given an acceptance of the personal construct psychology paradigm a coherent system of conversational technology will emerge. It will incorporate everything from Skinner boxes to client-centred therapy and ethological "live with them" methods to the interpretation of dreams. The reflexive use of the commonality, sociality, self-awareness and social awareness corollaries provides an experiential-behavioural framework from within which to understand what is going on. This insight offers a taxonomy of methodologies from which to choose methods appropriate to situations and purposes.

Complementality

Are the "social" corollaries so far proposed sufficient to provide firm theoretical framework for conversational investigations into social situations?

One of the social phenomena which has most intrigued man is the social complexity of insect communities (Ardrey, 1972). How can organisms which show no signs of consciousness or awareness organise themselves so complexly? Commonality is part of the answer. Each member of the community shares an innate construction of experience with its species-neighbours. But even in the most elementary of communities it is rare for all members to behave similarly. Males differ from females. The biology influences the construing. There is differentiation of function implying that specialists are endowed with different constructions; and yet the whole community functions as if the complexity of organisation arises not from total commonality but from a "complementality" of individual constructions of experience. The ethologists have described how these mesh together to form a social system which develops characteristics (Lorenz, 1977) that transcend the sum of the characteristics of the parts. Perhaps if personal construct psychology is to properly serve the needs of social investigation a "*complementality corollary*" should also be added to Kelly's original system. It might be framed as follows:

COMPLEMENTALITY COROLLARY. When people share in a common pool of events including each other, but by virtue of their position sample these events differently, their constructions of experience will develop to complement each other. This complementation will produce a social system which exhibits greater complexity of stable organisation than exists in the constructions of any individual contributing to it.

Thus the complementality corollary serves to link commonality to the other social corollaries and allows the concepts of organisation and institution to be introduced into the personal construct psychology approach to social systems. The participants share constructions of experience which embody implicit rules and regulations. For certain purposes they construe co-participants as objects and not as containers of alternate (or even similar) constructions of experience.

Another requirement for a conversational methodology of investigation is thus clarified. Repertory grid techniques must be expanded to include complementality. The form of the grid must not only contain the possibility of identifying commonality between the constructions of experience, one person to another, but the *sum of the grids* from the members of a group should reveal system properties not contained in the grids of any one.

Grids for Complementality

Where individuals share (at least partly) in the same events, grids can be elicited about these events. Personally elicited elements may be used as the basis for each individual grid. In theory such grids may have nothing in common, in practice they almost always overlap. Elements from all the original grids can now be contributed to a common mind-pool. Each participant is asked to do a second grid using all those elements in the mind-pool that have some meaning for him or her. Personal constructs still appear in each grid, but grids can be linked via their common elements. The PAIRS technique which was the basis of the SOCIO-GRIDS analysis, can be used to map one person's constructs on to another's. Inter-grid conversation now ensues to explicate the operant and verbal overlap of each two constructions of experience. Emphasis is placed on recognising regions in which the construction of experience differs. Thus grids, even after negotiation, only partly overlap; and each pair overlaps differently. The personal constructs are now added to the mind-pool and each individual constructs a final grid using all the elements and all the constructs in the mind-pool. Emphasis is given to the use of "don't know" and "not applicable" responses. Each grid is now mapped verbally and operantly onto every other grid. The resultant "system grid" can be treated as if it came from a system individual who would be seen as having a more complete construction of the experience of the total system than any individual contributing to it. A god-like observer, e.g. the ethologist, observing the insect community, can gain insight into the functioning of the social system. But more importantly in the real world of participative negotiation, the system grid and its various constituent parts can be used to raise the awareness by each individual of other individuals' constructions of experience. This technique is particularly appropriate for use in conjunction with such techniques as the socio-technical analysis of working groups pioneered by Trist, Bamforth and Rice and the examination of primitive technologies and artifacts carried out by anthropologists such as Mead (1970) and Levi-Strauss (1962). Thus the action research paradigm for social investigations pioneered in the post-war years and the sociological investigatory methods of, say, Goffman (1971), Reisman (1950) and White (1965), can be added to the separate strands from which the rich texture of a new generation of conversation methods is being woven. Mair's community of selves, and Pask's P-individuals communicating within one brain, offer the vision of the self having complementality characteristics which are more than the sum of the constructions of the internal communicants. Freud invented the unconscious to cope with this eventuality. Perhaps a more adequate conversational technology could be used reflexively as a form of psychotherapy. Seaborne-Jones (1972) offers the beginnings of such an analysis.

The Theory is the Method

This chapter has attempted to demonstrate that the paradigm of personal construct psychology provides the conceptual space within which alternate theories and different methods of investigation can be seen to supplement and complement each other. The shape of this space has been challenged. The fundamental postulate is as yet still fundamental, but the adequacy of the ten corollaries has been questioned. New ones have been suggested more in the spirit of Kelly's own method of inquiry than in any serious attempt to rewrite personal construct psychology. Self-awareness, social awareness, endowment and complementality would seem to require explanation.

Conversational technology can provide tools for building vehicles in which many different approaches to the understanding of living organisms can travel convivially together (Illich, 1973). Personal construct psychology offers this freedom because being a contentless model of man it contains the seeds, nay the seedlings, of a fully fledged meta-theory of psychological relativity. Public-content-laden theories and methods are construed as sources of nutrient in which systems for constructing personally relevant and viable meanings can feed. Each system is endowed with its own perspective and its own intentionality. Other systems are construed by it; and it construes other systems. Hence the relativity. There is no master construer, nor is there any one macro-programme containing the laws which coordinate the universe. Man invents himself and the space he occupies. Attempts to produce absolute systems of description and explanation will die away as the all-pervading media reveals the arbitrariness of the positions of all describers and explainers. The monolithic media will also die as its images become transparent and dissolve revealing the need for a technology that enables personal construct systems (people) to interact and to continually enrich and renew themselves.

Whilst most men believed that they lived within one or another coherent geographical, cultural and ideological position "objective explanations" were attempted and imposed upon everybody. The commonality of local construing provided the basis for unquestioning agreement about the nature of physical and social reality. Such self-supporting systems of local objectivity lean hard on the dissenter. Thus is madness manufactured. Even before the recent explosion in the means of apparent communication the conventional reality was never as unquestioned or monolithic as the belief in one objective reality might lead one to expect.

Unfortunately each questioner was, in self-preservation, driven to believe that his view contained the new, greater or more valid objectivity. Only the artist occasionally recognised that one man's personal reality was another man's prison. But then he probably distrusted his own reality to the point of madness, or drew a sharp line between the subjectivity of art and the objectivity of reality. A whole-hearted theory of psychological relativity would release a tremendous fund of creative energy. Theories and methods, Art and Science could be seen as tools for achieving shared purposes. Philosophy which is the arena within which intentionalities are clarified and non-trivial conflicts about purpose are negotiated, and conversational methodology which is the resource for building the vehicles in which personal, interpersonal and social space may be explored, become primary concerns of man. Personal construct psychology provides the meta-language in which man can explore his nature. The resolution of day-to-day affairs requires the construction of those interlocking systems of specific construing which serve the agreed common purposes of the participants. The creation of a negotiating technology frees people to negotiate. Recognition of the relativity of knowing leaves each person free to negotiate changes in the shared constructions, free to leave the group and join others with more compatible constructions or free to try to create a group by becoming the seed around which a new system of knowing can condense and grow. George Kelly was one such seed. An effective conversational technology can amplify the power of man to achieve such aspirations. George Kelly indicated the ground rules for the construction of such a methodology. Kelly is dead. Long live the spirit of Kelly.

References

Ardrey, R. (1972). "The Social Contract". Fontana, London.

Bannister, D. and Fransella, F. (1971). "Inquiring Man". Penguin, Harmondsworth.

Bannister, D. and Mair, J.M. (1968). "The Evaluation of Personal Constructs". Academic Press, London and New York.

Berne, E. (1972). "What do you say after you say Hello?". Grove Press, New York.

Bronowski, J. (1965). "Science and Human Values". Harper and Row, New York.

Bugental, J. F. T. (1967). "Challenge of Humanistic Psychology". McGraw-Hill, New York.

Castaneda, C. (1969). "The Teachings of Don Juan: A Yaqui Way of Knowledge". Ballentine, New York.

Duck, S. (1973). Similarity and perceived similarity of personal constructs as influences on friendship choice. *Br. J. Soc. Clin. Psychol.* **12,** 1–6.

Fransella, F. (1972). "Personal Change and Reconstruction: Research on a Treatment of Stuttering". Academic Press, London and New York.

Fransella, F. and Bannister, D. (1977). "A Manual for Repertory Grid Technique". Academic Press, London and New York.

Goffman, E. (1971). "The Presentation of Self in Everyday Life". Penguin, Harmondsworth.

Harri-Augstein, E. S. (1978). Reflecting on structures of meaning: A process of learning-to-learn. *In* "Personal Construct Psychology 1977" (Ed. F. Fransella). Academic Press, London and New York.

Harri-Augstein, E. S. (1978). Conversational procedures for the development of man-management skills and course evaluation. "Proceedings of BIOSS/Centre for the Study of Human Learning Repertory Grid Conference". Brunel University, Uxbridge.

Hull, C. L. (1932). The goal gradient hypothesis and maze learning. *Psychol. Rev.* **39**, 25–43.

Illich. I. D. (1973). "Celebration of Awareness". Penguin, Harmondsworth.

Kelly, G. A. (1955). "The Psychology of Personal Constructs", Vols 1 and 2. Norton, New York.

Kelly, G. A. (1970). Behaviour is an experiment. *In* "Perspective in Personal Construct Theory" (Ed. D. Bannister). Academic Press, London and New York.

Laing, R. D. (1970). "Knots". Penguin, Harmondsworth.

Levi-Strauss, C. (1962). "The Savage Mind". Weidenfeld and Nicholson, London.

Lorenz, K. (1977). "Behind the Mirror". Methuen, London.

Mair, M. (1977). Metaphors for living. *In* "Nebraska Symposium on Motivation 1976" (Ed. A. W. Landfield). University of Nebraska Press, Lincoln.

Mair, M. (1977). The community of self. *In* "New Perspectives in Personal Construct Theory" (Ed. D. Bannister). Academic Press, London and New York.

Mead, M. (1970). "Culture a Commitment: Study of the Generation Gap". Doubleday, New York.

Mendoza, S. and Thomas, L. F. (1972). The individual's construction of his visual world as projected by the repertory grid. Mimeo. Centre for the Study of Human Learning, Brunel University, Uxbridge.

Ogden, C. K. and Richards, I. A. (1923). "The Meaning of Meaning". Harcourt, New York.

Pask, G. (1973). "Conversation, Cognition and Learning". Elsevier Press, Amsterdam.

Pask, G. (1975). "The Cybernetics of Human Learning and Performance". Hutchinson Educational, London.

Pendleton, D. (1976). Intervening in the teacher/learner dialogue. *In* "Proceedings of U.K.R.A. Conference", Durham. Ward Lock, London.

Polanyi, M. (1967). "The Tacit Dimension". Routledge and Kegan Paul, London.

Pope, M. (1978). Monitoring and reflecting in teacher training. *In* "Personal Construct Psychology 1977" (Ed. F. Fransella). Academic Press, London and New York.

Popper, K. (1972). "Objective Knowledge: An Evolutionary Approach". Clarendon Press, Oxford.

Radley, A. (1977). Living on the horizon. *In* "New Perspectives in Personal Construct Theory" (Ed. D. Bannister). Academic Press, London and New York.

Reisman, D. (1950). "The Lonely Crowd". Yale University Press, New Haven.

Rogers, R. (1969). "Freedom to Learn". Charles E. Merrill, Columbus.

Rogers, R. and Coulson, W. R. (1968). "Man and Science of Man". Charles E. Merrill, Columbus.

Rosenthal, R. (1966). "Experimental Effects on Behavioral Research". Appleton-Century Crofts, New York.

Seaborne-Jones, G. (1972). "Treatment or Torture". Tavistock, London.

Sherrington, C. S. (1952). "Man in his Nature". Penguin, Harmondsworth.

Shotter, J. (1975). "Images of Man in Psychological Research". Methuen, London.

Skinner, B. F. (1971). "Beyond Freedom and Dignity". Alfred A. Knopf, New York.

Skinner, B. F. (1975). "Verbal Behavior". Appleton-Century Crofts, New York.

Slater, P. (Ed.) (1976). "Explorations of Intrapersonal Space by Grid Technique", Vol 1. Wiley, Chichester.

Stewart, V. (1976). Managers' views of management. Notes to a BIOSS Course. Brunel University, Uxbridge.

Thomas, L. F. (1968). DEMON and Double DEMON: Computer-aided Conversations with Yourself. Centre for the Study of Human Learning, Brunel University, Uxbridge.

Thomas, L. F. (1972). A Manual Grid Sorter. Centre for the Study of Human Learning, Brunel University, Uxbridge.

Thomas, L. F. (1976). Focusing: Exhibiting Meaning in a Grid. Centre for the Study of Human Learning. Brunel University, Uxbridge.

Thomas, L. F. (1978). "Spaced"—Manual for Visual Display of Repertory Grids. Centre for the Study of Human Learning, Brunel University, Uxbridge.

Thomas, L. F. and Harri-Augstein, E. S. (1977). Learning-to-learn: The personal construction and exchange of meaning. *In* "Adult Learning" (Ed. M. Howe). Wiley, Chichester.

Thomas, L. F. and Shaw, M. (1977). PEGASUS: A Manual for "Program Elicits A Grid and Sorts Using Similarities". Centre for the Study of Human Learning, Brunel University, Uxbridge.

Thomas, L. F., McKnight, C. and Shaw, M. (1976). Grids and Group Structure. Centre for the Study of Human Learning. Brunel University, Uxbridge.

Thomas L. F. *et al*. (1978). A personal construct approach to learning in education, training and therapy. *In* "Personal Construct Psychology 1977" (Ed. F. Fransella). Academic Press, London and New York.

Tinbergen, N. (1953). "Social Behaviour in Animals". Methuen, London.

Tolman, E. (1932) "Purposive Behaviour in Animals and Men". Appleton-Century Crofts, New York.

Tomkins, S. A. (1963). "Affect Imagery Consciousness. The Negative Affects" Vol II. Springer, New York.

White, R. W. (Ed.) (1965). "The Study of Lives". Atherton, New York.

Construing as Praxis

Alan Radley

The label "social psychology" describes the ground which most theories in social science attempt to cover, but upon which few will consent to stand. The psychology of personal constructs is no exception to the general situation, notwithstanding Kelly's (1955) description of a role as being "dependent upon cognate developments within a group of two or more people" (p. 98). His concept of role is grounded in the constructs of the *individuals* concerned, so that they may participate in a social process to the extent that they can subsume "aspects of the construction systems of those with whom [they] attempt to join in a social enterprise" (p. 97).

Kelly emphasised, however, that this should not be taken to imply that the execution of one's role is a cognitive exercise: it refers instead to an ongoing activity involving the person as "a participant, either in concert or in opposition, within a group movement" (p. 98). There is an indication here that the psychology of personal constructs might reach out toward the problems of social psychology, but the theory makes no theoretical advances in this particular direction. For Kelly's level of analysis was the individual person, not the society to which the individual belonged nor the particular groups within which he lived his life. And where Kelly did consider the larger social framework (Kelly, 1962), it was accounted for within the terms of constructs employed by persons treated as generalised individuals. Therefore, it is not surprising that the claim that personal construct theory be a valid starting point for social psychology should have been subjected to a detailed critique within the framework of the sociology of knowledge (Holland, 1977). Holland argues, amongst other things, that Kelly's definition of role was created in opposition to his poor understanding of the concept as framed by sociologists. He also indicates that much which is of interest to a social psychologist lies outside the range of useful application of a theory based upon personal (i.e. individual) constructs, or even of one based upon interpersonal understanding.

73

In this chapter we shall consider a number of specific questions drawn from the field of social psychology and attempt to re-frame them in a way which, while preserving their integrity, invites further consideration of Kelly's ideas. In doing this we, too, shall look the construct theory gift-horse in the mouth—a necessary attitude to a scientific offering. However, merely to demonstrate by repeated example that the theory as it stands does not encompass the field of social psychology will not be our aim, although this would not be difficult to achieve. It would seem like turning the horse around and continuing the exercise at the other end.

Personal Constructs and Social Action

"People, too, are events." The validation of constructs is carried out within the context of the groups of people with whom we live, and these other people, as persons, also act according to their anticipations. In this way Kelly (1955, p. 176) presented a picture of social life as maintained through the mutual validation of participants' construing, from which it follows that people behave similarly because they tend to expect the same things. Social roles are played out in the light of how other persons view the world, and we adjust our constructs to meet the various contingencies which arise in the course of events. However, there is a problem here if we describe both the expectations of "man-the-scientist" and those of the man in the street as simply examples of construing. Mischel (1964) has argued that while the former mode of construing can be described as predictive, the latter is better thought of as prescriptive.

Social actions are based upon intentions wrought within the bounds of what we can, may and ought to do (Heider, 1958). These prescriptive features often reveal themselves to us as obligations, expressed not only in terms of what other individuals expect from us as their rights, but in terms of what the group expects, society requires, or the law demands. It is to the rules of the situation that we appeal concerning these matters, rules which are not constituted solely *in* the views of individual persons, although depending upon persons' views *of them* for their institutional function. That is why rules have been described as appearing to individuals as if they were a "third person" (Thibaut and Kelley, 1959), or have been characterised conceptually as a "generalised other" (Mead, 1934).

It is a mark of so much of our social life that it does not require self-consciousness, or an explicit understanding of the rules which we presume guide our behaviour. However else we describe personal constructs, we cannot legitimately conceive of them only as a set of templates which we place over the social world in order to make sense of it, for, as co-participants, *we are already part of that world which we seek to understand*.

A person's role cannot follow from his constructs (interpretations) alone, nor from his deliberations about aspects of the construction systems of his fellows. Kelly seems to say this when he writes that

> . . . it is not enough that the role player organise his behaviour with an eye on what other people are thinking; he must be a participant, either in concert or in opposition, within a group movement. (1955, p. 98)

The problem still remains for us to say something about the nature of this participation within a group movement, without simply referring the reader back to a definition of role in terms of one person's constructs subsuming those of another. The view that sociality rests upon interpersonal predictions, or upon rule-following in the sense of individual choice is inadequate to this task. And in so far as personal constructs are defined within such a scheme, then questions regarding our social existence lie outside the scope of this approach.

The social world in which we live is indeed more than the interpersonal behaviour which we actually engage in, and we know it to be so. As a system of varied groupings, of classes with differing interests and as sets of institutionalised practices, people are confronted with them as social facts, the everyday reality of which they cannot deny. As Berger and Luckmann (1971) point out, it is only when we consider individuals born into a world which was created prior to their existence that we can talk about a social world at all. To a child the social world just "is" what it appears to be; it acquires through its historic form the status of an objective reality. Furthermore, throughout a person's life he continues to have actual first-hand knowledge of only a portion of the society of which he is one particular member. In this sense no comprehensive understanding of social life is reducible to the personal relationships of individuals who construe the construction processes of other individuals. The institutions of society may be the products of human endeavour, but in their objectified form they become part of the "real world" in which we live. Berger and Luckmann (1971) view this as a dialectical process in which, through changing their world, people are engaged collectively in constructing this objectivity which in turn shapes what they become.

For the personal construct theorist this means, in one sense, that the social world enjoys a similar status to the world which Kelly assumed to be "really out there" to be understood. It is a world which we first encounter only from the inside, in so far as it presents itself to us as what apparently must be. It is something which we can examine from the point of view of individual participants, by asking them how they interpret those aspects of society of which they have experience. And yet we would be mistaken if we were to limit our view of the social world to being a set of events lying passively within the constructs of individual people. The individual is himself formed by that world which he seeks to understand, and the institutions, roles and ideologies of his society are what he helps to shape through his interventions in social life.

Therefore, we shall need to abandon the idea of the person *interpreting* social events as the basis for a psychological understanding of social action, and turn towards an acknowledgement of the social relations in which people exist together. However, this does not mean that we should see society only as an external force which coerces individuals into doing things in spite of their interpretations of it. This would be the result of our reifying society, so that it appears *as if* it were a non-human or possibly supra-human phenomenon (Berger and Luckmann, 1971). To reify "society" and "individuals" is to set them inexorably apart, and to do this from the perspective of personal construct theory would lead either to denying the validity of *apparently* external social forces in shaping human action, or to vain attempts to assimilate such things as tradition, morality and law into a psychology of congregate individuals.

Of course, to many people the social world does appear to be *really* a foreign, coercive or dangerous place. People feel themselves to be in the grip of social forces which either carry them along or, in times of stability, seem to limit and hinder their efforts to express their individual capacities. There is a seeming paradox here about human activity, first explored in detail by Marx and summarised by Bernstein (1972) as follows:

> For it is man, or rather classes of men, who constantly and continuously create and reinforce the social institutions that pervade human life. These are the objectifications of social *praxis*. And yet these institutions—especially when understood in terms of political economy—have the consequence not of freeing *praxis* and creating those conditions which allows for the enjoyment of free individuality, but of enslaving man, dehumanising and alienating him. (p. 306)

This is not inconsistent with Kelly's own description of reification at the personal level, in which the individual forgets that he is the author of his own self-descriptions and believes himself to be *nothing but* the particular type of person defined by his constructs. The attitude of constructive alternativism extends to the individual the capacity to shape his life through his own constructions, even where that leads him to deny himself this potential by his belief in what he "really is" or "cannot be". The possibility of therapeutic change hinges upon the construct theorist's double acceptance of the relativity of events, *and* of the personal reality of the client's perceptions.

If we take this attitude into the realm of social psychology, the possibility of social change might be enhanced by our first extending *to people* the capacity to shape *their destiny* through *their actions together*. If we couple this with an acceptance of the present state of their situation—how they act within it and how they perceive it—then we will not pursue a line of inquiry which rests upon the alienation of persons from their social world. Just as we should not examine the inner world of the individual as a set of personality factors alien to the person, so we should not study the social world in its external reality apart from the people who constitute it.

Two facets of this alienation-in-theory will then be avoided. Social situations will not be treated as things apart, which act as variables in some way determining the thoughts and actions of the individuals involved. Were this to happen, it would make for a strange hybrid approach to social psychology in which the constructs of persons were understood within the framework of a society studied using the methods of positivistic science. Secondly, the acknowledgement of people's own social reality in particular situations means that what is to be understood are people living in the circumstances of their lives (Sève, 1975), rather than some "social man" born of the psychologist's abstractions.

This point might be clarifed by pursuing the comparison of social psychology with personality theory. Personal construct psychology eschews the mere categorisation of individuals as psychological theory in favour of comprehending the person's own constructions about his life. Similarly, social psychology might relinquish as its twin aims the study of how various categories of social situations affect individuals, together with the analysis of how different types of people react to the same social situations (Moscovici, 1972). Furthermore, the social psychologist who acknowledges the particular realities of people's lives can no longer preserve his standpoint as neutral in his scientific dealings with others. Just as the personal construct theorist must acknowledge the relativity of perceptions, so the social psychologist must admit to the relativity of the practical relations which he studies.

For the mere description of people's construct systems, and the plain documentation of social situations, leaves the standpoint of constructive alternativism and the acceptance of personal/social realities as separate attitudes. This separation diminishes the social scientist's effectiveness as an agent of social intervention. By comparison, it is in the personal construct therapist's engagement with the client through the grasp of his constructs that possibilities for change become apparent. It is in the therapeutic dialogue and in its transposition into action that change is effected, and we should strive for a similar attitude within the realm of social psychology. We shall have occasion to refer again to the work of Paulo Freire (1972), who said in his discussion of peasant education:

> the methodology proposed requires the investigators and the people (who would normally be considered objects of that investigation) to act as *co-investigators*.

> The more active an attitude men take in regard to the exploration of their
> thematics, the more they deepen their critical awareness of reality, and in spelling
> out those thematics, take possession of that reality. (p. 78)

It should be clear from this that we are not describing participant observation, nor an ethnomethodology aimed at description only. The standpoint
rests upon the acceptance of change; not only an individual's reconceptual-
isation of affairs, but people's practical endorsement of the possibilities
which their actions bring into view.

The personal construct theorist who would see people as shaping their
lives through action in unison or in conflict must also adjust to his field of
inquiry. For this capacity of people to intervene in human affairs, beyond the
mere reflection upon their situation, implies a fundamental shift in our
theoretical standpoint. By taking social action as the legitimate focus for
inquiry, and by according it a reality for our scientific endeavours, there
comes the possibility of *finding out afresh* what the basis for our theory
should be. By this we mean nothing short of the inevitable redefinition of
that basic but elusive term "construct"; a term whose operational definition
as "the way in which two things are alike and different from a third" is
grounded in the standpoint of the mental life of the individual. It is this
standpoint which is inadequate to encompass the field of social action.

The above suggestion should not seem at all radical to personal construct
psychologists who accept, as Kelly did, that all theory is temporary and that
scientific progress, as theoretical reconstruction, is premised upon experiment. It would seem inevitable that "construct"—in effect the *Theory* of
personal constructs—should be given a grounding in a further definition of
human action, or else be replaced by an alternative scheme altogether. This
is not a criticism intended to hasten the departure of the theory, for an undue
concern with the removal of established ideas is very similar in practical
attitude to the unfortunate need to conserve one's chosen explanation at all
costs.

What Form of Social Action do we Describe?

It is outside the scope of this chapter to undertake any detailed description of
a particular social situation, if only because I would have to speculate in ways
considered unacceptable given the remarks in the previous section. The
reappraisal of constructs must be sought in active inquiry, and cannot be
achieved through *a priori* definition. However, the assumption that people
have the capacity to shape their lives through social action, together with the
suggestion that we give credence to the actual relationships in which this
happens, requires that some form be given to this project.

The basic assumption is an affirmation which emphasises that persons act together in their world. It does not presume that they must always, or even should always act in unison, nor that we consider the word "people" to describe a homogeneous entity. Rather, it draws attention to man's transcendence of his situation through intervention in the world—through practical activity. Such socially constructive activity is not to be accounted for as "behaviour" which satisfies needs or verifies perceptions—it is not to be "predicted"—for it is assumed to be the basis of social and personal life. The question "Why does one individual relate to another?" is then seen to be as redundant as the question "What makes the person construe the world?". We take our standpoint in the interconnected actions of persons, in *praxis* (Bernstein, 1972; Janoušek, 1972.), rather than in the perceptions of individuals.

However, it is the actual situations in which people live which help form, and yet are transcended through *praxis*. It is the particular "here and now" which expresses the boundaries within which people must act together. Freire (1972) describes these "limit-situations" as "the impassable boundaries where possibilities end, but the real boundaries where all possibilities begin" (p. 71 ff.). He goes on to say:

> Men, as beings "in a situation", find themselves rooted in temporal-spatial conditions which mark them and which they also mark . . . . Men *are* because they *are in* a situation. And they *will be more* the more they not only critically reflect upon their existence but critically act upon it. (Freire, 1972, pp. 80–81)

These situations are not isolated, but are defined by people's relationships to other social groupings. So, for example, the Brazilian peasants of Freire's educational programme have their social being in relation to those whom he designates an oppressive class. An understanding of their situation is contingent upon attention to the particularities of this relationship, in which can be found what Freire calls the "generative themes" of that epoch. These themes he views as a universe of dialectically opposed ideas, values and hopes to which men in different situations enjoin themselves. His understanding of the peasant's outlook comes from Freire's attempt to liberate them, through education in literacy, from the social situation in which they are prevented from acting as whole human beings. Their awareness of themselves as a class, and of their own interests is limited by their social identity. This is characterised by the duality of their existence, in which their own needs and their wish to be like those who oppress them are in conflict. Their identity as a group and their ways of seeing themselves and their world is bound by their relationship to the dominant class. Freire gives an account of how, through educational intervention, the peasants are able to begin transforming this relationship and eventually to transcend it.

Freire's work is mentioned because it is just the kind of description of a particular social situation called for in the previous section. It illustrates the point that an understanding of any social grouping necessitates a comprehension of the wider context in which that grouping is located. More specifically, it is the relations in which social groupings stand that define their possibilities for action (Billig, 1976).

In our society groups and classes are in relationships which are "mediated" by the objective structures which are the institutionalised products of social action. The "limit-situations" are created by the differentiated social structure and the division of labour, through which various groups coordinate their actions within a network of tasks to be performed. The nature of this coordination will depend upon the forms of relation, in which case it might be a cooperative enterprise, a competitive exercise or a state of conflict. At this point all we wish to indicate is that social action is coordinated within a *praxis* which has as its object certain common features of the social world. Managers and workers, landowners and peasants are bound within relationships which are grounded in the "here and now" of the world which they must share. This means that, even when groups are clearly separated in their interests, their relationships are rooted in a reality towards which their very different intentions point in anticipation of their actions. The manager and worker comprehend the nature of the work to be done even though they might disagree about how the ends should be achieved. Similarly, living in different personal worlds, the landowner and peasant still grasp the needs of the land whose ownership divides them totally, but the demands of which bind them together.

There is no intention here to forge a spurious bond between these groupings; only to ascertain at the outset that *praxis* of whatever kind depends upon a coordination of groups about certain key features of their real world situation. It is this which is sometimes called the "Task" by social psychologists (Homans, 1951), and about which the group's survival must be framed. For Mead (1959) and for Schutz (1967) it is an aspect of the "vivid present" which reflects the continuity of human existence, an idea essential to our view of men transforming their world with a consciousness of their purpose.

The constraints of the institutionalised world, and in particular the modes of production seen in historical perspective, were a special contribution of Marx's writings on *praxis* (Janoušek, 1972). The point we would make here is different, though one also discussed by Marx (1975). It is that the actions of persons bent upon common endeavour constitute a unity of intention—of *anticipation*—in which their being is truly social. This is so even where group relations are in conflict, for the particular form of unity within the separate groups, and the form of the contextual relation in which they stand, depend upon the coordination of their actions together.

However, in each case the *particular* characteristics of this coordination remain to be described, and it is to this matter that we shall shortly turn our attention.

From the standpoint of the individual, he lives through or has his being in his participation in social action, the form of which *contains him* even as he lends himself to its transformation. In that sense, the nature of persons is inexplicable by reference to individuals taken separately, and indeed the extent to which persons in a given society consider themselves *to be individuals* is revealed by social analysis (Durkheim, 1972; Berger and Luckmann, 1971, p. 103). Our conclusion is that, living in relationship, there is a tacit basis to our existence, and this basis is fundamentally social. Far from being tucked away inside our "private subjectivities", those authentic aspects of ourselves most readily expressed in passion, and yet grasped with such difficulty on reflection, indicate the practical, relational nature of being human.

We may, as Kelly says, *live in anticipation,* but this is not like the expectations of the scientist who has already formulated his hypothesis. It is the co-participation in systems of action which have, as their object, the world in which we live. We might consider this intentional, organised activity through which the person knows himself and his world to be *construing* (Radley, 1977), except that action in this context is not individual behaviour, but *praxis*. This means that questions about the way in which a person contrues events are referred to the forms of social action in which he participates. It is not merely what an individual thinks or knows, but *how* he thinks or *what he knows with* which we would also need to understand. This requires consideration of the forms of social action in which people are involved, if we are to remain consistent in our argument that the person is a social being.

The Structure of Social Relations

If social groupings are in relationships constituted by their *praxis*, then we should inquire into the forms that these relationships might take. To pick up Freire's terms again, we should want to know about the "universe of themes" in which people participate, and the relative importance of these themes as they are expressed in the heterogeneity of social life. There is the question of the dominance of various groupings over others, the presence of conflict or cooperation, and the important question of the transformation of social relationships as men's *praxis*, of whatever kind, creates further thematic possibilities through changing their "limit-situations".

Not only might we expect certain social relationships to be dominant over others (for example, class or race relations), but assuming that change through action is characteristic of social life, there will be changes in the balance of relationship between the parties concerned. Freire's educational programme was just such an attempt to change the oppressive character of the relationship in which the lives of the peasants were defined and pre-scribed by the dominant class. If we think of social relations as being characterised by bipolar themes (not abstract, but practical contradictions), then the whole relationship is formed, in part, by the uneven development of each grouping with respect to the other. In the emergence and development of a relationship one group will play a principle determining part. This idea has been summarised by Mao Tse-Tung (1967):

> The nature of a thing is determined mainly by the principle aspect of a contradic-tion, the aspect which has gained the dominant position. (p. 333)

However, the principle aspect is not fixed, but changes from one "pole" to the other in the development of the relationship, so that the character of the whole situation is transformed. The structure of society may be seen to reflect such imbalances, not only in the wider sense (class relations), but in the relationships between smaller, specialised groups, e.g. behaviourist and phenomenological psychologists. A study of such relations must necessarily involve not only a description of the values and perceptions of the groups involved, but the ways in which these relations have become objectified in the framework of society. Within a Marxian framework, the imbalance is reflected in the products of men's efforts and in the unequal control which some men have in the means of production of material wealth. It is in these particular conditions that one might seek those features which contribute to the apparent stability of relations in our society. Indeed, to focus upon the actual conditions of social life is to reveal its heterogeneity, so that when we shall speak of "social relations" and of "social groupings" in abstract terms we do not mean to imply a study of "groupings in abstraction". Just as a construct only takes its full meaning if considered in the context of the system of *the living person* to whom it belongs, so any social relation needs to be appreciated in the context of the *real life circumstances* from which it has been referred.

Having made these points, we may now go on to discuss, not the actual conditions, but the *general* features of relationships in transformation. These are perhaps most striking in the struggles of groups attempting to claim their autonomy and to assert their identity in relation to others. For the group which is trying to claim for itself those things which it sees as currently held by others has its locus in the situation defined from the standpoint of the dominant grouping. To give some examples, the Scots and the Welsh live in a

Britain where many things are defined from the standpoint of the English, as present political events in the United Kingdom demonstrate. Supporters of women's movements have initially to speak as women defined in situations dominated by men. Personal construct psychologists must work from an actual basis of a discipline whose dominant paradigm is causal explanation coupled with experimental method. This is not to say that these examples are similar in other respects, but is only to indicate that there is no basis for assuming either equilibrium (or conflict) as being the constant state in all social relationships.

The example of the subordinate group, either in its dissent or in its early attempt to assert its own autonomy, is a useful illustration of some points in our discussion. For dissent of this kind is treated with respect to the normative practices of the relationship, in which it appears as an *incongruent object* (i.e. marked out as something to be corrected or resisted). It will appear as such particularly to the dominant group, and may also be apprehended in this way by those who dissent (Freire, 1972), for their identity is, as it were, contained within the practical definition of the relationship stated from the principal aspect. For example, a married woman who begins to seek autonomy as a woman continues to live within a relationship to her husband (to "men") which can evoke conflict and guilt in her about what she does. Similarly, when first putting aside statistics and the control of experimental variables a research psychologist may doubt, at times, that his work is "really scientific".

It is only when critical reflection is replaced by critical action that a clear change in this relationship can be seen. For then, either in struggle, in passionate argument or in carefully documented research the dissident grouping adopts its perspective *as a standpoint*, and realises it (i.e. makes it real) through action. We do not intend by use of these examples to convey the notion that such change is always sudden, passionate or revolutionary. There are many factors, special to each relationship, which will further the kind of transformation which we have just described. In the case of the English and Scottish nations, both the "external factor" of the dissolution of the British Empire and the "internal factor" of the discovery of oil in Scottish waters have contributed to gradual change in the political relationship between them.

The important point is that action by the subordinate party is the establishment of their position as a standpoint (or action perspective) from which they may critically realise themselves in relation to the opposing group. Having spoken for or acted from their position—having committed themselves to it—they may now apprehend the dominant position in an objectified form, and as itself something to be critically analysed. For the form of the relationship as it stood, maintained by the parties concerned, is that tacit basis to which we have referred and which becomes only fully available to people as they transform it through action.

As a part of this *praxis* the language which is used reflects this form, when, in simple terms, even the name of the dominant grouping may provide the nominative description of the whole, e.g. humanity is often referred to as "men" or "man". Indeed, the problem for any social group attempting to determine its position is that it must use the language of the relationship in its present form; so that, returning to our examples, women may try vainly to describe to men their domestic labours as "work", and phenomenological psychologists must establish to the satisfaction of their colleagues the "scientific" basis of their research. (We might note here that the deliberate manipulation of language is used by terrorist groups in an attempt to shift the balance of relations in the minds of the public, so that kidnap victims are sometimes "tried" and then "executed" for their "crimes".)

These linguistic structures are part of the *praxis* which we have described so that the norms of dominance are reflected in the ways in which events and actions are "marked out" against the background of what is accepted. This principle of imbalance may operate as a norm within a group, when, for example, certain animals or foods are taboo (Levi-Strauss, 1966, pp. 102-103); or else within individual construct systems in the establishment of one's own identity (Radley, 1973), and in one's perception of others (Adams-Webber and Benjafield, 1973). While we have no space here to discuss the interrelation between these levels of analysis, it is suggested (Radley, 1978) that they each reflect aspects of the *praxis* to which we have so far drawn attention.

However, this argument should not be seen to imply a form of social relativism in which people's situations merely determine their viewpoints about themselves and others. From our perspective, there is no validity in the generalised assertion that what a person does or says is merely a function of his class or group membership, and that he cannot comprehend things from an alternative standpoint (cf. Plamenatz, 1971). To say that a person's outlook is nothing but the view of a "bourgeois" or a "Marxist" or a "behaviourist" is to employ such typifications outside of the actual relations in which they take their meaning. For it is with respect to systems of specific relations (e.g. bourgeois–proletariat, Marxist–liberal, behaviourist–phenomenologist) that the relevant actions will be structured.

There are two aspects of social relations, as we have described them, which attest to a fundamental *relativity* of social action in contrast to the spurious "relativism" mentioned above. One concerns the example of the emerging group, whose actions will, at one time, take their meaning both in terms of the system of relations which they strive to alter, and in terms of the relations which that activity is bringing about. Critical intervention demands that people *live in anticipation* of the situation which they are trying to achieve, even as they must state it within the framework of the situation which they are attempting to overthrow (see also Freire, 1976, pp. 130–131). And this specific temporal characteristic of social life must be granted to the strivings of people in whatever particular relations they might act. (This, of course, does not deny this temporal characteristic to groups which are not "emerging" in the sense used here.)

Secondly, any relationship presupposes not only a separation of interests, but also their coordination within a framework which is common to both. Without this common framework no relationship between people would be possible. This does not mean that an object—say, a steel rolling mill—must mean the same to both workers and management, but that to be the (different) thing which it is for each *separate* group, it must be contemporaneous as an object within the perspectives of *both*. For *praxis* is *action in the world*, by which is meant that people relate to one another through their coordinated activities, directed towards the situations in which they find themselves. Social objects (such as a steel rolling mill) contribute to the definition of social relations because they set out, in objectified form, the constraints about which people's future action must be framed if they are to work with them successfully.

To simplify this argument let us suppose that, together with a friend, I am carrying a large trunk upstairs. Let us further suppose that, unbeknown to both of us, it is unevenly loaded and that I am holding the lighter end. The size and weight of the box, together with the angle and shape of the staircase, provide the constraints within which the task must be carried out. These, however, are not "given" to us directly, but are appreciated through our joint efforts to convey the trunk. For every movement which we make will be experienced quite differently at the heavier end as compared with the lighter end, as well as by the one carrying at the front as opposed to the person holding the back of the object. In a sense, in each person's experience a different "trunk" is being carried. However, these differential experiences arise simultaneously from the joint actions of both parties within a relationship framed about particular "moments" (of force, and in time) common to both. And indeed, as my friend struggles with his "heavy trunk" while I lift "mine" with relative ease, the uneven weighting of the object which we are moving (i.e. its *nature*), together with the unequal relationship of the endeavour are both revealed at the same time. Furthermore, what each person discovers is not something about himself as an isolated unit, but about himself as part of a relationship whose other aspect he must thereby apprehend in relation to his own.

The above example is meant to be an illustration, and is clearly not an explanation of social situations. It is intended, however, as a contribution to the argument that we cannot *assume* people's perspectives to be defined and wholly limited by their standpoints in society. That various groups are less able than others to perceive their situation is not disputed here. However, this remains to be accounted for, rather than being reflected back on to the social world as if it were the "natural" state of affairs.

We can also illustrate this problem by transposing the argument to the level of individual persons. Here we may consider each person's actions as falling, at any one time, within the context of the several groups to which he belongs. In effect, social action is not really constituted by oppositions or unities of discrete groupings of people, but by a *praxis* which expresses a multiplicity of relations at any one time. Far from this being an unfortunate problem for social analysis, it reveals how cautious we must be when, as in this chapter, we discuss persons *as if* they were members of single groups engaged in single relationships. Within the heterogeneous system of relations which we may describe society to be, every person is *at one time* a member of several social groups. To act in a social situation as a *person* is to act as a being whose social existence transcends the situation in which one is involved. Putting this in more graphic terms (but thereby rendering static a process of change), it is as if we were to consider a person to be defined by the multiplicity of social relations in which he participates. Yet it is not specific aspects which work individuals in any particular social relationship, but whole persons who act in relation to each other. Conceived in this manner, we can imagine (though this is a temporary, and ultimately a misleading notion) that a person is a nexus of social relations which are coordinated through his actions as an individual. The point is, however, that perspectives and standpoints do not act: people do. So it is that a person *exists simultaneously in multiple relations* even as he may *appear* to act, at that time, in one relationship only.

It is again the presence of the same events (in this case, people) within different relations at the same time which makes coordination of the individual's action possible (as a coherent, *enduring* personality). This would not be possible (nor indeed would a world of *praxis*) if individuals were "locked into" social standpoints conceived as separate from them as persons. This view of relativity as a key feature of both social and personal existence is expressed most succinctly in the later writings of George Mead (1959)* where it forms the basis of his concept of *sociality*. Mead used this term to mean, in the first instance, the capacity of being several things at once. Its relevance here is that by use of it he tried to show the inadequacy of a relativism in which an assumed "real world" could be viewed from several

*Unfortunately, recent critics of Mead's work (Janousek, 1972; Holland, 1977) do not consider these later writings, which (whatever the further criticisms) cannot be called either "subjectivist" or "individualistic".

alternative perspectives, and thereby appreciated as if it were a number of different things. This is very nearly Kelly's stated position at the outset of the "Theory of Personal Constructs". However, this philosophy pushes the "real world" beyond our consideration, while leaving us with a Subject who looks out from these perspectives (constructs) upon that world which he finds apparently ready-made. This position is consistent neither with a thoroughgoing psychology of personal constructs (Radley, 1977), nor with a social psychology based upon *praxis*.

Social Psychology and Personal Construct Theory

In an earlier section it was argued that personal construct psychology might have a practical recommendation to make to social psychologists. It was to adopt a "dual attitude" towards the social world, such that people are held to have the capacity to shape their lives through action, but must be understood in the actual situations of their lives together. The body of this chapter has been an attempt to give an outline form to this recommendation, though confining itself to the general features of social relations which are consistent with the adoption of this attitude.

With these arguments in mind, it can be seen that to ask questions from a standpoint of constructive alternativism conceived simply as "role-adoption" is to commit the error of idealising social life by projecting this generalised capacity for change upon the actual relations *in which* people exist. It is not disputed that critical reflection upon their circumstances provides people with possibilities for change, but we cannot begin from this standpoint if we are also to account for the ways in which people find their world structured and work to maintain or to transform that reality which they see. To conceive of people only as subjects who adopt alternative roles or societal positions is to fail to account for their social existence (conceived as a "becoming"); it is also to adopt, if only implicitly, a model of a ready-made social structure on to which, we imagine, people attach themselves in their attempts to change.

By contrast, to inquire into social relations as if they were things which existed "beneath" people, determining their lives, is to commit an error of a second kind. It is to reify social relations within social psychological inquiry so that they are made the object of study against the background of implicit assumptions about persons. This has the same effect as the former standpoint, in that people and their society are severed. However, from this perspective, it is the social structure which is held to predominate, while individuals are rendered passive. It is interesting to note that where individualism and social determinism are used as explanations in social science they appear as opposites which counter-support one another, and a focus upon one implies the co-existence of the other (cf. Holland, 1977, p. 108).

It is for this reason that the "dual attitude" to which we have referred may be of relevance if we are attempting to construct a *socio-personal* approach within which questions about individuals and actual social relations might be framed. If we begin with individuals and social structure as separate things for analysis, then inevitably there are difficulties concerning how the two relate together. It is partly for this reason that we did not proceed with an analysis of "role-theory", which in its various forms often seems to act as a cement to bind together individual and society, and yet also disguises how the analysis has itself helped to keep them separate. From the standpoint of such *individual-societal* approaches, which begin with established structures (either personality, or social institutions), questions of social relations inhabit a vague middle-ground which appears to be somewhere between psychology and sociology. It is this falsely termed "middle-ground" which we have sought to encourage as a theoretical perspective, from which the relational nature of social life is seen as basic to social psychological inquiry.

This attention to relations rather than to entities provides a parallel between such a social psychology and personal construct theory, and is grounded in the "dual attitude" which is the practical approach underlying both. Where one field is concerned with relations as constructs of individuals, the other reveals relations as *praxis*—as the practical endeavours of people in unity or in opposition to one another. However, these parallels do not arise from merely extending personal construct theory to the problems of inquiry into social life. It is only by attending to the field of social psychology *in its own terms* that a valid perspective can be established within which, at one time, problems can be grasped in a new way and theory itself is reconstructed. It is from such a perspective, or within such a social psychology, that the theory of personal constructs might be further appreciated in a critical way. Finally, it was argued that a recognition of the relativity of social relations implies (and this cannot be avoided) a change in the standpoint of the personal construct psychologist. Just as Kelly's theory removed the mask of "absolute knowledge" from the personality theorist, so this approach must remove from the personal construct theorist his role of "critical observer". For the theoretical framework outlined here indicates the necessity for critical *praxis* by social psychologists in addition to their critical reflection. Personal construct psychology has something to offer in this endeavour, and perhaps, in the trying, even more to gain.

References

Adams-Webber, J. R. and Benjafield, J. (1973). The relation between lexical marking and rating extremity in interpersonal judgement. *Can. J. Behav. Sci.* **5**, 234-241.

Berger, P. L. and Luckmann, T. (1971). "The Social Construction of Reality". Penguin Books, Harmondsworth.

Bernstein, R. J. (1972). "Praxis and Action". Duckworth, London.

Billig, M. (1976). "Social Psychology and Intergroup Relations". Academic Press, London and New York.

Durkheim, E. (1972). "Selected Writings", translated and edited by A. Giddens. Cambridge University Press, Cambridge.

Freire, P. (1972). "Pedagogy of the Oppressed". Penguin Books, Harmondsworth.

Freire, P. (1976). "Education: The Practice of Freedom". Writers and Readers Publishing Co-operative, London.

Heider, F. (1958). "The Psychology of Interpersonal Relations". Wiley, New York.

Holland, R. (1977). "Self and Social Context". Macmillan, London.

Homans, G. C. (1951). "The Human Group". Routledge and Kegan Paul, London.

Janoušek, J. (1972). On the Marxian concept of *Praxis*. In "The Context of Social Psychology" (Eds J. Israel and H. Tajfel), pp. 279-294. Academic Press, London and New York.

Kelly, G. A. (1955). "The Psychology of Personal Constructs", Vols 1 and 2. Norton, New York.

Kelly, G. A. (1962). Europe's matrix of decision. In "Nebraska Symposium on Motivation" (Ed. M. R. Jones), Vol. X, pp. 83–125. University of Nebraska Press, Lincoln, Nebraska.

Levi-Strauss, C. (1966). "The Savage Mind". Wiedenfeld and Nicolson, London.

Mao Tse-Tung (1967). On contradiction. In "Selected Works", Vol. 1, pp. 311-347. Foreign Language Press, Peking.

Marx, K. (1975). Economic and philosophic manuscripts of 1844. In "Marx/Engels—Collected Works", Vol. 3, pp. 229-346. Lawrence and Wishart, London.

Mead, G. H. (1934). "Mind, Self and Society". University of Chicago Press, Chicago.

Mead, G. H. (1959). "Philosophy of the Present". Open Court, Illinois.

Mischel, T. (1964). Personal constructs, rules, and the logic of clinical activity. *Psychol. Rev.* **71**, 180-192.

Moscovici, S. (1972). Society and theory in social psychology. In "The Context of Social Psychology" (Eds. J. Israel and H. Tajfel), pp. 17–68. Academic Press, London and New York.

Plamenatz, J. (1971). "Ideology". Macmillan, London.

Radley, A. R. (1973). "A study of self-elaboration through role change", Unpublished Ph.D. thesis, London University.

Radley, A. R. (1977). Living on the horizon. In "New Perspectives in Personal Construct Theory" (Ed. D. Bannister), pp. 221-249. Academic Press, London and New York.

Radley, A. R. (1978). Social relations and the principle of bipolarity. Seminar paper to a meeting of the Faculty of Social Sciences, The Open University, Walton Hall, England.

Schutz, A. (1967). "Collected Papers", Vol. 1. Martinus Nijhoff, The Hague.

Sève, L. (1975). "Marxism and the Theory of Human Personality". Lawrence and Wishart, London.

Thibaut, J. W. and Kelley, H. H. (1959). "The Social Psychology of Groups". Wiley, New York.

Individuals, Roles and Persons

Peter Stringer

Elucidation of the way in which Kelly (1955) used the terms "individual", "role" and "person" is essential to an appreciation of the relevance of his ideas for a psychology of social phenomena. In the light of the distinctions which I wish to make between the terms, Kelly sometimes used them in an unhelpful and confusing manner. The only one which was explicitly defined within the theory of personal constructs was "role". We shall find that this term has to bear much of the load in laying the foundations for a personal construct approach to social psychological issues. Indeed, Kelly wrote: "Personal-construct theory might have been called 'role theory'" (1955, p. 179).*

In positing and elaborating the fundamental postulate and corollaries of his theory, Kelly took unusual care to discuss the words in which they were framed. And yet "individual" and "person" are not explained satisfactorily. The fundamental postulate begins "A person's processes . . . ". The only weight given to "person" is to insist that it is "the individual person rather than any part of the person, any group of persons, or any particular process manifested in the person's behavior" (p. 47). Effectively the substance of psychology is indicated. "Person" is not defined and "individual" seems to be used as a rhetorical tautology.

The concept of individuality may have posed some problems for Kelly which he was not prepared to take up. It is treated in the second corollary, the first having introduced the notion of construing, which suggests some theoretical priority for it at least. But it is treated very briefly; only one page is devoted to it of the 57 in which the basic theory is laid down. No terms are formally discussed. Individuality is implicitly equated with individual differences.

In the light of this vagueness at the heart of the theory, and the fact that sociality is only introduced in the last of the corollaries, some critics have

* All references are to Kelly (1955).

91

been quick to dismiss the psychology of personal constructs as hopelessly individualistic and quite unequal to the task of explaining social psychological phenomena.

Models of Man-in-society

The significance of the terms "individual", "role" and "person" for social psychology can be indicated by making a rather crude distinction between three fundamental approaches to social psychology, which I will term "individualistic", "role theoretic" and "relational". Each of them is concerned with the relation between Man and society, but only the latter provides an integrated approach. The two former, to borrow Israel's (1972) terms, are, respectively, "individual-oriented" and "society-oriented".

Individualistic approaches include both behaviourism and humanism. In either case social phenomena are of interest primarily for their significance to the human organism as a unit. Despite disclaimers, the primary focus of, for example, social learning theory (e.g. Rotter *et al.*, 1972) is what happens to the individual or to a number of aggregated units in, or as a result of interaction with, the social environment. Process is used as an explanatory device, rather than as the thing to be explained. In social exchange theory (e.g. Chadwick-Jones, 1976) similarly, costs and rewards are outcomes for each member of the dyad considered separately; the dyad is no more than the vehicle within which exchange occurs. Humanistic theories are avowedly individualistic and serve to protect the individual against the pressure of social forces. Self-actualisation is only achieved by withstanding or denying existing social conditions. The humanistic self is unique and made available by essentially independent exercise.

Although role theory concerns itself with the individual, his behaviour is ultimately of interest only as the evidence for the working of socially based roles.

> The central theme of role theory is well known. Man has certain positions within the social system and related to these positions are normative expectations concerning the individual's behaviour and concerning relevant attributes. Positions are independent of a specific occupant. The same is true of the expectations directed towards a position; they are defined as the role of the incumbent of a position. (Israel, 1972, p. 140)

The explanatory basis of role theory requires the assumption that society is prior to the individual. A number of biological explanations of social behaviour are also society-oriented, in the sense that the species is taken as society.

An integrated, relational position gives priority to neither element. Man and society are defined in mutual relation to one another. Man is the sum of his social relations; society is the sum of social relations between men. Neither can be conceived of independently of the other. The relational model of Man can be illustrated by Marx and Mead. "The essence of Man is not an abstraction inherent in each particular individual. The real nature of Man is the totality of social relations" (Marx, 1964, p. 68). "A self can arise only where there is a social process within which this self had its initiation. It arises within that process" (Mead, 1956, pp. 41-42).

None of the three classes of model of Man are *defined* in the above remarks. They tend to take different shapes for different proponents. Often they are too implicit for clear definition. But they do represent certain logically guaranteed positions for a social psychology which deals with Man-in-society. Their interest in the present argument is that they give a basis for considering the terms "individual", "role" and "person". The reference of the two former should be evident. "Person" is equated with Man-in-relation.

An Experiment with the Repertory Grid

The confusion which these terms can generate in the reader of Kelly's work is exemplified in the repertory grid test, which persistently continues to be many psychologists' only point of contact with the work. The obsession with methods is as avid as the adherence to principles of disputation or rhetoric often was in mediaeval or Elizabethan times. At the risk of perpetuating a regrettable habit I shall describe an experiment carried out by Linda Mulley and myself (Stringer and Mulley, 1977) which used the repertory test.

It does not address the central issues which will be discussed in the greater part of this chapter to do with "role", "person" and "individual". But it is concerned with the rep grid at a level at which many exponents have worked. At that level the experiment yielded important methodological results which suggest that people should take care of the form of grid which they use. It may also form a convenient lead into the possibly less familiar theoretical issues discussed later.

For those who support the charge of individualism, the repertory grid—or the Role Construct Repertory Test to give it its most common label—poses a puzzle. Why is the individualist interested in "roles"? Another puzzle is the multiplicity of forms of the grid. Administration of the grid usually begins with a role title list. Persons may be nominated to fill the roles, and their names written on cards. The names are subsequently considered and construed by referring to the cards, independently of the role title list. In another and more common form, the named individuals may be written on a sheet of paper alongside the role titles, so that both are construed together. Or, the role titles alone may be construed. Bannister (1959), on the other hand, devised a grid form in which elements were simply 36 named individuals; role titles were not used to elicit names.

Neither Kelly, Bannister and Mair (1968) nor Fransella and Bannister (1977) spell out fully what might be the implications of using these different forms of grid. They are used fairly undiscriminatingly in rep grid studies. For this reason, we decided to compare some features of grids in which the elements were either role titles or named individuals.

In comparing the construing of roles and individuals our over-arching hypothesis was that the construing of roles would be less complex, less differentiated, on the grounds that constructs regarding roles are more consistently validated than constructs about particular individuals. Such a prediction can be derived from personal construct theory; and Bannister (1963, 1965) has shown that successive validation leads to a less elaborated and differentiated construct system, or tightening of construct relationships.

METHOD

The basis of the experimental method involved asking subjects to complete two repertory grids, one grid in which the elements were role titles, the other in which they were named individuals. Half the subjects did the roles grid first, and half the individuals grid. Personal constructs were elicited on whichever of the two grids was done first.

Eighty student served as subjects, 40 each for the "roles grid first" condition and 40 for the "individuals grid first" condition. The two sub-samples were matched for sex and faculty (arts/science), but the "individuals first" group were on average nine months older than the others. The overall mean age was a little over 21 years.

Grids were administered to groups of four subjects at a time, following a conventional procedure. Constructs were elicited on triads of elements, either role figures or named individuals. However, it is important to recognise that the named individuals *were* originally nominated in response to role titles. But once the nomination had been made, all subsequent references were to the individual by name and the role title was not mentioned again in this condition. Grids were completed by the subject rating, on a seven-point scale, each element on each construct.

A 24-hour interval fell between the subjects doing their two grids. On the second occasion, they were faced by a second and different list of role titles (Table I) which they construed either as individuals or as roles, contrary to their procedure for the first grid, but using the same personal constructs as those used in the first grid.

The roles and individuals grids were compared in respect of three measures derived from a principal components analysis of each grid (Slater,

TABLE I. *Role title lists*

---

1. Mother; a science student; a close friend of the opposite sex; a competent lecturer; a religious person; someone in a position of authority; an elderly person; a member of the working class; a neurotic person; a well-balanced person; self.

2. Father; an arts student; a best friend; an incompetent lecturer; a non-religious person; an admired person; a grand-parent; a housewife; an immature person; a mature person; self.

1977): the mean variance accounted for by each of the first five principal components, certain inter-element "distances", and patterns of construct loadings on the principal components. In addition, the face content of constructs elicited variously on roles and individuals was compared. A similar analysis is described in Stringer (1974).

Examination of these four types of data was guided by our general hypothesis that role construing would be less differentiated than individual construing. (1) It was hypothesised that the size of the first principal component would be larger for the role grids, and the sizes of the second and subsequent components would be smaller. (2) Hypotheses about the relative sizes of inter-element distances varied according to the elements examined, and will be specified below when the results are described. (3) The examination of construct loadings was not carried out for the purpose of hypothesis testing, but rather to explore the ways in which construing similar elements did or did not change according to whether they represented individuals or roles. (4) As regards the content of constructs, it was hypothesised that there would be more commonality in the face content of constructs elicited on roles than on individuals.

RESULTS

A three-way analysis of variance was used to examine the size of the principal components and of the inter-element distances. The three factors were the order in which the two grids were done, whether elements were roles or individuals, and the role title list used. The latter factor produced no significant differences between conditions and will not be discussed here.

(1) It was found that the first principal component accounted for significantly more variance in roles grids than in individuals grids, and the second

TABLE II. *Relative size of principal components: analysis of variance F values.*

	Principal components				
	1	2	3	4	5
Order of grids	0·06 n.s	0·12 n.s	0·51 n.s	0·75 n.s	1·17 n.s
Roles or individuals grid	15·28 $p \langle 0\cdot001$	8·75 $p \langle 0\cdot005$	9·92 $p \langle 0\cdot005$	0·54 n.s	0·57 n.s
Interaction	6·58 $p\ 0\cdot025$	10·19 $p\ 0\cdot005$	3·87 n.s	0·05 n.s	0·07 n.s

d.f. = 1,78

and third components accounted for significantly less (Table II). There were no differences on the fourth and fifth components. The order in which the grids were done made no difference to component sizes. But there was a significant interaction effect. The differences in the sizes of principal components were much more marked for the "individuals grid first" condition. And when constructs were elicited on individuals they gave a smaller first principle component in the persons grid than when constructs were elicited on roles. That is, constructs were not only used in a more differentiated way when construing individuals, but also when constructs were elicited on individuals. This is in line with our general hypothesis.

(2) Five inter-element distances were compared, the significance of the difference between role and individual grid means being tested by a *t*-test (Table IIIA). The distances were those for "self–competent lecturer", "self–science student", "self–mother", "mature–immature person", and "neurotic–well balanced person".

(a) No significant difference was found between the mean values of inter-element distances for "self" and "competent lecturer", whether competent lecturer was construed as a role or as an individual. This had been hypothesised on the assumption that lecturers would tend not to be well known as persons to our student subjects.

(b) Subjects saw themselves, as hypothesised, as more similar to science student", when "science student" was construed as an individual than as a role; the mean inter-element distance was smaller in the individuals grids. One assumes that students in a technological university, where the experiment was carried out, interact rather frequently with science students on a personal level.

TABLE III

(A) *Size of inter-element distances: role and individual construing:* t *values*

Self–competent lecturer	$t =$	-0.28	n.s	
Self–science student	$t =$	2.80	$p < 0.01$	
Self–mother	$t =$	-2.21	$p < 0.05$	
Neurotic–well-balanced person	$t =$	3.09	$p < 0.01$	
Mature–immature person	$t =$	3.31	$p < 0.01$	d.f. $= 78$

(B) *Self–mother inter-element distance: analysis of variance* F *values.*

Sex	$F =$	5.61	$p < 0.025$	
Roles/individuals grid	$F =$	4.54	$p < 0.05$	
Interaction	$F =$	1.41	n.s	d.f. $= 1,78$

(c) Contrary to hypothesis, subjects saw themselves as more like "mother" when she was construed as a role than as an individual. Further analysis showed that this effect was due in large measure to female subjects seeing themselves as significantly more similar to "mother" when she was construed as a role than an individual. Intuitively, this result seems reasonable (Table IIIB).

(d) The hypothesis that the distance between "neurotic and well-balanced" and "mature and immature" figures would be smaller in individual than in role construal was confirmed. Accepting one person as "neurotic" and another as "well-balanced" does not preclude the possibility that they will be construed as similar along other dimensions, when they are considered as specific individuals. This is less likely to occur, however, when they are considered simply as "neurotic" or "well-balanced" role figures.

(3) The pattern of construct use as between the two grids in their principal component decomposition can be summarised as follows: nine of the 80 subjects revealed the same underlying structure in the first two principal components when construing roles and individuals; 18 demonstrated a similar, but slightly altered, make-up for both components; 26 viewed roles and individuals through an essentially similar first component but a different second component; 16 sets of grids revealed an entirely different make-up in

the case of both the first two principal components. In other of the remaining 11 cases, the two major dimensions in individual construal were amalgamated to form the major principal component in role construal; or the first principal component of individuals became split into the first two components of role construal. In general, then, albeit with large differences between subjects, there were considerable alterations in the structure of their personal constructs when they moved from construing roles to construing individuals, or vice versa.

(4) Contrary to our hypothesis, there was considerably greater commonality among the constructs elicited in response to individuals than to roles (Table IV). Sixty-five per cent of the 400 constructs elicited on individuals but only 40% of those elicited on roles could be readily classified into categories with six or more constructs in each ($\chi^2=63.7$, d.f.$=1$, $p<0.001$). For both conditions the largest category was of constructs such as "stable–unstable" or "balanced–unbalanced", constructs indicative of mental equilibrium. Constructs which were more likely to be applied to individuals dealt with extraversion–introversion, sense of humour, flexibility, laziness, confidence, maturity, aggressiveness and popularity. On the other hand, some constructs were more confined to describing roles: socially powerful, commanding respect, affectionate, academic and egocentric. There was clearly a different focus of convenience of certain categories of construct as between construing individuals and roles.

TABLE IV. *Frequency[a] of elicitation of constructs on persons and roles* (n = 40).

Construct category	Persons	Roles
stable–unstable, secure–insecure	25	22
extraversion–introversion	25	⟨6
selfishness–altruism	20	8
sense of humour–dull	19	⟨6
broad minded–dogmatic	18	15
authoritative–submissive	15	9
religious–not religious	15	6
lively–lethargic	14	9
happy–unhappy	13	⟨6
intelligent–unintelligent	12	⟨6
close to me–not close to me	11	14
flexible–stubborn	10	⟨6
practical–unrealistic	10	7
calm–restless	⟨6	10

[a]Where the frequency is ⩾6 in either the Persons or Roles condition.

With one major exception, these results confirm our general hypothesis that the construing of individuals will be different from, and more differentiated than, role construing. The unpredicted finding that there was less commonality among constructs elicited on roles goes against a general explanation in terms of consensual validation. It may suggest that role construing is less of an ongoing process than the construing of individuals, and that the constructs are less readily available. Our subjects were using predominantly psychological constructs, which may not be those which are usually validated in respect of roles.

The methodological implication of these results is that the different forms of the grid referred to above do not elicit the same kinds of construing. This is a particularly important observation in respect of the very commonly used group form of the grid. People usually have available to them throughout the process of completing a grid both the role title list and the names of individuals nominated to represent the titles. There may be some ambiguity as to whether people are construing individuals, roles, or both, in the group form of grid. The ambiguity persists even if the role title list has been withdrawn; the role titles may be remembered and in a sense "colour" the individuals.

Role Titles

The significance of the experiment bears particularly on the many uses of the rep grid which are made with no, or very little, reference to personal construct theory. So often the grid's attraction is simply its ideographic nature. It is seen as a means of gaining access to an individual's "inner world", to his personal way of construing events which is assumed to differ from that of the experimenter or other subjects. It avoids the presumptions of nomothetic methods. "Individual" and "role" are taken in an everyday sense when the grid is used like this; they are not seen as problematic.

Kelly (1955) described the rep test as "aimed at role constructs . . . a direct approach to the elicitation of such constructs in the subjects whose personal-social behavior we wish to understand" (p. 219). The role titles used are "figures", defined primarily in terms of social position. Kelly's list of role titles was designed to ensure

> that the other people appearing as elements in the test be sufficiently representative of all the people with whom the subject must relate his self-construed role . . . Representative figures, with respect to whom people seem normally to have formed the most crucial personal role constructs, are incorporated in the list. (p. 230)

It might seem that Kelly was giving priority to social order in laying the rep test on such a base. At another point the issue of representative figures is discussed in a way which suggests that Kelly was aware of the problem he had posed, though without answering it. The psychologist

> must assume that the sample of figures is representative of those around whom the client must structure his life role. But it is not enough to say that the sample must be representative—it must be representative with respect to certain dimensions. It is only as a sample is representative along essential dimensional lines that it can be called representative of a population—but this is no place to launch a discussion of sampling theory . . . .What we must assume here is simply that the figures elicited by the Role Title List are representative of those with whom the client must interact and that the dimensions of their representation are relevant to those lines along which he has chosen to structure his life role. (pp. 270-271)

In this last sentence Kelly is on the horns of a dilemma. If one sees the grid as ideographic and individualistic, the figures should be representative in terms of the range of convenience of the client's construct system. This cannot be decided without prior knowledge of the construct system which the grid is to elucidate. The figures sampled are therefore those with whom the client "must interact"; or, alternatively, "with respect to whom people seem normally to have formed the most crucial personal role constructs" (p. 230). Given their definition in terms of social position, the figures are effectively sampled in terms of norms of social behaviour.

Kelly would not have drawn up the role title list as he did if he intended the grid to be thoroughly individualistic. Its form is an indication that he realised the necessity for a construct system to operate within a socially defined context. This is cloaked by the reluctant and uncertain assumption that the figures are representative both socially and psychologically.

A further influence on the form of the grid was the clinical setting in which it was designed principally to be used:

> the items of the test should be representative of the items the client faces in structuring his life. The psychometric task of the clinician is to elicit constructs in a form which will throw light upon the way they govern the subject's approach to elements of his world. (p. 209)

The clinician himself is socially situated. In his rationale of titles and sorts' (pp. 273-277) Kelly reveals quite clearly, though without any sense of disclosure, the clinical ethos within which he worked. The clear reflection of its social values in the titles and sorts makes it very difficult to interpret the grid as a solipsistic instrument, as some critics have claimed.

Role Constructs

So far I have been discussing "role", in relation to the Role Construct Repertory Test, only in so far as the test incorporates a role title list. But the key term is obviously "role construct". The first points in "The Psychology of Personal Constructs" at which the term is indexed are pp. 146-150 and p. 161, where there is a discussion of personal security within the context of a construct. In fact, the term is not used there! We only find "role-governing constructs". The discussion is of constructs which come to be symbolised by figures, such as "mother". One might conclude that role constructs were constructs which referred to roles, where role is interpreted in the familiar sense of a set of expectations and so on attached to its occupant. But Kelly meant something significantly different from this.

"Role constructs are . . . constructs which have other persons as elements in their contexts. More particularly, they are constructs which have the presumed constructs of other persons as elements in their contexts" (p. 209). Role constructs, then, have persons, not simply roles as their point of reference. But more than that, the persons are to be thought of as being construed, in terms of a role construct, as persons with certain constructs themselves.

Two of the six assumptions which Kelly discusses as underlying the rep test bear on role constructs.

> *The fourth assumption is that constructs will be elicited which subsume, in part, the construction systems of the element figures . . . .* The test assumes that a usable number of the constructs elicited by it do represent the subject's understanding, right or wrong, of the way other people look at things. If the subject gives only responses which describe his relationship to other people as if they were unthinking animals, the test has failed to elicit *role constructs . . . . The fifth assumption is that of the role regnancy of the constructs elicited.* If the subject entirely dissociates his own identity from the figures, or fails completely to organize his own behavior under the constructs elicited with respect to the figures in the test, then the constructs cannot be considered to be *role constructs.* (pp. 230-231)

In spelling out these assumptions Kelly made it clear that he intended the Role Construct Repertory Test to reflect that question of the self–other relation, or intersubjectivity, which has been at the centre of so much social theory and social philosophy. In the light of these explicit statements it is outrageous that Kelly's potential contribution to social psychology should have been ignored for so long. The irony of his situation is that despite a super-abundance of attention to the rep test, independently of the theoretical basis, its users have quite neglected essential aspects of its form. Most rep grid studies do indeed treat the test simply as a means of accessing private, subjective worlds. In concentrating in this way on the processes of the privatised subject, psychologists have pursued an individualistic social psychology and fostered the myth that Kelly shared their preconceptions.

Person

The irony is compounded when we turn again to examine Kelly's notion of "person". I noted at the beginning of the chapter that the term was not formally defined in the exposition of the basic theory of personal construct psychology. But it is given some attention in the chapter on the mathematical structure of psychological space. This chapter serves as a low-key prelude to what Little (1977) has called "griddles", the arcane number-crunching of the rep grid which has dominated much of the subsequent work associated with personal construct psychology (cf. Slater, 1977). It is as though Kelly wilfully camouflaged his treatment of the most important, to my mind, term in his theory by surrounding it with the strongest temptations and distractions known to contemporary psychology, quantification and instant "methodology". The camouflage has been very effective.

In the section headed "What is a person?" Kelly wrote: "From the standpoint of the psychology of personal constructs a person is perceived as the intersect of many personal dimensions" (p. 298). That is, another person is the particular set of anticipations which we make of him in terms of our respective construct systems. The person is constituted by the act of construing on the part of another. The term "person" is reserved for figures which are "*construed by someone* such as ourselves" (p. 300). The previous sentence quoted from Kelly is highly tautologous, in the definitional sense. A personal construct is a person-defining construct. It is not, in other words, a construct used by an individual, an idiosyncratic construct, as has often been assumed. The psychology of personal constructs is the psychology of the constituting of persons through constructs, or through construing.

The first volume of Kelly's work is subtitled "A theory of personality". It is not a personality theory in the usual sense. It is not a means to explain the operation of "natural and acquired impulses, and habits, interests and complexes, the sentiments and ideals, the opinions and beliefs" of the individual; nor of "the dynamic organisation within the individual of those psychophysical systems that determine his unique adjustments to his environment". It is a theory of *person*-ality which explains the constituting of persons, how persons come about. We shall return presently to the argument that this could be seen as the central question of social psychology.

The Sociality Corollary

One of the consequences of the coherent presentation of meta-theory, theory, method and application in Kelly's writings is that one may have to look at any or all of the four aspects to understand his position on a particular point. Although I have been suggesting that some of the most important ideas on social psychology are contained in two chapters which discuss the rep test, there are parts of the basic theory which provide a "take-off point for a social psychology", to use Kelly's own words in introducing the Sociality Corollary.

> By attempting to place at the forefront of psychology, the understanding of personal constructs, and by recognizing . . . the subsuming of other people's construing efforts as the basis for social interaction, we have said that social psychology must be a psychology of interpersonal understandings, not merely a psychology of common understandings. (p. 95)

This distinction serves to justify the inclusion of the Sociality Corollary in the theory. The Commonality Corollary had already taken account of simple similarity or overlap between the construing processes of two or more individuals. Sociality entails a deliberate attempt to achieve, not mere overlap, but the incorporation of another's constructs in one's own. The enterprise of driving in heavy traffic can be managed because there are a limited number of relatively inflexible common understandings between drivers. They do not need to talk to one another to attain their goals. But the enterprise of being married, even if it is reduced to the banal activities of maintaining a household and a social position, is sufficiently varied, at least in its earlier stages, as to demand an exploration by each partner of the other's construct system and a mutual construction of systems which take one another into account.

It should be clear by now that I have devoted myself to a reading of "The Psychology of Personal Constructs" which will permit me align it with a particular version of the purpose of social psychology. Others may judge whether or not the reading is a gross distortion. I have preferred to emphasise points which seem inescapably to be central to personal construct theory and which also allow a positive interpretation of its significance for social psychology, rather than to dwell on those parts which facilitate a destructive criticism. But they need not be ignored. Two instances can be found in Kelly's commentary on the Sociality Corollary, where therapist–client and leadership relationships are discussed.

Having introduced the idea of mutual understanding as being the core of social process, Kelly immediately turned to two examples of asymmetrical understanding, in which "One person may understand another better than he is understood" (p. 96). The leader attains his position because of his more general understanding of issues which concern a group of people. The therapist understands more about his client than the client does of his therapist. The discussion in these pages (96-102) of the two roles verges continuously on that form of individualism which reinterprets a social relation in terms of the attributes and capacities of one or other party in the relation, and which, more particularly, conceals a power-relation by reifying the attributes of the superior party (e.g. leadership quality, empathy).

An interpretation of this part of Kelly's argument could undoubtedly be made which countered the charge of individualism. But the important point is that the impression is given, and given strongly, in just that part of the basic theory, the Sociality Corollary, in which one would be looking for an indication of Kelly's position on social psychology. Both because of his own cultural background and because of his clinical and therapeutic interests, it was entirely reasonable that he should have been imbued with individualistic tendencies. But if on occasions they come through, it is in contradiction to the main theoretical assumptions. In his discussion of "the leadership role" (pp. 100-102), Kelly should be read as trying to demonstrate that the psychology of personal constructs takes neither an individualistic nor a role-theoretic stance, but rather a relational or person-oriented stance to the subject. He chose a very telling example for his purpose, since in many ways leadership is a paradigm instance of the possibility of the different approaches. But the argument is not elaborated or carefully enough defined to avoid ambiguities and misunderstanding.

Role

The crucial amplification of the Sociality Corollary lies in the definition of role. The corollary states: "To the extent that one person construes the construction processes of another, he may play a role in a social process involving the other person" (p. 95). The expression "play a role" is unfortunate. It could be taken to mean no more than "take part" or "play a part", in the everyday sense of the term. But the subsequent definition shows that it is much more than that.

Kelly emphasises (p. 98) that the notion of role is neither a stimulus-response nor a sociological notion. In other words, it corresponds neither to the individualistic nor the role-theoretic approaches. Similarly, it is not equivalent to the "self-concept". It does have to do with social process: the role-player "must be a participant, either in concert or in opposition, within a group movement" (p. 98). In passing, we may note that Kelly does not pre-empt either a consensus or conflict model of social process. There is a clear suggestion here that Kelly is interested in more than the dyad, two individuals in social interaction, despite assertions to the contrary by some critics.

Social process does not depend upon people construing the world in the same way as one another. Their constructs may be very similar in certain circumstances; this is acknowledged in the Commonality Corollary. The similarity may facilitate social process. But it does not guarantee it. Sociality and commonality are essentially independent of one another. One *may* subsume another's construct system in one's own without the respective constructs being similar; and the constructs may be similar without the subsuming occurring.

> To the extent that people understand each other or . . . that their construction systems subsume each other, their activities in relation to each other may be called *roles*, a role being a course of activity which is played out in the light of one's understanding of the behavior of one or more other people. (pp. 99–100)

I take this to be the crucial statement of Kelly's position on a social psychology, and interpret it as a commitment to a relational viewpoint. Despite the use of the term "role" in a personal construct theory exposition of social process it is not a role-theoretic concept.

There are, however, difficulties in this interpretation. The quotation comes at a point where Kelly is talking about people getting along in harmony with one another. Somewhat earlier he has said that "while one person may play a role in a social process involving the other person, through subsuming a version of that other person's way of seeing things, the understanding need not be reciprocated" (pp. 98–99). It looks as though Kelly is suggesting that one person can engage in a social process by himself. From a non-individualistic viewpoint that is nonsense as it stands.

At the end of the section which deals with the definition of role, a value position on the term is made explicit: "there is no greater tragedy than the failure to arrive at those understandings which permit this kind of role interrelationship" (p. 100)—that is the mutual understanding and constructive social interaction of a man and a woman, which is referred to as the finest example of role relationship. Inevitably in his work as a therapist Kelly would meet with many instances of potential role relationships which were frustrated by an absence of mutuality. Many of his clients would be people who had great difficulty in relating to others, in subsuming the construct systems of others. If, then, he expresses the possibility of someone engaging on his own in a social process, it may well be in reference to someone *attempting* to engage in a social process, but being frustrated by the other's lack of understanding.

At best, he could be referring to a situation in which the other was also engaging in a social process, but under different basic assumptions. The other might, for example, be a thoroughgoing individualist who was able to see his activity as being socially meaningful without it entailing any understanding of other people. Having adopted basic stipulations about the nature of Man and society one has to allow others to hold quite different views. From there it is a short step to the evaluative conclusion that the optimal forms of social process are those in which the actors are operating under the same assumptions as one another, and probably as oneself. A Kellyan and a non-Kellyan man might from their respective viewpoints be engaging in a social process, without reciprocal understanding (in personal construct theory terms). Presumably they would sooner or later appreciate their misalignment and reconsider what kind of process they were engaging in. Certainly from Kelly's viewpoint they would not be engaged in at all a fine example of a role relationship. And it would be best to say it was no role relationship at all.

The definition of role begins with this paragraph:

> In terms of the theory of personal constructs, a *role* is a psychological process based upon the role player's construction of aspects of the construction systems of those with whom he attempts to join in a social enterprise. In less precise but more familiar language, a role is an ongoing pattern of behavior that follows from a person's understanding of how the others who are associated with him in his task think. In idiomatic language, a role is a position that one can play on a certain team without even waiting for the signals. (pp. 97-98)

The paragraph is written as though it were re-stating the same idea in successively less specialised, more everyday terms. But if the words are to be taken seriously, each sentence adds something to the definition of role.

As I have said, the role-player should not be thought of as "playing" his role in the sense often meant by the term. He is not uncommitted. The role is not a part written out for him to follow by society or by other people. The role is based on the constructive process of actively making sense of the viewpoint of others; it is his intended creation. He makes sense of *aspects* of others' construct systems. It is not necessary for him to understand others totally. A series of roles *vis-à-vis* another may follow from construing different aspects of his construct system. The possibility is envisaged of the role-player construing aspects of several people's construct systems for the purpose of *a* social enterprise. Social process, once again, is clearly not limited to dyadic interaction. The social enterprise is something which one *attempts* and the attempt is in concert with others. It does not automatically follow from one's own actions, or independently of others' actions; others have to be doing the same sort of thing as oneself, in the same way and for the same reason. Otherwise, the social enterprise is frustrated.

The "less precise but more familiar" formulation tells us that a psychological process can be approximately seen as an ongoing pattern of behaviour. Kelly is so often dismissed as having nothing to say about behaviour that a reminder to the contrary is never out of place. The misinterpretation of "construct" as no more and no less than a verbal label is the most important source of the confusion. Anything that in everyday talk we call "behaviour" is in itself as much a matter of construing as is responding to a rep test. If we wish, we can construe an aspect of another's construct system as he walks down the street; since walking down the street is an instance of construing. Role is behaviour, in personal construct theory. It is not the rules for a pattern of behaviour or the norms or expectations.

The behaviour "follows from a person's understanding" of others, as well as being "based upon" it. Making sense of others is both a sufficient and a necessary condition for role-behaviour. The others to whom one's attention is directed in this case are *associated with him in a task*. It is the task through which they become associated; and the enterprise is thought of as a piece of work. Understanding others, subsuming their construct systems under one's own, is a piece of work, which they also engage in, as an inevitable result of which an association between all parties is formed.

The reference to team games is in metaphorical rather than idiomatic language. It provides an example of the kind of active association which can be achieved through such close, clear mutual understanding, that one can be two steps ahead in anticipation of other people's actions. Whether in cooperative or competitive game-playing, say football or chess, anticipation is of the essence. These two examples differ from the previous one of driving in heavy traffic. In that case the understanding of others and anticipation of their actions is based on laws, highly prescriptive rules and assumptions of biological priorities (staying alive, not killing your own). The task of driving is not a piece of work in association with other drivers. Arriving at one's destination is not a joint achievement, in the way performing a role is.

Playing football *for* a team and playing chess *against* an opponent can be differentiated from one another as well as from driving *in* heavy traffic. The mutual understanding that enables team players to play together efficiently by anticipating one another's moves, to which Kelly refers, is essentially a past achievement. As far as the team is concerned the game will give them little in the way of fresh mutual understanding as they play it; they will play in the light of what they already know of one another's tactics. But a chess-player, or anyone in competition (and some in cooperative play, of course), will play as much in the light of what he is learning about his opponent during the game. The mutual understanding of the two players will be constantly shifting, because they are trying to deceive one another. Because they are in competition, they will be "driving" one another's anticipations; moving the opponent on to new forms of (mistaken) understanding.

Many forms of role-based activity have the characteristic of attempting to move forward another's construction processes. In cooperative relations this will be aiming at a new and improved, rather than mistaken, understanding. If role-behaviour is based on or follows from construing others, that is not to say that it does not also involve in itself a further construing of others: "enactment of a role is more than merely an outcome of one's understanding of others; it is also a way to arrive at a further understanding of them" (pp. 1141-1142). Role-behaviour in relation to another will be followed by the other's construal of the role-player's construct system and by role-behaviour in relation to him. The other's behaviour will then offer the basis for reconstruing his construct system and a further understanding of him.

It should be clear that Kelly's definition not only suggests how it is possible to play in a football team, but also how one can engage in a conversation. With a stranger we start with certain assumptions about the nature of his construct system, on the basis for the most part of social norms and contextual cues. Having subsumed his construct system under our own we use this as the basis for role-behaviour—an ongoing activity in relation to the stranger—talk. Our initial utterances are at once a recognition that the stranger can construe our behaviour if he wishes; an expression of aspects of our construct system, including our construal of the stranger; and an invitation for him to construe us and engage in similar role-behaviour, that is to talk in reply. Language and talk is probably the most common way in which roles are enacted.

Figure and Person

The experiment which was reported in the first half of this chapter was an attempt, clumsy enough in the light of the subsequent discussion, to distinguish between role titles and persons as elements in a repertory grid. We have seen that the use of "role" in this instance can be misleading, when compared with Kelly's definition of "role". The term "figure" is preferable. In a discussion of aggression and hostility, Kelly illustrates how figure and person differ.

> The person with "authority problems" aggressively seeks to elaborate his field. He is too impatient to be able to learn to deal with people as *persons*. Instead he deals with them as *figures* . . . . He construes his relationship to other people as a matter of "social position", in terms of "status variables", by means of "class concepts", in the light of "subculture norms", rather than in terms of their unique identities and their personal viewpoints. He plays a *part* in relation to them, but it is not so much what we would call a *role* . . . . But it may not be in relation to the authority dimension only that his aggression leads him into difficulty; it may be in relation to any of his other construct dimensions which are based upon the *positional construing of human figures*. (p. 877)

Elsewhere Kelly refers to the possibility of a "relationship to other people as if they were unthinking animals" (p. 230) which also is not what he would call a role. He seems to have in mind something like the three-fold scheme with which this chapter was introduced. People can proceed as though others are simply organisms whose behaviour, independently of any construal processes, is to be examined, made sense of and reacted to; or they can be treated to all intents and purposes as no more than occupants of social positions; or they can be seen as persons, people who are trying to understand others, in the same way as we attempt to understand them.

In hoping that people will deal with one another "in terms of their unique identities and their personal viewpoints", Kelly is not proposing a form of individualism. He is suggesting that they recognise the possibility of using "I" and "you" in the way in which we do, intersubjectively, to create a we-relationship. To identify another as so-and-so, and as nobody else, and to construe him as having a construct system and to subsume it under one's own is to begin to constitute him as a person. If one then goes on to test out one's anticipations of his construct system through discourse, allowing him to do the same; and if this enterprise proceeds in a non-stereotyped way, not wholly determined by sets of rules, norms, habits and so on, then through discourse persons will have been brought into being in the context of a we-relation. The use of "we" will follow from the appreciation that mutual construing has been taking place.

The Rep Grid Again

Let us return to the rep test and the experiment reported earlier. We showed that there were differences between construing role titles and particular named instances of them. The latter were generally construed in a more complex, differentiated way. But what do we imagine people are doing when they complete either form of the grid? In the case of the role titles grid the evidence from the constructs elicited is that they were to a discernible extent construing roles as such; the constructs had a strong "positional" component. It would be surprising, however, if, for some role titles at least, subjects had not in mind one or two particular, individual instances.

This possibility seems especially strong for certain role titles or figures, of which there are prime instances—such as father or mother. Kelly discusses the mother figure:

> the child . . . actually develops two levels of meaning for *Mother* : the one referring to the actual behaviors of his mother, the other referring to *motherliness*. It is important . . . to stand ready to discriminate between these two levels of figure conceptualization. (pp. 297-298)

One can substitute for "actual behaviours", "construct system" in the case of one of our subjects who may have been construing mother as a person.

In a similar fashion, when individuals were construed, it seems likely that they were seen partly in terms of the role title as an instance of which they were selected. Subjects would be set to perceive their nominated individuals in the context of general role considerations or as instances of types. The wish to have a role title list which would cover representative figures makes this effect difficult to avoid. From the viewpoint of a social psychology, this may seem desirable. The procedure of nominating individuals to be construed in the rep test on the basis of role titles or other social categories could be seen as a means of having subjects construe others in some kind of social context. If the variety of social contexts used in the grid were broadened in scope—Kelly's Situational Resources Repertory Test gives an indication of what this might look like, with more explicit social reference—it could look a most apt instrument for examining aspects of the individual-in-society.

But if we pursue the question of what people were doing when they completed the individuals grid in our experiment, and ask whether or not they were construing *persons*, the answer is less satisfactory. In the usual forms in which the rep test is administered there is no way of knowing surely whether an element is being construed as an "unthinking animal", in positional terms or by subsuming that element's own construct system. Of course, certain kinds of construct are suggestive of one or other stance. For example, a situational construct, "lives in London", suggests one of the former two stances; a psychological construct "kind" the latter. But further exploration could reveal that "lives in London" subsumes a great deal of the other's construct system and entails considerable understanding of the way in which he is constructing his life. While "kind" might merely mean that the other exhibits that type of behaviour which is usually called "kind"; or that the other takes on a generally caring role in some social relationship or grouping.

The Psychologist in Relation

One means by which a psychologist might satisfy himself on this issue is to recognise the need to construe the construct systems of those whom he is studying. For any social psychologist, not only for a personal construct psychologist, it should be intolerable to continue to ignore the assumptions about Man-in-society which experimental subjects hold, or to proceed as though they were inevitably the same as one's own. Construing subjects' construct systems, rather than treating them only as cold data to be laid against your hypotheses, entails an acceptance of subjects construing your construct system. Once that has been accepted one is well on the road to a reflexive social psychology, and to a social psychology conducted by persons-in-relation to one another.

In terms of personal construct psychology, it is only possible to examine social relations by being-in-relation oneself with another. An account of the investigation should include a narrative of the relation, and from the viewpoints of both parties. Since the work of Orne (e.g. 1969) or Rosenthal (e.g. 1966) for example, it is commonplace to acknowledge that subjects actively interpret the experimental setting. However, although such observations have now attained the status of "fact" and are enshrined in textbooks, they are frequently ignored, or at best treated as confounding variables to be designed out of an experiment. The results of post-experimental questionnaires, for example, are very rarely used to provide independent variables for the analysis of data.

A personal construct psychology reminds us that the experimenter's and the subject's understanding of one another and of the investigation must all be a part of what is under investigation. These factors are contextual foreground, not background. The relation which is constructed between the two parties involved is not simply a method or procedure, it is an event like the events which are being investigated.

The technical questions which it raises are less important than the moral and epistemological ones. We have to consider the morality of the kinds of relation with others which we construct as psychologist, both in general and in specific instances, with the same seriousness which would apply to "ordinary" relations. Unless we can guarantee that there will be a high degree of generality in the relations which any one psychologist constructs while pursuing his business, or between the relations that numbers of psychologists construct, it will be very difficult to warrant the knowledge that results from those relations in the normal, scientific manner. Indeed it seems unlikely that one could. Among the consequences is the conclusion that personal construct psychology may tend toward an anarchic form of constructivism; and that in many instances the beneficiaries of the knowledge acquired through the practice of psychology will necessarily be strictly limited in number.

References

Bannister, D. (1959). "An application of personal construct theory (Kelly) to schizoid thinking". Unpublished Ph.D. thesis, University of London.

Bannister, D. (1963). The genesis of schizophrenic thought disorder : a serial invalidation hypothesis. *Br. J. Psychiat.* **109**, 680.

Bannister, D. (1965). The genesis of schizophrenic thought disorder : re-test of the serial invalidation hypothesis. *Br. J. Psychiat.* **111**, 377.

Bannister, D. and Mair, J. M. M. (1968). "The Evaluation of Personal Constructs". Academic Press, London and New York.

Chadwick-Jones, J. K. (1976). "Social Exchange Theory". Academic Press, London and New York.

Fransella, F. and Bannister, D. (1977). "A Manual for Repertory Grid Technique'. Academic Press, London and New York.

Israel, J. (1972). Stipulations and construction in the social sciences. *In* "The Context of Social Psychology" (Eds J. Israel and H. Tajfel). Academic Press, London and New York.

Kelly, G. A. (1955). "The Psychology of Personal Constructs". Norton, New York.

Little, B. (1977). St. George's Griddles. *Contemporary Psychology* **22**, 759.

Marx, K. (1964). "Selected Writings in Sociology and Philosophy" (Eds M. Bottomore and M. Rubel). McGraw-Hill, New York.

Mead, G. H. (1956). "The Social Psychology of G. H. Mead" (Ed. A. Strauss).University of Chicago Press, Chicago.

Orne, M. T. (1969). Demand characteristics and the concept of quasi-controls. *In* "Artifact in Behavioral Research" (Eds R. Rosenthal and R. L. Rosnow). Academic Press, New York and London.

Rosenthal, R. (1966). "Experimenter Effects in Behavioral Research". Appleton-Century-Crofts, New York.

Rotter, J. B., Chance, J. E. and Phares, E. J. (Eds) (1972). "Applications of a Social Learning Theory of Personality". Holt, Rinehart and Winston, New York.

Slater, P. (Ed.) (1977). "Dimensions of Intrapersonal Space". Wiley, London.

Stringer, P. (1974). A use of repertory grid measures for evaluating map formats. *Br. J. Psychol.* **65**, 23.

Stringer, P. and Mulley, L. (1978). Roles, individuals and persons in the repertory grid. *Bull. Br. Psychol. Soc.* **31**, 26.

Part II

Method

Self-organised Learning and the Relativity of Knowing: Towards a Conversational Methodology

Sheila Harri-Augstein
and Laurie F. Thomas

"God first made Angels bodilesse pure minds,
Then other things which mindlesse bodies bee;
Last he made man th' Horizon trixt both kinds,
In whom we do the worlds abridgement see."

Sir John Davies, Nosce Teipsum, 1599.
(From J. B. Bamborough "The Little World of Man"
Longmans Green and Co, London, 1952.)

Constructing Personal Destinies

At one point in "Beyond Freedom and Dignity" Skinner (1971) poses the question: who will use the behavioural technology he is advocating? "Until these issues are resolved", he writes, "a technology of behaviour will continue to be rejected, and with it possibly the only way to solve our problems." Skinner is offering his model of man as a basis for reflecting upon and then creating our own future. This would appear to be a very Kelly-like approach to the problem. Can (wo)man make (wo)man? For Skinner the answer is a very definite "YES". All we need to do is to design a culture in which "advantages accrue by emphasising contingencies of reinforcement in lieu of states of mind or feelings". Many of us may not feel that in stating the problem in this way Skinner has got it quite right. Who makes who? But there can be no doubt that in having the courage of his convictions about how people learn, Skinner is facing up to issues which concern us all, and to which we do not as yet seem able to envisage a coherent "humanistic" response.

The title of the first chapter in a recent book by Lorenz (1977) is "Life as a Process of Learning". Early on he writes:

> Life is an eminently active enterprise aimed at acquiring both a fund of energy and a stock of knowledge, the possession of one being instrumental to the acquisition of the other. The immense effectiveness of these two feedback cycles, coupled in multiplying interaction, is the precondition indeed the explanation, for the fact that life has the power to assert itself against the superior strength of the pitiless inorganic world.

Lorenz's purpose is if anything even more comprehensive than Skinner's. He is recruiting his life-long experience as an ethologist to reflect on the condition of man. Whilst not as overtly optimistic as Skinner about his ability to influence the outcome, he also sees our only salvation in re-viewing our nature. He believes that a new and different awareness of ourselves (as evolving living matter) and of the contexts we have constructed might enable the human race to avoid what he "knows" to be the inevitable consequences of the contemporary course of world civilisation. In this, his position is similar to that of George Kelly (1955). They both argue that human beings, life in its most complex form, have now evolved to the stage where they can, by reflecting on their own nature, take charge of their own destiny.

In the 1920s I. A. Richards wrote the "Meaning of Meaning" with C. K. Ogden (1923). Fifty years later in "Beyond" (Richards, 1973) he takes a different path in the same direction. Being a great teacher he does not believe that his conclusions are primary. He sets about the problem in a more "conversational" manner. He writes:

> an invitation offered to my readers to join me in entertaining certain notions, if only briefly. A number of works, from among the greatest, enter in various guises (whether dis-guises or not, is, partly, what the (inter)play is asking). They there confront one another. Being what they are—the spiritual ancestors: springs, headwaters, for the Helleno-centric and Judaic traditions, sources of our world and our very selves—what they do to one another, through the selected aspects I try to exhibit, provides the dramatic engagement. What the outcome may be is not to be presented here. If it could be set down (*down* is the word) the play would be needless. There will be more to these interactions and exchanges than any summary could report.

This is another road to awareness of our nature. The great literature of man reflects the very essence of our being. I. A. Richards is here offering to accompany us in our exploration of "the world's great word hoard": not to instruct us in what he knows, not even to guide us through literary country familiar to him, but to use his experience to help us equip ourselves for new expeditions into the ever-changing peaks of human understanding. As McCulloch (1965) asks, "What's in the Brain that Ink may Character?"

It is interesting to note that Rogers (1961), in battling with the problem of how to present the essential outcomes of his therapeutic investigations, eventually also opted for a "let the exchanges speak for themselves" style of presentation. This is the current dilemma of the "elders" of our civilisation. A life-time of thinking, feeling and acting has led them to constructions of experience which enable them to anticipate events in a manner which, they feel, would be of value to those of us following on. But the attempt to summarise, to state conclusions, not only antagonises many of their readers, but, usually for the best of them, fails to satisfy their own need to pass their experience on. This is also the new but perennial dilemma of (social) psychology. Its investigations lead to findings which are both significant and yet trivial. They are significant for the participants in their context. But remove the specific intentionality, the location in time, space and culture, and the attempts at objective generalisation appear to dissolve the substance, leaving only a shadow of understanding. That is why certain psychologists are tempted into alternate forms of expression (Bannister, 1979; Hudson, 1978; Skinner, 1948) and why certain writers are thought by laymen to be better psychologists than the psychologists (Wilson, 1972; Koestler, 1964). Kelly has identified these problems, stated the issues clearly and offered an original orientation to the description of what psychology might legitimately aim to achieve. Again it is significant to note that in most of his writing his style of presentation (e.g. Kelly, 1978) deliberately breaks the objective reportage mode which has been for so long equated with the valuing of scientific or professional work.

The theme of this paper is triadic. It attempts to view learning as synonomous with the process of living. It reflects on how (wo)man's images of (wo)man influence our alternate futures. And it offers the view that since in Kelly's terms thought, feeling and action are indivisible then psychological tool-making may be the most productive activity for advancing psychology through a period in which our modes of description must change at least as radically as did those of chemistry from the alchemists to the periodic table.

People as Self-organised Learners

The infant is conceived (lives), is born (lives), develops (l..s), struggles for understanding (l...s), reaches for self-awareness (l...s), blossoms (l...s), fades (l s), blossoms (l s), fades (l), blossoms (l), fades (l) and dies. This is learning. *How* we live is the question. Is what becomes of us due to happenstance or is it possible that some human beings construct their experience, reflect upon their constructions and converse with others to determine their own destiny? This issue recurs in surprisingly many areas of human experi-

ience. The universal appeal of a popular best-seller perhaps best illustrates this ubiquity.

> As he sank into the water, a strange hollow voice sounded within him. There's no
> way around it. I am a seagull. I am limited by my nature. If I were meant to learn so
> much about flying, I'd have charts for brains. If I were meant to fly at speed, I'd
> have a falcon's short wings, and live on mice instead of fish. My father was right. I
> must forget this foolishness. I must fly home to the Flock and be content as I am, as
> a poor limited seagull.
>
> When Jonathan Seagull joined the Flock on the beach, it was full night. He was
> dizzy and terribly tired. Yet in delight he flew a loop to landing, with a snap roll
> just before touch down. When they hear of it, he thought, of the Breakthrough,
> they'll be wild with joy. How much more there is now to living!. . . there's a reason
> to life! We can lift ourselves out of ignorance, we can find ourselves as creatures of
> excellence and intelligence and skill. We can be free! We can learn to fly!
>
> Whatever stands against that freedom must be set aside, be it ritual or superstition
> or limitation in any form. . .
> "There is no other". . .
> "Look at Fletcher! Lowell! Charles Roland! Judy Lee! Are they also special and
> gifted and Divine? No more than you are, no more than I am. The only difference,
> the very only one is that they have begun to understand what they really are and
> have begun to practise it.

("Jonathan Livingston Seagull" Richard Bach, Avon Books, New York.)

Psychology has been seriously disabled by specialist language. Its attempts
to converse more precisely continually pervert the everyday meanings of
words. The word "learning" is a good illustration. For Jonathan and his
friends living is learning. Theories of *learning* in psychology have been what
in common parlance would be called theories of *teaching* or instruction.
They describe how the experimenter must act to produce behaviours from
the learner which are then evaluated in terms defined by the experimenter.
Many other "psychological" words have suffered a similar fate. Rogers
(1969) in "Freedom to Learn" attempted to re-habilitate "learning". He
suggests it can be better understood if we recognise that:

> Human beings have a natural potentiality for learning. Significant learning takes
> place when the subject matter is perceived by the student as having relevance for
> his own purposes. Learning which involves a change in self-organisation—in the
> perception of oneself—is threatening and tends to be resisted. Much significant
> learning is acquired through doing.
>   Learning is facilitated when the student participates responsibly in the learning
> process.
>   Self-initiated learning which involves the whole person of the learner—feelings
> as well as intellect—is the most lasting and pervasive.
>   Independence, creativity and self-reliance are all facilitated when self-criticism
> and self-evaluation are basic and evaluation by others is of secondary importance.

> The most socially useful learning in the modern world is the learning of the process of learning, a continuing openness to experience and incorporation into oneself of the process of change.

This resonates with Rogers' view of the fully functioning person and with what Maslow (1962) describes as self-actualisation. Learning entails the complete person. It involves more than just theories of memory, problem solving, skill and motivation. It does, as Rogers rightly indicates, involve more than contemporary theories of learning (i.e. teaching or instruction) offer. The whole is more than the sum of the parts; the (human) system as a whole develops characteristics which cannot be predicted from the characteristics of the subsystems considered in isolation (von Foerster, 1960). It is from this perspective that PCP is most likely to illuminate our view of people as learners. PEOPLE SEEK MEANING. THE CREATION OF MEANING, THE PROCESS OF ACHIEVING PERSONAL KNOWING IS LEARNING.

Kelly's view of man as scientist, revised to read personal scientist, does treat the learner as a whole person. But this analogy between the anticipations achieved by construing the replications of events, and the theory building and testing activities of scientists, has its limitations. If it is interpreted in conjunction with, say, Popper (1972), Polanyi (1967), or Koestler (1964), it offers some exciting ideas about how people might live their lives. But for most of us the ways of the scientist seem less than completely human. What about man as personal artist?

Pirsig (1976) has made the most telling recent statement about what he calls the difference between classical understanding and romantic understanding. The modes in which experience is constructed totally shape the anticipations with which the Kelly-person lives in the world. Pirsig again uses a form of presentation which allows him to play ideas and their consequences back and fore, sometimes offering almost textbook (or workshop manual) passages of explanation and sometimes pursuing the narrator's own journey to illustrate his meanings. To heal the classical versus romantic split Pirsig identifies "Quality" as prior. Quality is that valued event which may, later, for purposes of analysis, be sliced into subject and object. Pirsig uses the term "event", as does Kelly. Maslow prefers the terms "peak experience or creative encounter". A creative encounter cannot be valued except by using criteria which arise within the encounter itself. Evaluation is thus self-referent and retrospective, a method of describing and reviewing where one has been. Experience is neither subjective nor objective, quality does not reside in the object, nor is it "just what you like". It is "significantly what you like" and this makes it identical with what Rogers refers to in his third criteria for a fully functioning person:

This person would find his organism a trustworthy means of arriving at the most satisfying behaviour in each existential situation.

The personal scientist must be *person* before *scientist*. By fully living in events, trusting his organism as the sounding board for validating constructions of experience, he uses behaviour not as a series of experiments each designed to test some micro-hypothesis, but as the continuing test-bed for his system of construing. This is what Polanyi (1967) meant by tacit knowing. This is self-organised learning. Pirsig identifies this state:

> Mountains should be climbed with as little effort as possible and without desire. . . each footstep isn't just a means to an end but a unique event in itself. This leaf has jagged edges. This rock looks loose . . . . It's the sides of the mountain which sustain life: not the top . . .
>
> If you watch a bad workman and compare his expression with that of a craftsman whose work you know to be excellent, you'll see the difference. The craftsman isn't ever following a single line of instruction. He's making decisions as he goes along. For that reason he'll be absorbed and attentive to what he's doing even though he doesn't deliberately contrive this. His motions and the machine are in a kind of harmony . . .
>
> "Sounds like art". . . . "Well, it is art," I say "This divorce of art from technology is completely unnatural."

In all the Oriental religions great value is placed on the Sanskrit doctrine of Tat tvam asi, "Thou art that", which asserts that everything you think you are, and everything you think you perceive are undivided. To realise fully this lack of division is for Eastern mystics the way to become enlightened.

The personal scientist, the Zen master, the fully functioning person, the self-actualising individual, the excellent craftsman and mountain climber are all self-organised learners. They are all optimistic images of man.

Colin Wilson's (1972) robots are images of what many people fear might be the outcome of Skinner's design of a culture. Wilson describes how when composing a manuscript he is unaware of the typewriter and yet trusts his typing robot to strike the right keys to transfer the ideas in his head into typed words on paper. He then goes on to describe amusingly some of the other robots that service the real Wilson. This propensity of man to become so skilled that routine tasks become non-conscious or habitual has great advantages; and disadvantages. Wilson expresses the fear that his robots may take him over and that his capacity for fully experiencing may be impaired. This is a dramatic expression of our concern with alienation, boredom and the deprivation of self. It embodies the other-organised learner; someone who is controlled by his or her environment and cannot reflect sufficiently to escape. The system of contingencies takes over. Whether we assign the locus of control to a robot inside our skins or to forces in the environment, is as irrelevant as the object/subject dichotomy is in Zen.

What is important is to recognise the dimension defined by the gumption—non-conscious dichotomy or by the difference between self-awareness and the subconscious. Man is a learner. How a person's learning is organised, where the locus of control resides, is the key question. Kelly offers an answer. He suggests that if the focus of construing lies higher in the hierarchy of constructs than that being construed, a person is exercising free will. If the locations are reversed the person is determined. Skinner is more cynical. He suggests that,

> The self-knower is almost always a product of social contingencies, but the self that is known may come from other sources. The controlling self (the conscience or superego) is of social origin, but the controlled self is more likely to be the product of genetic susceptibilities to reinforcement (the id, or the Old Adam).

The controlling self generally represents the interests of others, the controlled self the interests of the individual. Where does this leave man the self-organised learner? Self-organised learners control their own destinies. Other-organised learners are victims of their fate. We are all both.

Public Knowledge and Personal Knowing

Part of the message of the preceding sections is that we have positions not only in time and space but also in meaning. The pursuit of one objective reality is as self-defeating as the assumption that everything is totally subjective. We are not simple automata to be moulded by patterns of contingencies of reinforcement; nor are we able to invent any personal reality we choose and then operate freely within it.

If a sheet of plate glass is placed across a trail that is familiar, not knowing it was there would not allow us to walk through it. The behaviour of others occupies our experience. The hidden observers who placed the glass in our path would perceive us behaving in a manner compatible with their constructions. Our behaviour would occupy their experience. But this does not mean that members of the Ojibwa tribe, exposed to the same experience would necessarily construe it as walking into a sheet of plate glass. As members of Western civilisation we have arrived at a point where we construe certain events as encounters with sheets of glass. Replications of such encounters with shop fronts, bathroom shelves and glass-topped tables in the context of others stabilise our constructions of such experiences. We construct our social reality.

Among members of an isolated close-knit community the human capacity to construct individual meaning poses little difficulty. Events are shared and constructions of experience are mutually cross-validated. So they go unquestioned. The artifacts and technologies are familiar to everybody. Skills are shared and passed from one generation to the next. Culture,

society and its institutions remain static or evolve so slowly that the awareness of the process of construction remains minimal. The encoded knowledge of the community, the writings, the music, the visual arts and technology are incorporated into the contemporary constructions of experience. If
life is hard, hazardous or demanding, common immediate needs create a
system of intentionalities which is shared by all members of the community.

Anthropologists have provided gradually improving descriptions of such
shared and unquestioned realities. But the anthropologist also inhabits a
social reality of his own. Levi-Strauss (1962) has gone some way in showing
how the very patterns of individual psychological function are moulded by
and yet contribute to such shared systems of meaning. He illuminates both
the integrative functions which they serve for their participants (e.g. the
naming of the Penan) and their incomprehensibility to outsiders (e.g.
Needham's inability to enter the husband's construing of the dangers to
himself during childbirth and the first few weeks of the infant's life). The
social psychology of Mead (1934) and the writings of Shutz (1967) also
illustrate man's struggle to come to grips with his own nature. Each in his
own way grapples with this problem of public knowledge and personal
knowing. But they remain constrained by the dichotomy between subject
and object which Pirsig disavows. Paradoxically it is this very dichotomy
which prevents us from fully understanding what it is to be an individual.

Personal knowing does not take the same form as public knowledge. The
individual who attempts to achieve it by carving pretty pieces from the public
store and stringing them into a necklace to be worn with pride does not meet
Rogers' criteria. But this is what most educational institutions value. Their
content preoccupied examinations succeed in seducing the learner away
from his or her own involvements into a false valuing of public knowledge,
not even for its own sake, but for public recognition. Only the eccentrics and
mavericks waste their time whittling away at the products of their own
experience to produce beautiful and functional clothing of their own.
Leonardo da Vinci has expressed this as follows (MacCurdy, 1938):

> Those who are inventors and interpreters between nature and man as compared
> with the reciters and trumpeters of the works of others, are to be considered
> simply as is an object in front of a mirror in comparison with its image when seen
> in the mirror, the one being something in itself, the other nothing: people whose
> debt to nature is small, for it seems only by chance that they wear human form.

The self-organised learner interacts with the mind-pool of human culture
(Harri-Augstein, 1978) to construct personally satisfying, significant and
viable meanings. Such meanings allow the individual to continue to transact
effectively with the events, people and objects which make up the realities of
his or her world. These personal understandings offer better insights into

individuals' own processes and enhanced communication with the processes of others. Awareness and control of the process by which meaning is attributed enables the self-organised individual to act in ways which facilitate competency in ongoing creative transactions with chosen realities.

Learning how to learn frees the personal scientist from the shackles of the mind-pool and the robot in man becomes servant rather than master. The maverick converses with the social system of public meaning, remaining free to interact with it in personally meaningful terms, so that living, by doing, talking, thinking, feeling, investigating and sharing becomes a creative experience as individuals seek to express and find themselves within their social context, the content and the purposes of the mind-pool itself becomes changed. Personal knowing and public knowledge are part of the dynamics of individual and social learning processes.

The Relativity of Personal Knowing

Each person lives within their own system of meaning. But their personal meanings are part of a larger system of meanings within which they have some location, albeit changing and not totally specifiable. In the study of learning this relativity of personal knowing can be used to illuminate some crucial issues. Learning is not an observable fact; it is (as is everything worth knowing) an inference which can be drawn from behaviour and/or experience. Who is to draw the inference? Ninety per cent of all the evidence on which theories of learning are based derives from observations made by the teacher (experimenter) in terms which he had carefully planned before the event. In a few studies the learner is his own experimenter. He is given a purpose and evaluates his own behaviour and experience in terms of prospectively determined criteria. Only in the more fringe literature (Harri-Augstein and Thomas, 1977b) is the learner encouraged to experiment openly and then to evaluate the outcomes retrospectively. Yet, these are the conditions of the creative encounter and the peak experience. The following three by two classification indicates six perspectives from which learning can be inferred (Fig. 1). In addition to the point of view of the observer(s) there is also the time perspective.

These perspectives all offer possible constructions of the experience of the same event, but each on its own leads to a very different psychology of learning.

Such personal systems of meaning might be envisaged in descriptive terms. If each person has a system of personal constructions, then to the extent that there is commonality between personal systems they map one on to another. An analogy would be to a series of aerial photographs. By careful scrutiny and by allowing for the distortion introduced by the perspective,

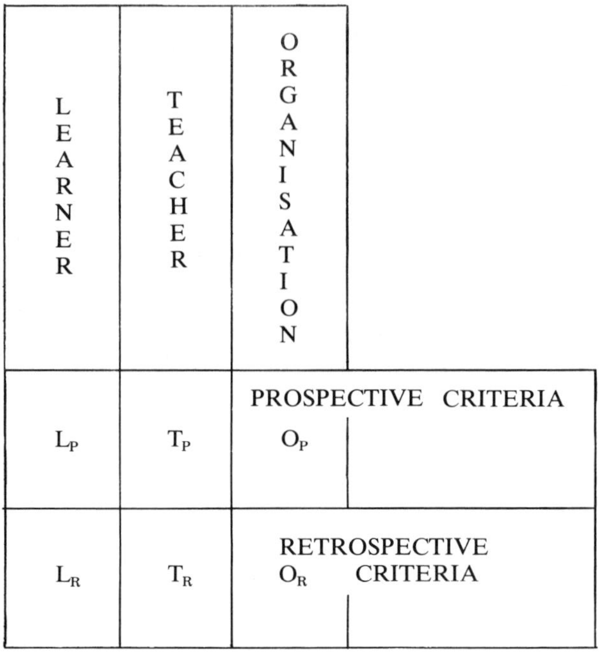

L E A R N E R	T E A C H E R	O R G A N I S A T I O N	
L_P	T_P	O_P	PROSPECTIVE CRITERIA
L_R	T_R	O_R	RETROSPECTIVE CRITERIA

Fig.1

distance and angle from which each photograph was taken, a composite view of the whole terrain could be achieved. This is the rationale behind any belief in objective reality. The analogy serves well for a social system in which experience is widely shared, change is slow and in which intentionality is coherent for the whole community. Ethologists studying insect communities or the social systems of animals (Ardrey, 1972) are, from a behavioural viewpoint, able to achieve just this type of description. But people are in a funny position when they turn to the study of people. Imagine the inspectorate, teachers and pupils in a large comprehensive school in East London. Is there any one coherent system of meaning which could contain each personal knowing as a part? It is extrapolation from the circumstances of the behavioural biologist that has led so much of sociology astray; and with it those components of psychology that rely on concepts deriving from this approach. It is here that Kelly's message sounds loudest and most clearly. It is not the study of behaviour in itself which will improve our understanding of people. It is the exploration of how constructions of experience relate to behaviour and how the consequences of behaviour relate to the reconstruction of experience which offers the most fruitful openings for increasing our awareness of ourselves. It is by pushing himself to the limit that Jonathan Seagull discovers himself.

Systems of construing, the construction of personal experience, is prior. It is the only place that each of us has to start from. This is why Rogers and others have gradually come to insist that the prime evaluation is necessarily self-referent. It was Descartes' base. Rephrased he might have written "I construe therefore I am" or "I think, feel and act, therefore I am becoming". Juxtaposed with this is the feeling "I can occasionally know nature or another, therefore I have value or quality in Pirsig's terms". How can we grasp this nettle? One way through is to take this redefinition of Descartes' position totally seriously. Seek to know thyself. Meditation, archery, religious experience, boxing, acting, prostitution, flower arrangement, have all been claimed as vehicles for coming closer to a full understanding of "self". The Upanishads (Muller, 1962) probably contain the most comprehensive analysis of man studied from within. Physiology and the new brain studies (Blakemore, 1977) would locate the sources of awareness centrally in the brain. As the brain both lives within the body and controls it, this symbiotic relationship offers a solid "scientific" basis for believing such exploration possible. The Yogi is more practical living proof.

Achieving the awareness that allows precise, thorough and delicate control over one's own processes, not necessarily construing them in physiological terms, would appear to be one significant aspect of becoming fully functioning or self-actualising. Skinner argues that the body is merely the continuation of the system of external contingencies within the skin. But for him the relative privacy of what goes on in there makes this area of experience less amenable to control. Disciples and fellow-travellers in the behaviourist tradition have taken up this challenge and studies in self-control (Goldfried and Merbaum, 1973) raise some very fundamental philosophical issues. If the person once accepts responsibility and takes control of his or her own programme of training, is he or she not seizing an opportunity for self-actualisation with all the technology of behaviour available as a resource? Listening to internal processes to reinforce the ones you value is behaviourally almost identical to meditation! Perhaps the constructions of experience are different!

One important aspect of the relativity of personal knowing derives from the inescapable fact that we see ourselves as members of varieties of the same species. To turn inwards is to turn to what we all have in common. The common humanity of man is perhaps no more, but is certainly no less than that we all live in symbiotic relationship with very similar organisms.

There is no reason to doubt that in common with other species human beings are born with certain constructions of experience. At one level this may be no more than the selectivity produced by the particular sensory systems with which we are endowed. But the endowment probably also influences the ways in which sensory information is processed. Patterns of processing common to all members of a species may well explain replicating myths and archetypes.

The Miracle of Conversation

Jung (1933) has postulated a group unconscious and has explored what he saw as the repeating patterns in the mythologies of man. For this he is popularly either dismissed as a mystic or revered as a mystic: but there has always been an undercurrent of serious interest in Jung's work and this could now be re-emerging into the mainstream of psychology. Chenault (1969) attempts to rehabilitate the word "syntony". She has written,

> Specific, partial exceptions to the traditional Aristotelian bind can be found in certain aspects of Jung's self-actualisation, Adler's creative self, Framm's concept of man as both part of nature and separate from it, Allport's proprium which rejects the self as a discrete entity, Rogers' continuing process of becoming, and Maslow's rejection of the traditional distinctions between sickness and health.

Working from quite a different locus of attention, Pask (1975) has introduced the notion of P-individual as a necessary aspect of what he calls the new cybernetics (in contrast to classical cybernetics). For Pask the P(psychological) individual is an entity arising out of the properties of a communication network. For the authors this concept of P-individual has served to contain certain elusive ideas. Pask has a well specified definition for his entity. To avoid possible confusion by our less rigorous usage, the term "C-indi" will serve our purposes for reasons which will emerge later. Experience is prior. Personal knowing is immediate experience. It is only as we reflect upon our knowing that difficulties or doubts about perspective arise; but it is only by reflecting upon our knowing that we increase our capacity for knowing in the future. Thus "P-individual" can be seen as a convenient label for that which has psychological coherence for the duration of an event, encounter or occurrence. It is that which can converse (i.e. participate in a conversation). For Mair (1977) a person may be construed as a community of selves: for Henry Kissinger, nation might speak unto nation., For Pirsig, and in "Zen", there are periods in which man and nature merge.

These periods of psychological coherence are the essence of the conversational exchange: but they leave us facing a dilemma. The whole frame of our manner of thinking about these issues is challenged. Communication consists in the exchange of messages. At the behavioural level we can see and hear it happening. A Bales' interaction recorder will enable us to record who talks to whom, when. Communication networks remind us of the telephone system. There is sender, message and receiver. Two-way communication gets a little more complicated. The participants alternate the functions of sending and receiving. The two person system (people) as a whole takes on characteristics which were not inherent in the individuals as separate entities. The properties arise out of how the parts exchange meaning together. How do they link? Two systems running separately can temporarily synchronise becoming one. Their functions interrelate. One conversationalist is not empty of meaning while the other is talking, nor is he or she necessarily receiving the message which is being sent. Both participants if they are actively engaged, are running a developing system of personal meaning. The exchange influences both systems and occasionally, in the creative encounter, the two temporarily coalesce to form one C-indi. After the event the two individual people go their own ways carrying their own constructions of the event with them.

It is this experience which proves Descartes wrong; or not completely right. He came upon his insight after a long period of isolated meditation. Had he been in love, or on a walking tour in beautiful country he might have created a different insight. For example: "I can occasionally know nature or another, therefore I have value (or Quality)" suggests that it is the miracle of conversation which might better be accepted as the basis of our becoming. This assumption clears many psychological and philosophical obstacles out of our path. Coupled with the C-indi proposition the way looks clear.

(1) Parts of me can converse, therefore I am becoming.
(2) I can converse with nature and with others, therefore I have value and can experience quality.
(3) Conversing is not pre-emptive, it does not imply identity of meaning, only the sharing of experience.
(4) Therefore all personal knowing is prior but is positioned in conversational space. That is where meaning lies.
(5) Each position in conversational space has its own perspective. Both with respect to others and with reference to time. Thus, it is only by achieving a full relativity of meaning that conversation can be enhanced and we can all as self-organised learners be free. We might even learn to fly.

Towards a Conversational Paradigm

The miracle of conversation is then the starting point. The "human scientific" enterprise (Giorgi, 1978) is to be constructed around this assumption. If people are to understand people they must converse. Not only must they record behaviour but they must also seek those constructions of experience which the behaviour expresses. In the absence of true conversational events such evidence will not emerge and cannot be transmitted. A conversational media for the exchange of human research findings is also a prerequisite for the growth (or even birth) of such a human science. It is the need to create these conversational media which has led so many potential human scientists to experiment with novel ways of transmitting their ideas to others (e.g. Carl Rogers' workshops, I. A. Richards' "Beyond", the bar at a conference and the PEGASUS online computer program). It also explains the incredible repeating disappearance of the person from psychology. This can now be seen as perfectly natural phenomena, like attempting to transport liquid nitrogen in open tanks exposed to air at normal temperatures. It disappears. Psychology's formal attempts to transmit our condensations of the person fail when we do not formally create the minimal conversational conditions in which this can be done. The person evaporates. More infuriatingly, informal or lay psychologists and even psychologists when they are being lay or informal, already have a tacit understanding of the experiential technology required. They talk to each other; not in the frozen exchanges of pre-programmed messages or po-faced texts which sink an increasingly opaque barrier into attempts to converse; but responsively, creating little islands of conversational event which just occasionally gel into a fully fledged encounter.

What are the requirements for a conversational methodology? They are the conditions for creating conversational space. What are these conditions?

A first approximation would be to have two or more people in the same place at the same time. This is certainly a crude technique for enriching the strength of the solution in which conversational material is dissolved, but it will not in itself precipitate out any conversational events. Nor is more than one person necessary. Pirsig's narrator appears to converse with his motorcycle. You, the reader, may feel you are conversing with this article; and the authors have experienced conversation whilst seated alone at a computer terminal. But these are conversations in which the C-indis involved are not the entities of the apparent subject/object relationship. The C-indis all extend into the human being. (The evidence is that two motorcycles cannot converse) but one C-indi at least entails some part of the object, e.g. motorcycle. (The evidence is that removal of the motorcycle would disrupt the conversation.)

What are the conditions for the creation of conversational space? They are as yet not fully known. When two people appear to converse the C-indis involved are not necessarily, or even often, co-existent with the objects within the separate skins. Personal meaning exists in conversational space. Conversational space is created only in the presence of personal meaning. Under certain conditions the space will shrink, reducing the meaning. In other conditions the space will expand, allowing the growth of meaning. Conversational space is experienced as the context of personal meaning. It has no fixed dimensions, being always created to contain at least two systems of personal meaning. It is defined by the modes of expression in which these meanings are exchanged. It is the manner in which these two systems of personal meaning interrelate that determines the dimensionality and thus the capacity for decay or development. Languages in the most general sense are the modes in which the interrelations are negotiated. Meta-languages are the modes in which the process of interrelating is itself negotiable. The power of the meta-language determines the capacity for growth. Tacit understanding of the required experiential technology shows that the design of a conversational amplifier should present few problems. Part of this design will be found in Chapter 4.

Earlier work (Harri-Augstein and Thomas, 1976) has explored the nature of a "learning conversation". This was found to entail at least three inter-woven dialogues, one about *process,* one relating to emotional *support* and one concerned with the creation of *personal referents* to replace the external contingencies of reinforcement. The ways in which these dialogues combine create the conditions for conversational space. This is probably best con-strued as non-euclidian since it appears to have levels corresponding to the time-span or perspective involved. In learning conversations it is found useful to construct at least three levels. The central level is the *content of the learning*; in one direction this connects with life. The *life conversation* is about the relevance of learning. It is about the construction of personal knowing. The other direction is towards the process of learning, awareness of this enables *learning-to-learn.*

The concept of a conversational methodology points to the contribution which psychology might make to the evolution of man. By construing our task as that of psychological tool-making we move away from the description of people in our terms and move towards a systematic technology for enabling each individual to become more aware of his or herself in their own terms.

Conversational tools may take the form of contentless heuristics (e.g. the repertory grid, structures of meaning (Harri-Augstein, 1978) and client centred therapy) which control the form of the conversation whilst leaving the content to be contributed by the participant. Court procedures offer a similar paradigm. Other conversational tools have more specific purposes enabling certain parts of the conversation to be enriched beyond the capac-ity of the individuals involved. Many existing psychological techniques take on new meaning when they are perceived from this perspective. Tests can be used not as the measuring devices of a secret society, but as awareness raising devices. The responses are behaviours, which mirrored back to the behaver heighten awareness. The measure becomes negotiable in conversa-tion and it no longer acts as stigma or accolade. Even a selection procedure can become truly conversational leading to an agreement which includes a large measure of self-evaluation. But the mirror must be clean. In learning conversations the authors have developed and used extensively a series of specific tools which record learning behaviour and use the behavioural record to talk the conversational learner back into a re-construction of the learning experience. This heightened awareness acts as a pre-condition to significant conversationally-aided change.

By definition a conversational tool is essentially a crutch or aid to conversation which becomes redundant as the structure is internalised by the participants, who can then control the conversation from within themselves. Thus, by taking the apparently meek role of tool-maker we enter our true domain, the person.

Psychological Relativity

All knowing is relative. This thought lies behind all nihilistic philosophies. It is also expressed (Evans-Wentz, 1960) in the Sunyavada of Nagarjuna's Mahayana Buddhism. Meaning is relative. The conception of Kelly-like systems of personal meaning existing in conversational space offers the ground rules for development of a theory of psychological relativity. The conversational methodology would give such a position a cutting edge which would enable it to function effectively: serving as the conceptual basis for all manner of negotiation and collaboration. This operational effectiveness would steer it clear of the emptiness of extreme nihilism.

Relativity is one of a system of associated concepts which have transformed both the power and the appearance of modern natural science. Uncertainty (Heisenberg, 1930), discontinuity (Max Planck, 1949) and relativity (Einstein, 1950) are all characteristics of the now public meanings which are differentially attributed to reality in our personal systems. Each of these has its equivalent in descriptive systems available to the psychologist. trophe theory stand ready for a full-blooded relativism to remove the absolutist base of much of our residual thinking. Each node of personal meaning offers a perspective from which to view and/or re-view the others.

Personal construct psychology offers a perspective on behaviourism which may serve to close the gap between the experiential and behaviourist technologies. In PCP validation serves an apparently similar function to reinforcement in operant conditioning. The immediate validation of the construction of experience which triggered certain behaviour, functions only if the anticipations inherent in that construction of experience are validated by the reinforcement. After a few trials the constructions would lead to the anticipation of the reinforcement. The learner could trust his habitual constructions of experience and Rogers' criteria for significant learning would be met. But as experience grows, the construction of experience is elaborated and the anticipations become longer-term. By analogy to the structure of the TOTE system (Miller *et al.*, 1960) the higher order construing would require an increased time-span before validation. This delayed gratification or validation of longer-term anticipation, is one of the characteristics of civilised man. It is here that humanistic and behavioural psychology meet. The humanistic approach allows us the freedom to invent our own understanding of "what influences what". It allows us to view events selectively; anticipating acting and construing the perceived short- and long-term consequences of our actions. Thus, by changing our ideas about what relates to what, we change the direction of our search for validation of our anticipations. Our models of the world influence how we may be in it. For the behaviourist the patterns of reinforcement are given. The contingencies of reinforcement are prior. Control in the conversation lies firmly with the constructor of the environment. Religions vary in their views on this issue; Richards' (1973) introduction to great literature points to the same issue. Freedom exists in the acquisition of a meta-language in which to construe and therefore control the conducting of conversations with others of our species, with other species, with nature and within ourselves. By construing their own nature the human race can create their own destiny. By construing the nature of the universe we have the freedom to explore it and so change our minds.

References

Ardrey, R. (1972). "The Social Contract". Fontana, London.

Bannister, D. (1979). "Sam Chard". Routledge and Kegan Paul, London.

Blakemore, C. (1977). "The Mechanics of the Mind". Cambridge University Press, Cambridge.

Chenault, J. (1969). Syntony: A philosophical premise for theory and research. *In* "Readings in Humanistic Psychology" (Eds A. J. Sutich and M. A. Vich). Collier-MacMillan, London.

Einstein, A. (1950). "The Meaning of Relativity" (4th edn). Methuen, London.

Evans-Wentz, W. Y. (1960). "The Tibetan Book of the Dead". Oxford University Press, Oxford.

von Foerster, H. (1960). On self-organising systems and their environments. *In* "Self-Organising Systems" (Eds M. C. Yovitts and S. Cameron). Pergamon Press, Oxford.

Giorgi, A. (1978). Problems encountered in developing a phenomenological approach to research in psychology. *In* "Personal Construct Psychology 1977" (Ed. F. Fransella). Academic Press, London and New York.

Goldfried, M. R. and Merbaum, M. (1973). "Behaviour Change through Self-Control". Holt, Rinehart and Winston, New York.

Harri-Augstein, E. S. (1978). Reflecting on structures of meaning: A process of learning-to-learn. *In* "Personal Construct Psychology 1977" (Ed. F. Fransella). Academic Press, London and New York.

Harri-Augstein, E. S. and Thomas, L. F. (1976). The Self-Organised Learner and the Printed Word. Final Report to SSRC, London.

Harri-Augstein, E. S. and Thomas, L. F. (1977b). The Art and Science of Getting a Degree. Centre for the Study of Human Learning, Brunel University, Uxbridge.

Heisenberg, W. K. (1930). "The Physical Principles of the Quantum Theory". Leipzig.

Hudson, L. (1978). "The Nympholepts". Jonathan Cape, London.

Jung, C., (1933). "Modern Man in Search of His Soul". Kegan Paul, London.

Kelly, G. A. (1955). "The Psychology of Personal Constructs", Vols 1 and 2. Norton, New York.

Kelly, G. A. (1978). Confusion and the clock. *In* "Personal Construct Psychology 1977" (Ed. F. Fransella). Academic Press, London and New York.

Koestler, A. (1964). "The Act of Creation". Hutchinson, London.

Levi-Strauss, C. (1962). "The Savage Mind". Weidenfeld and Nicholson, London.

Lorenz, K. (1977). "Behind the Mirror". Methuen, London.

McCulloch, W. S. (1965). "Embodiments of Mind". MIT Press, Cambridge.

MacCurdy, E. (1938). "Notebooks of Leonardo da Vinci". Jonathan Cape, London.

Mair, J. M. M. (1977). The community of self. *In* "New Perspectives in Personal Construct Theory" (Ed. D. Bannister). Academic Press, London and New York.

Maslow, A. H. (1962). Notes on being-psychology. *J. Humanistic Psychol.* **1**, 47–71.

Mead, G. H. (1934). "Mind, Self and Society". University of Chicago Press, Chicago.

Miller, G., Galanter, E. and Pribram, K. H. (1960). "Plans and the Structure of Behavior". Holt, Rinehart and Winston, New York.

Muller, F. M. (1962). "The Upanishads", 2 Vols. Dover, New York.

Ogden, C. K. and Richards, I. A. (1923). "The Meaning of Meaning". Harcourt, New York.

Pask, G. (1975). "The Cybernetics of Human Learning and Performance". Hutchinson Education, London.

Popper, K. (1972). "Objective Knowledge: An Evolutionary Approach". Clarendon Press, Oxford.

Pirsig, R. (1976). "Zen and the Art of Motorcycle Maintenance". Corgi, London.

Planck, P. (1949). "Scientific Autobiography and Other Papers". New York.

Polanyi, M. (1967). "The Tacit Dimension". Routledge and Kegan Paul, London.

Richards, I. A. (1973). "Beyond". Harcourt, Brace and Jovanovich, London.

Rogers, C. (1961). "On Becoming a Person". Constable, London.

Rogers, C. (1969). "Freedom to Learn". Charles E. Denill, Columbus.

Schutz, A. (1967). "The Phenomenology of the Social World". Northwestern University Press, Evanston.

Skinner, B. F. (1948). "Walden Two". The MacMillan Co., New York.

Skinner, B. F. (1971). "Beyond Freedom and Dignity". A. Knopf, New York.

Wilson, C. (1972). Existential psychology: A novelist's approach. *In* "Challenges of Humanistic Psychology" (Ed. F. T. Bugental). McGraw Hill, New York.

Zaden, L. A. (1971). Towards a theory of fuzzy systems. *In* "Aspects of Network and System Theory" (Eds R. E. Kalman and N. Declares). Holt, Rinehart and Winston, New York.

Exploring Socialization through the Interpersonal Transaction Group

A. W. Landfield

This chapter outlines the efforts of several investigators who have elaborated the psychology of George A. Kelly within the context of the Interpersonal Transaction group. This group process is of particular interest since it shows how a strategy of change and research methods for evaluating that change can be derivations from the same theoretical position—"The Psychology of Personal Constructs" (1955).

When George A. Kelly lectured on personal construct psychology, he sometimes would invite his audience to suspend their preoccupations with other theories and to imagine life as a personal construction with its many elaborations. In extending this invitation to enter *his* world, he was also asking them to function within his Sociality Corollary: "To the extent that one person construes the construction processes of another, he may play a role in a social process involving the other person" (p. 95). If this definition of social role is extended to Kelly, himself, the following statement seems to logically follow: To the extent that Kelly could understand something about the theoretical systems of his audience, including their thoughts, feelings and values, he could play a reciprocal social role in relation to them.

Kelly's statement of the Sociality Corollary suggests that the most sensitive interpersonal roles are those in which one's behavior reflects some attempt to understand the viewpoints of the other person. Although human beings may treat one another as though the person is "just" a behavior or "just" a social norm, the most vital ways of relating to others involve a willingness to listen to the other person's feelings, attitudes and values. Speaking reflexively, the majority of us presumably feel most understood when someone cares enough to ascertain our views and the reasons for them in an open-minded way. Now understanding another's view is more than just observing a sequence of behavior or agreeing with a particular choice or decision. One tries to infer a structure of feelings, attitudes and values which are linked to the person's choices, decisions and behavior.

133

Kelly, in defining social process in relation to construing the other person's outlook, presumably was urging psychologists to depart from more conventional definitions. Although one can define social role as behavior occurring within a social context or in relation to a stereotype about some group of persons, Kelly wanted to incorporate an appreciation of that which contributes vitally to our being both human and humane. In the process of trying to construe the other person's outlook, one may become more sensitive to his ways of thinking, feeling, valuing and being. Even as one disagrees with another's behavior, one can feel more sympathetic toward him because he becomes more than an object which merely supports or frustrates the behavior of others. He becomes a person with viewpoints and emotions—similar to oneself.

Elaborating the idea of Kellyan sociality, one may reason that the most effective interpersonal exchanges are generated by more valid conceptions of how the other person is feeling and thinking. However, this accuracy of conception does not mean that one necessarily views the world in exactly the same ways as the other person. Kelly was quite explicit on this point. In construing the outlooks of the other person, it is possible to encompass these outlooks within a system which is broader, more abstract, and somewhat different from that of the other person. This is what perspective is all about (Landfield, 1977b). And, it is perspective which carries the social role process beyond empathy. To take perspective, the empathic person must construe the particular viewpoints of others within a broader or more abstract system. For example, one may understand with considerable feeling how another person could assume that life is against him. At the same time, one may have such an understanding of the other person without accepting the idea that life is most validly reflected by negative construction. Perspective-taking may also be exemplified by the feeling or assumption that one can learn by listening to others or that really caring means to listen well.

Just as sociality can be related to empathy and larger perspectives, it seems reasonable to presume that increasing sociality would be associated with increments in meaningfulness of others as well as heightened positive regard for them. Now relating meaningfulness and positiveness to Kellyan sociality may not seem as straightforward as linking empathic predictive accuracy within the other's system to sociality. It might be argued that one can assign great meaningfulness and positiveness to the other person without projecting any feelings, thoughts or values into his behavior. Even granting this strange possibility, the construct theorist can maintain that within a context designed to promote sociality, meaningfulness of others and favorableness of regard for them should generally increase along with the ability to anticipate their decisions within their frames of meaning.

As one stretches out his own system to understand more about the other person's system of meaning, one is engaging in a social role process that can generate more profound understandings of the other's role behavior. As one begins to construe the other person as a feeling, thinking, valuing and anticipating creature, like oneself, the other person becomes more meaningful within one's own system. The other person becomes more than just a set of disembodied behaviors. The other person can become meaningful in the same ways that one is meaningful to himself. Restating this point, understanding more about how the other person feels and thinks expands the base from which he may be understood. Additionally, increased understanding of the other's framework of meaning can induce increased sympathy for the other person—even though there may be disagreement with his behavior. There are, of course, instances where better understanding of the other's values could turn one against him. Nevertheless, it seems reasonable to theorize that dislike for others often relates to a lack of understanding about their life struggles. Greater sympathy for others is associated with knowing more about what it might feel like to be the other person.

Beginning with these elaborations of Kellyan sociality, the Interpersonal Transaction (IT) group was devised as a way of studying and facilitating the interpersonal process. Essentially, the IT group focuses on dyadic interactions among persons, a process which emphasizes sharing and listening. Research measures used in conjunction with the IT group, such as meaningfulness, positiveness of regard and predictive accuracy, are also based on an appreciation of construct theory. The IT group will now be defined and explored as a way of studying and facilitating an increasing sociality among persons.

Introduction to IT

Within the structure of the Sociality Corollary and its elaborations, the following question was posed: What kind of strategy might encourage the development of a context in which persons become more open to each other's constructions? It seems reasonable that an investigator of "Kellyan" sociality would encourage persons to both share and listen to each other. But, what kind of interchange would optimize sharing and listening? For example, should the focus be on dyadic interactions or would a larger group provide the better context for sharing and careful listening?

An investigator could argue that a larger group protects the person from interactions that are too prolonged and intense. A group member has the option of allowing others to take the initiative, thus avoiding the feeling of being constantly spotlighted. Extending this point, the person may briefly withdraw into his psychological shell if he feels overwhelmed and confused. He can do this without feeling conspicuous about it. Taking another perspective on the larger group, it could also be argued that the larger group can be dominated by a few members. Such dominance by the few may encourage the more passive members to perseverate in their less active or less sharing roles. Even when all members of the larger group actively participate, there still is a tendency for conversation to focus on several group members. In other words, there tends to be an unevenness about the dyadic interactions that occur within a larger group. Perhaps it is this unevenness of dyadic interaction that accounts, in part, for the observation that the same group which is experienced constructively by one person may be experienced as a "downer" by another person.

Even as the larger group may contribute to an experience of failure for a particular person, it can be argued that the exclusive, face-to-face interaction between two persons can have its special problems. The intensity of the dyadic interaction could lead to a type of confrontation from which the person cannot easily disengage.Although such confrontation might seem desirable to those psychologists who believe that interpersonal buffeting and angry interchange is the way to honest relationships, vigorous and argumentative confrontation can also lead to excessive anxiety, threat and hostility.

Since the terms anxiety, threat and hostility are used in special ways within construct theory, these terms should be defined or paraphrased. *Anxiety* occurs when the person feels unable to encompass certain important events within his construct system. Experiencing the inability to understand a person could provoke anxiety.*Threat* is the awareness of an imminent, comprehensive change in core structure. Restated, the person experiences threat when he becomes sensitive, at some level of awareness, to an impending and vital change in his life constructions and behavior. Threat refers to something which has not happened but which could happen. As the person relates to another, he may become uncertain about his role. In this context of uncertainty, he may envision, if only remotely, the possibility of suddenly playing a role which he devalues. Alternatively, he could anticipate, at some level of awareness, the possibility of suddenly playing a most constructive role, but one with which he has had little experience. This too can be threatening. As Kelly often stated, the anticipation of change, of whatever nature, can be threatening. Now the third term, *hostility*, is uniquely defined as the person's attempt to extort validational evidence. One tries to force outcomes that cannot be forced. One may argue endlessly with another person about some particular point.

Applying these terms to the dyadic as well as to the larger group, the position could be taken that the larger group offers a greater possibility for disengaging from interactions which are becoming too anxiety provoking, threatening or hostile. It would seem that intense anxiety, threat and hostility might promote an unwillingness to share, to listen carefully and to understand. Conversely, it could be argued that exclusive, face-to-face, dyadic interaction provides more information about how all members of a group construe their worlds.

The Dyadic Solution

Taking into consideration the positive and negative features of both dyadic and larger group interaction, we developed a context in which the person has many brief dyadic encounters. The brevity of interaction, e.g. four to eight minutes, and the opportunity to meet as many as nine other persons reduces the threat and anxiety of several less than favorable interactions. Additionally, three other structures are provided which may reduce threat and anxiety. First of all, topics introduced for discussion are general in nature. Topics of a more general nature allow the person greater freedom and control over what he shares in each dyad. Secondly, participants are urged to share as much or as little as they wish, thereby giving them greater control over what is shared. They are also urged to listen actively, asking for clarification, but they are cautioned not to question the values or statements of the other person. Each person has a right to his own viewpoints. In this regard, our conduct of the IT group runs directly counter to groups which encourage argument and criticism. One "confrontation" group leader, who will not be identified, used paid "agitators" to stir up argument and hostility among group members. The idea of his group might be defined as "letting it all hang out" and hostility hangs out best.

Another interesting feature of the IT group is evident in the first session and represents a concern for defining the personal construct as more than just words. In the first session, participants are instructed to introduce themselves to the other persons in the dyads by communicating in gestures. This gesture experience lasts only four minutes. After each person has met the other group members in the gesture experience, they again rotate through the dyads, remaining four mintues in each dyad. This time they discuss the gesture experience.

Now the value of this gesture instruction is three-fold. First, members recognize that even though it is difficult to communicate by gestures, much may be learned beyond the intended communications. Second, the highly verbal and more extrovertive person may be as seriously handicapped or even more so than his more introvertive or quieter partner. Third, group members tend to find the gesture experience hilarious. In this spirit of fun, members anticipate returning for the second session.

Another instruction used routinely at each of the two hour sessions is the Mood Tag. Each member, at the beginning and end of each session, records how "I feel and don't feel at the moment" on a slip of paper which is then taped to his clothing. He also places his first name on the Mood Tag. After the person has "hung" his Mood Tag, he circulates among the other members and reads their tags. At the close of the session, the person again records his feelings and anti-feelings on the reverse side of the tag and circulates among his fellow members. Now the Mood Tag not only sensitizes each person to the mood constructs of the other person, but it also serves a diagnostic purpose for the investigator. Much can be learned about how group members anticipate each session and what impact the session has had on them. Typically, Mood Tags at the beginning are egocentric. Members talk about their feelings of tiredness, elation, boredom, anxiety, curiosity and hope. Later, members talk about their feelings for members of the group, individually and collectively. That which begins with intrapersonal construction shifts to themes which are interpersonal.

Summarizing the sequence of IT events, the two hour session begins with the Mood Tags and is followed by dyadic experiences. Rotational orders for the dyadic experience are presented in Table I. Although these instructions are only given for groups of eight and ten persons, the investigator of IT may wish to study groups of other sizes. However, the group size must be limited to even numbers. Now the use of even numbers can present a problem when there is one absence. On such an occasion, the group administrator may substitute for the missing person or he may ask each person to sit "contemplatively" opposite the empty chair for that dyad. Following the dyadic experience and prior to re-hanging the Mood Tags at the end of the session, participants pull their chairs into a circle and talk about the session for approximately 15 minutes. The primary function of the "large group" experience is to allow members to unwind from the intensity of dyadic interaction. A secondary function of the large group is to obtain immediate and direct feedback from group members about the sessions.

Brief Description of Measurements

The IT strategy was first employed with college students who volunteered for a research project in which they "might" learn more about themselves in relation to others. In IT Groups 1, 2, and 3 there were ten persons, both male and female, who met weekly for eight two-hour sessions. Prior to the first session, all persons completed a rep test modified by Landfield (1971). In this rep test procedure, 15 contrasting descriptions of "outside" acquaintances were elicited from each subject. These fifteen contrasting descriptions or verbalized constructs were then placed at the poles of 13 point scales with zero mid-points. This was done by the investigator who also made xerox copies of each person's scales. These Personal Construct Scales (PCS) were then used in three ways. First, the person rated himself and the nine other group members on his own PCS, Next, he predicted how the other persons might rate him, using their PCS. Finally, he predicted how each of the other persons might rate himself, again using the PCS of the other person. These procedures are described in greater detail by Landfield and Rivers (1975), Landfield and Barr (1976) and Landfield (1977a).

A fourth procedure is used in conjunction with the rep test. Each group member is asked to value code each of his own construct poles by placing a plus, minus, ? (can't decide) or N (values don't apply) beside it. Experience with this method indicates that the person should determine his own values. The following descriptions were *positively* valued by the persons who originally contributed them: "concerned with self; average intelligence, headstrong; easy going; works for today; direct; outward; idealistic; innocent; realistic; emotional; unpredictable; striving; relaxed". The following descriptions were *negatively* valued: "a scientist; flamboyant; a wee bit self centered; dependent on others; knows no real goal yet; good mother; quiet; experienced; hard nosed; practical joker; unemotional; predictable".

A panel of nine psychology graduate students were asked to judge the value of these and other construct poles elicited from these subjects. Not only did these judges sharply disagree among themselves as to how best to value code construct poles, but their majority vote led to a miscoding of 15% of the constructs. The judges could not believe that there would be such disagreement either among themselves or with the subjects of the IT group. Here is an excellent example of how "objectivity" may preclude an accurate perception of the other person.

Using the above procedures led to several interesting measures which we have called predictive accuracy, meaningfulness and positiveness. Each of these measures would seem to have implications for the development of sociality.

Predictive Accuracy is used with both the predicition of the other person's view of himself and the prediction of how the other person will view the predictor. This kind of measurement, in which the predictor enters the construct systems of other group members, is a direct application of the Sociality Corollary in which making inferences about the other person's outlooks are emphasized. Predictive accuracy, as it relates to self and empathy, is elaborated by Landfield and Rivers (1975).

A measure of empathy may be derived by asking each member to predict how others will rate him as well as how others will rate themselves, predictions being made on the other person's scales. In this measurement, the 13-point scale is reduced to 3 points: left side (1), middle (0), and right side (2). The reason for reducing the scale to one of sideness and mid-position can be illustrated. Take the example of Person A who rates himself on his own personal construct scale at position plus 2, but is predicted by Person B at plus 5 and by Person C at minus 1. Using our scale of minus 6 to zero to plus 6, Persons B and C predict Person A equally well. However, Persons A and B are more in agreement because they understand A on the plus side. Moreover, giving greater weight to sidedness makes good sense within personal construct theory. Therefore, our 13-point scales are scored as a 3-point measurement instrument. (p. 367)

Meaningfulness of self or others is measured by the total rating scale polarization score derived from adding the scale points rated on the 15 scales of the PCS. Since the PCS can be rated from six to zero to six and points in between, the total possible score on one PCS scored for meaningfulness is 90 points. The person may rate another group member at this maximum level by using all six point ratings on 15 scales. The person may also rate each of the other nine group members at this level for a grand total of 810 points. Employing each person's ratings of the nine other members, one may elicit two kinds of information. First, there is the meaningfulness of the group to the person. Second, there is the meaningfulness of the person to the group. In the latter case, one sums the ratings of a person done by other group members. For a further discussion of rating scale polarization refer to Bonarius (1970) and Landfield (1977a).

Positiveness of regard for self or others also may be inferred from the PCS by using the value codings of group members. Just as predictive accuracy is estimated by breaking down the 13 point scale into sidedness, positiveness is determined by the number of times the person rates others on the positively valued side of his construct scales. If a particular person rates each of the nine other members consistently on the positive side of his constructs, all of which have a positive coding, his total possible score for positiveness toward others would be 135. Just as meaningfulness and predictive accuracy may be scored in two ways, positiveness may be considered from the perspective of the "person on the group" or conversely, the "group on the person".

Research Studies

Specific studies of the first three IT groups focused on predictive accuracy and a "cognitive complexity" measure derived from rep grid scoring patterns called functionally independent construction or FIC (Landfield, 1971). Bigley (1972) found that Group 2 members, functioning extensively within dyads, tended to be more certain about and accurate in predictions of others after eight sessions than Group 1 members who functioned more within the larger group than within dyads. Barr (1972) found some evidence that FIC score change on external grids tends to parallel the direction of change on internal grids. The external grid required subjects to rate 15 "outside" acquaintances on 15 elicited construct dimensions. The internal grid required subjects to rate self and nine other group members across the previously elicited constructs.

Barr (1977), again working with organizational scores from grids, used constructs elicited from both acquaintances and IT group members. She asked normal subjects who participated in 16 sessions to fill out PCS on self and nine other group members at intervals of four weeks. Constructs based on outside acquaintances were alternated with constructs based on group members. She found a gradual decrease in the size of FIC scores, suggesting less complexity of construction at the end of the group. Another measure called ordination or 0 was also used (Landfield and Barr, 1976; Landfield, 1977). The 0 score—a measure of meaningfulness levels derived from variations in degree of rating scale polarization—theoretically points to some capacity to think hierarchically or integratively. To be able to employ different levels of meaningfulness suggests that the person can handle hierarchical structure. Now the 0 score showed a sharp decrease at the eighth session and then a more gradual rise to the end of the group, but not to the level of initial scoring. This sharp decrease in the 0 score was related to the employment of more zero ratings and a restricted range of scoring to the middle of the PCS scales. In other words, there was a loss of meaningfulness and of meaningfulness levels at mid-group.

Landfield and Rivers (1975), in their 20 week groups, 4 and 5, found beginning to end of group decreases in FIC and 0 scores, suggesting simplification of conceptual structure. However, mid-group ratings were not obtained. Now it is possible that the sharp decrease, at mid-group, in meaningfulness of others found in Barr's second study also obtained in Groups 4 and 5. However, the decrease in the 0 score at the *end* of group experience in these latter groups ($\chi^2 = 12\cdot8, p >0\cdot001$) is accompanied by a constriction of ratings to higher levels of meaningfulness, a condition occurring in the Barr study as well.

Although it is impossible to relate fully data from the Barr study to data obtained by Landfield and Rivers, an hypothesis may be stated: IT group members tend initially to project greater meaningfulness on to new acquaintances than they rightfully should. Later, after group members have had more extensive experience with one another, these first projections become invalidated, associated with less meaningfulness. Then, a reconstruction process begins, accompanied by increases in meaningfulness attributed to others. Such an hypothesis should come as no surprise to investigators of impression formation. An amazing array of meanings may be attributed to persons whom one scarcely knows. As laymen, we often remark that one must be careful about first impressions—knowing full well that we will probably change our minds. Then, with more than a little pomposity and a great need for unity (Landfield, 1977), we plunge ahead, characterizing new acquaintances as though we know them intimately. We preface our characterizations with "I wonder if" and "I suspect that," if we have recently experienced being wrong. More likely we will say, "I'll make a bet on it!" and "You just wait and see!"

In another study, which combined information from Groups 2, 3, 4, and 5, Landfield and Barr (1976) and Landfield (1977) defined confusion by high FIC and low 0 scores, i.e., high "cognitive complexity" without the capacity to hierarchically order one's constructs. In other words, high complexity in the absence of integrative skills points to confusion rather than to a healthy complexity. Exploring with several patterns of organizational scoring, it was found that high FIC and low 0 scores occur in the interpersonal contexts of less positive regard, less meaningfulness and greater inability to predict accurately within the other person's construct system. This finding has important implications for research on cognitive complexity which has not taken into account the possibility that persons may relate their constructs in some hierarchical fashion. Questions may also be raised about the appropriateness of correlational and factoring techniques for assessing hierarchical relations when such procedures assume mutual relationships between two variables, i.e. A leads to B and B leads to A. This point is elaborated by Landfield (1977a; in press).

Although our understanding of the IT experience primarily comes from observations within seven IT groups and one control group, all designed within a formal research format, the IT group has been used in other contexts with interesting results. Robert Neimeyer (1978) used several IT groups, numbering less than ten, in a class which focused on conceptions of death. He found that larger group discussion was greatly enhanced by first introducing topics in the dyadic context. He also reported the results of a class evaluation. Using a 5-point scale, ranging from 1 (completely worthless) to 5 (very worthwhile), the class rated the IT experience at an average of 4·0. In response to another question, 94% of the class replied that the IT group should definitely be used in future courses on death and dying. Rivers *et al.* (1978) currently have IT research in progress involving three groups of alcohol counselors. Data was collected at three points in time over an eight session period. Preliminary analysis suggests a gradual and even growth in meaningfulness within the groups. Moreover, counselors who are recovered alcoholics tend to show less increase in meaningfulness attributed to others than other counselors. Landfield, employing IT in a graduate seminar, observed the same large group effect. These classroom experiences suggest that IT methodology would be useful for professors who complain that students are unwilling to engage in class discussions. By increasing sociality through dyadic interaction, students may feel more comfortable in expressing themselves in the larger class situation. Another interesting application of IT has been made by Gavin Fairbairn (personel communication, January 1978). Fairbairn reports that the IT group has proven useful in the context of a "long stay" ward at Chricton Royal Hospital, Scotland. He states,

The ladies have begun to talk more freely both in the dyads and in the larger group. They pay more attention to one another in the group; they listen more attentively than they did. They initiate conversations quicker and more easily. They ask more questions both of each other and of the therapists which is particularly noticeable in the larger group. Changes have been noticed outside the group, eg. nurses commenting on the fact that certain ladies seem to engage more in conversations. Therapists who have met members of groups in other parts of the hospital have had friendly and spontaneous chats with them.

Longer-term IT Groups

The shorter-term, eight week IT groups were lengthened to a period of 20 weeks by Landfield and Rivers (1975) for a study of persons with alcohol related problems. Members who comprised Groups 4 and 5 were drawn from a subject pool of "volunteers" who had been arrested by city police for driving while intoxicated. Although these subjects volunteered for the group experience, they were expected to become involved in several "personal improvement" projects. This project was one of the several alternatives. To some degree then, participation was like asking a child whether he wanted to wear his red or white gloves. The IT group probably was chosen as the best of several poor alternatives. The choice of persons with alcohol related problems was suggested by Rivers, director of an alcohol studies program. He maintained that many alcoholics have difficulties in relating to others and what may appear like socialization is often quite superficial.

Since the investigators would be working with persons who might have more serious psychological problems, the decision was made to have a third person organize and administrate the groups, allowing the investigators to become regular members of the groups. Although there was no evidence that the IT group would be destructive, it seemed ethically sound to have first-hand impressions of group members. Moreover, it seemed important that the investigators know what it feels like to be engaged in the IT process. Sometimes objectivity can be carried to the point of being ignorant about obvious factors that may affect one's studies.

In their roles as participants, the investigators were identified as professors of psychology who would be regular group members. However, they were only identified by their first names as were other group members. One investigator knew he had really become a part of the group when one member asked him, "Where did you drift in from?" Since the investigators enjoyed playing their "ordinary," non-professional selves in the dyads, they were accepted by other group members. It became obvious that the administrator was considered the "real" psychologist, a role thoroughly enjoyed by the graduate student administrator.

Members of Groups 4 and 5 varied in age from 21 to 60, the oldest person being a grandmother. Occupationally, they were highly varied. Occupations included: secretary, janitor, teacher, stock analyst, sales manager, student, bar girl, hospital maintenance worker, military officer, cleaning lady, housewife, bank teller, office manager, mutual funds salesperson, Vietnam veteran, and a former pilot. Twelve males and eight females participated in the studies. In regard to their problems with alcohol, about half were taking antabuse. Many were members of Alcoholics Anonymous. Several of them had been hospitalized for alcoholism and two persons had received private psychological treatment. At the six months follow-up after IT termination, only one alcoholic member was known to have been drinking and he was hospitalized for one month.

In personality, the subjects were certainly a "mixed bag". Two members at the beginning of the groups seemed to have suicidal ideation. For example, one person stated that life was like looking through the wrong end of a telescope and the telescope was becoming elongated. The Vietnam veteran was somewhat withdrawn, cynical and suspicious. A recent divorcee seemed to feel proud of having visited a dozen bars in one evening. Another woman used jokes as a primary vehicle for relating to others. The salesmanager was noticeably jittery in his behavior, presumably a symptom of alcohol withdrawal. One attractive, highly intelligent young woman who seemed most mature was living with a man of violent disposition and a criminal record. The former pilot, a woman, was most calm and reassuring in her interactions with others. One student made it clear, again and again, that he was a "born again Christian". The military officer's earlier traffic offense involved crashing into a police car. The bar girl seemed frightened and alienated. One male member who had frequented many jails played the role of sophisticated boredom.

Groups 4 and 5 began with Mood Tags and an orientation about what to expect. A rep test was administered; however, part of it could be finished at home. The first session concluded with a brief larger group discussion of the evening and a re-hanging of Mood Tags. Sessions were limited to two hours. Coffee was served at each session. Session 2 focused on the gesture experience which was described earlier. Special instructions were given in regard to careful listening, sharing and respecting others' views. Session 3 focused on the topic, "Who are you?" Formal research was begun at Session 4, employing the rating scale methodologies outlined earlier which provided information about interpersonal meaningfulness, positiveness, and predictive accuracy within the other's system. The same research instruments were again used 14 weeks later. Sessions between the two research periods focused on such topics as: Sharing something you value and don't value; Discuss ways in which people see me accurately and inaccurately; Exchange

TABLE I. *Order of dyadic interactions for eight and ten members.*

1	2	3	4	5	6	7	8	9	10
2	1	4	3	6	5	8	7	10	9
3	5	1	6	2	4	9	10	7	8
4	6	9	1	8	2	10	5	3	7
5	4	7	2	1	10	3	9	8	6
6	7	8	9	10	1	2	3	4	5
7	8	5	10	3	9	1	2	6	4
8	9	10	5	4	7	6	1	2	3
9	10	6	8	7	3	5	4	1	2
10	3	2	7	9	8	4	6	5	1

1	2	3	4	5	6	7	8
2	1	4	3	6	5	8	7
6	5	7	8	2	1	3	4
4	7	5	1	3	8	2	6
5	4	8	2	1	7	6	3
7	8	6	5	4	3	1	2
3	6	1	7	8	2	4	5
8	3	2	6	7	4	5	1

and discuss each other's Mood Tags; and, Talk about anything important to you. Further information on the IT format is found in Landfield and Rivers (1975). The rep test modification is described by Landfield (1971) and Landfield and Barr (1976).

The Control Group for Groups 4 and 5, referred to as the C Group, was comprised of University students who were each paid 20 dollars for participating in five IT Group sessions. The first four sessions paralleled those held with the two regular groups. However, an interval of 14 weeks preceded the fifth session. At this session, members were re-introduced, hung their Mood Tags, and circulated. As usual, first names were written on their tags. Care was taken that each person was correctly identified by other members prior to re-doing the research task of session four.

Change and the Long-term groups

Interpersonal meaningfulness, positiveness of regard and predictive accuracy within the other person's construct system was discussed in a previous section. These measures will now be applied to Groups 4, 5 and C in the context of two questions. First, do a significant number of persons in Groups 4 and 5 increase their scores on these measures? For example, how many persons increase in the total meaningfulness attributed to the nine other group members? Reversing this question, how many persons in the group receive an increased attribution of meaningfulness from the nine other group members? In the first instance, one refers to the "person on the group". In the latter instance, the terminology of the "group on the person" is employed.

The next analysis focuses on a comparison of each IT Group, 4 and 5, with the Control (C) Group. The second question being asked is whether (as predicted) the amounts of increase in individual members of Groups 4 and 5 on the interpersonal measures will be significantly greater than that found among members of Group C. Although a greater increase among members of Groups 4 and 5 was predicted as a function of socialization, one could argue that repeated testing might encourage a systematic increase on the research measures. This possibility would be revealed in Group C.

Proceeding now to the first question, Table II indicates that a significantly large number of persons in Groups 4 and 5, combined, increase in meaningfulness (col. 1), positiveness (col. 2), ability to predict the other's view of the predictor (col. 3), and ability to predict the other's view of himself (col. 4). This increase holds within the contexts of both the "person on the group" and the "group on the person".

The answer to the second question is found in Table III. Groups 4 and 5, considered separately, show significantly greater increases on the interpersonal measures in every comparison with the control group. Additionally, there is no evidence that Group C members tend to increase on the various measures (see Table IV).

TABLE II. *Number of persons increasing in interpersonal meaningfulness, positiveness and predictive accuracy in combined IT Groups 4 and 5 with total n of 20.*

	Meaningfulness	Positiveness	Prediction A	Prediction B
Person on group	17 $\chi^2 = 9.8$, $p < 0.01$	18 $\chi^2 = 12.8$, $p < 0.001$	17 $\chi^2 = 9.8$, $p < 0.01$	20 $\chi^2 = 20$, $p < 0.001$
Group on person	19 $\chi^2 = 16.2$, $p < 0.001$	18 $\chi^2 = 12.8$, $p < 0.001$	17 $\chi^2 = 9.8$, $p < 0.01$	17 $\chi^2 = 9.8$, $p < 0.01$

Prediction A: other person's view of you within other's constructs.
Prediction B: other person's view of himself within other's constructs.

TABLE III. *Comparisons of Groups 4 and 5 with Control (C) Group on degree of increases on meaningfulness, positiveness and predictive accuracy.*

	Meaningfulness	Positiveness	Prediction A	Prediction B
Person on group	Gp 4⟩ C U= 13, *p* ⟨0·01 Gp 5⟩ C U= 17, *p* ⟨0·01	U= 24·5, *p* ⟨0·005 U= 10, *p*⟨0·001	U= 10·5, *p* ⟨0·01 U= 5, *p* ⟨0·001	U= 8·5, *p* ⟨0·001 U= 2, *p* ⟨0·001
Group on person	Gp 4⟩ C U= 2, *p* ⟨0·001 Gp 5⟩ C U= 3, *p* ⟨0·001	U= 18·5, *p* ⟨0·01 U= 1, *p* ⟨0·001	U= 13·5, *p* ⟨0·01 U= 9, *p* ⟨0·001	U= 16·5, *p* ⟨0·01 U= 12, *p* ⟨0·01

Mann-Whitney U test of distribution differences is used with score frequencies. The *p* level is used with a 1 tailed test.

TABLE IV. *Number of persons increasing in interpersonal meaningfulness, positiveness and predictive accuracy in Group C with total n of 10.*

	Meaningfulness	Positiveness	Prediction A	Prediction B
Person on group	3 χ^2= 1·6, *p* ⟨0·30	5 χ^2= 0, *p* ⟨0·99	5 χ^2= 0, *p* ⟨0·99	6 χ^2= 0·4, *p* ⟨0·70
Group on person	3 χ^2= 1·6, *p* ⟨ ·30	4 χ^2= 0·4, *p* ⟨0·70	3 χ^2= 1·6, *p* ⟨0·30	3 χ^2= 1·6, *p* ⟨0·30

The data from the above tables tend to support the social facilitation value of the IT group. However, it cannot be stated that the increasing social process seen in the group necessarily generalizes to outside the group. Fairbairn is the only investigator who has had the opportunity to directly observe such generalization. In the absence of such direct information, anecdotal evidence will now be given from the six months follow-up with Groups 4 and 5 which point to increments in feelings of well-being and improved socialization in many group members.

Subject A quit her job as a bar girl, completed high school by taking evening classes, acquired secretarial training, and is now employed as a full-time secretary. Subject B returned to his role of responsible military officer. Although somewhat shy, this person recently gave a humorous talk about his battles with alcoholism before a distinguished audience which included a state governor. Subject C quit his job as a hospital maintenance man, acquired training in carpet installation, and produced metal sculptures for a retail store. Several months after the group experience, he visited a grandfather whom he had never seen. He talked about establishing his roots. Subject D, who had lived a very unstable existence, married and settled down to what at one time would have been a "hum drum" existence, one which she might have previously referred to as "cold mush". Subject E, a most egocentric person, took an interest in a family next door. She had lived beside this family for five years without knowing anything about them. She took the initiative in getting acquainted and now feels close to the wife and shows a motherly concern for the children. Subject F, the sales manager who could not argue with his boss, was able to tactfully inform him that he was in disagreement with some of his policies and procedures. Much to F's surprize, his boss listened to him. At the follow-up meeting, F's jitteriness seemed to have subsided. Subject G courageously, but not without some perspective, married a widower with four children. Subject H continued his role as a "born again Christian", showing a genuine interest and compassion for other group members. Subject I returned to alcohol even while taking antabuse. He was treated for one month in a special institutional program. Subject J quit the University even though he was doing well in his subjects. He sought special training as a refrigeration unit expert, something he wanted to do for himself, but something which would create difficulties between himself and his father—a man whom he respected. Subject K married the boyfriend with the violent temper. Subject L changed jobs from office work to selling mutual funds in the community. Little information is available about the other problem drinkers.

Socialization and Construct Congruency

It has been shown that members of Groups 4 and 5 increase on measures of interpersonal meaningfulness, positiveness of regard and predictive accuracy. It has also been shown that this increase in interpersonal scoring is not just a function of repeated testing. Now there is a third question which an investigator may wish to explore. To what extent is the increment in social-ization within the group related to a homogenization of constructs among group members? In other words, is the process of socialization within the IT group primarily a matter of persons beginning to think alike? A partial answer to this question will be sought in an analysis of the content of rep tests taken at the beginning and end of the group experience. This analysis involves post-coding the meanings of construct poles, obtaining congruency coefficients for each dyad, and noting the direction of congruency change.

More specifically, the content coding system was developed by Landfield (1971) for studying client–therapist congruency as a predictor of premature termination in psychotherapy. The system was later used by Fransella (1972) in her research on stuttering. This content post-coding system is comprised of 32 categories and subcategories within which a construct pole may be fitted. Since multiple scoring is possible, a particular description can be categorized in several ways. For example, the description, "a kindly social extrovert", could be coded as high social interaction, high forcefulness and high tenderness. The description, "very confused", could be coded as low organization and extreme description. Now there are problems with such a coding system which are suggested by construct theory itself and have been highlighted in research. First of all, the data base for the post-coding is far from ideal. It would be better to work from construct poles which have been exemplified and elaborated by subjects. A recent classroom exercise showed that subjects post-code their own constructs in more categories than an "objective judge". Secondly, post-coding categories are those on which the judges can most readily agree. The problem here is that the coding system is itself a personal construct framework attuned only to easy cultural agree-ment. Knowing the shortcomings of post-coding, but appreciating its useful-ness in previous research, we decided to post-code.

A comparison of pre-post dyadic congruency scores revealed a systematic lessening in congruency scoring. Seventeen of the 20 group members showed more dyadic decreases than increases in congruency. Since this pervasive decrease in congruency was not anticipated, the mechanics of coding were carefully studied. For example, could the assignment of fewer coding categories on the second rep test restrict the possibility of increases in congruency? Although there was some lessening of content category assignment at second testing, the trend was not significant ($\chi^2 = 1 \cdot 8$, $p < 0 \cdot 30$). Moreover, Group 4 did not contribute to the trend. A second analysis of total frequency of content scoring across the categories did not support any relation between total score decrease in a person's content and the number of dyads in which he showed decreased congruency.

Although the evidence from content coding suggests that persons did not become more alike in their construct focus on the rep test, group members may have internalized the three superordinate (perspective-taking) constructs and their polar values which were provided through IT group instructions. The constructs provided by instructions were listening *versus* not listening; sharing *versus* not sharing; and, respecting *versus* not respecting others. The preferred poles were listening carefully; sharing, but not to the point of great discomfort; trying to be understanding without invalidating the other person's viewpoint. In theory, these superordinate constructions with their preferred poles should help IT group members bridge the gaps between their own conceptual structures and those of other group members. When members of one longer term group were asked about changes in the group, they agreed that "others" had become good listeners.

Taking Perspective on IT

Further developments in IT procedure should be oriented toward enlivening the experience without increasing the potential for threat. In addition to designing more useful topics generally, and for special groups, in particular, some effort should be directed toward pre-structuring the group in regard to different ratios of higher and lower levels of congruency in the content and organization of personal construct systems. Research by Landfield (1971) outside the context of the IT group suggests that crises in relationship may occur when dyadic content congruency falls below the coefficient of 0·56. Below this level, premature termination in individual psychotherapy tends to occur. Although one cannot generalize much from the setting of individual psychotherapy to the IT group experience, the research on premature termination does raise an interesting question.

Group pre-structuring in relation to organizational styles is also suggested by experience with Group 6, in particular. For the first time, investigators of IT were seriously confronted with the problem of absences from and criticisms of the group. These absences and criticisms seemed related to a particular kind of rep test organization. It seemed that whenever a person's rep grid implied few orthogonal constructions and little organizational hierarchy, the person would complain more about boredom and ambiguous interactions, and show some anger. Observations of this group, a short-term one, suggest that persons who function from simple, tight structures may face a bewildering array of new events in the IT group. These people may suffer from Kellyan anxiety. Assuming this to be the case, an investigator might experiment with different combinations of construing styles. He might also experiment with discussion topics which have a more concrete structure. For example, group members might be asked to share a particular construct of choice from their own rep tests. This was actually tried in Group 6 with interesting results. Two persons who construed in simpler ways stated that it was the best session. One girl whose organizational scores implied both complexity and hierarchy commented that the session format was unnecessary.

Further research on IT might also focus on facilitating classroom discussion, professional and lay group interaction, friendship formation, counselor training, and psychological treatment. Work with such groups should also include an assessment of the extent to which the themes and processes of IT become incorporated into the construct systems and lives of members outside the group. Anecdotal evidence does suggest that there may be such generalization.

Finally, it should be remembered that the vitality of IT for the construct theorist is embedded in George A. Kelly's "Psychology of Personal Constructs" and in the pursuit of implications and elaborations of his Sociality Corollary.

References

Barr, M. A. (1972)."Change viewed within personal construct theory and the method of rotating dyads". Unpublished M.A. thesis, University of Missouri.

Barr, M. A. (1977). "An investigation of cognitive differentiation and integration within personal construct theory". Unpublished Ph.D. dissertation, University of Nebraska.

Bigley, S. A. (1972). "An analysis of accurate perception of others' feelings toward oneself in interpersonal groups". Unpublished M.A. thesis, University of Missouri.

Bonarius, J. C. J. (1970). Personal construct psychology and extreme response style. An interaction model of meaningfulness, maladjustment, and communication. University of Groningen, The Netherlands.

Fransella, F. (1972). "Personal Change and Reconstruction". Academic Press, London and New York.

Kelly, G. A. (1955). "The Psychology of Personal Constructs". Norton, New York.

Landfield, A. W. (1971). "Personal Construct Systems in Psychotheraphy". Rand McNally, Chicago.

Landfield, A. W. (1977a). *In* "Nebraska Symposium on Motivation, 1976, Personal Construct Psychology" (Ed. A. Landfield), pp. 127–177. University of Nebraska Press, Lincoln and London.

Landfield, A. W. (1977b). The person as perspectivist, literalist and chaotic fragmentalist. Unpublished manuscript.

Landfield, A. W. (in press). Personal construct psychology: A theory to be elaborated. *In* "Cognition and Clinical Science" (Ed. M. Mahoney). Plenum, New York.

Landfield, A. W. and Barr, M. A. (1976). Ordination: A new measure of concept organization. Unpublished manuscript.

Landfield, A. W. and Rivers, P. C. (1975). Interpersonal transaction and rotating dyads. *Psychotherapy: Theory, Research and Practice* **12**, 366–374.

Neimeyer, R. (1978). The interpersonal transaction group in death education. Unpublished manuscript, University of Nebraska.

Rivers, P. C., Adams, J. and Meyer, J. (1978). Research in progress on the use of IT with alcohol counselors. University of Nebraska, Lincoln.

Social Networks and Interpersonal Constructs

C. P. Hargreaves

Phenomenological arguments have pointed to the immense problems of studying interpersonal perception. It is not only impossible to see exactly what another person "sees", but also impossible to know exactly what he means by his words, most of the time. In particular, traits perceived in other people tend to be a highly personal affair of the viewer. Admittedly rather general traits may be a form of Schutzian "typification", but the more specific the trait seen in another person, the more personal a matter it is for the viewer. This is principally because the other person will have a very personal relevance to the individual, in terms of both social structure and personal "project".

Thus the following is an attempt to study personal construct systems, not in terms of constructs labels, but rather in terms of the element patternings upon constructs. It relates interpersonal relational structures to subjects' cognitive structuring of a group of elements, not just the specific thoughts about each individual element. The use of a particular construct label has been explained sometimes by the specific form of a dyadic relationship of which the subject is part. However, to explain the complex patterning of all the elements upon constructs, one needs to study the others' interrelationships as well as the subject's relationships with each of them.

Thus instead of treating a subject's interpersonal behaviour in terms of dyadic interaction, one needs a framework within which one can analyse a person's overall situation within his social world. This is not a new departure, for it fits in with a paradigm that has been developing for some while. Within philosophy, existentialism has indicated how a person is not a single element in contradistinction to each single separate other, but rather he is involved via a "project" in a particular world, not as an onlooker, but as a being at one with that world, a being-in-the-world, a being-with-others.

Feuerbach was the first to point out, in 1843, the meaninglessness of "I" without its complement, "You". The point came up much later in the works of people such as Buber, Scheler, Husserl, Heidegger and Sartre, to name just a few. Note however that this construct of "I–You" provides a distinction between two objects already seen together within a world. The "I" and the "You", and the "Him", "Her", etc., are all seen together as existing; one has an awareness of the objects before one starts to separate out the "I", the "You" and so on.

George Herbert Mead also tended away from analysis of dyadic interaction with his concept of the generalised other, and he studied that aspect of the self, as a being amongst others, with his analysis of the concept "Me". Furthermore, he thought that a child develops an awareness of other selves *before* developing an awareness of his own self, as the latter only arises through response to others:

> the appearance of the self is antedated by the tendencies to take the attitudes of the others, so that the existence of the others is not a reflection of his self-experience into other individuals. The others are not relative to his self, but his self and the others are relative to the perspective of his self organism. (Mead, 1938, p. 153)

It must be stressed that this is not simply saying that the self or one other is viewed against a background of others. Instead, each element, self or other, is viewed as together within the totality of existence for the viewer, his being-in-the-world. I hope to show how not just a person's own relationships with other elements are relevant to his cognitive structuring of his social world, but instead the whole network of relationships between elements, where the self is viewed as just one more element. The specific significance of the self element arises just from its being the central connecting element in a star-shaped network.

The viewer sees his self and others together within a *social* world. At a pre-cognitive level, he is faced instantly with a social world that has a definite structure. Some results from Balance Theory studies

> strongly suggest that there exists a cognitive bias which favours the learning of interpersonal over attitudinal relations . . . (The former) constitute perhaps mnemonic "anchors" for the learning of other relationships in the structures. (Zajonc and Burnstein, 1965)

Bittner (1931) also shows how Mead's concept of the self implies the precedence of social consciousness over physical consciousness.

Taking this further, one could say that a person is existentially confronted with a specific network structure. He then "makes sense of " the given structure by imposing constructs upon it in such a way that the constructs (with their element patterns) portray the given element structure as well and efficiently as possible. In line with Kelly's Minimax principle, enough construct dimensions will be created to reflect back the structure, while superflous construct dimensions will be avoided. Thus the complexity of a person's construct system will be directly related to the complexity of the network structure. Partial evidence for a relationship between cognitive complexity and network complexity has already been found by E. O. Laumann (1973).

In this article, the structure of the network is, however, not considered in terms of actual patterns of frequency of interaction. It is considered solely from the subject's viewpoint—that is, who he thinks interacts more with whom, and whether they like each other or not. Methodologically it would have been almost impossible to find out what "actually" happened, even if that could be defined objectively. Thus the subject's construct system is compared to his own description of his social network.

For this reason, it is worth noting that most people generally assume a neutral to positive link between other people, unless given evidence to the contrary. Thus events which "stand out", needing definite explanation, are the negative or strong positive relationships. It was felt that there would be a strong tendency for "psychological" constructs to arise in order to explain these relationships and to differentiate elements within the same network subsets or cliques.

One can create many hypotheses between depth of knowledge of interpersonal relationships and the types of constructs needed to explain them. However, the types of constructs will not be differentiated. Suffice it to say that, possibly because the subjects were interviewed upon their relatively close friendship networks, almost every construct elicited was of an "interactional" or "psychological" nature. Here, I will only try to show how the personal network structures directly relate to the element structures within construct systems.

Research Design and Data Collection Methods

The major difficulty in relating network structure to repertory grids is that most people's social networks are continuously in a state of flux. One needs not only to see if the grid changes as the network changes, but equally whether the grid does not change if the network does not. It would be too risky to just leave to chance the possibility of no change. However, a set of very useful subjects was available—American students visiting Edinburgh University for a year. They had a home network in America with which they naturally had very little interaction, and at the same time they were forming a new social network in Edinburgh. Although they came over in organised programmes, only one of my subjects knew anybody on the programme or in Edinburgh before joining the programme.

Thus it was possible to study their interaction with and thoughts about their new developing social network at the same time as studying their

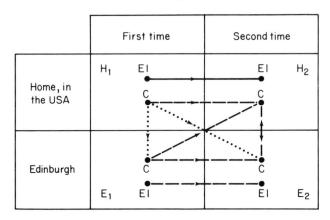

Fig. 1. Research design. El = element structure; C = construct structure. Arrows show hypothesised causal effect: →— strong; – – –→ – – average; ....>.. weak.

thoughts about the old static network. As this involved two completely separate social worlds, repertory grids were taken separately upon each. Grids were carried out twice, upon arrival here and about five months later, which gave a simple two by two design as in Fig. 1. For simplicity of exposition the four grids will be referred to as H1, H2, E1, and E2, standing for home time 1, home time 2, Edinburgh time 1, and Edinburgh time 2 respectively.

With this design it was possible to see how constructs and their structure changed over time, with a constant and a developing network. It permitted comparison of the home element structures at time 1 and at time 2, but only a partial comparison of element structures was possible with the Edinburgh networks, because on the second occasion some new elements replaced some old, as new contacts replaced old in the changing network.

The two main hypotheses associated with this design were as follows:

(1) There would be a general development of new constructs arising through new networks. H1 would include largely personal evaluative constructs. E1 would use some of the H1 constructs but involve many less personal, socially classificatory constructs befitting people not known very well. H2 would include some of the old H1 constructs but many new ones arising in E1 and E2. E2 would include mostly new constructs with just a few old ones from E1. The main point is that H2 would not include the same constructs as H1 even though it had the same elements.

(2) The four elements structures would relate directly to the structure of the social networks. Very good friends would be viewed similarly in general. Two people disliking each other would be seen as similar upon some dimensions as they are connected, but also as dissimilar upon other dimensions to

explain the negativity of the relationship. Two unconnected people from different sectors of the personal network would be viewed differently and so be largely set apart upon the constructs. Apart from the relations of grids to networks, one would expect the element structures, in H1 and H2, to be the same even though the constructs change. As far as it can be measured, one would not expect the same consistency of element structure between E1 and E2 as the Edinburgh network developed.

To summarise, the hypothesis is that the constructs originate to explain the relationships and structure of the social network. That is, the network comes first, as it were, and the constructs are more attributions to explain patterns than descriptions *per se* of individuals as individuals. This leads to many other hypotheses upon issues such as triad splitting and dimensionality of grids, right up to theories of the "self", causes of mental disturbance, and so on. Although the latter ramifications of the hypothesis are in fact very, very interesting, there is not enough space here to discuss it fully and it will be developed elsewhere. It might anyhow be better to prove the hypothesis first, rather than indulge in interesting speculation.

To test these hypotheses, data was collected as follows. Each subject was interviewed four times, twice at the beginning of the winter term and twice at the end of the spring term of the university. The order was H1, E1, H2, E2. Between H1 and E1, and between H2 and E2, subjects completed diary sheets for two weeks. Upon these they recorded what they did, when, where and with whom. Results from these will be reported elsewhere.

At each interview the first task after introductions, was sorting out a set of elements to use. For the home network the subjects were asked where they spent last year, and to name people they were involved with. They were told that the idea was to obtain a representative selection of contacts and not just the people they liked best. Fourteen names were obtained, often with a little probing, and mutual agreement as to who to include and who not, if more names were forthcoming. For the Edinburgh network grids, a set of elements was derived via the diary contact lists.

The subjects wrote each name upon a separate small piece of card, which was five-sided, rectangular at one end and coming to a point at the other (see Fig. 2). Their own name was also written on one card.

After the cards were jumbled up, the subjects were asked to lay the cards out upon the table in whatever pattern came to mind and meant something to them. They often asked for more details than this, but were carefully given no clues at all and told to do just whatever they wanted. To prevent any discussion while they did this, and so that they did not feel watched or rushed, I would instantly offer them coffee. Even if they did not want any, I made myself a cup which entailed leaving the room to go to the kitchen. Through various ways I was able to avoid interrupting them, and I only rejoined them at the table after they had finished.

Fig. 2. Element card.

When they had finished, I put a large sheet of thin paper over the cards and traced their positions. I asked the subjects to explain the pattern; why were these cards here and those there, was there any reason for this card being next to that one, and so on. This proved to be a very easy task that subjects found both amusing and interesting. These particular patterns will be referred to as the "layouts" below.

The cards were shuffled and the names written down in a random order. A standard cyclic (1, 2, 5) design was used to obtain 15 sets of three names, triads, such that each name occurred three times always with different people. Each triad was used in the cyclic order, so that the same name did not occur in consecutive triads and normally occurred three, four or five triads later. Most standard design texts describe how to find such a design for any number of constructs or elements. On the first and second occasions, subjects were given the same triads as far as possible, though in a different order.

To elicit constructs from each triad, the subjects were asked to give a way in which they saw two elements as similar and at the same time different to the third. They were also asked for a different construct to one they had named before. They were handed a long sheet of plain white paper (100 × 10 cm), and were asked to write down one pole of the construct at one end and the other at the other end of the piece of paper, whichever way round they liked.

They were asked to space out the cards upon the sheet of paper, using the pointed end of the card to show where a person was on that dimension relative to the others. By having the cards pointed, the subjects were able to be very precise if they wanted. When the cards had been laid out, their positions were noted with a dot and name on the sheet of paper. The subjects were asked where the division was from one side to the other of the construct and where they would ideally like to be upon the dimension. An example of the sort of result is shown in Fig. 3.

The beauty of this technique was the great ease with which subjects could represent not only the order of the elements upon the dimensions, but also their relative positions. It provided results similar to a rating scale without bothering the subject with numbers. The scale could also in imagination go on to infinity and was not bounded by zero and a hundred, or any other chosen numbers. Before now I have had subjects reject the idea of assigning

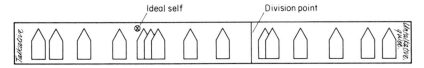

Fig. 3. An example construct pattern.

ratings to people; it seemed to have unacceptable moral overtones, which would also probably have affected the constructs they thought of. However, with this technique all went very smoothly. Another factor of great value was the speed with which one could elicit the grid.

I also found it better if the subjects did not have a card entitled "ideal self" to fit in with the other elements. This would have brought in moral and other overtones for some subjects. It was better to ask where they would ideally like to be, after the elements had been placed, and to mark where they pointed to, rather than make something concrete and "overtly meaningful" by the term "ideal self".

After 15 constructs had been elicited the subjects were asked to lay the cards out upon another sheet of paper in such a way as to represent their personal preferences, from best friends down. They were asked whether they would call the first person best friend or not, and so on down to where it was very good friends, good friends, friends, acquaintances and any dislikes. After the interview, the elements were also numbered from one up to a possible 14, according to their place in the preference orders, irrespective of the categories.

Naturally, there were some occasions where there was a negative evaluation of a person very well known to the subject, whereupon the subject was unsure whether to place the person high up or low down, but this happened quite seldom. They were also asked to do the same, as far as possible, for each other contact. That is, upon other sheets, the subject would try to represent what he thought each other person's preference ordering would be. The subject was asked to leave off the sheet any people in the 15 that the contact had not met.

Obviously this is not a "true" picture of the network but, in general, the subjects' ideas seemed to be relatively good mappings of the basic structures of their social networks. The mappings tended, naturally, to be loosest in the middle ranges, i.e. whether, for example, Joan would call Margaret a friend or an acquaintance, and which of two acquaintances was liked more. At the best friend and opposite level, the subjects' mappings of the networks seemed quite reliable.

All this was done in one interview, which lasted anything from two to four hours. Most subjects found the interviews interesting and enjoyable, though admittedly, both they and I were often quite tired by the end. Apart from four such interviews, they also filled in the diary sheets twice for two weeks. Although there is no space to report the results from the diaries, it is worth commenting that they correspond very well to the network pictures gained in the interviews.

Given the above data the results below have been obtained so far. To give the description a reference point, I will describe the specific results for the two subjects that were flatmates, as this affords some useful cross comparisons as naturally they had some common contacts in the Edinburgh networks. The results from their data are quite typical. All the names have of course been changed. I will describe in order results from the analysis of the layouts, the triad splitting, the element mappings and the inter-element correlations. Lastly the conclusion contains a summary of the basic results and their implications.

"Layouts"

Every time the subjects laid out the cards in their own pattern, they did so with personal interrelationships in mind. This was without any prompting to that effect. The patterns ranged from simple to complex. The simplest were just the subject's personal preference order, but this happened only twice in 68 layouts. These two occurred where the subjects had a very weak network in Edinburgh. The lack of social involvement led to little awareness of the others' contacts. This was coupled with very simple, highly evaluative grids. I remember well a sense of worrying, self-perpetuating isolation. The highly evaluative overtone of comments, and little awareness of others' responsibilities, might have made it hard for the subjects to establish stronger relationships and thus extricate themselves from the situation.

The patterns became more complex as the subjects tried to picture their social networks in more detail and as the networks became more complex. Figure 4 shows the first pattern that Hilary produced for her home network. Here are her comments: "The height implies something in my mind— importance to me". The six in a circle pointing in are

> my primary group that I interact with—not ordered in height—pointing in as interacting together as far as my perspective is concerned. Charles is a male friend, once boyfriend. Leslie is my best friend. Last year she lived on the same floor, unintentionally. Claire was my roommate and Dinah was also on the same floor last year. Margaret, like me, is majoring in journalism. Alice was Leslie's room-mate, unintentionally. She was in the same contact environment as the primary group, but I do not share with her the same emotional relationship as with the others, hence she is pointing out.
>
> Pamela links Ohio and Abington, borders on primary/secondary, pointing upwards as more in my primary group. Amanda, Celia and Mark are the group in Abington that I like. Mark is pointing in, implying more important than the other two. Milo is under Abington group, heading in the same direction as Celia and Amanda: if more important I would have put him pointing the other way. Shaun is pointing down to differentiate him from the rest, and at the bottom as I don't

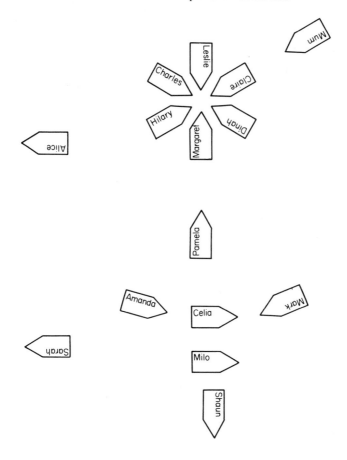

Fig. 4. Hilary's first home layout.

esteem him as highly as the others. Sarah is in the environmental context of Abington but not the same emotional importance. Like Alice, she's on the fringe. Mum's here, highest, as I interact with her at the same primary level as the top group, but not directly within the context of the group. Hence she is outside, but pointing in.

A few extra points can be added. The patterning in the primary group reflects the fact that Charles, Leslie and Margaret were better friends of Hilary in that group. Claire and Leslie mutually called each other best friends after Hilary. Margaret, Claire and Dinah had visited Abington and met people there; Leslie and Charles had not. Celia and Mark were stronger friends than Amanda and Mark. Milo was friends with Celia, Mark and Shaun but had only just met Amanda. Milo was also the link from Shaun and

Celia to Mark. Sarah's only mutual friendship was with Amanda. Mum had met Claire and Dinah but not Alice, which may be another reason why Mum's across to the right.

This sort of pattern is quite typical. The contacts are sorted according to personal preference and then placed according to their interconnections. The idea of the cards pointing in a particular direction was oft°n, though not always, used to reflect further detail. Above all, however, never once in 68 layouts did anybody place people near each other because of a construct such as "equally humorous" or "artistic" and so on. The nearest thing to this was when students met in the same class, say a literature seminar. They may have been all "interested in literature" but in the layouts it was never said like this. Instead the subject would only mention that they all went to the same class.

The general result was that subjects patterned contacts instantly always upon network grounds. At a fundamental level the peoples' interrelationships came first, and intrinsically these gave the contacts a structure. One could say that this structure is implanted in the mind first, and then constructs arise to explain this structure. Then, through the principle of construct economy, the construct structure will relate to the network structure in terms of complexity and in many other ways.

The Triad Splitting

After the layouts, the grid was elicited from the subjects using triads to derive the constructs. It was of great interest to see how the triads were split. Very often subjects would take the three cards and almost instantly pair two together and separate out the third, even though they were actually unaware why. Occasionally they would even say that "These two definitely go together, but I'm not sure why", and then they might say "Ah yes, of course, those two are much more adventuresome" or whatever the construct was that came to mind. Thus one had the impression that the structure was there, before the construct arose to explain it.

This led to the following hypotheses. Firstly, given the subjects' preference ordering, there would be a tendency for the triad to be split in one of the two ways that did not put together the most liked and the least liked. Also, if two were at a preference level very distinct from the third, then they would be paired; for example, two very good friends of the subject paired in contrast to an acquaintance, or, less strongly, two average friends of the subject paired in contrast to a well liked acquaintance. Secondly, pairs that are strongly connected will tend to be placed together. Thus, if the subject likes, for example, John more than Mary, and Mary more than Peter, then if John and Mary are strongly linked and neither is as strongly linked to Peter, then John and Mary will be paired together.

Now these hypotheses are sometimes contradictory, for example: the least and most liked might be very good mutual friends that have not met the third person. Which factor prevails depends upon the relative differences in the subject's preference ordering and the strength of the network tie. This meant that with the new Edinburgh network one would expect the personal preference ordering to dominate. As the network develops, becoming more connected, network ties might become more important. Equally, as time passes, with the home grids one would expect the personal preference ordering to become more important as the subject's memory of all the interpersonal relationships fades.

Thus when the subjects were given the same triads when eliciting the second home grid, it was expected that there would be a tendency for the triads to be split in the same way, as the network had basically not changed as far as the subject knew. This proved to be very evident. Normally at least ten out of 15 triads were split in the same way, sometimes all 15. When the triad splits did change, it was normally to fit a slightly changed preference ordering, due, for example, to receiving letters from one person in particular. It must be stressed, however, that the reason for the triads being split in the same way was not because the same construct was used. Normally on the second occasion only one or two constructs arose that were verbally similar, and only five or six had similar overtones, but almost never did these arise with the same triads.

With the Edinburgh grids, subjects were given the same triads as far as possible, except that some new elements replaced old ones. This triad splitting analysis naturally only relates to those triads that were identical the second time round—that is they were made up by the same three people. Where the Edinburgh network had changed, it was not expected that the identical triads would be split in the same way. Only if that section of the network had basically not changed was the same split expected. Appropriately, normally only a third of the identical triads were split in the same way, much less than on the home grids.

There is not enough space here to list in detail long series of triads, showing how and why they were split in the way they were. Suffice it to say that not only gross distinctions such as "good friends" versus "not mets" are relevant, but also much finer structural detail, especially where the network is highly connected. Structural equivalence was also involved on occasion.

This analysis was carried out as the triad splitting and construct elicitation is, in a sense, the closest one can get to construct formation. The dominant impression is that affective relationships of the personal network are sensed immediately. The network thereby gains a structure which the subject then explains by fitting constructs across it. The constructs often thus turn out to be more attributions than descriptions.

It was also noted that when the network contained completely disconnected sectors, triads that involved people from different sectors seemed to lead to lower level constructs, almost more mundane. This reflects badly upon the role procedure for sorting out a list of elements to use on the grid. One may well obtain a very disconnected set of people leading to relatively superficial constructs and relatively random placings on the constructs, particularly towards the centre of the dimension. Further comment on this will be left until later.

Repertory Grid Mappings

Having used a triad to elicit a construct, the subject then placed the cards on a sheet as described earlier. The 15 constructs were then analysed with the help of the computer and a programme, called "MDPref", that produces mappings in basically the same way as "Ingrid".

The mappings of the elements in all four grids were expected to relate to the social network structures. This meant that the two home element mappings should have been very similar even though the constructs had changed. With the Edinburgh grids it was expected that patterns would change as far as the network changed. This proved to be the case almost without exception across 68 grids.

As an example here are the four mappings of Sandra's grids (Figs 5–8) with a brief explanation of the dominant structures. Comparing the first home mapping to Sandra's network description, one notices the following pairs close to each other:

(1) Caroline and Sally, mutual best friends, adjoined by Karah and Kenny, both good friends. The four make up a central clique, although Karah is a little separate.

(2) Julia and Teresa are mutual best friends. Teresa's likes and dislikes do not parallel other people's as closely as Julia's do, and this may be why she is put further out than Julia.

(3) The relation between Patricia and Melanie is best friend from Patricia to Melanie, and good friend from Melanie to Patricia. This connection relates to them being placed first and third upon the third dimension. Upon the first two dimensions they are evidently separated as Melanie is liked by all, but Patricia is not (in particular Melanie is good friends with Sally). There are six negative relations to Patricia from others—Jenny from whom she is separated on dimension one, from Caroline on dimensions one and two, from Julia on dimension two, from Desmond on dimension three, from Karah on dimension one and, lastly, from Sandra on all three dimensions.

(4) Kay and Desmond are two people difficult to join up to any particular group in the network. They are mutual good friends. Kay apparently found the housing cooperative a little difficult and moved out at the end of the

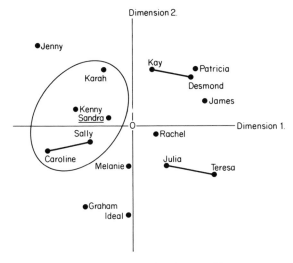

Fig. 5. Sandra's first home grid.

previous year; Desmond lived out anyway. Thus it appears that the top right quadrant generally holds people who did not fit very well in the cooperative, or who lived outside it.

(5) James's position may be partially explained in terms of the fact that he has negative relations with ten of the others. The remaining four, to whom he has positive relations, include Julia, Teresa and Rachel, all of whom he is reasonably close to in the mapping.

(6) The only remaining mutual best friend pair are Rachel and Jenny. Jenny is much more of an outsider to Sandra's central clique. She has weaker relations to the clique than Rachel. Also Rachel and Sandra were in the stage of becoming very good friends, exchanging many letters. Rachel, like Sandra, had come to Europe for the year, although, admittedly, to Paris. In contrast, Sandra said that she was not at all interested in seeing Jenny when she went back to the States.

(7) Finally, Graham was an "advisor" in the cooperative and was said to interact with others much more upon an individual basis, not as part of the group. This may explain why he is separated out. Also appropriately his strongest ties are with Caroline, Sally, Julia and Teresa, and his only negative relation is to James.

Looking now at Fig. 6, one notices that the mapping is basically very similar indeed to Fig. 5. The network also turns out to be almost identical. To take it even further, the few slight changes in the network do relate to slight changes in the grid mapping. The tie to Desmond from Karah becomes slightly negative, and another tie to Desmond, from Patricia, becomes

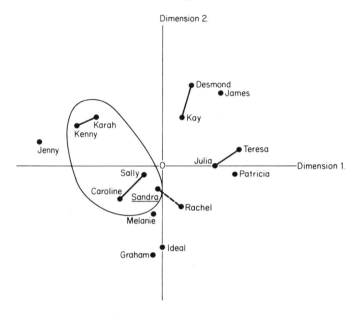

Fig. 6. Sandra's second home grid.

mutually negative. Accordingly he is further away from Karah and even more from Patricia. Desmond and Sally's relation has cooled from best friends to just friends. Kenny and Karah's relation has risen from friend to good friend, and accordingly they are closer. Also both Julia and Teresa's relations to Graham have cooled from good friends and friends respectively to low acquaintances. This may be why they have moved up, around and away from Graham. Rachel is also more in a category on her own, being in France, and has a stronger relation to Sandra.

Thus the two element mappings relate very strongly to the network structure and its few changes. It is worth pointing out that none of the three major components (which account for 70% of the variance) are of the evaluative type. Even dimension two, upon which the ideal self stands out, is totally unrelated to Sandra's preference orderings on either occasion. This points to the possibility that as everybody here at least knew each other, the network structure dominated over Sandra's preference orderings. None of the lesser components relate to her preference ordering either.

However, when it comes to the disconnected networks in Edinburgh, the preference ordering springs up, becoming strongly related to the first dimension. This was quite evident throughout all the grids. Personal evaluation became much more important as the elements became increasingly disconnected. This relates, of course, very interestingly to other studies that show and emphasise the supposedly ever-present evaluative dimension.

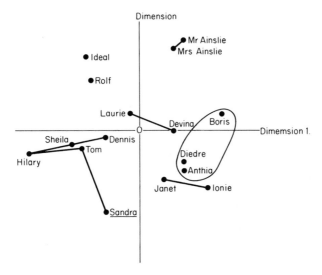

Fig. 7. Sandra's first Edinburgh grid.

In Fig. 7 is shown the mapping of Sandra's first Edinburgh grid. The network falls into quite distinct sections, relating to the network subsets. There are the Ainslies with whom Sandra and Hilary are living. Being their landlords and 30 years older than everyone else they are set apart quite distinctly on their own. There are Boris, Diedre and Anthia, members of Sandra's English tutorial group, who know nobody else. Boris is separated out a bit, and further away from Sandra at the same time, as Sandra felt rather negative towards him.

Devina and Laurie are in similar positions structurally in the network though Sandra underestimated their interrelationship; they are reasonably close on all dimensions. Janet and Ionie are members of Sandra's Economic History tutorial and appropriately Sandra felt closer to Janet than Ionie. Rolf was an acquaintance met a few times only through Hilary. He was in a class of Hilary's but was not a friend of hers, and knew nobody else. Sheila and Dennis are mutual friends, met in another class of Sandra's, and were good friends of Sandra. Sheila was also a friend of Hilary's but Dennis had not met Hilary. Tom was Sandra's best friend and he was also a very good friend of Hilary. He had met nobody else except Laurie with whom he was acquainted.

In general, in the bottom right quadrant one has Sandra's own acquaintances, not met by Hilary. To the top right are the Ainslies that they both knew, but on a very different level to the rest. To the top left are Hilary's acquaintances, naturally not represented so strongly. Finally, to the bottom left are Sandra's strong contacts, all shared with Hilary.

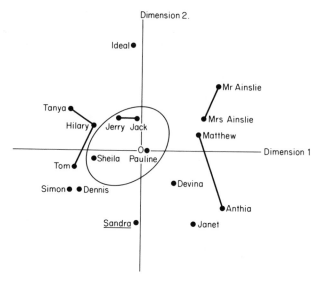

Fig. 8. Sandra's second Edinburgh grid.

When it comes to her second Edinburgh grid (see Fig. 8), the structure is similar in certain ways though five new contacts have been substituted— Pauline, Jerry, Jack, Simon and Matthew replace Laurie, Rolf, Ionie, Diedre and Boris. Janet, Matthew and Anthia are again just classmates, not related to anyone else. Of these only Matthew and Anthia are related, for they are in the same class. The Ainslies are basically placed together; their separation on the third dimension may be due to a development, by Sandra, of distinct relationships to each of them. Indeed, it would have been surprising if differences between them had not arisen with time.

Jerry and Jack are mutual best friends that are equally just friends of Sandra. Appropriately they are very close on all dimensions in the mapping. They are also the core of a clique that strongly includes Sheila and Pauline, together with, although more weakly, Hilary and Simon. Simon is in fact disliked by Jerry and Jack as well as Sheila which may be why he is out down to the left. Dennis only knows Sheila and Sandra, and is also disliked by them. This may be why Dennis is close to Simon (although he did not know him), for Dennis and Simon are the only people in the grid disliked by anyone. Noticeably, Dennis is strongly separated from Sheila on the third dimension.

Tom only knows Hilary and Sandra and is very loosely between the two. Tom did not live in Edinburgh and the third dimension seems to separate the best Edinburgh friends, Hilary and Sheila with Sandra, from the other good friends, Tom and Devina, who are both relative isolates in the network. The last person is Tanya who is an acquaintance met through Hilary. As she knows nobody else she is appropriately placed near to Hilary.

As a final comment, one notes that in both the Edinburgh grids Sandra places herself almost out on her own and far away from her ideal self. This is in strong contrast to the home grids where she places herself in the middle and not so far from her ideal self, particularly on the second occasion. This may well relate to the fact that she did not develop a strong network at all in Edinburgh. She was never considered as part of any clique, but always a bit different. As time went by, Hilary developed very different non-student contacts which were not shared with Sandra at all. On the whole Sandra was not very happy, and as time passed looked forward increasingly to seeing her old contact, Rachel (to whom she wrote a large number of letters), and her other friends back home.

This also relates to her layouts. In the two home layouts she places herself right in the centre of everyone, her card overlapping those representing her best friends. In strong contrast, in the Edinburgh layouts she is on one side. On the first Edinburgh layout she is on the long side of a rough rectangle, and on the second she is on the narrow side of a rectangle, with all the others stretching away to the right. Also with the home layouts, the cards overlapping hers were all pointing in towards herself. On the first Edinburgh layout the cards point in all sorts of directions. On the second Edinburgh layout none are pointing towards her and her card is pointing away from them. Thus it appears that her element mappings in the grids relate not only to the network structures and partially to her preferences, but also to her fundamental attitude towards the network as a whole, and her sense of her place within it.

Inter-element Correlations

Having looked at the general mapping of elements, the inter-element correlations were then studied in detail. For each element, correlations with the other elements were ordered and then related to the element's network ties. The results of the previous section were again supported. In general stronger ties tended to be at the top of these orderings, weaker at the bottom. In most grids there are often several "not mets", making ordinal correlations between the two orders impossible. With Sandra's home networks, however, one could calculate them as all the contacts knew each other. The rank correlations were all positive, except for two, and ranged from -0.04 up to 0.56. This was taking into account the ties in both directions as far as possible. Considering only the ties away from the source, the correlations ranged from zero to 0.6, with one exception which was -0.2. How this was done, may be clearer after the following example.

TABLE I

Order of correlations	Karah's ties	Returned ties	Order of mutual ties
1	F 4	F 3	4
2	A 12	K 4	9
3	K 6	F 6	6
4	B 1	B 1	1
5	K 9	A 11	11
6	B 2	G 5	2
7	F 3	F 12	5
8	F 5	G 8	3
9	K 8	F 6	7
10	A-14	A 13	14
11	A 10	K 6	10
12	A-13	A 6	13
13	A 11	A 13	12
14	K 7	F 8	8

B = best friend; G = good friend; F = friend;
K = know well: A = aquaintance; A- = negative acquaintance.

Table I shows how the order was derived for Karah in Sandra's first home grid. The second column shows her own preference ordering listed in order from the element with which she has the highest correlation down to the element with which she has the lowest. The third column shows the ties to her from the other elements; the figures in this column do not relate to each other. The strongest mutual tie is the B1,B1; the next the B2,G5 and so on. This ordering is in the fourth column. The Spearman's rank correlations between the correlations and Karah's own ties is 0·44, and with the mutual tie ordering it is 0·53.

If one uses partial correlations, partialling out the effect of Sandra herself, the partials fit the model better. In the Edinburgh grids where the network is relatively disconnected, the partials between connected pairs have a strong tendency to rise, compared to standard correlations. In the Edinburgh networks, there were a lot of "not mets". In the first one, people only knew on average three others in Sandra's network. Six people knew only two others, and five, one other only. In all the orders of dyads from grid correlations, any best friend dyads were in the highest five, and the other relationships were mostly in the top ten. The bottom four were almost all "not mets". Basically the same happens on the second occasion.

The general result is that high correlations relate to network connectedness and only secondarily to negative relations. This is quite appropriate for negative relations must be between people who at least interact, and hence probably have something in common. Thus they are separated on some dimensions, but are close on others, making the correlations not as low as between people who have not met.

One can see the subject relating differently to different sectors of the network, and thus construing them differently. The subject plays a different role in each sector. Thence different sectors are not just at opposite poles on some constructs, but generally construed differently. This again shows how the diversity of the construct system is not an individual psychological factor, but is due to the diversity of the person's social network. Given that people's networks are increasingly felt to be much more a matter of happenstance, it is surely the network diversity that creates the construct complexity, rather than vice versa.

Upon the structure of construction, Kelly once wrote, "Construction is systematic in that it falls into a pattern having features of regularity" (Kelly, 1955, p. 72). But what is a "pattern showing features of regularity"? Kelly's idea of "tight versus loose" construing needs a lot of reworking. It needs to be considered both in terms of the dimensionality of the cognitive map, and in terms of clustering within that space.

Finally, it had been hypothesised that the number of significant dimensions in the grids would increase over time with the Edinburgh grids, and decrease with the home grids. This would relate to the Edinburgh network developing, and the details of the home network fading in the memory. In Sandra's grids, for example, the number of dimensions, with eigen values greater than or equal to one, drops from five to four, from first to second time with the home grids, and it rises from four to five, from first to second time with the Edinburgh grids. This sort of pattern was in fact found for every single subject. This further reinforces the idea that the causality is from the social network to the grid instead of the other way around.

Conclusion

It was felt that the most interesting form of data collected were the "layouts". In a sense they parallel the self-description technique, but whereas that is more for looking at construct structures, the layouts show the main element structures that the subjects perceive. Like the self-description technique, the subjects normally found the layouts interesting and revealing. The two techniques both involve a certain exploration of their own "world", while doing them. The subjects often notice things that seem to be new revelations to them. This was noticed sometimes with the layouts, when the subjects began to explain the pattern that they had made. It was often worthwhile noting what the subjects seemed to see as "new revelations", and how they seemed to have come to them.

Now, to summarise the results, we have the following. The layouts show a very basic domination of social network structures in the determination of element structures. The construct-eliciting triads seem to be split almost always upon network criteria, and, only after a triad had been split, was a construct found in order to explain the split. In the grid mappings, the placings of the elements related strongly to the overall network structures. The inter-element correlations tend to relate to network connectedness, as do the pairings. The element mappings of the two home grids were very similar, even though the constructs had changed; this related to the relatively stable view of the home network structure. The Edinburgh element mappings appropriately showed more change as the network developed.

It has been seen that two elements are generally unrelated in the grids if they are socially disconnected, and vice versa they are related if socially connected. If there is a positive relationship between two elements, they will tend to be close on all dimensions. If there is a negative relationship between two elements, they will be close upon some dimensions to explain their connectedness, and strongly separated on some other dimensions to explain why the relationship is negative.

With regard to the constructs, the general picture is of new constructs evolving to explain the new network. These new constructs were mixed with the few prevailing ones from the old grids. One thus has a fairly straightforward image of slow construct change as a person involves himself with new contacts, or as the structure of the present contacts changes.

The dominant result, however, is that the cognitive structure is directly related to the network structure, and not to the structures of the semantic fields used to perceive the contacts. This·creates a very interesting image of the self as a function of the person's social network. Each person is a distinct individual, with his own construct system, as each has his own distinct social network and relation to it. This fits in well with the developing paradigm referred to in the introduction.

In fact, the results relate well to many ideas about the "self" in modern society. Within psychology, an interesting parallel can be made, for example, to L. A. Zurcher's "mutable self". Within social psychology, a parallel can be made to the whole symbolic interaction literature and role theory. Within sociology, one has, for example, the concept of the "other-directed" self. Within philosophy, one has the existentialist view of a person as a "being-in-the-world", a "being-with-others". The important thing, however, is that results do not just confirm principles of socialisation and so on, but they describe a concrete way in which we seem to internalise and structure our social reality. And only after this, do we then attribute meanings to the internalised structure as we try to explain it.

Within personal construct theory itself, the results are rather disturbing. Firstly they infer that constructs are not the initial basic structuring factor, but arise secondarily to explain already internalised structures. As such, constructs are often more in the nature of "attributions" than perceptive descriptions. Secondly, the structure of interpersonal constructs is not self-determined, but dependent upon the structure of the person's social network. The often quoted example of a tightly construing army major probably relates to the fact that he has a very rigidly structured social framework, within which each person has a specific function and should not be related to in any other way.

Thirdly, the results have obvious implications for grid technique. If a person's grid is basically related to his personal immediate network structure, one is liable to obtain false results if one uses the role idea for obtaining a set of elements to use. One may well obtain very old and infrequent contacts that are totally unconnected to each other. This may adversely affect the structure, and lead to rather random placings on constructs that are only related to the new social network. Equally one may force the creation of constructs that are not actually used by the subject when interacting with his present social world.

Finally, there are implications for when one is trying to help people, possibly clients or patients, with problems. The results possibly imply two different approaches, based on the idea that change can be usefully created by changing the person's social "world". One is to try to alter the person's network structure by altering his own ways of appraising others. This is rather tricky, as it is felt that the person's feelings for others are formed at a level before construing is involved; if this is so, one might easily cause more, rather than less, anxiety for the person. The other approach is simply to try to change his network directly. By this I do not mean interference with his present contacts. Rather it would involve the person coming to group discussions, being introduced to new people, and hopefully establishing new contacts. As long as this is done in a reasonable way, this is surely the more humane way. Within the supposedly depersonalised modern technological world, it often appears that problems with one's social network are the cause of most people's personal problems. Thus, the emphasis should possibly be moved away from studying a client's internal cognitive "world", to studying his personal social network.

Acknowledgements

This research was carried out with the advice and encouragement of Rosemary Johnson and Professor T. Burns (Edinburgh University Department of Sociology), to whom I am extremely thankful.

References

Bannister, D. (Ed.) (1970). "Perspectives in Personal Construct Theory". Academic Press, London and New York.

Bittner, C. J. (1931). Mead's social concept of the self. *Sociology Soc. Res.* **16**, 6–22.

Buber, M. (1937). "I and Thou", translated by R. Gregor Smith. T. T. Clark, Edinburgh.

Dagenais, J. J. (1972). "Models of Man; a phenomenological critique of some paradigms in the human sciences". Martinus Nijhoff, The Hague.

Denzin, N. K. (1972). The genesis of self in early childhood. *Sociol. Q.* **13** (Summer), 291–314.

Duck, S. W. (1973). "Personal Relationships and Personal Construct Theory". Wiley, London.

Feuerbach, L. A. (1843). "Grundsatze der Philosophie der Zukunft". Berlag der Literarifchen Comptoirs, Zurich.

Goffman, E. (1959). "The Presentation of Self in Everyday Life". Garden City, Doubleday.

Heidegger, M. (1973). "Being and Time", translated by J. Macquarrie and E. Robinson. Blackwell, Oxford.

Heider, F. (1958). "The Psychology of Interpersonal Relations". Wiley, New York.

Holland, R. (1972). "Self and Social Context". Macmillan, London.

Homans, G. C. (1950). "The Human Group". Harper, New York.

Husserl, S. (1931). "Ideas: General Introduction to Pure Phenomenology", translated by W. R. Boyce Gibson. Macmillan, New York.

James, W. (1890). "Principles of Psychology", Vols 1 and 2. Holt, New York.

Kelly, G. A. (1955). "Psychology of Personal Constructs", Vols 1 and 2. Norton, Norton.

Laing, R. D. (1960). "The Divided Self". Tavistock, London.

Laing, R. D. (1961). "Self and Others". Tavistock, London.

Laumann, E. O. (1973). "Bonds of Pluralism: the form and substance of urban social networks". Wiley Series in Urban Research, New York.

Lee, D. (1959). "Freedom and Culture". Prentice Hall, Englewood Cliffs.

Leinhardt, S. (1977). "Social Networks: A Developing Paradigm". Academic Press, New York and London.

MDPref: part of the MDS(X) Series of the Multidimensional Scaling Programs. Source: J. D. Carroll and J. J. Chang. Any enquiries about the package, or the series should be made to Professor A. P. M. Coxon, Department of Sociology, University College, P.O. Box 78, Cardiff.

Mead, G. H. (1932). "The Philosophy of the Present" (Ed. A. E. Murphy). Open Court, Chicago.

Mead, G. H. (1934). "Mind, Self and Society" (Ed. C. W. Morris). University of Chicago Press, Chicago.

Mead, G. H. (1938). "The Philosophy of the Act" (Ed. C. W. Morris). University of Chicago Press, Chicago.

Meltzer, B. N., Petras J. W. and Reynolds, L. T. (1975). "Symbolic Interactionism; Genesis, Varieties and Criticism". Routledge and Kegan Paul, London.

Merleau-Ponty, M. (1962). "The Phenomenology of Perception", translated by Colin Smith. Humanities Press, New York.

Natanson, M. (1956). "The Social Dynamics of George H. Mead". Public Affairs Press, Washington, D.C.

Pfeutze, P. (1954). "Self, Society and Existence". Harper and Brothers, New York.

Sartre, J-P. (1958). "Being and Nothingness", translated by H. E. Barnes. Methuen, London.

Scheler, M. (1973). "Selected Philosophical Essays", translated by D. R. Lachterman. Northwestern University Press, Evanston.

Schutz, A. (1962–6). "Collected Papers", 3 Vols. Martinus Nijhoff, The Hague.

Schutz, A. (1967). "The Phenomenology of the Social World", translated by G. Walsh and F. Lehnert. Northwestern University Press, Evanston.

Slater, P. (1964). "The Principal Components of a Repertory Grid". Vincent Andrews, London.

Slater, P. (1976). "The Measurement of Intrapersonal Space by Grid Technique", Vols 1 and 2. Wiley, London.

Straus, E. (1963). "The Primary World of the Senses: a vindication of sensory experience", translated by J. Needleman. Free Press of Glencoe, New York.

Straus, E. (1966). "Phenomenological Psychology: Selected Papers", edited and translated in part by E. Eng. Basic Books, New York.

Taguiri, R. and Petrullo, L. (1958). "Personal Perception and Interpersonal Behaviour". University Press, Standford.

White, H. C. and Lorraine, F. (1971). Structural equivalence of individuals in social networks. *J. Math. Soc.* **1**.

Zajonc, R. B. and Burnstein, E. (1965). The learning of balanced and unbalanced social structures. *J. Pers.* **33**, 153–163.

Zurcher, L. A. Jr. (1977). "The Mutable Self: a self-concept for social change". Sage Publications, London.

Self-disclosure and the Reptest Interaction Technique (RIT)

Fred. A. Eland, Franz R. Epting and Han Bonarius

Truth is a matter of the imagination. (Ursula K. Le Guin)

In his paper on the Interaction Model of Communication, Bonarius (1976) describes three different models of professional practice: the predicting model, the reflecting model, and the communicating model.

Under the predicting model the individual takes a test or answers interview questions. The information thus gained from the individual is to be compared with standard knowledge of the population of which the individual is a member. The resulting statement of the psychologist is about the individual as-an-object, a member of the population. Those statements are essentially long-term predictions, since they usually refer to aspects of the individual thought to be relatively permanent. One generally believes those statements to have some "objective truth".

The reflective model stresses the unique aspects of the individual (e.g. Rogers, 1951) and this implies an important change in the relationship between professional and the individual. Together, the professional and the client explore the client's personal experiences and perceptions of the world. The individual client is perceived as an equal, active and responsible for his actions. Essentially, any statement is a short-term statement and its immediate value is further exploration of the self, of the phenomenal world of the individual. The psychologist can no longer rely on scientific background; more important are conditions like genuineness, unconditional positive regard, and empathic understanding (Rogers, 1957).

One can imagine such interaction taking place between two non-professionals. This is thought to be the case in the communicating model. The essential difference with the reflecting model is the complete symmetry between the participants in the interaction. The emphasis is on intrapersonal explorations and interpersonal understanding. Statements emerging from such interactions are not intended to represent any "outside" truth, rather they are meant "to clarify, for each individual, a conception of his own being, the anticipation of his own future, and his experience with the other individual" (Bonarius, 1976, p. 304). As the professional no longer participates in the interaction, his task, of course, will be a different one. The study of the communication process, its impact upon the partners, and the development of more articulated communication techniques, are important issues of the research conducted within this model. The focus of the research may be upon the communication between two non-professionals or upon the interaction between a professional and his individual client.

From this perspective, one may wonder whether existing assessment techniques can be adapted to serve the purpose of facilitating communication. One such technique is the Role Construct Repertory Test (Reptest), introduced by George A. Kelly (1955), and embedded in the psychology of personal constructs. The Reptest is a technique to obtain a number of role constructs, relevant to and representative of the individual's construct system. From the content of the individual's responses to the Reptest, the psychologist may derive hypotheses about the way the person views himself and others, and about the way he acts upon his world.

There is no doubt that the Reptest was introduced within the classical tradition of personality assessment, and as such it belongs under the predicting model. It was shown (Bonarius, 1976) that the Reptest could be transformed into a Reptest Interaction Technique (RIT), so that it would fit the communicating model. The purpose of the RIT would then be to structure the process of personal clarification and interpersonal understanding of the two persons playing the RIT. Several features of the Reptest seem to simplify the transformation into an interaction technique: unlike many other personality inventories, the Reptest already allows the individual to describe his experiences in his own words. Also, the *grid* form of the Reptest proved a convenient and practical way to organize the given information.

One could say that the RIT is the administration of a Reptest by two people to each other. In order to make the RIT meaningful and acceptable as an interaction technique, it is presented in the form of a game, the instructions taking the form of a set of rules. It is to be played by two people who are interested in getting to know each other better.

As Kelly (1955) pointed out in his Sociality Corollary, it is crucial to have an acceptance of a person and of his way of seeing things, if one is to play a constructive role in a social process involving that person. The RIT, it is hoped, allows both partners to become aware of each other's construct systems. They get familiar with the words the other person uses to describe his experiences, and they can begin to grasp the way the other construes his world.

In order to test some of the ideas mentioned above, an experiment was carried out, focusing on the concept of self-disclosure. But before entering into the details of the study, we would like to expand a little more on the RIT itself. The illustrations are drawn from the experiment.

The RIT

The participants begin by studying the manual* that explains the rules of the game. Having familiarized themselves with the procedure of the RIT and its purpose, the participants begin with the first phase of the RIT.

The partners are presented a "person form". This form offers a role-title list, containing 14 roles. Each participant writes down the names of at least nine persons fitting the roles of the list. The participants are not allowed to list their partner's name yet. The partners take turns and everything is said aloud. In all phases of the RIT, the partners are stimulated to ask questions and to help each other clarify their thoughts.

It was our observation that the first part of the RIT is an important one, especially when two strangers are playing the game. It is as though the tone is set for the rest of the interaction. Afterwards, most participants indicated that they did not feel threatened or uncomfortable, rather they thought it an easy way to get acquainted.

After exchanging the names of nine people, the partners begin the second phase of the RIT. Each individual fits a sheet with the names of the nine persons above the first nine columns of his grid. Next, the personal constructs are elicited. This is done with the help of the triads indicated on the RIT grid (see Fig. 1). In this way 12 constructs are formulated and written down at the left of the grid. Again, the participants take turns; everything is said aloud.

In a follow-up interview, some participants indicated that they started very carefully, waiting to see their partner's reactions. It was our impression that participants tended to answer openness with openness. It is interesting to note that most pairs had some constructs in common. Several students indicated that they appreciated the help and feedback from their partner. This atmosphere of cooperation is perhaps best illustrated by the remark of one of the participants: "I could never have done it alone". Some people found it hard, especially with the first triads, to find a construct dimension that they felt to be appropriate. Occasionally participants needed help with the first construct to get started.

In the third phase of the RIT, all constructs are applied to all nine persons.

---

*Special thanks are due to Peter Dingemans, who, in collaboration with Cindy Gallois, reviewed and adapted the manual to fit the experiment.

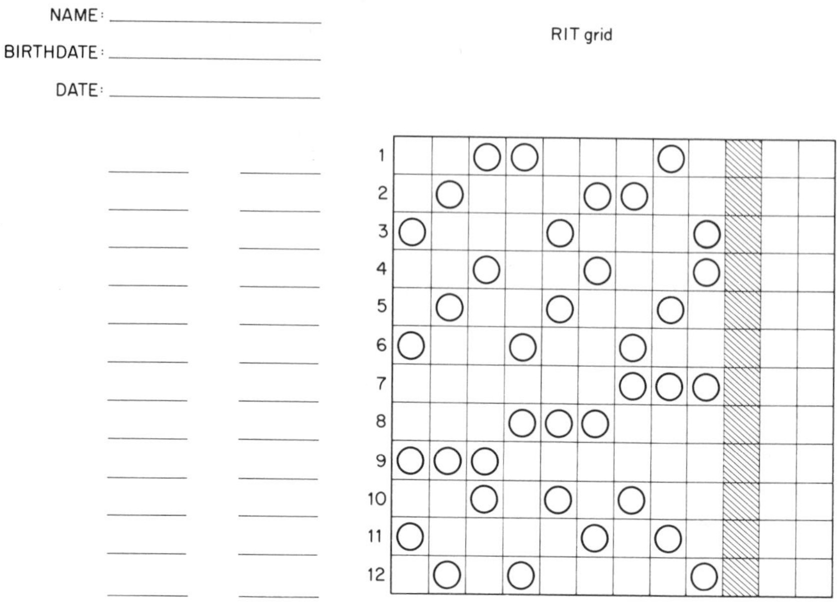

Fred A. Eland et al.

Fig. 1. Example of recording form worksheet, Reptest Interaction Technique.

People start with the first construct dimension and decide to which persons the construct pole applies and to which the contrast is applicable.

Sometimes participants had to adjust construct dimensions in order to be able to apply construct or contrast to all personal others. Occasionally people avoided forced choices. Participants often thought this to be the least interesting part of the RIT. "A lot of work", observed one student. It seemed that not all participants were that much interested in how their partner applied the constructs to all other persons.

The final part of the RIT is the personal encounter in which the construct dimensions are applied to themselves and to their partner in the experiment. For some participants this created some tension. Two pairs of subjects decided not to discuss their application of the constructs to self and other. It appeared that the partners, who happened to be strangers, did not particularly like each other. Most participants, however, were pleased with the feedback they received from their partner.

As we anticipated that the RIT, when used in an experimental setting, could possibly create tension or discomfort to the participants, we offered help if people wanted to talk about their experience. Fortunately, this precaution appeared to be a superfluous one. Apart from that, it was explicitly stated in the manual that the participants should terminate the RIT if one or both of the partners became too much threatened by the experience.

The Experiment

To play the RIT involves revealing oneself to the other person, in other words: self-disclosure. The importance of the concept of self-disclosure was first pointed out by Sidney M. Jourard (1958) and since then it has been studied extensively (Jourard, 1964, 1968, 1971; Culbert, 1968; Cozby, 1973; Goodstein and Reinecker, 1974; Derlega and Chaikin, 1975; Epting *et al.*, 1977).

Jourard and Lasakow (1958) defined self-disclosure as "the process of making the self known to the other person" (p. 91). In their reconceptualization of the concept of self-disclosure, Goodstein and Reinecker (1974) state that sharing information that is both central and private is essential. Epting *et al.* (1977) emphasize authenticity of disclosure as opposed to a false presentation of the self. In this study we choose self-disclosure to mean: sharing intimate and private information that one believes to be true about oneself at that particular moment.

Jourard's Self-Disclosure Questionnaires (Jourard, 1971) are often used to assess individual differences in self-disclosure. Typically, such questionnaires consist of 40–60 items. The subjects are asked to indicate the extent to which they disclosed themselves on such topics as:

the different kinds of play and recreation I enjoy;
what I am most afraid of;
feelings about my adequacy in sexual behavior—my abilities to perform adequately in sexual relationships. (Jourard and Resnick, 1970, pp. 86–87)

One of the problems related to the assessment of self-disclosure is who decides on the quantity and quality of a person's self-disclosure. Goodstein and Reinecker (1974) suggest three different perspectives for solving this problem: the sender, the recipient, and some objective and neutral observer. It is clear that discloser and recipient do not necessarily have to agree on the disclosure-value of a particular statement or communication. Also, a neutral observer might have an opinion that is different from both the discloser's and the recipient's. In an interpersonal interaction one might ask the discloser and the recipient for their experienced and perceived self-disclosure. The term "experienced self-disclosure" (ESD) is proposed to define the way a person values a statement or communication in which he reveals himself to another person. The term "perceived self-disclosure" (PSD) could then be used to denominate the recipient's impression of the other person's self-disclosure. The point of view of the objective observer is reflected in the concept of "actual self-disclosure" (ASD). (In a way, the neutral judge's opinion on the intimacy of the disclosure relates to the concept of perceived self-disclosure. Ideally, however, judges are trained, they are not involved in the interaction, and their task is quite specific.)

As suggested in the literature (Cozby, 1973; Goodstein and Reinecker, 1974; Davis, 1977; Epting *et al.*, 1977) self-disclosure between strangers is different from disclosure between acquaintances or friends. Taylor (1968) studied self-disclosure between male roommates from the first week of their acquaintance onwards at different points in time. Subjects reported a substantial increase in self-disclosure over time: a gradual increase in intimate self-disclosure and a fairly rapid increase in non-intimate disclosure.

Friends and acquaintances will have shared at least some minimal amount of intimacy, and some communication about the nature of the relationship, whether explicitly or not, will have taken place. Also, they have a certain trust in the other person. A "friendship effect" was hypothesized: in general, friends and acquaintances are expected to be more open with one another than with a stranger. Therefore, it was expected that subjects with an acquaintance as a partner would experience and perceive more disclosure than subjects interacting with a stranger.

It was further assumed that prior experiences in self-disclosure and reported willingness to disclose to a stranger (as reflected in the self-disclosure questionnaire) play an important role in the way people experience and perceive self-disclosure.

It was speculated that people who experienced less self-disclosure in the past and who were less willing to disclose to a stranger ("Low disclosers" on the self-disclosure questionnaire) would feel they revealed more while playing the RIT than they would expect of themselves. In comparison, "high disclosers" playing the RIT would feel they revealed less than in other situations. Therefore, it was expected that subjects scoring low on the pretest self-disclosure questionnaire would experience more self-disclosure (after the RIT was done) than subjects scoring high on the questionnaire. Likewise, it was expected that subjects scoring low on the self-disclosure questionnaire would perceive more disclosure on the part of the partner than subjects scoring high on the questionnaire. This hypothetical process could be summarized in the term "surprise effect".

We assumed this effect to apply to experienced and perceived self-disclosure only. The relationship between scores on a self-disclosure questionnaire and actual self-disclosure in a situation seems to be a limited one (Cozby, 1973; Goodstein and Reinecker, 1974). The reason may well be that scores on most self-disclosure questionnaires reflect people's experienced self-disclosure in the past, rather than their actual disclosure at that time.

A final aspect of this study relates to the question of how well participants think they came to know themselves and their partner while doing the RIT. No specific hypotheses were formulated, although it was speculated that the RIT would be more rewarding to acquaintances than to strangers. It may be important to note that the RIT was originally intended to be used by people who already know each other and who are interested in getting to know each other better (Bonarius, 1976).

METHOD

Subjects

Two different groups of subjects were formed. The first group consisted of 42 male and female undergraduate students, ranging from 17–25 years of age, and fulfilling a psychology course requirement. They were paired arbitrarily in like-sex dyads that had no prior acquaintance (stranger condition). A second group was formed by asking 21 undergraduates, fulfilling a psychology course requirement, to bring to the experiment a person of the same sex whom they would like to know better: a friend, roommate, or classmate. There were some restrictions, however: the subjects were asked not to bring a relative; the partners should not know each other longer than six months, and no great personal problems should exist between the subjects and their partner in the experiment. In this way 21 like-sex dyads were formed (10 male and 11 female dyads). All subjects in this group were between 18 and 25 years of age. All pairs of subjects completed the experiment.

In this study, subjects were paired in like-sex dyads only. We assumed that dyads composed of male and female subjects would make interpretations extremely difficult. Factors like the wish to make a good impression, sexual attraction, or a certain diffidence or shyness to disclose intimate information to an (unknown) partner of the opposite sex, would make comparisons with other groups and conditions no more than an almost random guess.

ESD and PSD

After the RIT was completed, the subjects were asked to answer a number of questions on a nine-point scale.

The scores on questions 1 and 2 were combined to form an index of experienced self-disclosure (ESD):
  (1) How much do you feel you revealed about yourself to the other person? (Scored from very much to very little.)
  (2) In general, how intimate do you feel the information was that you revealed to the other person? (Scored from very intimate to not intimate at all.)

Perceived self-disclosure (PSD) was operationalized by adding the scores on questions 3 and 4:

(3) How much do you feel the other person revealed to you? (Scored from very much to very little.)

(4) In general, how intimate do you feel the information was that your partner revealed to you? (Scored from very intimate to not intimate at all.)

Other questions were as follows:

(5) How well do you think you got to know the other person during the experiment? (Scored from extremely well to did not get to know him/her at all.)

(6) How well do you feel you got to know yourself in this experiment? (Scored from very well to not at all.)

(7) How well did you like the experiment? (Scored from like very much to dislike very much.)

ASD and the evaluation of the constructs

In order to get a measure of actual self-disclosure (ASD), the content of the constructs was evaluated. Based on studies by Landfield (1971) and Duck (1973) three categories were distinguished: (1) *self-reference constructs* (like me/unlike me, feel comfortable with/feel uncomfortable with, enjoy their company/do not enjoy their company), (2) *psychologically meaningful constructs* (sociable/shy, introverted/extraverted, romantic/cynical, quick tempered/even tempered, mature/immature), (3) *superficial constructs* (rich/poor, tall/small, skinny/obese, blue eyes/brown eyes, young/old, male/female, smoker/non-smoker).

Every categorization is somewhat arbitrary and it can be argued that no construct is "superficial" in itself as it holds a meaning to the person. However, for this purpose (ASD) we feel this distinction to be tenable and relevant.

A self-reference construct was rated two points, a psychologically meaningful construct one point, and superficial constructs were awarded no points. Scores were simply added to form an index of actual self-disclosure (ASD).

If either construct or contrast was rated as superficial and the other one as meaningful, the whole construct was counted as a psychologically meaningful one. If both construct and contrast were used more than once in exactly the same words, they were counted only once.

The problem in all judgement and evaluation tasks is to obtain an acceptable level of objectivity and reliability. In order to accomplish this aim we decided to use pairs of judges instead of the usual individual judges. Four undergraduate students were invited to participate in the evaluation task.

Two pairs of judges were formed to evaluate the construct dimensions. Before the actual rating task the judges were instructed in the categories and their application. The pairs of judges rated the construct dimensions independently, the forms were in random order, and the judges were not aware of the rationale behind the evaluation. Both judges in a pair had to agree on the categorization before assigning a score. In this way an interjudge reliability between both pairs of judges of $r = 0.84$ was reached.

PROCEDURE

First, subjects were asked how long they had known each other and they were also asked to specify their relationship.

Then, Jourard's Self-Disclosure Questionnaire (Jourard and Resnick, 1970) was administered. Part two of the instructions was changed to: "Check those topics you would be willing to discuss fully with a partner, who would be an unknown person of your same sex, age, and peer group". Topic 38 was changed to "how I feel about new fashion styles".

Next, the RIT was presented. The subjects were handed the manual and they were asked to study the procedure and the rules of the game. After making sure the subjects understood the rules and the meaning of the different forms coming with the RIT, the participants were left alone to play the game. As the RIT is presented in the form of a game, we tried to make the experiment a non-threatening experience. Subjects were free to take a break any time, and an experimenter was always nearby to answer questions.

After finishing the RIT, the subjects were separated and they were asked to answer some questions (see "ESD and PDS").

The data were collected in one session. It took most subjects two and a half to three and a half hours to complete the RIT and to answer the questions.

RESULTS

The "friendship effect"

Table I shows the results of an analysis of variance of experienced self-disclosure (ESD). It was hypothesized that subjects interacting with an acquaintance would score higher on ESD than subjects interacting with a stranger (friendship effect). An analysis of variance for simple effects revealed that male acquaintances scored higher than male strangers, $F (1, 80) = 6.23, p < 0.05$; female acquaintances scored higher than female strangers, $F (1, 80) = 36.30, p < 0.001$.

TABLE I. *Analysis of variance of experienced self-disclosure.*

Source	d.f.	MS	F	p
Sex	1	58·466	4·83	⟨0·05
Stranger/acquaintance	1	439·418	36·301	⟨0·001
Interaction	1	75·457	6·234	⟨0·05
Residual	80	12·105		

As shown in Table II, our prediction of a friendship effect with respect to PSD was confirmed: subjects interacting with an acquaintance ($\overline{X}$ = 10·83) scored higher than subjects interacting with a stranger ($\overline{X}$ = 7·59).

The "surprise effect"

To test the hypotheses concerning a surprise effect, the subjects were divided into low and high disclosers. The median score on Jourard's Self-disclosure Questionnaire (SDQ) was computed (median score 56·5; possible range 0–80) and subjects were divided accordingly into high and low disclosers.

Our prediction that subjects scoring low on the SDQ would score higher on ESD than subjects scoring high, was not confirmed, F (1,80) = 0·01.

As for PSD, our prediction that low disclosers would score higher than higher disclosers, was only partially supported. In the stranger condition low disclosers ($\overline{X}$ = 9·00) scored higher than high disclosers ($\overline{X}$ = 6·32). This difference was significant beyond the 0·05 level of confidence, F (1, 80) = 5·4.

Interpersonal and intrapersonal understanding

After the RIT was played, the participants were asked how well they thought they came to know their partner in the experiment (question 5). Acquaintances scored higher than strangers ($\overline{X}$ = 6·31 *vs* $\overline{X}$ = 5·03), a difference

TABLE II. *Analysis of variance of perceived self-disclosure.*

Source	d.f.	MS	F	p
Sex	*1*	28·039	1·948	
Stranger/acquaintance	1	227·230	15·784	⟨0·001
Interaction	1	22·209	1·543	
Residual	80	14·396		

TABLE III. *Analysis of variance of actual self-disclosure.*

Source	d.f.	MS	F	p
Sex	1	137·704	15·403	⟨·001
Stranger/acquaintance	1	28·371	3·173	
Interaction	1	9·611	1·075	
Residual	80	8·940		

significant beyond the 0·001 level of confidence, F (1, 80) = 10·81. The main effect for sex did not approach significance, F (1, 80) = 0·58.

Participants were also asked how well they thought they came to know themselves in the experiment (question 6). Subjects in the acquaintance condition scored higher on this question than subjects in the stranger condition, F (1, 80) = 5·66, $p<0.05$. Again, no difference was found between male and female participants, F (1, 80) = 1·50.

DISCUSSION

The data in the present study seem to suggest that different perspectives as to the question of amount and intimacy of self-disclosure provide different answers. Subjects interacting with an acquaintance experienced significantly more self-disclosure than subjects interacting with a stranger. Also, subjects who played the RIT with an acquaintance perceived more self-disclosure on the part of their partner. However, as shown in Table III, an analysis of variance revealed no difference in actual self-disclosure between strangers and acquaintances. In other words, in comparison to subjects in the stranger condition, subjects in the acquaintance condition experienced and perceived more self-disclosure, although they did not necessarily use more self-reference and psychologically meaningful constructs. The "friendship effect" may help clarify this phenomenon: people generally feel they can be more open, more honest, and more personal to an acquaintance or friend. That is also what is expected of a friendship. People have a certain trust that the communication will be maintained as confidential, and there is a certain faith in the other person's good intentions. These two factors are mentioned by Epting *et al.* (1977) as related to the authenticity of self-disclosure. People are more or less motivated to get to know each other better. Self-disclosure is perceived as "functional", as it were. The partner is perceived as disclosing a lot of intimate information, because he is communicating with a friend, too. The friendship effect may be compared, then, to a "set", or the expectancy of a certain kind of experience.

Acquaintances, more so than strangers, perceived a balance between input and output. Perceived reciprocity (operationalized as the correlation between ESD and PSD) was $r = 0.82$ for acquaintances and $r = 0.65$ for strangers.

The view that communication with an acquaintance or friend, as compared to communication with a stranger, is perceived differently, seems to be supported by the finding of a "surprise effect" in the stranger condition only. Low disclosers playing the RIT with a stranger perceived more self-disclosure on the part of the other person than high disclosers. Although as to experienced self-disclosure no such relationship was found in the stranger condition, the results were in the predicted direction ($\overline{X} = 8.2$ for low disclosers and $\overline{X} = 7.5$ for high disclosers).

The data strongly suggest that strangers in a disclosure situation tend to value or judge their partner's openness more according to their own prior experiences in self-disclosure and their willingness to disclose to a stranger. People with a high barrier to self-disclosure seem to be "surprised" by their partner's self-disclosure. For acquaintances, earlier experiences in self-disclosure seem to count less as a standard for judging the other person's openness. Interacting with an acquaintance or friend, one is not that easily surprised: communication about the nature of the relationship itself is likely to have occurred and a certain pattern of behaviors and expectancies may already be established.

Although the findings of the influence of sex on self-disclosure are not conclusive (Jourard, 1964; Pederson and Breglio, 1968; Weigel *et al.*, 1969; Goodstein and Reinecker, 1974), Cozby (1973) concluded that "the fact that no study reported greater male disclosure may be indicative of actual sex differences" (p. 76). It is interesting to note that an analysis of variance revealed no difference between male and female subjects on the self-disclosure questionnaire, $F(1, 80) = 1.42.$* However, as shown in Table III, while playing the RIT, female subjects scored significantly higher on actual self-disclosure ($\overline{X} = 9.21$ vs $\overline{X} = 6.59$), using more psychologically meaningful and self-reference constructs. Within this context, another finding is worth mentioning. As shown in Table I, a sex difference was found with respect to experienced self-disclosure. An analysis of variance for simple effects revealed that in the stranger condition, male subjects scored higher than female subjects, $F = (1, 80) = 11.01, p < 001$. No sex difference was found with respect to perceived self-disclosure.

As to experienced self-disclosure, one might assume, again, some "surprise effect": for men in our society it is still rather uncommon to talk to a stranger in an intimate way about relatives and acquaintances. Accordingly,

---

*The analysis of variance revealed no difference between subjects in the stranger condition and subjects in the acquaintance condition, either, $F(1, 80) = 0.40$.

after playing the RIT, they might have felt they were very open, while in fact they used considerably more superficial constructs, compared to female participants. As this is a *post hoc* reasoning, of course, replication of the results would be desirable.

The scores on the self-disclosure questionnaire did not correlate strongly with our measure of actual self-disclosure ($r = 0.07$). An analysis of variance revealed no differences between high and low disclosers with respect to actual self-disclosure, $F (1, 80) = 0.067$. These findings tend to confirm the limited relationship between Jourard's self-disclosure questionnaires and actual self-disclosure in a situation. The problem becomes even more complicated when participants in an interaction give their own impressions on the quality and quantity of self-disclosure. The data in this study at least seem to suggest some relationship between scores on the self-disclosure questionnaire and perceived self-disclosure for strangers.

It can be argued that the impressions and feelings of the people directly involved in the communication are just as important, if not more important, than some neutral judge's opinion. After all, in everyday life one is only concerned with experienced and perceived self-disclosure.

The distinction between the different aspects of self-disclosure is an important one. To mention just one implication: in a counselling or therapy situation the participants start off as strangers to each other. The client tells about himself, his feelings and his situation, and he might experience considerable self-disclosure. The therapist, on the other hand, is quite used to intimate information and he is also convinced of the necessity of considerable disclosure for the good of the client. He probably perceives the client's disclosure differently; he might think, for instance, the client is still holding back or he might even note resistance. He might push the client to more self-disclosure or intimacy than the client can handle in the first phases of therapy.

Subjects in the acquaintance condition scored higher on intrapersonal and interpersonal understanding than subjects in the stranger condition. Obvious as it may sound, these findings can be interpreted to mean that communication with an acquaintance or friend is perceived as more rewarding, more beneficial, than intimate communication with a stranger. It reminds us, however, that self-disclosure is a phenomenon that does belong within the context of friendship formation and the development and deepening of relationships between acquaintances, relatives, friends and lovers. All too often the phenomenon is taken out of its context and studied in some unnatural environment. Therefore, studies of self-disclosure preferably should be performed with subjects who are already acquainted with each other and who are sincerely interested in getting to know each other better.

Finally, it may be concluded from our data that the RIT can be useful as a vehicle for personal, intimate communication between two people. Although the time spent on the experiment by each subject was rather long, the experience was valued quite positively: the average score on the question of how well subjects like the experiment was $\bar{X} = 7\cdot71$ (s.d. $= 1\cdot41$) on a nine point scale. Female subjects tended to like the experiment better than male subjects, $F(1, 80) = 5\cdot58, p<0\cdot05$. The difference between strangers and acquaintances did not approach significance, $F(1, 80) = 1\cdot03$. It was our impression that the time spent on the RIT was directly related to a positive evaluation of the experience. Unfortunately, time was not recorded for all pairs of subjects.

Concluding Remarks

The data in the present study seem to indicate that the distinction between the different perspective from which self-disclosure can be approached (the discloser's, the recipient's, and the objective judge's perspective), is a relevant one.

Emphasis on the context of the process of self-disclosure seems to be crucial in obtaining a thorough understanding of the nature of the process. Therefore, it seems important to study self-disclosure with people who already know each other and who are motivated to get to know each other better. The study of self-disclosure between strangers should focus on specific situations, such as the first stages of the psychotherapeutic process.

The data also seem to indicate that the RIT, as an interaction technique, can be useful, especially when people are already acquainted and have a sincere wish to get to know each other better.

Acknowledgements

The authors would like to express their gratitude to the following people for their help and support: Karin Buschell, John Crum, Peter Dingemans, Jody Lehman, Jim Orr, Cory Schafer, and Roger Owens.

References

Bonarius, J. C. J. (1976). The interaction model of communication: Through experimental research towards existential relevance. *In* "Nebraska Symposium on Motivation (Eds J. Cole and A. W. Landfield), Vol. 24. University of Nebraska Press, Lincoln.

Cozby, P. C. (1973). Self-disclosure: A literature review. *Psychol. Bull.* **79**, 73–91.

Culbert, S. A. (1968). "The Interpersonal Process of Self-disclosure: It takes two to see one". Renaissance Editions, New York.

Davis, J. D. (1977). Effects of communication about interpersonal process on the evolution of self-disclosure in dyads. *J. Personal. Soc. Psychol.* **35**, 31–37.

Derlega, S. W. and Chaikin, A. L. (1975). "Sharing Intimacy". Prentice Hall, Englewood Cliffs, New Jersey.

Duck, S. W. (1973). "Personal Relationships and Personal Constructs". Wiley, London.

Epting, F. R., Suchman, D. and Barker, E. N. (1977). Some aspects of revealingness and disclosure. *In* "Frontiers of Human Psychology". Gardner Press, New York.

Goodstein, L. D. and Reinecker, V. M. (1974). Factors affecting self-disclosure: A review of the literature. *In* "Progress in Experimental Personality Research (Ed. B. A. Maher), Vol. 7. Academic Press, New York and London.

Jourard, S. M. (1958). A study in self-disclosure. *Scientific American* **198** (May), 77–82.

Jourard, S. M. (1964). "The Transparant Self". Van Nostrand-Reinhold, Princeton, New Jersey.

Jourard, S. M. (1968). "Disclosing Man to Himself". Van Nostrand-Reinhold, Princeton, New Jersey.

Jourard, S. M. (1971). "Self-disclosure: An Experimental Analysis of the Transparent Self". Wiley, New York.

Jourard, S. M. and Lasakow, P. (1958). Some factors in self-disclosure. *J. Abnorm. Soc. Psychol.* **56**, 91–98.

Jourard, S. M. and Resnick, J. L. (1970). Some effects of self-disclosure among college women. *J. Humanistic Psychol.* **10**, 84–93.

Kelly, G. A. (1955). "The Psychology of Personal Constructs". Norton, New York.

Landfield, A. W. (1971). "Personal Construct Systems in Psychotherapy". Rand McNally, Chicago.

Pederson, D. M. and Breglio, V. J. (1968). Personality correlates of actual self-disclosure. *Psychol. Rep.* **22**, 495–501.

Rogers, C. R. (1951). "Client-centered Therapy". Houghton Mifflin, Boston.

Rogers, C. R. (1957). The necessary and sufficient conditions of therapeutic personality change. *J. Consult. Psychol.* **21**, 95–103.

Taylor, D. A. (1968). The development of interpersonal relationships: Social penetration process. *J. Soc. Psychol.* **75**, 79–90.

Weigel, R. G., Weigel, V. M. and Chadwick, P. C. (1969). Reported and projected self-disclosure. *Psychol. Rep.* **24**, 283–287.

Part III

Substantive Contributions

Construing Persons in Social Contexts

J. Adams-Webber

From the standpoint of personal construct theory, interpersonal relations can be understood in terms of three principles which Kelly derived from his Fundamental Postulate: "A person's processes are psychologically channelized by the ways in which he anticipates events" (Kelly, 1955, p. 46). Firstly, the *Individuality Corollary* asserts that "persons differ from each other in their constructions of events" (Kelly, 1970; p. 12). Secondly, the *Commonality Corollary* states that "to the extent that one person employs a construction of experience which is similar to that employed by another, his psychological processes are similar to those of the other person" (Kelly, 1970, p. 20). Finally, the *Sociality Corollary* stipulates that "to the extent that one person construes the construction processes of another, he may play a role in a social process involving the other person" (Kelly, 1970; p. 22). The purpose of this discussion will be to elaborate some of the implications of these three propositions in the light of the results of more than twenty-five years of research in the psychology of personal constructs.

The *Individuality Corollary* is logically prior to the other two, since without it, neither of them would be necessary. That is, if it were not the case that persons differed from one another in their constructions of events, then "commonality" would be the rule, and "sociality" would not be problematic. For example, Duck (1977; p. 392) infers that "the more similar one's constructs are to those of another person, the easier it will be to grasp the other person's psychological processes and play a role in social behaviour with him". The Individuality Corollary must be an implicit assumption in this argument, since without individuality, commonality would be universal, and therefore the latter would not require special attention as an antecedent condition for sociality.

These three corollaries have provided the logical foundation for the development of a specific model of interpersonal relations within the framework of personal construct theory. At first, research carried out within the context of this model dealt almost exclusively with implications of the

Individuality Corollary. This work primarily emphasized the influence of individual differences in the structure and content of personal construct systems on the way in which people interpret the behaviour of others in social contexts (see reviews by Adams-Webber, 1978a; Bannister and Fransella, 1971; Bonarius, 1965). During the last decade, however, the range of convenience of this model has been extended to include the investigation of how individuals make inferences about the personal construct systems of other people as a basis for effective communication and mutual understanding, that is, "sociality" (e.g. Adams-Webber, 1969; Adams-Webber *et al.*, 1972; Mair, 1970a,b; Ryle 1975; Thomas, 1977; Smail, 1972). Another problem which has received a great deal of attention recently is the role of similarities between persons in terms of the content of their personal construct systems (i.e. "commonality") in the development of interpersonal relationships (e.g. Duck, 1973, 1975, 1977; Duck and Spencer, 1972; Landfield, 1971; Weigel *et al.*, 1973). Finally, the experimental analysis of basic structural commonalities underlying the ways in which we organize information about our social environment has just begun to emerge as an area of research in personal construct theory (e.g. Adams-Webber, 1977a, b, 1978a,b; Adams-Webber and Benjafield, 1973, 1976; Adams-Webber and Davidson, 1979; Benjafield and Adams-Webber, 1975, 1976; Benjafield and Green, 1978; Benjafield and Pomeroy, 1978; Cochran, 1973, 1977). These four topics will provide the main foci of the following discussion.

Personal Axes of Reference

Kelly (1955, 1969, 1970) proposes that each individual develops his own system of cognitive dimensions for interpreting and anticipating behaviour—his own as well as that of others. As Schneider (1973) notes, this system of interpersonal constructs can be viewed as an "implicit personality theory" (cf. Bruner and Taguiri, 1954). There is now ample evidence that *individuals exhibit stable idiosyncratic preferences for using particular sets of constructs in characterizing themselves and other persons* (Bonarius, 1965; Fager, 1954; Fjeld and Landfield, 1961; Hunt, 1951, Isaacson, 1966; Isaacson and Landfield, 1965; Landfield, 1965; Oswalt, 1974). People also seem to be consistent over time in terms of the number of different constructs which they employ to describe persons whom they know (Bieri and Blacker, 1956; Crockett, 1965). Thus, interpersonal construct systems appear to be stable with respect to both their content and "cognitive complexity" (i.e. differentiation; cf. Crockett, 1965).

In addition, *people tend to judge themselves and others more extremely ("more meaningfully") on the basis of personal constructs elicited from themselves than on the basis of dimensions supplied to them from other sources* (Adams-Webber, 1970a; Adams-Webber and Benjafield, 1973; Bender, 1968; Bonarius, 1965, 1966, 1967, 1968, 1970, 1977; Cromwell and Caldwell, 1962; Isaacson, 1966; Isaacson and Landfield, 1965; Landfield, 1965, 1968, 1971; Meertens, 1967; Tajfel and Wilkes, 1963). The only discrepant finding (Warr and Coffman, 1970) could be a methodological artefact (cf. Bender, 1974). Moreover, Mitsos (1961) indicates that elicited constructs are, on average, relatively more saturated with "meaning" in terms of the three major Semantic Differential factors (cf. Osgood *et al.*, 1957).

Bonarius (1970) suggests that the personal meaningfulness of any construct used by a particular individual will depend in part on its idiographic context of usage, that is, the specific domain of events to which he typically applies it (cf. Kelly, 1955). This implies that differences between elicited and supplied constructs in terms of polarization ("meaningfulness") should be more pronounced when we describe our own families and closest associates than when we describe more remote figures in our lives. This specific hypothesis of Bonarius' is supported by the results of several experiments (Bonarius, 1968, 1970; M. Bonarius, 1968; Van Os, 1968; Wissema, 1968). This work clearly demonstrates the importance of the *interaction between a given construct and its specific context of usage in determining its personal meaningfulness for each individual who employs it.*

Lemon and Warren (1974) argue that the personal meaningfulness of a construct will depend also on its "implicative potential", that is, the number of specific inferences that an individual can make from a particular construct to other related constructs within his own system (cf. Hinkle, 1965). Lemon (1975), summarized below, has shown that a given construct can have more "meaning" in terms of its range of implications for the same individual within one domain of his experience than within another domain. There is also some experimental evidence which indicates that elicited constructs are more personally meaningful than supplied dimensions in terms of their implicative potential. For example, Cochran (1977a) demonstrated that elicited constructs have more implications than supplied ones in evaluating career opportunities.

In the sphere of interpersonal judgement, Delia *et al.* (1970) reasoned that when information about people is encoded in terms of an individual's own elicited constructs, it can be assimilated into his interpersonal construct system more easily and completely, and consequently, he will be able to derive more inferences from it than from information presented in terms of supplied constructs. In support of this hypothesis, they found that judges were able to form more differentiated impressions of an individual's personality when all the information available about him was presented to them in terms of their own elicited constructs than when all or some of it was presented in terms of less personally relevant, "normative" dimensions. Furthermore, the predominant valence of the impression as a whole tended to be negative when only negative information was based on elicited constructs and positive when only positive information was based on elicited constructs. In addition, Stringer (1972) indicates that elicited constructs have different structural properties than supplied ones, and the former also have wider ranges of convenience.

Lemon and Warren (1974) also provide evidence that elicited constructs have more "self-relevance" than provided ones, in that the former are considered by individuals to be more important in their own self-characterizations. This is consistent with the finding that people tend to differentiate between themselves and others to a greater extent on the basis of elicited constructs than on the basis of supplied ones (Adams-Webber, 1968; Adams-Webber and Benjafield, 1976; Benjafield *et al.*, 1976). Another relevant finding is that judges are able to predict a stranger's self-ratings following a brief conversation with him or her more accurately in terms of personal constructs elicited from the latter than in terms of constructs elicited from other persons (Adams-Webber, 1968). The results of these studies, considered together, suggest that persons are able to formulate clearer conceptions of their identities within the specific context of their own personal constructs than in terms of standard lists of dimensions supplied to them by psychologists.

The general assumption that people customarily rely upon particular personal construct systems to interpret and anticipate their own actions also implies that specific information concerning the content of those systems should prove useful to others who are attempting to understand and predict their behaviour. For instance, Payne (1956) asked subjects to predict the social questionnaire responses of two strangers on the basis of a set of personal constructs previously elicited from one of them and descriptions of the other formulated by a group of peers. Predictions derived from personal constructs were more accurate. In a similar vein, Shoemaker (1952) reasoned that, if persons elaborate their "self-concepts" primarily in terms of their own personal constructs, then the content of those constructs should manifest itself to some extent in their social behaviour. It was found that judges who had observed an individual during a social interaction were able to exceed chance expectations in picking out his or her elicited constructs from a list which included constructs elicited from other persons.

Social Development

The research which we have considered so far has a distinctively "idiographic" character (cf. Allport, 1958) in the sense that it involves eliciting personal constructs from each subject individually. This emphasis is dictated by the basic logic of the Individuality Corollary. It is also consistent with the evidence; that is, as Bonarius (1965; p. 26) notes, "the research has shown convincingly that the individual prefers to express himself and to describe others by using his own personal constructs". On the other hand, this general approach to the understanding of "social perception" has not precluded the formulation of so-called "nomothetic" generalizations concerning the way in which psychological construing develops. We now have considerable evidence that *as children mature they employ progressively more "psychological" constructs in describing persons*, that is, constructs which refer to personality traits and other psychological characteristics.

Studies in both the United States (Barratt, 1976, 1977; Scarlett *et al.*, 1971) and England (Brierley, 1967; Duck, 1975; Little, 1968) have shown consistently that there is a decrease with age in the relative frequency of usage of constructs which refer to people's "appearance" (e.g. "She is tall"), "social roles" (e.g. "He is captain of the football team") and "behaviour" (e.g. "Bill fights a lot"), while there is a corresponding increase in the use of "personality" constructs (e.g. "Mary is quite shy"). In the youngest age groups sampled so far—eight and younger—appearance and role constructs are used more often than either behaviour or personality constructs. At intermediate ages—from eight to ten—behaviour constructs are used most frequently. During puberty and early adolescence—from 12 to 15—the use of personality constructs increases dramatically; and by mid-adolescence, they are the most prevalent of all. Girls tend to employ more personality constructs than boys at every age surveyed in these studies. Barratt (1977, p. 351) also indicates that as children mature, their social construing becomes "more adequately descriptive, less likely to involve a personal frame of reference [cf. Scarlett *et al.*, 1971], of greater "depth", and of increasing discriminatory potential . . . [and] girls are generally precocious with respect to these transformations".

In addition, Scarlett *et al.* (1971) found that there is a steady increase with age in the number of different constructs which children use to describe their peers, which is Crockett's (1965) operational definition of "cognitive complexity" (differentiation). Crockett (1965, p. 63) hypothesizes specifically that "an individual's constructs relative to others with whom he interacts frequently and intimately will be more complex than his constructs relevant to categories of people with whom he interacts less frequently". For example, the more frequently people interact with their immediate neighbours, the more constructs they use to describe them (Zalot and Adams-Webber, 1977). Assuming that the interpersonal experience of most children increases as they mature, it is not surprising to find that older children tend to employ more constructs to describe people than younger ones. Moreover, individual differences in this form of "cognitive complexity" have been found to correlate with other indices of social development such as the ability to reconcile inconsistencies in the information available about a particular person (Nidorff and Crockett, 1965; Radley, 1974) and ease in assimilating unbalanced social structures (Delia and Crockett, 1973; Press *et al.*, 1969).

Thus, from the standpoint of personal construct theory, social development involves systematic transformations in both the structure and content (cf. Bannister and Mair, 1968) of interpersonal construct systems. A progressive increase in terms of the number of different constructs that are used to describe people, i.e. complexity, is accompanied by a gradual shift of emphasis from a primary concern with appearance, social roles and behaviour to a predominant interest in personality. As Duck (1973) suggests, this process may reflect a general change from viewing others mainly in terms of "stereotypes" to a greater "individuation" and "differentiation" of them as persons (cf. Barratt, 1977).

According to Kelly (1955), forming an impression of an individual's "personality" is not simply a matter of characterizing his or her behaviour on the basis of one's own personal constructs. It also involves making inferences about the psychological processes of the other. We have seen that Kelly's Sociality Corollary asserts that "to the extent that one person construes the construction processes of another, he may play a role in a social process involving the other" (Kelly, 1970, p. 22). In the context of personal construct theory, the term role is defined explicitly as "a course of activity which is played out in the light of one's construction of one or more other persons' construct systems" (Kelly, 1955, p. 177).

Salmon (1970) notes that there is a close parallel between Kelly's elaboration of the implications of the Sociality Corollary and Cameron's role theory in that both of these approaches to the study of interpersonal relations emphasize understanding the outlooks of other persons (cf. Adams-Webber, 1970b). For instance, Cameron (1947, p. 167) contends that "the less practiced a person is in sharing the perspectives of others the less opportunity he will have of finding out how different from himself other ordinary persons can be". In support of this hypothesis, Adams-Webber *et al.* (1972) found that the more accurate a person is in discriminating between two new acquaintances in terms of their elicited constructs, the greater the extent to which he differentiates between himself and others on the basis of his own personal constructs (cf. Adams-Webber, 1969).

There are obviously many other attributes of people which can be used to distinguish between them without taking into consideration individual differences with respect to the ways in which they characteristically interpret events. Nonetheless, skill in inferring differences between people in terms of the structure and content of their personal construct systems allows one to make a variety of distinctions between their personalities, and, as we shall see in the next section, it may play a major role in the formation and development of role relationships.

Role Relationships

Landfield (1971, p. 7) notes that, according to Kelly, "the critical factor in the development of productive role interaction or sociality lies in the ability of one or both participants in a dyadic relationship to subsume the points of view of the other person". Thomas (1977) argues that this form of sociality depends upon our being able to hold similar and elaborate sets of related constructs simultaneously in mind, comparing them, and locating common areas of reference. It is possible that the more constructs an individual is able to bring to bear on a social interaction ("cognitive complexity"), the better position he is in to construe it from several different perspectives at once and to make inferences about the points of view of the other persons involved (Adams-Webber, 1969, 1970b). In support of this hypothesis, Olson and Partington (1977, p. 14) found evidence that "an individual's ability to reconcile simultaneous different perspectives in an interaction is directly related to the complexity of organization of the constructs by which he structures his world". The index of "cognitive complexity" employed by Olson and Partington also correlates with accuracy in making inferences about the personal constructs of other people (Adams-Webber, 1969).

It was pointed out above that Kelly's model of interpersonal relations implies that the probability that one person will be able to understand the constructions of another also should increase with the degree of similarity between their personal construct systems (cf. Duck, 1977). That is, as Eiser and Stroebe (1972, p. 205) note, "the 'commonality' and 'sociality corollaries', taken together predict, among other things, that individuals who are cognitively similar will be able to communicate more effectively with each other". On the other hand, Kelly himself (1955, p. 99) claims that "commonality can exist between two people who are in contact with each other without either of them being able to understand the other well enough to engage in a social process with him". Thus, according to Kelly, commonality is not a sufficient condition for sociality. He does allow, however, that "commonality between construction systems may make it more likely that one construction system can subsume part of another" (Kelly, 1955, p. 99; cf. Landfield, 1971).

This hypothesis has been put to the test in the context of group psychotherapy by Smail (1972). He found a substantial correlation ($r = 0\cdot84$) between the accuracy of each participant in predicting another participant's rankings of all members of the group on an elicited construct and the initial degree of similarity between both participants with respect to their rankings of group members on that particular construct. In a related study, Landfield (1971, p. 16) reasoned that "some commonality is necessary for the development of interpersonal communication between client and therapist" in the context of individual psychotherapy. He specifically observed that clients who drop out of therapy early manifest less commonality with their therapists in terms of elicited constructs than do clients who do not terminate therapy prematurely. Furthermore, the degree of this relationship is enhanced when consideration is limited to those constructs which have the highest "implication potential" within the clients' interpersonal construct systems (cf. Crockett and Meisel, 1974).

If "commonality" is in fact an important antecedent condition for "sociality", then, according to Duck (1973), the former should play a significant role in the formation of friendships. A series of recent studies (Duck, 1973, 1975, 1977; Duck and Spencer, 1972) have demonstrated that this is indeed the case. He has found repeatedly that *friends typically exhibit more similarity in terms of elicited constructs than do pairs of individuals who are not friends*. Moreover, similarity with respect to elicited constructs has proved to be a much better predictor of friendship choices than similarity in terms of responses to standard psychological tests such as the Allport-Vernon Study of Values or the California Psychological Inventory. This is hardly surprising in the light of all the evidence reviewed above that people find their own elicited constructs more personally meaningful than supplied dimensions for characterizing themselves and others.

Duck and Spencer (1972) also found that similarity between persons in terms of the content of their personal construct systems tends to be a precursor of friendship formation and not merely its product. In a further study, Duck (1973) was able to predict in which of two groups the greater number of friendships would be established on the basis of the initial degree of commonality among all groups members. This provides more indirect evidence that commonality facilitates sociality.

There is also evidence that individuals tend to be aware of the degree of similarity between themselves and their friends with respect to the content of their construct systems, in fact, they show a slight tendency to overestimate it. Duck (1973) interprets the latter finding as lending support to his hypothesis that it is "consensually validating" to find that our personal constructions are shared by others since this provides a source of subjective evidence that our construing is relevant and accurate. This factor is, according to Duck, especially important in the sphere of social judgement where "objective" evidence is usually lacking. As Crockett and Meisel (1974, p. 290) point out, interpersonal construct systems "develop out of the perceiver's experience with other people and with socially shared interpretations of people's behaviour".

Duck's work also indicates that there are gradual changes in the nature of commonality between friends as their relationship develops. Once a friendship has become firmly established, similarity in terms of *psychological constructs* seems more important than similarity in terms of other types of constructs. He proposes that there may be two distinct stages through which the development of a role relationship typically progresses. In the initial stage, each partner is concerned primarily with the non-psychological construing of the other. In the later stage, interaction between friends will involve communication mostly in terms of one another's psychological constructions. This implies that commonality in terms of non-psychological constructs may facilitate interactions between new acquaintances, whereas similarity in terms of psychological constructs should become increasingly important as their relationship continues to develop. The results of several of Duck's experiments support this specific hypothesis (cf. Duck, 1973).

He has also shown that persons tend to employ fewer psychological constructs in characterizing people whom they have just met for the first time than close friends and other old acquaintances. In addition, more psychological constructs are used to describe new acquaintances met in person than remote public figures known only through the media. Moreover, the relative number of psychological constructs used to describe new acquaintances depends in part on the nature of the situation in which we meet them. For example, Duck (1973) observed that more psychological constructs are used to characterize people met during a minimally structured, "social" encounter than those met in a more formal setting.

These findings based on people's impressions of new acquaintances are consistent with the differences found between the successive stages of friendship formation. That is, while in the early phases of friendship, overall commonality with respect to personal constructs is observed, at later stages, commonality in terms of psychological constructs seems to be the most important factor. Duck (1973) discusses these trends in the light of his own "filter hypothesis", which implies that as the basis of a role relationship expands, there will be a progressive shift of interest away from factual information to a greater concern with understanding one another's psychological processes, that is, "sociality". He maintains that

> the shift away from a major concern with construal of another's behaviour towards construal of his construct system marks an important change in emphasis and is also the stage where the greater differences are possible between individuals. (Duck, 1973, p. 138)

Surprisingly, Weigel *et al.* (1973) found no significant differences between married couples and randomly assigned pairs in terms of the number of shared construct preferences. Perhaps this outcome is attributable to the fact that they simply asked people to select ten preferred constructs from a standard list of 40 rather than eliciting personal constructs from them individually, as was done in most of the other studies considered here. Another relevant factor may be that, although commonality with respect to personal constructs influences the choice of friends of both sexes by women, it appears to relate only to the choice of male friends on the part of men, who may "look for something else when choosing between potential female friends", including wives (Duck, 1973, p. 73).

Finally, Duck (1975) has found evidence of developmental changes in the nature of commonality between friends. This research relates to earlier studies which have shown that older children tend to employ more psychological constructs, and fewer appearance, social role, and behaviour constructs, than younger children (Barratt, 1977; Brierley, 1967; Little, 1968). Duck (1975) not only confirmed this general pattern of developmental transformations in the content of personal construct systems, but also showed that similarities in terms of different kinds of constructs relate to friendship choices at different ages. He points out that this finding goes beyond the previously observed increases with age in the relative frequency of usage of various kinds of constructs in showing that "it is *similarities* between constructs of particular types (rather than absolute numbers) which are associated with friendship choices of adolescents at different ages" (Duck, 1975, 359–360). This is also consistent with evidence that children tend to use a disproportionate number of constructs that are typical of their current level of development in describing those peers whom they know best (Scarlett *et al.*, 1971).

Another form of commonality, "organizational congruence", has been investigated by Landfield (1971) in terms of the role relationship between therapist and client. He presents evidence that clients whose personal construct systems are tightly organized profit more from interacting with a therapist whose own construct system is more loosely structured; and conversely, therapists whose constructs tend to be highly interrelated are more effective with clients who exhibit lower levels of construct relatedness. Moreover, Landfield reports that improvement in the course of psychotherapy is accompanied by a gradual convergence between client and therapist with respect to the level of organization of their personal construct systems.

Unfortunately, initial "organizational incongruence" between therapists and clients is associated not only with improvement during therapy, but also with premature termination by the client. We noted at the beginning of this section that clients who drop out of therapy early also exhibit lower levels of commonality with their therapists in terms of the content of their construct systems. In short, "premature termination may be related to lower client-therapist congruence in both the content and organization of their personal construct systems" (Landfield, 1971, p. 79). Landfield (1971, p. 82) suggests that it is "a moderate amount of client-therapist organizational incongruency, found in the context of content congruency, that appears to facilitate improvement".

So far, there have been no direct investigations of the effects of "organizational congruence-incongruence" in terms of other kinds of role relationships such as that between parent and child, husband and wife, or worker and supervisor. There is some indirect evidence, however, which suggests that organizational congruence between parents and their children may be an important factor in cognitive development. Specifically, Winter (1975) found a correlation of 0·55 between the level of construct relatedness of a group of schizophrenics and that of their parents. The corresponding correlation for a group of control patients and their parents was 0·65. A related finding is that the parents of thought-disordered schizophrenics exhibit significantly lower levels of construct relatedness than do the parents of non-thought-disordered patients (Muntz and Power, 1970). This evidence is consistent with the general notion that interpersonal experience, especially with one's parents, is the predominant factor in the genesis of clinical thought disorder (e.g. Bannister and Salmon, 1966; Bateson *et al.*, 1956; Laing and Esterson, 1964; Lidz, 1968).

Organizational congruence has also been observed among individuals working together in the same institutional setting. Adams-Webber and Mirc (1976) found that the average level of interrelationship among a set of "professional role constructs" for teachers in seven different schools correlated 0·75 with the corresponding scores of their respective principals. In addition, the degree of organizational incongruence between experienced teachers and student teachers in the same schools decreased from a significant level to almost zero during a period in which the latter were engaged in supervised, practice teaching in the classrooms of the former. These changes were specific to "professional role constructs" and did not generalize to other sectors of the student teachers' personal construct systems.

In general, the effects of organizational congruence on the development of role relationships could be as pervasive and theoretically significant as those of commonality in terms of the content of personal construct systems. The former, however, are considerably more difficult to evaluate and have received far less attention to date. This has created an important gap to be filled by future research.

Formal Principles of Social Judgment

It has been demonstrated in a series of recent experiments that *whenever persons categorize people on the basis of bipolar constructs* (e.g. *happy/sad*), *they tend to assign them to the negative poles* (e.g. *sad*) *approximately*

37–38% of the time (Adams-Webber, 1977a, 1978b; Adams-Webber and Benjafield, 1973; Adams-Webber and Davidson, 1979; Benjafield and Adams-Webber, 1975, 1976; Benjafield and Green, 1978; Benjafield and Pomeroy, 1978). This finding has been generalized across a variety of different constructs, subject populations and alternative methods of measurement. Its explanation may lie partly in early Greek philosophy and partly in modern information theory.

Pythagoras, the presocratic philosopher and mathematician, developed a complex system of numbers and geometrical shapes to which he and his followers attributed great moral significance (Wheelwright, 1966). A central concept in this system was the "golden section" of a line segment, which can be constructed by dividing a line AB by a point C in such a way that the ratio AC:CB = CB:AB (see Fig. 1). If we assume that the entire line

Fig. 1. The golden section of a line segment (from Adams-Webber, 1978a "Personal Construct Theory: Concepts and Applications", Wiley, New York and Chichester).

segment AB is of unit length, and let CB = φ, then AC = 1−φ. It follows that $\varphi^2 + \varphi - 1 = 0$. If we disregard the negative root (which is extraneous since this ratio is always positive) and solve for φ, we find that $\varphi = (5^{1/2} - 1)/2 = 0.61803$.

Berlyne (1971) points out that this particular proportion has had an ubiquitous influence on Western culture; and, at least since Fechner (1876), psychologists have been interested in its aesthetic properties. For instance, the rectangle which many people find most pleasing is the "golden rectangle", whose sides are in the ratio 1:φ (e.g. Benjafield, 1976). On the other hand, it may not be for purely aesthetic reasons that we tend to assign the positive poles of constructs to people approximately 62% of the time.

As Berlyne (1971) notes, this proportion is related closely to Frank's (1959, 1964) operational definition of "strikingness" (salience), as well as the concept of *average information* (cf. Attneave, 1959). Frank, summarized by Berlyne (1971), submits that the "strikingness" of any event can be measured in terms of its relative frequency of occurrence (p_i) and the amount of "information" which it contains ($\log_2 1/p_i$). His specific index is the product of these two values: $p_i \log_2 1/p_i$. This expression is equivalent to the contribution of any category of event to "average information" (H) in the Shannon-Wiener formula: $H = \Sigma p_i \log_2 1/p_i$ (Attneave, 1959, p. 8). The value of $p_i \log_2 1/p_i$ as a function of p_i reaches its maximum when $p_i = 1/e$, which works out to approximately 0·368 (Berlyne, 1971, p. 232). This value is quite close to the minor element in the "golden section", i.e. $1 - \varphi = 0·382$.

Benjafield and Adams-Webber (1976, p. 14) speculate, in the light of this relationship, that we tend to assign the negative poles of constructs to people about 37–38% of the time so as to render our negative judgments, considered as a whole, maximally salient; that is, "by arranging his judgments in the golden section ratio, the person is able to pay special attention to negative events" (cf. Adams-Webber, 1978b). This hypothesis is consistent with other evidence that negative impressions are generally more salient than positive ones (cf. Warr, 1974); and it lends precise quantitative form to Kanouse and Hanson's (1972) notion that positive information, because it is so common (cf. Boucher and Osgood, 1969; Warr, 1971), serves as the perceptual ground against which negative information stands out as "figure" (cf. Peeters, 1971).

It also has been demonstrated that *people have a general tendency to assign the "self" and other persons to the same poles of constructs, both elicited and provided ones, approximately 62–63% of the time* (Adams-Webber, 1977b; Adams-Webber and Benjafield, 1974, 1976; Adams-Webber and Davidson, 1979; Benjafield *et al.*, 1976; Charlton, 1978; Clyne, 1975). About the same proportion of "like-self" judgments is observed when people describe strangers whom they have just met for the first time as when they characterize their own parents and siblings (Adams-Webber, 1977b). This distribution of "like-self/unlike self" judgments seems to have stabilized at approximately 63–37 by mid-adolescence (Adams-Webber and Davidson, 1979).

Kelly (1955, p. 131) asserts that "the self is, when considered in the appropriate context, a proper concept or construct. It refers to a group of events which are alike in a certain way and, in the same way, necessarily different from other events". It follows that each individual has a clear and distinct notion of his or her own identity only to the extent that she or he can discern a specific pattern of similarities and differences between the "self" and others (Adams-Webber, 1970c, 1977b, 1978a; Adams-Webber *et al.*, 1972; Adams-Webber and Benjafield, 1976; Bannister and Agnew, 1977; Benjafield and Adams-Webber, 1975). Lemon and Warren (1974, p. 123) hypothesize that a person's judgments of others "automatically involve a kind of self-comparison process" in which "the self-construct will act as an anchoring point to produce the effects of assimilation and contrast familiar in psychophysics and from Hovland and Sherif (1952)". In a similar vein, Bannister and Agnew (1977) propose that "the ways in which we elaborate our construing of the self must be essentially those ways in which we elaborate our construing of others for we have not a concept of self but a bipolar construct of self-not self". Adams-Webber (1977b, 1978a) suggests further, in light of the evidence cited above, that it is perceived differences between oneself and others which define the contours of the self as "figure" against a general background of similarities, since we organize our social judgments in such a way that these differences occupy that proportion of all of our impressions which should render them maximally salient.

An important problem for future research is the nature of the relationship, if any, between the way in which persons structure their self-concepts and their general propensity to assign people to the "positive" and "negative" poles of constructs in the "golden section" ratio. Osgood and Richards (1973, p. 381) maintain that the distinction between positive and negative is more fundamental than the three major components of connotative meaning, that is, "*strong* and *active*, as well as *good*, are somehow psychologically positive as compared with their opposites" (cf. Adams-Webber, 1978a,b; Benjafield and Green, 1978). The tendency to assign the same poles of constructs to the self and others approximately 62% of the time could be a "side-effect" of a more general propensity to assign events to the alternative poles of constructs in the "golden section" ratio; however, it could still have the effect of making perceived differences between ourselves and others stand out as maximally salient. A more extensive analysis of this problem is provided elsewhere (Adams-Webber, 1978a).

Public Versus Private Psychologic

Kelly (1970, p. 12) explains that his Individuality Corollary implies that people not only impose different constructions on the same events, but also it is unlikely that any two persons put their construct systems together in terms of the same "logical relationships". Nonetheless, there appears to be some degree of general consensus concerning patterns of relationships between constructs. This is a very important area of investigation within the context of personal construct theory because it is assumed that the meaning of any given construct depends in part upon its specific linkages with other constructs, that is, its "implications" (cf. Hinkle, 1965). This problem also has clinical relevance since deviations from the "typical" pattern of relationships between constructs relate to the diagnosis and judged severity of thought disorder in schizophrenics (Bannister *et al*., 1971; McPherson *et al*., 1973; Higgins and Schwarz, 1976).

Bannister (1962) found that when people categorized photographs of strangers on the basis of seven different constructs, there was a significant level of intersubject agreement concerning the overall pattern of interrelationship among constructs despite the fact that there was little agreement in terms of how particular photographs were categorized. Applebee (1975, 1976) also showed that the degree of consensus among children about relationships between specific constructs increases with age. As did Bannister (1962), Applebee observed more intersubject agreement concerning relationships between constructs than about the ratings assigned to particular elements. In the light of these findings, Fransella and Bannister (1977, p. 87) suggest that we could "establish a kind of dictionary of average relationships between constructs".

Further work along these lines should take into account that the positive poles of constructs seem to be more closely interrelated than their negative counterparts (Adams-Webber, 1977c), and also there seems to be more consensus concerning specific relationships between the former (Adams-Webber, 1977a). These factors, if not adequately controlled, are likely to serve as a source of bias in developing "norms" involving construct relationships. Adams-Webber (1978a) speculates that people may attempt to keep their usage of the positive poles of constructs as consistent as possible with what they understand to be the commonly accepted "public" meanings, whereas they may employ the negative poles somewhat more idiosyncratically in the light of their own personal experience. Perhaps by exercising more "degrees of freedom" in applying the negative pole of a given construct to events an individual is able to rotate the meaning of the dimension as a whole slightly away from what Mair (1967) calls the "logic of public language" so as to achieve the best possible fit in terms of the organization of his or her own personal construct system. In the language of Kelly's corollaries, we might expect more "commonality" in the use of the positive poles of constructs, and more "individuality" in the use of their negative opposites.

There also has been considerable interest in the problem of how an individual's social experience affects the "logical structure" of his personal construct system. Lemon (1975) hypothesizes that certain kinds of social linguistic contexts can directly influence relationships between constructs which are immediately relevant to experience in those contexts. For example, he observed that Tanzanian school children, who typically speak only English while studying geography in school and Swahili while interacting with peers outside of school, exhibited relatively higher levels of construct relatedness in judging nations on the basis of "English constructs" and their peers on "Swahili constructs". A parallel finding is that student teachers, during their first six weeks of classroom experience, showed gains in the average level of relationship between constructs which were used to define their professional roles while that among "irrelevant" constructs remained constant (Adams-Webber and Mirc, 1976). Another related finding is that a consistent effect of "sensitivity training" groups is an increase in the overall degree of relatedness between the participants "psychological" constructs (Baldwin, 1972; Benjafield *et al.*, 1976). Further relevant evidence, based on the social role construing of stutterers, has been presented by Fransella (1972).

The logical organization of personal construct systems also can be affected by the perception of "inconsistency" in the behaviour of other people. Bannister and Mair (1968, p. 211) explicitly define an "inconsistent figure" as a person whose profile in terms of a specific set of interrelated constructs used by a particular individual is not consistent with the pattern of relationships between those constructs (i.e. their "implications") within his own personal construct system. They suggest that an attempt to understand such inconsistent figures can initiate the elaboration of new constructs and construct relationships. Adams-Webber (1968, 1970b) also argues that new structure evolves within a personal construct system to accommodate events which are ambiguous in terms of its current "logical structure". Du Preez (1975, p. 269) provides an excellent example of this process:

> What has changed is the government's model of political relations in South Africa. The units are no longer races, they are nations, and South Africa is multinational rather than multiracial for the purposes of political decision. A problem from the government point of view is that this introduces contradictions: racialism justifies compulsory social segregation, whereas multinationalism does not. To cope with this, a new superordinate construct has been introduced; *international-intranational*. When an event is international, limited forms of social mixing are permitted and racial distinctions are temporarily allowed to lapse . . . Racial inequality may now be applied at a domestic level without contradicting a policy of co-operation on equal terms with blacks from other countries including the "home-lands" of South Africa which are being prepared for self-government by blacks.

Experiments by Cochran (1973, 1976a,b, 1977b) have revealed some specific effects of "inconsistent" information on the structure of personal construct systems. He reports that in two independent studies (Cochran, 1973, 1977b) people who initially exhibited relatively high levels of interrelationship among their constructs reacted to inconsistency by weakening construct relationships, whereas people with relatively low levels of interrelationship tended to strengthen construct relationships under the same conditions. In a related study, Higgins and Schwarz (1976) also showed that when people were validated for applying "typically related constructs" (e.g. *kind* and *sincere*) to persons in "an atypical, inversely related manner", there was a progressive loosening of construct relationships. Both Cochran (1977b) and Higgins and Schwarz (1976) discuss the implications of their findings in terms of Bannister's (1963, 1965) "serial invalidation" explanation of the aetiology of clinical thought disorder, which is marked by a gradual loss of relationships between constructs. Recently, an attempt has been made to increase the degree of interrelationship among the constructs of thought-disordered patients by presenting them with examples of "consistent" behaviour (Bannister *et al.*, 1975).

Applications

Thomas (1977) has developed a technique on the basis of personal construct theory for facilitating interpersonal understanding between two people. First, person *A* rates a list of elements on a set of personal constructs elicited from himself. Then, person *B* is asked to pretend that he is *A* and rate all the same elements on the latter's constructs. The two resulting matrices are superimposed and any areas of mismatch are located and then discussed by *A* and *B* together. This entire sequence can be repeated several times until some predetermined level of agreement is eventually reached. To this extent, we can say that *B* now understands that sector of *A*'s personal construct system which is represented by the constructs and elements included in the "exchange". Meanwhile, *A* can undertake a series of "like-*B*" exchanges until he also arrives at the desired level of understanding (i.e. "sociality"). The overall difficulty of each participant's task could depend in part of the relative degree of "logical organization" of both their personal construct systems (Adams-Webber, 1973; Landfield, 1971). Thomas (1977) indicates that the effectiveness of such exchanges will depend also upon the ability of the two participants to "take the constructs and elements apart", that is to move down through the hierarchy of meanings until all misunderstandings have been identified and resolved through direct reference to specific events in the common experience of both partners. He reports that many couples have found that this process results in greater refinement of shared meanings and often produces the experience of reconstruing the same events in a different way with an increase in mutual understanding.

Honikman (1976a, b) has adopted a similar approach to assisting architects in understanding the specific needs of their clients in designing homes for them. He has developed a procedure for articulating idiosyncratic patterns of meaning relating a client's superordinate goals to physical features of houses, for example, we can trace the implications of the abstract value "sense of home, security, and family" down through subordinate networks of constructs such as "friendly" and "homely" to specific concrete details, for instance, "rough bricks" or "fireplace" (Honikman, 1976a). Honikman (1976b, p. 89), himself an architect, points out that it is necessary 'to recognize the individuality or personal nature with which events are experienced'. Some alternative techniques for facilitating the development of sociality between persons which also have been derived from personal construct theory are Mair's (1970a, b) "conversational model", Bannister and Bott's (1973) "duo grid", and Ryle's (1975) "double dyad grid".

Finally, the range of convenience of the psychology of personal constructs is not limited to the study of "implicit personality theories", as the work of Honikman, described above, illustrates. Harrison and Sarre (1971, p. 365) point out that "Kelly's model, and the empirical methods associated with it, were developed in the field of interpersonal psychology but come very close to being a ready-made approach to the study of environmental images". Personal construct theory has been applied to the analysis of how people organize information about many important aspects of their socio-cultural environment. Recent studies have dealt with such diverse topics as the choice of a university (Rowles, 1972; Reid and Holley, 1972), housing preferences (Betak, 1977; Rawson, 1973); urban planning and design (Downs, 1970; Harrison, 1973; Hudson, 1974; Stringer, 1974); perception of political parties (Du Preez, 1977; Fransella and Bannister, 1967); and the understanding of drama (Moss, 1974a, b) and painting (Bonarius, 1970; O'Hare and Gordon, 1976). Stringer (1976a, b) provides comprehensive reviews of much of this work, which is beyond the scope of the present discussion (cf. Downs, 1976).

Summary

Within the framework of personal construct theory, an explicit model of interpersonal relations has been derived from the Individuality, Commonality and Sociality Corollaries. Research informed by these three principles has shown that people tend to rely on particular constructs to interpret their social environment ("individuality"); and that they can form more definite and complex judgments from information encoded in terms of their own personal constructs. Thus, it is hardly surprising that persons choose as friends other people who employ the same constructs as themselves. There is now considerable evidence that this form of "commonality" facilitates the development of role relationships in general, i.e. "sociality".

Several investigators also have observed systematic changes in the nature of children's social construing as they mature. Younger children use mostly appearance, behaviour and social role constructions to describe people, whereas older children show more interest in psychological processes. Older children also form more differentiated impressions of the personalities of others. Thus, sociality seems to develop with interpersonal experience.

Recent studies also have revealed that we adopt a general strategy of organizing our social judgments which could make perceived differences between ourselves and others stand out maximally as "figure" against a diffuse background of similarities. We also tend to organize our impressions of persons into more or less coherent systems in which one alternative construction of behaviour will have specific "implications" in terms of other possible interpretations. A major factor in this process may be the extent to which the behaviour of other people seems consistent in terms of the "logical structure" of our own personal construct systems. The latter may derive in part from public "norms" and partly from private experience.

References

Adams-Webber, J. (1968). "Construct and figure interactions within a personal construct system". Unpublished Ph.D. thesis, Brandeis University.

Adams-Webber, J. (1969). Cognitive complexity and sociality. *Br. J. Soc. Clin. Psychol.* **8**, 211–216.

Adams-Webber, J. (1970a). Elicited versus provided constructs in repertory grid technique. *Br. J. Med. Psychol.* **43**, 349–354.

Adams-Webber, J. (1970b). Actual structure and potential chaos. *In* "Perspectives in Personal Construct Theory" (Ed. D. Bannister). Academic Press, London and New York.

Adams-Webber, J. (1970c). An analysis of the discriminant validity of several repertory grid indices. *Br. J. Psychol.* **61**, 83–90.

Adams-Webber, J. (1973). The complexity of the target as a factor in interpersonal judgment. *Soc. Behav. Pers.* **1**, 35–38.

Adams-Webber, J. (1977a). Assimilation and contrast in dichotomous construction processes. Paper presented at the Second International Congress on Personal Construct Psychology, Oxford University.

Adams-Webber, J. (1977b). The golden section and the structure of self-concepts. *Percptl Mtr Skls* **45**, 703–706.

Adams-Webber, J. (1977c). The organization of judgments based on positive and negative adjectives in the Bannister-Fransella Grid Test. *Br. J. Med. Psychol.* **50**, 173–176.

Adams-Webber, J. (1978a). "Personal Construct Theory: Concepts and Applications". Wiley, New York and Chichester.

Adams-Webber, J. (1978b). A further test of the golden section hypothesis. *Br. J. Psychol.* **69**, 439–442.

Adams-Webber, J. and Benjafield, J. (1973). The relation between lexical marking and rating extremity in interpersonal judgment. *Can. J. Behav. Sci.* **5**, 234–241.

Adams-Webber, J. and Benjafield, J. (1974). Pollyanna's private self. Paper presented at the Annual Meeting of the Canadian Psychological Association, Windsor.

Adams-Webber, J. and Benjafield, J. (1976). The relationship between cognitive complexity and assimilative projection in terms of personal constructs. *Bull. Br. Psychol. Soc.* **29**, 219.

Adams-Webber, J. and Davidson, D. (1979). Maximum contrast between self and others in personal judgments. *Br. J. Psychol* (in press).

Adams-Webber, J. and Mirc, E. (1976). Assessing the development of student teachers' role conceptions. *Br. J. Educ. Psychol.* **46**, 388–340.

Adams-Webber, J., Schwenker, B. and Barbeau, D. (1972). Personal constructs and the perception of individual differences. *Can. J. Behav. Sci.* **4**, 218–224.

Allport, G. (1958). What units shall we employ? *In* "The Assessment of Human Motives" (Ed. G. Lindzey). Rinehart, New York.

Applebee, A. N. (1975). Developmental changes in consensus within a specified domain. *Br. J. Psychol.* **66**, 473–480.

Applebee, A. N. (1976). The development of children's responses to repertory grids. *Br. J. Soc. Clin. Psychol.* **15**, 101–102.

Attneave, F. (1959). "Applications of Information Theory to Psychology". Holt, Rinehart and Winston, New York.

Baldwin, B. (1974). Change in interpersonal cognitive complexity as a function of a training group experience. *Psychol. Rep.* **30**, 935–940.

Bannister, D. (1962). Personal construct theory: a summary and experimental paradigm. *Acta Psychologica* **20**, 104–120.

Bannister, D. (1963). The genesis of schizophrenic thought disorder: a serial invalidation hypothesis. *Br. J. Psychiat.* **109**, 680–686.

Bannister, D. (1965). The genesis of schizophrenic thought disorder: a retest of the serial invalidation hypothesis. *Br. J. Psychiat.* **111**, 377–382.

Bannister, D. and Agnew, J. (1977). The child's construing of self. *In* "Nebraska Symposium on Motivation, 1976: Personal Construct Psychology" (Eds J. Cole and A. W. Landfield). University of Nebraska Press, Lincoln and London.

Bannister, D. and Bott, M. (1973). Evaluating the person. *In* "New Approaches in Psychological Measurement" (Ed. P. Kline). Wiley, New York and Chichester.

Bannister, D. and Fransella, F. (1971). "Inquiring Man: The Theory of Personal Constructs". Penguin, Harmondsworth, Middlesex and Baltimore.

Bannister, D. and Mair, J. M. M. (1968). "The Evaluation of Personal Constructs". Academic Press, New York and London.

Bannister, D. and Salmon, P. (1966). Schizophrenic thought disorder: specific or diffuse? *Br. J. Med. Psychol.* **39**, 215–219.

Bannister, D., Fransella, F. and Agnew, J. (1971). Characteristics and validity of the grid test of thought disorder. *Br. J. Soc. Clin. Psychol.* **10**, 144–151.

Bannister, D., Adams-Webber, J., Penn, W. and Radley, A. R. (1975). Reversing the process of thought disorder. *Br. J. Soc. Clin. Psychol.* **14**, 169–180.

Barratt, B. B. (1976). "Studies of peer perception and social development in childhood and early adolescence". Unpublished Ph.D. thesis, Harvard University.

Barratt, B. B. (1977). The development of peer perception systems in childhood and early adolescence. *Soc. Behav. Pers.* **5**, 351–360.

Bateson, G., Jackson, D., Haley, J. and Weakland, J. (1956). Towards a theory of schizophrenia. *Behav. Sci.* **1**, 252–264.

Bender, M. P. (1968). "Friendship formation, stability and communication amongst students". Unpublished M.A. thesis, University of Edinburgh.

Bender, M. P. (1974). Provided versus elicited constructs: an explanation of Warr and Coffman's (1970) anomalous finding. *Br. J. Soc. Clin. Psychol.* **13**, 329–330.

Benjafield, J. (1976). The golden rectangle: some new data. *Am. J. Psychol.* **89**, 737–743.

Benjafield, J. and Adams-Webber, J. (1975). Assimilative projection and construct balance in the repertory grid. *Br. J. Psychol.* **66**, 169–173.

Benjafield, J. and Adams-Webber, J. (1976). The golden section hypothesis. *Br. J. Psychol.* **67**, 11–15.

Benjafield, J. and Green, T. R. G. (1978). Golden section relations in interpersonal judgment. *Br. J. Psychol.* **69**, 25–35.

Benjafield, J. and Pomeroy, E. (1978). A possible ideal underlying interpersonal descriptions. *Br. J. Soc. Clin. Psychol.* **17**, 339–340.

Benjafield, J., Jordan, D. and Pomeroy, E. (1976). Encounter groups: a return to the fundamental. *Psychotherapy* **13**, 387–389.

Berlyne, D. E. (1971). "Aesthetics and Psychobiology". Appleton-Century-Crofts, New York.

Betak, J. (1977). Personal construct theory and multioperationism in studies of environmental cognition and spatial choice. Paper presented at the Second International Congress on Personal Construct Psychology, Oxford University.

Bieri, J. and Blacker, E. (1956). The generality of cognitive complexity in the perception of people and inkblots. *J. Abnorm. Soc. Psychol.* **53**, 112–117.

Bonarius, J. C. J. (1965). Research in the personal construct theory of George A. Kelly. *In* "Progress in Experimental Personality Theory" (Ed. B. A. Maher), Vol. 2. Academic Press, New York and London.

Bonarius, J. C. J. (1966). Persoonlijke constructen als zinvolle beoordeling-scategorieën. *Hypothese* **10**, 70–80.

Bonarius, J. C. J. (1967). Extreme beoordelingen en persoonlijke constructen: een vergelijking van verschillende indices van extremeit. *Hypothese* **12**, 46–57.

Bonarius, J. C. J. (1968). Personal constructs and extremity of ratings. *In* "Proceedings of XVIth International Congress of Applied Psychology", pp. 595–599. Swets and Zeitlinger, Amsterdam.

Bonarius, J. C. J. (1970). "Personal construct psychology and extreme response style: an interaction model of meaningfulness and communication". Doctoral dissertation, University of Groningen.

Bonarius, J. C. J. (1977). The interaction model of communication: through experimental research towards existential relevance. *In* "Nebraska Symposium on Motivation, 1976: Personal Construct Psychology" (Eds J. Cole and A. W. Landfield). University of Nebraska Press, Lincoln.

Bonarius, M. (1968). Henkilökohtaiset konstruktiot ja äärimmäis-luokittelun käyttö. Unpublished data, University of Gronigen.

Boucher, J. and Osgood, C. E. (1969). The Pollyanna hypothesis. *J. Verb. Lrng. Verb. Behav.* **8**, 1–8.

Brierley, D. W. (1967). "The use of personality constructs by children of three different ages". Unpublished Ph.D. thesis, University of London.

Bruner, J. S. and Tagiuri, R. (1954). The perception of people. *In* "Handbook of Social Psychology" (Ed. G. Lindzey) Addison-Wesley, Reading, Mass.

Cameron, N. (1947). "The Psychology of the Behavior Disorders". Houghton Mifflin, Boston.

Charlton, S. (1978). "Some correlates of creative behaviour". Unpublished B.A. thesis, Brock University.

Clyne, S. (1975). "The effects of cognitive complexity and assimilative projection on preference for the definitive or extensive role in an elaborative choice situation". Unpublished M.A. thesis, University of Windsor.

Cochran, L. (1973). "The effects of integrating structurally incompatible information on cognitive organization". Unpublished Ph.D. thesis, University of Utah.

Cochran, L. (1976a). Categorization and change in conceptual relatedness. *Can. J. Behav. Sci.* **8**, 275–286.

Cochran, L. (1976b). The effect of inconsistency on the categorization of people. *Soc. Behav. Pers.* **4**, 33–39.

Cochran, L. (1977a). Differences between supplied and elicited considerations in career evaluation. *Soc. Behav. Pers.* **5**, 241–248.

Cochran, L. (1977b). Inconsistency and change in conceptual organization. *Br. J. Med. Psychol.* **50**, 319–328.

Crockett, W. H. (1965). Cognitive complexity and impression formation. *In* "Progress in Experimental Personality Research" (Ed. B. A. Mather). Academic Press, New York and London.

Crockett, W. H. and Meisel, P. (1974). Construct connectedness, strength of disconfirmation and impression change. *J. Pers.* **42**, 290–299.

Cromwell, R. and Caldwell, D. (1962). A comparison of ratings based on personal constructs of self and others. *J. Clin. Psychol.* **18**, 43–46.

Delia, J. G. and Crockett, W. H. (1973). Social schemas, cognitive complexity and the learning of social structures. *J. Pers.* **41**, 413–429.

Delia, J. G., Gonyea, A. H. and Crockett, W. H. (1970). The effects of subject generated and normative constructs upon the formation of impressions. *Br. J. Soc. Clin. Psychol.* **10**, 301–305.

Downs, R. M. (1970). The cognitive structure of an urban shopping centre. *Environ. Behav.* **2**, 13–29.

Downs, R. M. (1976). Personal constructions of personal construct theory. *In* "Environmental Knowing: Theories, Research and Methods" (Eds G. T. Moore and R. G. Golledge). Dowden, Huchinson and Ross, Stroudsberg, Pa.

Duck, S. W. (1973). "Personal Relationships and Personal Constructs: A Study of Friendship Formation". Wiley, New York and Chichester.

Duck, S. W. (1975). Personality similarity and friendship choices by adolescents. *Eur. J. Soc. Psychol.* **5**, 351–365.

Duck, S. W. (1977). Inquiry, hypotheses, and the quest for validation: personal construct systems in the development of acquaintance. *In* "Theory and Practice of Interpersonal Attraction" (Ed. S. W. Duck). Academic Press, London and New York.

Duck, S. W. and Spencer, C. (1972). Personal constructs and friendship formation. *J. Pers. Soc. Psychol.* **23**, 40–45.

Du Preez, P. D. (1975). The application of Kelly's personal construct theory to the analysis of political debates. *J. Soc. Psychol.* **95**, 267–270.

Du Preez, P. D. (1977). Kelly's "Matrix of Decision" and the politics of identity. Paper presented at the Second International Congress on Personal Construct Psychology, Oxford University.

Eiser, J. R. and Stroebe, W. (1972). "Categorization and Social Judgment". Academic Press, New York and London.

Fager, R. E. (1954). "Communication in personal construct theory". Unpublished Ph.D. thesis, Ohio State University.

Fechner, G. T. (1876). "Vorschule der Ästhetik". Breitkopf and Härtel, Leipzig.

Fjeld, S. P. and Landfield, A. W. (1961). Personal construct consistency. *Psychol. Rep.* **8**, 127–129.

Frank, H. (1959). "Grundlagenprobleme der Informationsästhetik und erste Anwendung auf die mime pure. Schnelle, Quickborn.

Frank, H. (1964). "Kybernetische Analysen subjektiver Sachverhalte". Schnelle, Quickborn.

Fransella, F. (1972). "Personal Change and Reconstruction". Academic Press, London and New York.

Fransella, F. and Bannister, D. (1967). A validation of repertory grid technique as a measure of political construing. *Acta Psychologica* **26**, 197–106.

Fransella, F. and Bannister, D. (1977). "A Manual for Repertory Grid Technique". Academic Press, London and New York.

Harrison, J. (1973). "Retailers' mental images of the environment". Unpublished Ph.D. thesis, Bristol University.

Harrison, J. and Sarre, P. (1971). Personal construct theory in the measurement of environmental images: problems and methods. *Environ. Behav.* **3**, 351–374.

Higgins, K. and Schwarz, J. C. (1976). Use of reinforcement to produce loose construing: differential effects for schizotypic and non-schizotypic normals. *Psychol. Rep.* **38**, 799–806.

Hinkle, D. N. (1965). "The change of personal constructs from the viewpoint of a theory of implications". Unpublished Ph.D. thesis, Ohio State University.

Honikman, B. (1976a). Construct theory as an approach to architectural and environmental design. *In* "Explorations of Intrapersonal Space" (Ed. P. Slater), Vol. 1. Wiley, New York and Chichester.

Honikman, B. (1976b). Personal construct theory and environmental meaning: applications to urban design. *In* "Environmental Knowing: Theories, Research and Methods" (Eds G. T. Moore and R. G. Golledge). Dowden, Hutchinson and Ross, Stroudsberg, Pa.

Hovland, C. I. and Sherif, M. (1952). Judgmental phenomena and scales of attitude measurement. *J. Abnorm. Soc. Psychol.* **47**, 822–832.

Hudson, R. (1974). Images of the retailing environment: an example of the use of repertory grid methodology. *Environ. Behav.* **6**, 470–495.

Hunt, D. E. (1951). "Studies in role construct repertory: conceptual consistency". Unpublished M.A. thesis, Ohio State University.

Isaacson, G. I. (1966). "A comparative study of the meaningfulness of personal and common constructs". Unpublished Ph.D. thesis, University of Missouri.

Isaacson, G. I. and Landfield, A. W. (1965). The meaningfulness of personal and common constructs. *J. Indiv. Psychol.* **21**, 160–166.

Kanouse, D. E. and Hanson, L. R. (1972). "Negativity in Evaluations". General Learning Press, Morristown, New Jersey.

Kelly, G. A. (1955). "The Psychology of Personal Constructs". Norton, New York.

Kelly, G. A. (1969). "Clinical Psychology and Personality: The Selected Papers of George Kelly" (Ed. B. A. Maher). Wiley, New York and Chichester.

Kelly, G. A. (1970). A brief introduction to personal construct theory. *In* "Perspectives in Personal Construct Theory (Ed. D. Bannister). Academic Press, London and New York.

Laing, R. D. and Esterson, A. (1964). "Sanity, Madness and the Family". Tavistock Publications, London.

Landfield, A. W. (1965). Meaningfulness of self, ideal and other as related to own versus therapist's personal constructs. *Psychol. Rep.* **16**, 605–608.

Landfield, A. W. (1968). The extremity of rating revised within the context of personal construct theory. *Br. J. Soc. Clin. Psychol.* **7**, 135–139.

Landfield, A. W. (1971). "Personal Construct Systems in Psychotherapy". Rand McNally, Chicago.

Lemon, N. (1975). Linguistic development and conceptualization. *J. Cross-Cultural Psychol.* **6**, 173–188.

Lemon, N. and Warren, N. (1974). Salience, centrality and self-relevance of traits in construing others. *Br. J. Soc. Clin. Psychol.* **13**, 119–124.

Lidz, T. (1968). The family and the transmission of schizophrenia. *J. Psychiat. Res. Supp.* **1**, 175–184.

Little, B. R. (1968). Factors affecting the use of psychological versus non-psychological constructs on the rep test. *Bull. Br. Psychol. Soc.* **21**, 34.

Mair, J. M. M. (1967). Some problems in repertory grid measurement: 1. The use of bipolar constructs. *Br. J. Psychol.* **58**, 261–270.

Mair, J. M. M. (1970a). Psychologists are human too. *In* "Perspectives in Personal Construct Theory" (Ed. D. Bannister). Academic Press, London and New York.

Mair, J. M. M. (1970b). Experimenting with individuals. *Br. J. Med. Psychol.* **43**, 245–256.

McPherson, F. M., Blackburn, I. M., Draffan, J. W. and McFayden, M. (1973). A further study of the grid test of thought disorder. *Br. J. Soc. Clin. Psychol.* **12**, 420–427.

Meertens, R. W. (1967). "Zinvolheid van beoordelingscategorieën". Unpublished thesis, University of Groningen.

Mitsos, S. B. (1961). Personal constructs and the semantic differential. *J. Abnorm. Soc. Psychol.* **62**, 433–434.

Moss, A. E. St. G. (1974a). Hamlet and role-construct theory. *Br. J. Med. Psychol.* **47**, 253–264.

Moss, A. E. St. G. (1974b). Shakespeare and role-construct therapy. *Br. J. Med. Psychol.* **47**, 235–252.

Muntz, H. J. and Power, R. (1970). Thought disorder in the parents of thought-disordered schizophrenics. *Br. J. Psychiat.* **117**, 707–708.

Nidorff, L. J. and Crockett, W. H. (1965). Cognitive complexity and the integration of conflicting information in written impressions. *J. Soc. Psychol.* **66**, 165–169.

O'Hare, D. P. A. and Gordon, I. E. (1976). An application of repertory grid technique to aesthetic measurement. *Percptl Mtr Skls* **42**, 1183–1192.

Olson, J. M. and Partington, J. T. (1977). An integrative analysis of two cognitive models of interpersonal effectiveness. *Br. J. Soc. Clin. Psychol.* **16**, 13–14.

Osgood, C. E. and Richards, M. M. (1973). From Yang to Yin to *and* and *but*. *Language* **49**, 380–412.

Osgood, C. E., Suci, G. J. and Tannenbaum, P. H. (1957). "The Measurement of Meaning". University of Illinois Press, Urbana, Illinois.

Oswalt, R. M. (1974). Person perception: subject-determined and investigator-determined concepts. *J. Soc. Psychol.* **94**, 281–285.

Payne, D. E. (1956). "Role constructs versus part constructs and interpersonal understanding". Unpublished Ph.D. thesis, Ohio State University.

Peeters, G. (1971). The positive-negative asymmetry: on cognitive consistency and positive bias. *Eur. J. Soc. Psychol.* **1**, 455–474.

Press, A. N., Crockett, W. H. and Rosenkrantz, P. S. (1969). Cognitive complexity and the learning of balanced and unbalanced social structures. *J. Pers.* **37**, 541–553.

Radley, A. R. (1974). Schizophrenic thought disorder and the nature of personal constructs. *Br. J. Soc. Clin. Psychol.* **13,** 315–321.

Rawson, K. (1973). "Residential mobility and housing preferences". Unpublished thesis, School of Architecture, University of Kansas.

Reid, W. A. and Holley, B. J. (1972). An application of repertory grid techniques to the study of choice of university. *Br. J. Educ. Psychol.* **42**, 52–59.

Rowles, G. D. (1972). "Choice in geographic space: exploring a phenomenological approach to location decision making". Unpublished M.Sc. thesis, University of Bristol.

Ryle, A. (1975). "Frames and Cages: The Repertory Grid Approach to Human Understanding". University of Sussex Press, London.

Salmon, P. (1970). A psychology of personal growth. *In* "Perspectives in Personal Construct Theory" (Ed. D. Bannister). Adademic Press, London and New York.

Scarlett, H. H., Press, A. N. and Crockett, W. H. (1971). Children's description of their peers. *Child Develop.* **42**, 439–453.

Schneider, D. J. (1973). Implicit personality theory: a review. *Psychol. Bull.* **79**, 294–309.

Shoemaker, D. J. (1952). "The relation between personal constructs and observed behavior". Unpublished M.A. thesis, Ohio State University.

Smail, D. J. (1972). A grid measure of empathy in an experimental group. *Br. J. Med. Psychol.* **45**, 165–169.

Stringer, P. (1972). Psychological significance in personal and supplied construct systems: a defining experiment. *Eur. J. Soc. Psychol.* **2**, 437–447.

Stringer, P. (1974). A use of repertory grid measures for evaluating map formats. *Br. J. Psychol.* **65**, 23–34.

Stringer, P. (1976a). Repertory grids in the study of environmental perception. *In* "Explorations in Intrapersonal Space" (Ed. P. Slater), Vol. 1. Wiley, New York and Chichester.

Stringer, P. (1976b). The demands of personal construct theory: a commentary. *In* "Environmental Knowing: Theories, Research and Methods" (Eds G. T. Moore and R. G. Golledge). Dowden, Hutchinson and Ross, Stroudsberg, Pa.

Tajfel, H. and Wilkes, A. L. (1963). Salience of attributes and commitment to extreme judgments in the perception of people. *Br. J. Soc. Clin. Psychol.* **2**, 40–49.

Thomas, L. F. (1977). Psycho grid analysis: the development of psychic mirroring devices. Paper presented at the Second International Congress on Personal Construct Psychology, Oxford University.

Van Os, H. (1968). "De mate van extremiteit in beoordelingen van pubers en volwassenen". Unpublished thesis, University of Groningen.

Warr, P. B. (1971). Pollyanna's personal judgments. *Eur. J. Soc. Psychol.* **1**, 327–338.

Warr, P. B. (1974). Inference magnitude, range and evaluative direction as factors affecting relative importance of cues in impression formation. *J. Pers. Soc. Psychol.* **30**, 191–197.

Warr, P. B. and Coffman, T. (1970). Personality, involvement and extremity of judgment. *Br. J. Soc. Clin. Psychol.* **9**, 108–121.

Weigel, R. G., Weigel, V. M. and Richardson, F. C. (1973). Congruence of spouses personal constructs and reported marital success: pitfalls in instrumentation. *Psychol. Rep.* **33**, 212–214.

Wheelwright, P. (1966). "The Presocratics". Odyssey Press, New York.

Winter, D. A. (1975). Some characteristics of schizophrenics and their parents. *Br. J. Soc. Clin. Psychol.* **14**, 279–290.

Wissema, A. (1968). Zinvolheid en onverenigbaarheid. Unpublished data, University of Groningen.

Zalot, G. and Adams-Webber, J. (1977). Cognitive complexity in the perception of neighbors. *Soc. Behav. Pers.* **5**, 281–283.

Children as Social Beings: A Kellyan View

Phil Salmon

In this chapter, I will be writing about the social lives of children; and I would like to begin with an aspect that most people would probably see as fairly central to social life—interpersonal relationships. Here are some sample sentences from a summary of this area in one reputable, recent, and widely used text on social development:

> For parents, the training of the child's "personality" and patterns of interpersonal relationships are among the main concerns. The child must be "socialized" to fit into her society . . .
> Of particular concern to parents are the child's aggression, and attachment or dependency . . .
> Individual differences in early attachments are partially determined by the mother's child-care practices, although the child's temperament may be influential too . . .
> Individual differences among children in aggression are marked. Boys show more aggression on the average, particularly more physical aggression, at nearly all ages. Consistency in aggressiveness throughout the lifetime is also more apparent in males than in females . . .
> There is good reason to suppose that the baby comes equipped with a link between frustration and aggression, so that aggression is a very common response to frustration in all children. Other responses to frustration can, however, be learned . . .
> During the elementary school years, children band together in clear "in-groups", nearly always same-sex groups. At adolescence same-sex groups gradually give way to heterosexual groups . . .
> Peer acceptance and popularity are associated with friendliness and outgoingness, with brightness, with being born later in a family, and with being large and husky (at least among boys).
> (Taken from "The Developing Child" (1975) by Helen Bee.)

I suppose these pronouncements can be taken as a fairly representative sample of the current official expertise in psychology about how children function and develop in their relationships with others. I wonder how all this strikes most people who read it. To me, there are a number of features which need thinking about. One of these is the universality which is implied in the account. What is being put forward is not claimed to be true of children in a particular cultural or historical context—in fact the question of context is not considered; the statements seem to purport to describe all children, at all times, everywhere. The actual content of the account is a description of attributes rather than processes. The terms are those of properties of persons, again highly generalised. So there are references to dependency and aggression in abstract, without any mention of the social context or the kind of activity which might be involved. When it comes to the kind of explanations which are offered, what is striking is that no reference is made to any mediation or agency on the part of the child. The cause–effect relationships claimed are of an essentially mechanical kind; for example, age, gender and family position, all of which are cited as causal factors, are put forward as though they had an absolute causative power, without any consideration of the symbolic significance they might have for children.

There are also some features of the tone of this account which I think are worth considering. It strikes me that the statements are made in a very definite, even dogmatic way; there is nothing tentative or provisional about them. Even more striking, to me, is the impersonal tone which pervades the account. It is almost as though the author were writing about another species. The language is very distancing, and the concepts are those of a total outsider. You could never guess from this account that the writer had been a child herself—or that, as she reveals in the preface, she has a young daughter. I think the impersonality of the account is heightened by a feature which is, in fact, present in nearly all texts of child development—illustrative photographs of children. You do not generally find such illustrations in psychological texts about adults; and to me, their presence seems to reinforce the feeling that it is an unknown species we are considering.

If Kelly is associated with any single remark, it is probably his suggestion that if you want to know something about someone, you should ask him. It is from this point that I would like to start in trying to trace some of the things that would follow from a personal construct theory view of children as social beings, and how the account might be different from the sort of picture we have been considering. Patently, to ask children themselves about their lives is something which few developmental psychologists do. But it is what Moore and Clautour (1976) did in an interesting small-scale study of the way children generally construed life. What emerged from the kind of questions they asked—questions like "What do you think is the best age to be?" and "Do you think it will be nice to be grown up?"—were some quite strongly held and generally shared ideas about the course of human development from childhood to adulthood. There was general agreement, for instance, that the late teens were the best time of life, between the irksome routines of school and the burdens of work and family. In fact, a marked theme running through the remarks of both older and younger children was that of freedom and responsibility—something that does not seem to play much of a part in the official account of social psychological development.

If the content of growing up, as described by children, is rather different to the content which psychological texts present, the same difference between subjective and objective accounts appears, I think, when it comes to questions of the chapters and dividing lines of development. For the past few years, I have been asking students on the Masters course in Child Development, in my department, to divide their lives, up to adulthood, into what seem like separable chapters. What emerges from this retrospective exercise, year after year, is again at variance with the conventional wisdom. The stages are typically not those of the textbooks, with the exception that starting school usually marks a fresh chapter. The crucial event which defines new departures seems almost invariably to be a change in social setting, or a change within the familiar social setting. Retrospectively at least, new chapters in young life are introduced by such experiences as moving from one country to another, or merely from one house to another, changing schools or classes, leaving school or changing jobs, a new baby in the family, the arrival of a step-parent, a brother or a grandmother, a death in the family, or a change of neighbours. Talking about the significance of such events, students generally refer to the changes they brought in one's standing with others, and the new social worlds they introduced in which one had to learn unfamiliar rules and ways of being. A glaring omission from all such accounts, so far, has been the definition of puberty as the marker of a new stage in life, which is how it is defined in the texts about this area. It is not that sexual interest is absent from the descriptions students give; but this is part of the ongoing themes of personal experience, in which other, social rather than biological events are seen as critical in signalling new life phases.

The phenomenological approach which personal construct theory would bring to any understanding of children's social lives represents an obvious contrast with the kind of account we began by considering. It is a surprising fact, I think, that the psychology of social development has characteristically NOT adopted a subjective viewpoint, whereas the psychology of cognitive development, to some extent, has—I suppose because of the influence of Piaget. To me it is rather strange that the child's relationship with the world of physical objects should be conceptualised in terms referring to his personal understanding, intentions and agency; yet his relations with other human beings, where subjectivity plays so crucial a role, should be understood in essentially mechanistic and impersonal terms.

There are, of course, many different kinds of phenomenological approach which might be adopted towards the psychology of social development. What I think is distinctive about Kelly's psychology is that he saw people as essentially ENGAGED IN LIVING. To take this view seriously in the way we regard the social lives of children would, I believe, produce a different and interesting kind of psychology. In the first place, I think it would give a distinctive character to the particular kind of phenomenological perspective adopted. It would mean more than merely viewing children as having an inside story to tell; they would be seen as unique authorities, having owner-ship of their personal domain because they are, in a positive sense, living their lives.

Seeing children as persons engaged in life would necessarily introduce something which now seems totally absent from developmental social psychology—an experienced time dimension. Time is an aspect of experi-ence of which children are conscious from quite an early age. Both the future and the past are surely represented in the moment-to-moment awareness of most children. A fair amount of conversation in many families consists of the rehearsing of memorable events in the child's earlier life, and for many children there are visual mementoes of their earlier selves displayed at home. Children themselves often have an acute, even poignant sense of endings in their own lives, of people, phases and experiences that will not come again. As for the future, this is certainly entailed in the intentionality and purpose with which a child engages himself in his personal projects. There is also, of course, a good deal of explicit reference to children's future lives by adults who are involved with them, as well as among children themselves; and some children seem to live in anticipation of a distant as well as an immediate future. The time scale of human life is also present, I think, to the experience of children simply through their engagement with others who are at different points in the life span. Through knowing intimately the old man who is her grandfather, a little girl comes to know something of what it is to be old, just as she witnesses, in seeing her baby brother, an earlier phase of life through which, though she does not remember it, she knows she herself passed. This engagement with other people also makes available a sort of anticipation of what may come in the future. Having intimate access to the sister who is taking an exam, the brother who is getting married, the father who is laid off, the grandmother who falls sick and dies, means, in a sense, experiencing these things, and partly knowing, therefore, how it will be if they happen to oneself.

To emphasise the engagement of children would also carry major implica-tions for the view we took of the social contexts of their lives. The way these are seen in conventional social psychology is as major socialising agencies; family, school and peer group therefore make up the list of contexts with which social psychology concerns itself. A perspective on children as engaged in their lives, rather than as merely the recipients of socialising influences, would, I think, mean viewing families, schools and peers very differently, as well as necessitating attention to other kinds of places and people in children's lives.

Any view of social contexts which was inspired by Kelly would certainly be likely to incorporate his strong sense of cultural and historical relativity. Looking at the kinds of context in which children in our own society are engaged would mean being aware of the recentness of the institution of school, the changes that have occurred in family structure and function, and the differences in these kinds of institution within other cultures. More broadly, it is obviously important to take account of the way childhood is viewed in the society one is looking at. Legal and institutional provision, of course, explicitly direct and channel the lives of children; but beyond these official means are a host of assumptions and expectations, via the mass media and the general public, which govern the kind of ecology in which children live, and the social opportunities available to them. Just to take one aspect of all this, perhaps a distinctive feature of our own society is that the young are very much segregated from the adult world. This becomes more evident if one looks at a minority group within this society—gypsies. It is not just that gypsies do not send their children to school if they can help it. Gypsy children are very much a part of the same world that their parents experience and act in; it is taken for granted that they will pull their weight in working, domestic and family jobs. One gypsy community, in Surrey, was the subject of a study which Rosemary Sturt (1976) carried out. What she found was that gypsy children do not seem to experience the same disjunction that non-gypsy children do, as between children and adults; for them, the world of people is not divided up like that.

Because the official psychological expertise excludes social settings where children are not clearly in receipt of "socialisation", many places and situations which form part of a child's everyday experience have been almost completely overlooked. Early on in life, children learn about a variety of public contexts, and appropriate ways of conducting oneself in them. The street, the park, shops, clinics, social security offices, buses, cafés, the cinema—all these places feature in the lives of most children in our society, and in them, a child soon becomes expert in knowing the sort of behaviour expected of him, as well as the kinds of social negotiation that go on in each sort of setting. Part of the social learning that must occur is likely to concern the attitude to be taken towards particular kinds of people. Quite early on, children assimilate the sense that a policeman is a friend and an ally, or that he is on the other side, to be given as wide a berth as possible, that social security officials are for us or against us, that, as an Indian, you can pass the time of day with the local Indian storekeeper, but you keep the lowest possible profile on buses and in the street. Behaviour in public, which is part of children's social repertoire, is surely complex and subtle, as well as highly differentiated across social and ethnic groups, for public places must be very different depending on who is experiencing them.

Public settings, and children's place in them, would not, I think, be neglected by a psychology which emphasised the engagements of childhood. For children do take a social part in their neighbourhood, both directly, as participants, and as involved spectators of transactions between others, and the nature of their particular engagements is certainly affected by the social group of which they are part, with its allegiances, rivalries or antagonisms. A focus on children's engagements would also be likely to redefine some other social contexts. All developmental psychologists do, of course, place great weight upon families in the social development of children. But a Kellyan perspective might view the family as important for rather different reasons.

In the conventional wisdom, families represent the major setting in which children are socialised, acquiring the norms and roles that operate in their society. Because this is the view, certain figures within the family are emphasised to the exclusion of others, and these figures are seen only in terms of the explicitly socialising roles they are supposed to play. In practice, this means that parents are seen as overwhelmingly important, with other family members barely getting a look in. Siblings, in so far as they are granted any significance, are viewed as sex role models and rivals in competence—and that is about all. Grandparents, aunts, uncles, let alone more remote kin, are not generally featured at all; nor, of course, are non-kin members of households. This is partly due to the nuclear family model which is still rigidly adhered to in the texts, despite its increasing atypicality; that is something I want to come on to later. But I think the family-as-socialising-agent picture is what is basically responsible for this very one-sided attention to family members. By contrast, I think the view of families as settings in which children are extensively and intimately engaged with others would be sure to bring other members of the family circle into the picture. To look at children's ongoing relationships within their families would necessitate an awareness of the importance of other people as well as parents. Parents, too, would perhaps be seen rather differently.

What would it mean to see families as settings in which children are engaged? At its broadest, it would imply, I think, a view of the family as defining for the child what sort of engagements are possible for someone living in the world. As I see it, this is what is implied in the notion, explored by Berger and Luckmann (1966), of families as mediating social reality for the child. And, of course, families do constantly engage in the interpretation of life, in explicit and, still more, in implicit ways. This is obviously true at many different levels; but just one example would be the complex of attitudes to television. So far from children receiving, in the simple and direct way which is usually implied, the messages put over by the makers of news, documentary or fictional programmes, these must necessarily come over to any child through the interpretative filter of his family's feelings towards political and official agencies, the commercial world, education, fantasy and so on.

Families also serve as the involved audience for the engagements of their members in the world outside themselves. To the sounding board of family members, the episodes that constitute day-to-day experience can be represented, one's part in them applauded or criticised, their significance mulled over and perhaps reinterpreted. Because close relationships mean that people can enter, to some extent, into each other's experience, children come in this way to know something of the ongoing lives of the adults as well as the other children in their family circle. The sharing of experience also includes the rehearsal of times and events which are long past, and through this means a small girl can come to have access to what life was like for her grandfather in his childhood. What is also likely to be shared among family members is the anticipation of future events and projects, so that those involved play a part in defining and planning each other's potential future engagements in the world.

Seen in this way, the family setting represents a place where the life project that each person is living is intimately known and closely followed. And, of course, family members play a direct part in each other's lives, through their very intimacy, as well as in the activities they jointly undertake. This seems likely to be true of all families; but some major differences within families must make a difference to the kind of engagements that their members have with each other. For example, something which differs across families is the significance that is accorded to age and gender. Whereas in many American families it is the lives of the children that are seen as being of paramount importance, in most Asian families the older family members, and the males, are granted the greatest status. This must govern the degree to which family attention is focused upon the day-to-day lives of some members rather than others, and a girl growing up in a Sikh household will perhaps experience her everyday life as having a lesser salience than that of her brothers or of the adults in her family. Families differ, too, in the continuity of their composition, and this must affect how far their relationships are sustained, as well as the degree of continuity in their access to the history of each other's lives. In families which become reconstituted through remarriage, adoption or fostering, in ethnic groups whose family composition is fluid, in families where a child is regularly or for a long time away from home, because of a residential court order, attendance at boarding school or being boarded out, for instance—in these circumstances the quality of a child's family engagements must be episodic rather than totally continuous, with the experience of some transitions. But perhaps this is true to some extent in all families. It seems likely that the nature of any child's engagements with other family members changes as he passes from infancy to adulthood. At one phase of his life a boy may be closest of all to his mother; later it may be his brother with whom he is able to share experiences most fully, and at another time, perhaps, it is a marginal member of the household, as with Joyce Cary (1976) whose uncle's "dog-man" stood to him as a figure of the greatest moral authority, defining honour and shame.

Where would this view take us with respect to the setting of school? Here again, the usual perspective on the child as the passive recipient of socialisation has meant an over-emphasis on the adults as against the children in the setting, on what is explicit at the expense of what is implicit, and on what the child is receiving rather than on what he is engaged in doing. All this adds up to a serious neglect of schools as complex social worlds which each child must enter as a stranger, somehow to learn the rules that operate there and define new engagements for himself within them. For, of course, children do engage themselves in school life. It is surely only the blinkered focus of most developmental psychologists on the formal and official side of classroom processes which has resulted in the ignoring of this rather obvious fact. Yet perhaps rather few of children's engagements at school are easily subsumed by their role as pupils. A study of children in schools which looked at their relationships with each other, not only in the classroom but in the playground, corridors and around the place generally, would be likely to reveal the complexity and the subtlety of the ways in which children or adolescents engage with each other, the joint action which they undertake, and the interpretative negotiations through which events are woven into the fabric of the whole social project which is school life.

I would guess that for many children and adolescents, the engagements of school have much more to do with each other than they do with teachers. Anyway, it seems impossible to talk about school life without talking about the relationships between children. Again, the conventional textbook psychology about children's interrelationships seems very inadequate. The peer group—a chapter heading in nearly every text—implies a monolithic aggregate, which is seen as operating a direct socialising influence on the child, supposedly against the norms of adults and towards deviance in norms and values. To anyone who thinks back to his own childhood experience, this concept of a monolithic group must make nonsense. It can only be for the adult who sees children in terms of the categories of age and gender that a class of 30 11-year-old boys represents a homogeneous and undifferentiated group—it would certainly not be so for any of the boys themselves. I do not think the degrees of feeling towards other people are any less fine and subtle for children than they are for adults. A girl at school is likely to feel all the shades of attraction and dislike, unease, fear, jealousy, indifference and so on, towards the other children who people her class. Age and gender, which define the peer group for developmental psychologists, are probably specially irrelevant for friendship in places where—because of the way schools are organised—children are already segregated into groups on the basis of similar age and, sometimes, gender.

For virtually all children in our society, school constitutes a major part of their daily experience. Obviously, though, different children live school lives of very different kinds. Whereas for many secondary school pupils, the relationships and activities in which they personally invest themselves are fundamentally supportive of the goals and values of the school authorities, in other cases this is patently not so. It may be that the ongoing life of pupil groups is actively and explicitly opposed to teachers and the authority of the school; or it may be that pupils are engaged in conducting among themselves projects of an altogether different kind, to which the formal educational side of school is simply irrelevant. The kind of social life outside school, of which a child is part, must affect the degree to which any individual pupil involves himself in activities that are at variance with, supportive of, or at a tangent to those that formal education endorses. A child who has grown up in a household where education is respected, valued and felt to have contributed to the life progress of the adults in the family, will find it more natural to engage himself in pro-school kinds of activities, than a child whose family places no such positive value on schools and what they stand for. Social and cultural differences surely also matter when it comes to how far children involve themselves closely with other children at school. The restrictions, for example, to which Muslim girls are subject in their associations with non-Muslim girls, and still more, with boys, probably does more than limit the opportunity to join up with other pupils outside school hours; it is likely, too, to impose a sense of inhibition on the freedom with which a Muslim girl can enter into relationships with her peers even in the classroom.

Given that within this society, we create a social world for children in which they are mostly segregated from the social world of adults, among large numbers of other children, the kinds of engagements that a child creates with his peers must be very important, and they are far from simple. To enter the complex and informal social reality of children's group lives, to establish a place for himself within it, to create projects for himself that will have significance for others, and forward their collective life—this is surely the difficult task that any child must undertake in engaging with his peers. One thing which must be necessary to achieve the task is some degree of continuity in the peer group itself. Certainly this conclusion is suggested by a study which Wooster and Harris (1972) carried out into the effects of constant changes of school on adolescent boys whose fathers were serving in the army. What these boys lacked, according to the findings, was any stable and consistent system for understanding themselves and other boys, as people. As Wooster and Harris put it, the absence of a stable audience against whom to play out a social role is likely to leave one without any coherent view of oneself in relation to others. That integration into the world of one's peers takes time, is also, as I see it, the meaning of a finding I obtained myself in a study I once carried out (Salmon, 1969) into the social values of primary school boys. Among the measures which I used, when the boys were aged eight and ten, were indices of popularity with other boys, conformity to peer or adult norms, insight into the content of such norms, and the adoption of peer or adult values. What I found was that, surprisingly, peer group orientation, in terms of conforming, insight and values, was more closely associated with popularity among peers two years earlier, than with current popularity. I take this to mean that it is necessary to have experienced personal acceptability to the group of one's peers, over quite a long time, in order to have had access to the whole network of meanings which constitute its salient values and perspectives.

So far, I have been emphasising the sense of people engaged in living, which I think would be a characteristically Kellyan perspective on children's social lives. Finally, though, I want to say something about the significance, for developmental social psychology, of a different feature of Kelly's approach—his concern with reflexivity. Making sense of their own sense-making is something which social psychologists seldom do; yet to examine the ground from which official psychology looks at children's social development would tell us a good deal about its particular character. Textbook psychology, like any other kind of understanding, is necessarily a particular kind of social reality, constructed in a particular historical and cultural context by people in a particular position in their society. Inevitably, it puts forward one version of reality. In order to see what biases and blind spots it may incorporate in its account of children's lives, we have to ask the question, whose social reality does it represent?

I think it would be very difficult to deny that the conventional psychology about social development is extremely ethnocentric, and has marked cultural and class biases. It seems to me that this is true in almost every aspect one considers. It is particularly obvious in its account of the family. A simple two-generation nuclear family pattern is universally assumed, despite the fact that this pattern is no longer standard even for middle-class indigenous whites. One-parent families, reconstituted families, extended kinship groups, families whose composition is fluid and changing—none of these structures is acknowledged to exist in the textbook account of family settings. And it is not merely that such accounts are grossly inaccurate in describing the family lives of many of the children in our society. What is perhaps more insidiously harmful is that imputations are made, because of the assumption that the nuclear pattern is normal, about the pathological significance of other modes. An example of this is the treatment of "father absence" in families. In West Indian families, which are characteristically matricentric in structure, and very often without a single permanent father-figure, this feature is seen as a symptom of social inadequacy, having pathogenic consequences for children.

The same kind of biases are also evident in the way textbook psychology treats other aspects of children's social lives. For instance, the very different ways in which children are likely to regard and experience school, depending on their ethnic and social background, are completely disregarded; school is assumed to have a standard significance for every child. When it comes to the discussion of young people's occupational choices and roles, these are viewed from an equally unrepresentative position. Neither the variety and level of vocational possibilities, nor the kinds of dimension involved in the selection and experience of work, which are put forward in the usual accounts of adolescents' occupational lives, are likely to constitute the experience of most young people in our society. The situation of being unemployed is, of course, never considered. A similar white, middle-class bias shows, too, in the kinds of leisure contexts which may be considered—children's camps and Boy Scouts, for instance, rather than football matches, Boys Brigade or discos. In general, developmental social psychology has extrapolated a particular life-style as a universal one.

Developmental social psychology is also undoubtedly sexist. The whole body of work on maternal deprivation is based on unquestioned, though questionable, assumptions about the motherhood role. The content of con-ventional sex roles is also quite uncritically incorporated into the account offered. Boys as more aggressive, more adventurous, girls as more depen-dent, more nurturant: this is seen to be the natural order of things. Because the major dimensions of sex roles in our society are viewed like this, rather than being seen as a social construction, all the more subtle aspects of sex roles, and how children come to learn them, are passed over. So no attention is given to the ways in which girls acquire feminine, rather than masculine, ways of using personal space, and placing one's limbs, in public, or how they come to view themselves and present themselves, as physical objects. Nor do social psychologists seem to ask how it is that a girl learns that females are expected to defer to males in conversation and to use indirect rather than direct ways of influencing others. Least of all is it asked how boys and girls are able to learn the very complicated rules that our society operates about sexuality, and the differential expectations which these incorporate towards the two genders.

What I have been urging here, drawing on Kelly's insights, adds up, I think, to a distinctive kind of social psychology. It would be one which viewed children's lives as complex and serious, as a matter of developing engagements rather than acquiring attributes, and as taking place within a particular cultural, historical context, in which we, as psychologists, are also living our lives.

References

Bee, H. (1975). "The Developing Child". Harper International Edition, New York, Hagerstown, San Francisco, London.

Berger, P. L. and Luckmann, T. (1966). "The Social Construction of Reality". Penguin Books, Harmondsworth.

Cary, Joyce (1976). "Selected Essays". Michael Joseph, London.

Moore, T. and Clautour, S. E. (1976). Attitudes to life in children and young adolescents. *Scand. J. Psychol.*

Salmon, P. (1969). Differential conforming as a developmental process. *Br. J. Soc. Clin. Psychol.* **8**, 22–31.

Sturt, R. (1976). Unpublished thesis, Diploma in Child Development, Institute of Education, University of London.

Wooster, A. D. and Harris, G. (1972). Concepts of self and others in highly mobile service boys. *Educ. Research* **12**, 46–52.

Personal Constructs
and Social Competence

Fraser Reid

It is significant that many of the issues Kelly addressed nearly a quarter century ago regarding the person's efforts to make sense of his world are finding fresh expression in contemporary social psychological thinking. In this chapter we shall focus on his treatment of one issue, the dual role of personal constructs as speculative predictions and as controls on the person's outlook, which has foreshadowed recent developments in attribution theory and social theories of personality. In particular, we shall examine how these contrasting facets of personal construing contribute to an understanding of a person's competence in forming social relationships and managing social encounters.

The objectives we set are two-fold. The primary task will be to formulate a definition of social competence from the vantage point of personal construct theory. The secondary task will be to derive from this definition a rationale for methods to promote social competence. In pursuing the first task, we first examine two contemporary views of the socially competent individual, views which lead to conflicting prescriptions until they are reconciled within the scheme of personal construct theory. In the second section, we critically examine Kelly's statements regarding the functioning of personal constructs, and identify contrasting outlooks in which the person either affirms his beliefs in the social world, or constructs speculative theories about it. These outlooks are traced in the third section to distinctive, and frequently conflicting, needs either to understand or to achieve a sense of mastery over the social world. These dual needs, central to Kelly's theory of social action, provide the backbone of a definition of social competence, and in the fourth section the manner in which these needs mesh with the exigencies of social interaction is examined. In the final section, Kelly's view that the articulation of these needs provides the person with the maximum opportunity to test and revise his personal constructs is extended to provide a rationale for promoting social competence.

Reconciling Two Paradigms

The declining popularity of the traditional trait approach to personality (see, for example, Argyle, 1976) has shifted the theoretical focus in studies of social competence away from global dispositions toward competencies in assessing the rules prevailing in social settings and in constructing appropriate lines of conduct (Mischel, 1973). Despite the dangers of glossing individual differences in the search for the situational determinants of behaviour (Bowers, 1973), or of supplanting the proliferation of traits with the practice of "rule-hunting" (Robinson, 1977), the heuristic value of this shift of focus is substantial. In recognising the situational specificity of much of social behaviour the door is opened to an examination of the demands that social settings impose on individuals, the manner in which these demands influence the construction of social behaviour, and the ways that individuals fashion social settings to their own liking (Bandura, 1974).

With this shift of focus two contrasting paradigms for conceptualising social competence have emerged. In the first, an attempt is made to identify the prescriptive elements in social situations by using a variety of procedures to "discover" the rules that are assumed to underlie and steer social conduct. Social competence is usually defined in terms of a knowledge of appropriate rules and the individual's ability to meet their prescriptive requirements. We might term this paradigm the "rule-following paradigm".

Whilst rules have a place in the second paradigm, they are not viewed as intrinsic to situations but as cognitive and behavioural schemes for solving problems of a social kind. Of interest here is not so much what the person *typically* does but what he may *potentially* do. The logic of inquiry in this paradigm is to assess the capacity to intelligently manipulate and transform information and to generate adaptive social behaviours. As competence pivots upon the individual's resourcefulness and constructional abilities, we might term this the "problem-solving paradigm".

Our task is to present personal construct theory as a means of reconciling, *en dépassant*, these contrasting paradigms. We might briefly illustrate them by examining two recent examples. With a rather literal analogy to Chomsky's (1957) generative grammar, Argyle (1976) puts forward an approach to personality in which situations are regarded as sources of generative rules for demarcating the set, or "behavioural category", of relevant, meaningful and appropriate social acts. The more formal the social setting, the more salient and rigorously prescriptive the generative rules, and the smaller the role of person variables (such as ability, motivation, style, etc.). In less formal settings there is greater scope, and exchanges are organised into episodes bounded by a general theme or goal. Each episode embodies rules governing behaviour within it, and participants cooperate to perform the episode as a joint social act. Moreover, the selection and sequencing of episodes requires the participants to negotiate them by means of verbal and non-verbal signals.

Envisaging social behaviour as a sequence of communicative events structured by a kind of "social grammar" calls for procedures to recover this grammar from the "surface structure" of everyday social behaviour. Methods for partitioning, categorising and analysing the rules for sequencing in conversational exchanges have been developed and tested in a number of studies (Clarke, 1975, 1977; Shapiro, 1976a,b; Kent *et al.*, 1978).

Although the development of the generative-rule model marks a broadening of Argyle's approach to social behaviour, his familiar social skills model (Argyle, 1972) continues to play a key role in his definition of social competence. If we were to extend the analogy to Chomsky's generative grammar a stage further, Argyle's recent writings would then appear to be concerned with the basic "rewriting rules" which steer the choice of category of social action appropriate to social settings. The stress he places on the feedback and control of meshing, sequencing and rewarding of social behaviour in his most recent formulation of social skill (Trower *et al.*, 1978) then appears to correspond to the "transformational rules" which govern the generation of surface structure behaviour. A lack of knowledge or facility in applying either class or rule leads to a failure of social competence.

The spirit of the problem-solving paradigm contrasts markedly with these views and is best exemplified in the writings of de Waele and Harré (1976). Rather than embodying prescriptive rules, social episodes are constructed and endowed with meaning by participants who negotiate that meaning in search of a definition. Situations thus present the person with problems of a social kind, and the solutions arrived at are precarious in the sense of representing a delicate and alterable balance of human and physical factors (Gonos, 1977). Instead of grading situations by reference to the formality of rules of selection and conduct, de Waele and Harré mark off settings for which prepared solutions are ready to hand, and those for which solutions must be improvised and negotiated.

In both cases social action is generated by transforming a cognitive structure (variously termed "template", "plan" and "rule") into a linear behaviour sequence; in the former the template exists as a standard and habitual routine whilst in the latter it is constructed in advance of or during an encounter.

In addition to instrumentally shaping his actions and the setting according to constructed or ready-made solutions, the person has considerable choice in the expressive style with which he qualifies his actions. He engineers a "persona", or situated identity (Alexander and Lauderdale, 1977) by manipulating the perceptions that others form of his dispositional character.

Social competence depends not on knowing the rules, but on the cognitive resources necessary for negotiating or deploying instrumental and expressive solutions to situations, and for monitoring their adequacy and propriety as the encounter unfolds. Such resources will include the capacity to transform social information and construct a range of potential behaviours and, above all, to reorganise behaviour in the light of changes in the behaviour of other persons.

The task we have set is to dovetail the rule-following and problem-solving paradigms by considering them from the perspective of a personal construct theory interpretation of social competence. The view to be put forward is that personal constructs and personal construct systems may function *either* as prescriptive statements about oneself, other people and social settings, steering behaviour and simplifying the task of social decision-making in the manner of social rules, *or* as descriptive propositions functioning as hypotheses and subject to validation by events in the progressive effort to solve the problems that encounters present. Further, personal construct theory envisages these orientations as alternative states of the same system, as typical shifts in the sequence of constructions which people employ in order to meet everyday situations. Social competence may then be described in terms compatible with both the rule-following and problem-solving paradigms as the capacity to engage in social situations with an appropriate constructional orientation and to adjust this orientation as the demands of the situations change and different needs become salient.

To refine this definition to the point where a rationale for enhancing competence may be devised requires first an examination of the conditions under which each orientation can be expected to occur and their function for the individual's construct system. Secondly, we must consider their consequences for social judgement and interaction and their relationship to the course of events in social episodes.

Rules and Hypotheses

In the first volume of "The Psychology of Personal Constructs", Kelly (1955) attempted to fix the metaphor of *man-the-scientist* firmly in the mind of the reader. Personal constructs were defined as speculative interpretations placed on events, as "working hypotheses" put to the test of experience and revised or replaced according to their validational outcomes. The question we must now ask, and it is one that Kelly himself addressed, is whether this is a complete description of a person's constructional processes. In particular, do personal constructs always function as hypotheses for making predictions regarding the course of events?

It is a key feature of Kelly's reasoning that a person's tests of a construct's predictive efficiency may sometimes be redundant either because in making the test he acts in such a way as to predispose certain outcomes, or because he imposes restrictions on construing the implications of events for cherished constructs. However, Kelly refused to part with the terms "prediction" and "anticipation" for these activities.

This is not simply a quibble over Kelly's use of terms. Whilst Kelly might have admitted that a "prediction" which fixes, fudges or ignores the data of experience is no prediction at all, what is at issue here is the precise relationship between the course of events, the person's interpretational efforts, and his behaviour towards those events. The set of relationships that obtain when constructs predispose particular outcomes, whether they be real or imagined, cannot be described in terms of their predictive properties. What the person may be predicting, however, is the *effect* of fixing, fudging and ignoring the data. He predicts that by cooking the books he might make events more manageable and thereby purchase a measure of certainty about them at the expense of a complete understanding. The constructs organising his behaviour function no longer as "working hypotheses" and he anticipates, *at a superordinate level*, the consequences of construing in this fashion. Seeking to establish more precise control over events not only involves construing preemptively, as Kelly had suggested but, as we shall see, *prescriptively* as well.

Kelly's uncritical use of the concepts of "hypothesis" and "prediction" to describe this mode of construing did not pass unnoticed and was explicitly challenged some years ago by T. Mischel (1964). The theme of Mischel's critique was that a close inspection of examples of "predictive" construing reveals radical differences between the use of hypotheses to make predictions and the process of construing. Mischel used a particular instance of behaviour, "I insult my boss", to demonstrate three ways in which the construing process leading up to the behaviour might depart from Kelly's hypothetico-deductive model.

Firstly, Mischel pointed out that Kelly would say that if I construe my boss as "dominating", I might expect (predict) him to attempt to dominate me and interpret his demands for overtime in this way. If, in addition, I construe myself as "dominating" and expect (predict) to dominate others, I may choose to insult my boss because otherwise he will succeed in dominating me. But Mischel observed that by insulting my boss I am not making a prediction about what I will do based on the evidence of the kind of person my boss is. Instead, I am expressing an intention, or *decision* to act in a certain way, and my judgement about my boss provides me with a justification for my actions. In short, I could be said to be following a regulative rule (Searle, 1970) of the form, "*If* my boss is dominating, *then* insult him".

Secondly, does construing my boss as dominating mean that I entertain this proposition as a prediction? Mischel pointed to a variety of ways in which such a construction might depart from the normal sense of "prediction". By insulting him, for example, I may give him no choice but to lay down the law and thus confirm my suppositions in the manner of a self-fulfilling prophecy. On the other hand, I may choose to regard his demand for overtime as an act of domination, even though to you it might seem a reasonable request. What is at issue here is our capacity to determine accurately the boss' intentions in making the request. Without some kind of admission from him my interpretation of his motives stands on an equal footing with yours. Even perhaps, in spite of such an admission I might find ways to palter with the evidence, arguing that my boss is lying, or unaware of his own hostility, and so on. In short, I may perceive my boss in terms of a stereotype and follow a constitutive rule (Searle, 1970) of the form, "A person with such and such characteristics *is* a dominating sort of person".

Finally, Mischel noted that construing not only involves a description but also an evaluation of events, and it is this latter component that channelises behaviour. Thus, having characterised my boss as a dominating person, negatively valuing "being dominated" will lead me to act towards him in one way rather than another. But a prediction never evaluates what it predicts.

From this analysis, Mischel concluded that constructs do not function as hypotheses for making predictions but as rules for making decisions, and consequently are justificatory reasons for prescribing what should be (or what has already been) done. His decisive demonstration of this was his analysis of Kelly's example of the old maid who "predicts" eventual marriage to a man who never comes along:

> She, too, has *predicted* a husband in terms of the intersect of a number of conceptual dimensions. But there are altogether too many dimensions involved and nobody ever lands on the precise point where all of them converge. Her long-standing *anticipation* is never fulfilled; she continues to be a spinster. (Kelly, 1955, p. 121; my italics)

But as Mischel put it:

> She is not predicting what will happen, but is expressing her intention to marry that kind of man. She has *decided* that this is the 'right' sort of man for her . . . In following the rule she makes things happen—i.e. she turns down this suitor and that because he does not have the requisite characteristics. The rule she follows thus tends to bring about what it prescribes; indeed, that is its function. (1964, p. 184)

Whilst concurring with Mischel's view that constructs can and do function in the manner of rules for making social decisions, we wish to avoid his generalisation that they always function in this way. Certainly, constructs may function as hypotheses, no more noticeably so than when, as Popper (1977) puts it, we encounter events which require "the solution of problems of a non-routine kind". Such events disappoint our "unconscious expectations" and demand that we take stock of ourselves. It is then that we become aware of our expectations and their rule-like qualities.

We are not always able, however, to take advantage of such disappointments to extend our understanding of events. In their classic "trick card" experiment, for example, where recognition thresholds for incongruous playing cards (e.g. red six of spades, black eight of hearts, etc.) were measured, Bruner and Postman (1949) found two responses which attest to Mischel's observations of reactions to construct invalidation. In "dominance" responses, Bruner and Postman found a tendency to perceptually deny the incongruous elements of the stimulus pattern in an attempt to render the stimulus congruent with expectancies. Thus, some subjects persisted in perceiving, say, a red six of spades as the six of hearts for exposure durations well beyond other subjects' recognition threshold for the same "trick" card. In "compromise" reactions, trick cards were identified as compromise objects, embodying elements of both the expected and the provided stimulus attributes. So, for example, a red six of spades might be perceived as a "brown" or "purple" six of hearts. Dominance and compromise reactions represent attempts to "paper over the cracks" in perceptual expectancies, to prevaricate in the face of invalidating events.

It was in the disruption of the perceptual process, however, that the task of identifying trick cards became a full-fledged "problem of a non-routine kind". Bruner and Postman observed that the failure to organise the perceptual field into an identifiable configuration was accompanied by a loss of confidence, perceptual confusion and discomposure. Subjects became uncomfortably aware of their inability to make sense of their perceptual experience. Only through a sense of the "wrongness" of the stimulus was it possible for them to observe, dissemble and reassemble their expectancies and eventually achieve successful recognition of the unexpected qualities of the trick cards. The implications are clear—it is through reflective appraisal, an "awareness of some fate of the construct system" (McCoy, 1977) that the rule-like character of deep-seated expectations is challenged and changed. Bruner and Postman observed that the greatest single barrier to the recognition of incongruity is the tendency for perceptual hypotheses to fixate after receiving a minimum of confirmation. We are proposing that hypotheses which are so readily confirmed are more reasonably considered as rules for organising the perceptual world.

Radley (1977) remarks that to participate in the world is silently to ask questions, questions for which we may or may not form explicit answers. Forming explicit answers is an activity that is forced upon us by events in an attempt to render them meaningful and orderly. But such objectives may be achieved in two ways. We may form answers either to bring us closer to a more complete understanding of events, or to provide us with evidence that we are able to control them. These two outcomes are not always coincident. Indeed, we may consider them to be the objectives of two distinct, frequently conflicting, needs.

Understanding and Control

In his discussion of causal attribution in social interaction, Harold H. Kelley (1972) observes that attributional phenomena include processes which involve systematic bias in the way available information is used as well as rational causal reasoning. These departures from rationality suggest to Kelley that the attribution process is to be understood both as a means of providing the person with a veridical outlook on his world and of maintaining effective control of events within it. That is, the scientist in man is not pure but applied. He is not simply a seeker after knowledge, but is pursuing "feelings of efficacy" in his interaction with the environment (White, 1959).

Kelley suggests that the control of environmental events entails a compromise between controlling the *controllable* and controlling the *important*:

> Thus, on the one hand, controlling tendencies will persist only if a person has some success in exercising control. So it is essential that his control efforts be directed toward realms in which he has some chance of being effective. On the other hand, what is controllable is not always what is more important. To persist in attempting control with respect to important but intractable conditions is to experience repeated failure, and, usually, to dampen one's control efforts. But *not to attempt* to exert control in relation to such circumstances is unnecessarily to delimit the quality of one's life. Thus, some sort of compromise must be reached between limiting and extending one's control attempts. (1972, p. 22)

Kelley goes on to suggest that many of the attributional biases that have received intensive study in recent years may be viewed as attempts to exact reinforcement from the environment for one's control attempts. They reflect a system biased in support of an internal locus of control orientation. Thus, the individual will more readily engage with situations in which he may exert control over the course of events. When confronted with events that resist his control attempts, he will focus on whatever evidence that is available that reflects his success at control. In fact, he may distort the available evidence in order to meet this need. To extend Kelley's reasoning, we might say the compromise the individual seeks to achieve is between two distinct needs—a need for a veridical understanding of events in order to predict them with greater efficiency, and a need to ensure that whatever understanding he has enables his mastery over the course of events. When the need to understand is salient, he seeks to perceive events apart from whatever hopes and fears he might otherwise attach to them. The latter need becomes salient when he is confronted by short-comings in his grasp of events and the anxieties which ensue. We propose that White's (1959) account of effectance motivation confuses two distinct needs—a need for effectance and a need for the *feeling* of effectance.

To return to George Kelly's thinking, we can see that he, too, was concerned with these distinct needs. He realised that feelings of effectance and control were purchased at the price of a complete understanding of events. He recognised three modes for achieving this need. In the first, the person construes events *preemptively*. That is, he adopts a "this-and-this-only" point of view, narrowing his interpretation of events to a single meaningful dimension. Preemption has the effect of ruling out other constructions as irrelevant, allowing the person to take a ready-made stand without the need to exercise judgement. In an ambiguous social situation where effective control may require several aspects to be simultaneously considered, the anxious person, recognising that what confronts him is beyond the scope of his construct system, concentrates on that construction through which he may most readily organise his response.

The second mode of control Kelly described as *constriction*. In contrast to preemption, constriction entails ruling out parts of the perceptual field in order to make control more feasible. Thus, the person "minimises the apparent incompatibility of his construction systems by drawing in the outer boundaries of his perceptual field" (p. 477). If preemption involves restricting the interpretation of events, constriction entails restricting the events to be interpreted. The person approaches situations ponderously and methodically, simplifying his construing in order to deal with one issue at a time and ignoring events which cannot immediately be made meaningful.

Kelly's third mode of control, *choice*, is one which he viewed as central to the explanation of action and is therefore embodied in his Choice Corollary. "A person chooses for himself that alternative in a dichotomised construct through which he anticipates the greater possibility for extension and definition of his system" (p. 64). Preemption and constriction imply that the person selects an aspect of the situation to deal with simply because he can deal with it. How he deals with it, however, is determined by the alternatives with which his construing presents him.

For Kelly, choice between alternatives is always "elaborative"—the person chooses either to extend his understanding, to test *as a hypothesis* that alternative which, on balance, will provide the information necessary to augment his construct system, or he opts for definition and confirms for himself in greater detail that interpretation of the situation which *he already believes* to be the case.

Together, these modes of construing provide a strategy for maintaining feelings of control. To use Kelly's example, the young man who, the morning after a quarrel with his girlfriend, considers only the bare events of the last evening (constriction), reasons that it was nothing but a "break-up" (preemption) about which he can do only one thing, say, bury himself in his studies (decision). If the need to understand his dilemma was salient, on the other hand, he would "broaden his perceptual field in an attempt to reorganise it on a more comprehensive level" and consider other events, such as failing an important exam the day before, which might have a bearing on the quarrel (dilation). Furthermore, he may consider a series of alternative interpretations of the events of the evening (circumspection), so that, for example, the heated exchange with his girlfriend amounted not to a quarrel and break-up, but simply to a momentary loss of a frayed temper which might, perhaps, be smoothed over by a little discreet flattery (prediction).

Following Mischel's critique of the practical application of construct theory, we may describe the young man's reasoning in the former case as reasoning by *deduction from a rule*. He combines the evidence to hand with an *a priori* rule for interpreting it in such a way as to use the evidence to justify the inference he draws. In the latter case, however, the young man's inferences reflect his attempts to construct an explanation for the effects he has observed. He considers the events of the evening and draws generalisations about them which have the character of *inductive hypotheses* to be put to an imaginative or behavioural test.

Kelly's distinction between constriction–dilation and preemption–circumspection now becomes clearer. In his studies of language and attributional reasoning, Kanouse (1972) distinguishes reasoning from evidence bearing on the subject of propositions (subject-specific evidence) and reasoning based on evidence about propositional predicates (object-specific evidence). Forming inductive hypotheses from subject-specific evidence entails dilating the perceptual field in order to consider additional elements from the perspective of a particular construct. A person may wonder, for example, what sort of people his friends are. Of his friends he recalls that Peter occasionally tells tall stories, that Paul, he has discovered, falsifies his tax returns, and that Mary is cheating on her husband. Are the people he calls friends "dishonest"? Forming inductive hypotheses from object-specific evidence, on the other hand, corresponds to the circumspective construing of a single element from the perspective of two or more alternative constructions. Not only does Paul falsify his tax returns, he also cheats at cards. Is Paul a harmless fraud? Or is he a crook?

A similar distinction applies when control needs are salient and construing is narrowed to particular interpretations of particular events. In forming a deduction from subject-specific evidence, a female party-goer, for example, who holds the belief that "married men who flirt at parties are insecure about their masculinity" may observe that Peter is engrossed in intimate conversation with an attractive and unattached woman whilst his wife is out of the room. Choosing to avoid considering what his wife might be doing and that other married men present are also talking to women other than their wives (constriction), she concludes that Peter is flirting and is, therefore, insecure about his masculinity. Conversely; she may reason from object-specific evidence that since she knows Peter is insecure about his masculinity (preemption) he must be behaving flirtatiously. In either case, this "heads I win, tails you lose" logic is tailored to be consistent with her belief that she has Peter "summed up" and that she will show him what's what if he tries to flirt with her!

Whilst these contrasting patterns of construing appear to be stylistic approaches to social judgements of this kind, Kelly also conceived of them as typical shifts in construction. Thus, in the course of a social encounter the person might follow "a sequence of construction involving, in succession, circumspection, preemption, and control, and leading to a choice which precipitates the person into a particular situation" (p. 515). However, depending on whether the need for understanding or for control is most salient, specific steps in this, the C–P–C cycle, may be protracted, attenuated or passed over entirely. For example, Kelly defines "impulsivity" as an unduly shortened period of circumspection prior to making a decision. Similarly, confusion and indecision are symptoms of lodgement in circumspection.

We may now phrase our earlier definition of social competence in greater detail; it is the capacity to articulate the needs for understanding and control and their associated constructional outlooks to the exigencies of social situations. Through dilation and circumspection the individual speculates about his social world and puts his theories to the test. Through constriction and preemption, he affirms his social world as this rather than that, and this he verifies in action. We now turn to consider what form social exigencies take and the manner in which they are met by the constructional outlooks the individual adopts.

The Demands of Social Interaction

In their example of the mountain-path encounter of two travellers, de Waele and Harré (1976) draw attention to the dual possibilities that exist in all encounters. On the one hand, the travellers may share a set of conventions for defining appropriate conduct within such meetings. They preempt their construction of the encounter by making a number of assumptions on the basis of those conventions—that they have correctly interpreted what kind of social episode it is, that the other person shares this interpretation, and that the events which subsequently take place confirm this interpretation (McHugh, 1968). It is a routine episode in which a reliable and familiar pattern is followed; greetings are exchanged, the man travelling upward allows the downward traveller to pass, farewells are exchanged and they part. These events do not challenge their assumptions. All the travellers do is assess correctly what the situation ought to be and then act accordingly. It is for such episodes that the rule-following paradigm is patently appropriate.

However, de Waele and Harré ask us to consider the case where either a common set of conventions has not been established or, to the discomfiture of the travellers, they find that they hold conflicting conventions regarding appropriate conduct. The encounter then poses a problem for which a solution must be improvised. And as the solution requires the travellers to fit together their separate lines of behaviour it must be cooperatively produced. They must bring their imperatives into agreement by means of some kind of contract. The focal point of this contract will be each traveller's interpretation of the encounter and it is from this interpretation that their character parts and lines of action will flow. In bargaining to contract each traveller will seek the best possible compromise between his own goals and the demands of the other, so that as bargaining proceeds "each succeeding response, by either participant, contains, as a major element, an assenting or denying term limiting variability in performance further and further" (Weinstein and Deutschberger, 1964, p. 454).

Situations of this kind exhibit the intrinsic indeterminacy of all social encounters. Routine situations are simply those in which participants' preemptive construing is more or less shared and more or less efficient in predicting events. As McCall and Simmons put it, "all that is needed is a sufficient lack of disagreement about one another for each to proceed with his own plans of action" (1966, p. 127). It is only when disagreement becomes inescapably evident that encounters pose problems of a non-routine kind.

Many writers, and in particular Kelly, have stressed that trouble-free interaction can occur only when individuals accurately "construe the construction processes of the other". Weinstein (1971) analyses this proposition in greater detail. He points out that a kind of "symbolic skill" is necessary for the individual to entertain multiple perspectives simultaneously. He must be able imaginatively to "take the role of the other" and avoid confusing this perspective with his own. Secondly, he needs to be sensitive to those cues in the other's behaviour which have inferential relevance for the perspective he holds regarding the interaction. The empathic understanding that individuals achieve by these means is, then, a necessary condition for harmonious interaction in both routine and non-routine encounters.

However, not all students of social interaction hold this view. Two recent critiques of Kelly's Sociality Corollary stress important reservations. Holland (1977) suggests that Kelly's concept of role cannot contend with situations where the individual must interact with an entire social group. Because he has neither the time nor the capacity to form separate impressions of the construction processes of all those involved he must resort to labels and categories in order to abstract rough rules to steer his conduct. Secondly, Young (1977) observes that a reliance on empathic understanding is likely to lead to more errors in judgement than the use of such rules. Moreover, he notes that the preoccupation with the imagined views of others is a characteristic of neurotic self-consciousness and leads to a disruption of, rather than improvement in, social behaviour.

These two critiques highlight the ways in which constructional outlooks respond to situational exigencies. In interaction with a social group, the individual has to be content that his understanding of others is sufficient to steer his behaviour towards them. He meets the call for behavioural commitment by preempting his construction of the group and organising his behaviour on the basis of ready-made generalisations about the expectations usually held by people similar to those present. But it is possible that the behaviour of the group fails to confirm these generalisations and he will be forced to re-examine his assumptions. The preoccupation of the neurotic is a distrust of precisely these assumptions. It is a preoccupation with establishing a sense of mastery in the face of overwhelming uncertainty. But the same uncertainty undermines all attempts to preempt his construing and leaves him lodged in circumspection. The demands for decision and action imposed upon him by encounters are resisted or inappropriately dealt with, and he shuns committing himself to a line of action which he feels he cannot justify.

The view we are proposing coincides precisely with the obsession of the neurotic—all social encounters are ambiguous and fraught with difficulties. What distinguishes ours from the view of the neurotic, however, is that in answer to the press for feelings of mastery individuals can commit themselves wholeheartedly to a line of action. Routine social encounters exhibit, *a fortiori*, this commitment. In them individuals collude, as it were, in staging an encounter according to supposedly shared rules. The interpersonal tasks of politely passing on the mountain-path, asking the way to the station, borrowing five pounds from a friend—all become the "figure" of the interaction whilst the constructions which support task-oriented behaviour retreat into the "ground" (McCall and Simmons, 1966). But to the extent that the rules are evidently *not* shared, a figure-ground reversal follows and task performance is suspended until the working agreement can be restored or renegotiated. The encounter presses for a circumspective outlook from individuals as the need for empathic understanding becomes salient.

However, the individual may not respond to this exigency. He may strive, instead, to re-establish control at the soonest opportunity by attenuating circumspection and reverting to rules to guide his interpretation of the encounter. The intrusion of rules into his construing may take a variety of forms. By employing an implicit and "common-sense" theory about which personality characteristics covary in other people (Bruner and Tagiuri, 1954), he might size up the other person as a "nosey-parker", "know-all", "loud-mouth", and so on. Or he might use a similar theory about what behaviours are likely to co-occur in what situations (Wish and Kaplan, 1977) and what actions are most appropriate (Price and Bouffard, 1974) in order to draw conclusions about the encounter. He may even have a theory about the type of person normally encountered in particular social positions (Weinstein, 1971), so that bank clerks are "timid", civil servants "officious", and used-car salesmen "unscrupulous". In short, the need for control in encounters may be sufficiently pressing for the individual to cut corners in his judgements of other people.

Such judgements, however, shape the lines of action he improvises in his encounters. As efforts to control the course of the encounter they may have some predictive validity; but frequently, they do not. Decades of research on person perception have emphasised the enduring effects of these short-cuts to an understanding of other people. First impressions continue to count long after contradictory information becomes available in the encounter (Anderson and Jacobson, 1965). This reluctance to adapt to new contingencies, Mischel (1973) observes, reflects a defensive reaction of an individual who seeks to maintain the sense of his mastery over events.

When events fail to confirm a person's beliefs about others, four courses of action are open to him: he may reluctantly concede that the rules he follows are invalid and that he is confronted with a person whose actions demand explication; he may discount what he sees as exceptional; he may selectively attend only to those behaviours which are consistent with his judgements; or he can try to force the other person to act in a way that confirms his beliefs. Kelly defined this last tactic as "hostility", as an attempt "to collect on a wager that has already been lost". The person strives to prove to himself that his rules still apply by manipulating the behavioural options available to the other person. He endeavours to "altercast" the other person with a role (Weinstein and Deutschberger, 1972) which bolsters his beliefs about himself (Secord and Backman, 1965) or his beliefs about them (Snyder and Swann, 1977).

This need not be a deliberate strategem. The person may even believe he is approaching the encounter with an open mind. But, as in Kelly's example of the man who construes his neighbour as "hostile" and so throws stones at his dog just to check that he is not wrong, the illusion that his construct system is capable of coping with events leads the person to construct, rather than test, reality. He will become blissfully unaware, observe Snyder and Swann, of the causal role that his own behaviour plays in generating the evidence that erroneously confirms his expectations, inferences and attributional labels.

The varying demands arising in social interaction for speculative reflection and active commitment may be resisted by the individual. In particular, we have considered the consequences of avoiding the uncertainties of circumspection and negotiation by reverting to rules to simplify the task of social decision-making. The individual's version of social reality comes to be affirmed both imaginatively, in his selective attention to, and distortion of, the data of experience, and behaviourally, in the moulding of events to a preformed cast.

Promoting Superordinate Control

The task we set at the outset was to achieve two objectives: to define social competence from within a personal construct theory perspective, and to derive from that definition the broad requirements of practical methods for enhancing social competence. We are now in a position to complete the first task and embark on the second.

We have attempted to dovetail two contrasting approaches to social competence, the rule-following and problem-solving paradigms, by proposing that they reflect dual demands of social interaction and dual constructional possibilities for the individual. Thus, social episodes may be approached either by recourse to rules which prescribe what "ought" to be done and what "ought" to happen, or by speculations about the nature of episodes and the meanings to be attributed to events within them. We proposed that these constructional orientations are responses to distinct needs—for a sense of mastery over events on the one hand, and for a more complete understanding of them on the other. Moreover, we have indicated that these needs become differentially salient as social episodes unfold. Social interaction imposes fluctuating demands on the individual—at one moment he is pressed to commit himself in decision and action, at another to reflect on events and negotiate their meanings with other participants. He may meet these exigencies by recognising the kind of constructional orientation that each requires. Or he may resist such demands, preferring instead to meet his own needs in the interaction. Thus, reluctant to commit himself to a single, definite course of action, he withdraws in doubt and uncertainty. Or he casts caution to the wind and adopts a line of behaviour which effectively brings about what he believes ought to happen. In short, his constructional outlook may not coincide with the situational exigencies that confront him.

However, the outlooks he adopts are responses to those exigencies. They reflect his awareness of the fate of his construct system. As McCoy (1977) remarks, "awareness of construing is via yet another construction" (p. 99). The individual anticipates that by preempting his construing events become more manageable, and that, if they resist, he can make them manageable. Alternatively, he anticipates that the situation will make sense only if he can discern the way that others interpret it. Both outlooks stem, as McCoy puts it, from a "recognition of construct system functionality". The outlooks differ only in terms of the anticipated consequences of circumspective or preemptive construing for the exigencies with which he is confronted. These exigencies and the functional capacity of the construct system to meet them are thus construed at a *superordinate level*. Superordinate construing in this sense has a more specific meaning to that proposed by Kelly. To be sure, we do imply that "a superordinate construct is one which includes another as one of the elements in its context" (Kelly, 1955, p. 532). However, we refer specifically to that system of constructs through which the functioning of subordinate constructs is evaluated. Such a system, however, may become stabilised as constructional outlooks develop into habitual and stylistic responses to situational exigencies. Thus, Bannister identifies failures to elaborate personal construing as stemming from two primary sources; either because the construct system has become too tight and "too restricted to particular strategies for handling experiment and evidence", or because constructs become so loose that "they cannot act as a guide to any formulated venture" (1975, p. 132). The individual becomes lodged in either the preemptive or circumspective outlooks. He does not respond to environmental demands in an appropriate way. Lodgement in circumspection alienates the person from interaction and he fails to meet his "involvement obligations" (Goffman, 1972). He becomes preoccupied with himself as someone who is faring well or badly, with the perceptions that others form of him and with the way the interaction is proceeding. Lodgement in preemption unduly narrows and stabilises the assumptions underlying encounters and, confirmed and reconfirmed in the course of events, they become progressively more resistant to inspection and revision. It is this feature that characterises many enduring relationships and the sense of "security" engendered by marriage (Berger and Kellner, 1975).

Social competence, then, pivots upon the capacity of the superordinate construct system to appraise situational exigencies and their consequences for interpersonal construing. The socially adroit person brings to bear superordinate constructs which enable him to articulate control and circumspection according to the demands of social situations as he perceives them. It is precisely these perceptions that Kelly advises the therapist to manipulate. In a sense, the therapist temporarily usurps his client's superordinate system, inducing him to preempt or circumspect according to his understanding of the client's conceptual response to his environment. However, Kelly does not offer the advice necessary to enhance the superordinate system directly. Indeed, in therapies which seek to equip the client with strategies for coping with life's difficulties, its development occurs by chance rather than by design.

To meet this need, practical methods for enhancing social competence will have as their primary objective the elaboration of the superordinate system through which the individual appraises the demands of his social world and his capacities to meet those demands. Put quite baldly, the task is to train the individual to become his own therapist, to discern for himself at what point loosened construing and circumspection is required, and at what point events call for tightened construing and committed action. Rather than simply providing a therapeutic environment in which he can explore and experiment with alternative constructions of the situations with which he is confronted, we require methods which will accelerate the development of the *capacity* to engage in cycles of construction as circumstances in the social world press him to adapt and change. The goal, as Rogers has put it, is not that the individual move from "a fixity, or homeostasis, to a new fixity", but from "fixity to changingness, from rigid structure to flow, from stasis to process" (1958, p. 143).

To provide a framework for operationalising these idealised objectives we may identify three assumptions which follow from our definition of social competence. Firstly, it is assumed that inappropriate or stabilised constructional outlooks are maintained by self-perpetuating cycles of superordinate construction. Lodgement in preemption follows from the superordinate belief that people are nothing but what they seem and that they are best dealt with in those terms. As we have seen, the effect of preemptive construing is to justify, both imaginatively and behaviourally, the inferences the person draws concerning his social world. Similarly, lodgement in circumspection follows from the superordinate belief that people are invariably other than they seem, and that conclusions about them rarely provide a sufficiently firm foundation for committed action. Circumspective construing will always provide the evidence necessary to sustain this belief. The constructional outlooks adopted by the individual fuel these beliefs and they become established as superordinate rules for prescribing the fate of subordinate constructs.

The second assumption is that stabilised constructional outlooks are alterable by interrupting these self-perpetuating cycles. Rather than seek to equip the person with more "normal" or "rational" explanations for social behaviour, the focus of training will be to enhance his superordinate perspective on the explanations that he habitually employs. Ideally, he acquires a capacity similar to the therapist for assessing his constructional behaviour. That is, he learns to recognise those cues that have inferential relevance for his interpersonal construing. To do this, he must acquire the information regarding the functional consequences of his constructional outlooks that his superordinate construing denies him. In a sense, he must develop perceptual skills for discriminating the conceptual processes in which he engages. Extending this rationale, we might then conceive of practical methods for providing him with an extrinsic source of feedback concerning the functioning of his constructs. The role of this feedback will be to draw the individual's attention to intrinsic cues that arise from his constructional behaviour in social situations, so that, eventually, the control and articulation of his constructional processes may be taken over by these cues (Holding, 1965). Clearly, the success of this feedback may be measured in terms of the acquisition of internal control of constructional behaviour and the individual's eventual independence of extrinsic sources of information.

A final assumption concerns the intended results of practical methods for enhancing social competence. Whilst feedback regarding construing habits is intended to bring constructional behaviour under cognitive appraisal, it is not the intention to create states of self-consciousness that might disrupt social behaviour. Psychoanalysis distinguishes two kinds of insight, emotional and intellectual. Intellectual insight enables the individual "to understand and control aspects of himself from which he remains alienated" (Rycroft, 1972, p. 72). It is classed as an obsessional defence because the individual insulates the effect of his observations by suppressing their emotional significance. In emotional insight observations effect changes in behaviour by providing silent answers to the silently asked questions which Radley (1977) associates with the "posture of anticipation". More specifically, Meichenbaum (1976) indicates three avenues through which emotional insight influences behaviour; in appraising the emotional significance of forthcoming events, in the attributional labels applied to events and in the feelings of efficacy aroused by events. Thus, the individual's capacity to implicitly form answers to the questions, What is going to happen? Why is it happening? What can I do about it?, is enhanced only through emotional insight.

These three assumptions are embodied in a paradigm developed by Thomas and his co-workers (Thomas and Augstein, 1974; Augstein and Thomas, 1975; Thomas *et al.*, 1977) to develop superordinate control of learning skills in educational contexts. Termed "cognitive mirroring", the paradigm comprises a set of techniques for training the learner to detect, interrupt and revise habitual learning strategies. The cognitive mirroring paradigm provides a basic framework of three phases of operation around which techniques for reviewing interpersonal construing may be coordinated. A first requirement is that observational records of social behaviours and their explanation be collected from one or more participants. As Orvis *et al*. (1976) observe, conflict between the explanations that individuals form to account for their behaviour is frequently irresolvable for a number of reasons. The complexity of the behavioural evidence, the difficulty of recovering its causal history, the multiple plausible interpretations to which it is subjected, and the justificatory social context in which accounts are voiced—all combine to obscure the relationship between events and their explanation. As these become the substrate for subsequent appraisal, methods for directly recording interpersonal events and obtaining immediate interpretations are to be preferred (e.g. the videotape procedures of Kaswan and Love, 1969). However, methods involving the recall of interpersonal events and their present interpretations are also suitable (e.g. repertory grid technique).

In the second phase of the paradigm procedures are applied for classifying and displaying to the participants the functional characteristics of their construing in the first phase. Choice of procedures clearly depends on the form of the observed records. These procedures will include methods for categorising constructs according to defined features (e.g. the tendency for dichotomous reasoning; Meichenbaum, 1976), assessing the extent to which constructs covary in their application to events and, conversely, the covariation of events in terms of their interpretation (e.g. the cluster analysis and "focusing" of repertory grids; Thomas *et al*., 1977), obtaining perceived implication relationships between constructs (e.g. Hinkle's "implications grid", described in Fransella and Bannister, 1977), assessing commonality and understanding between participants (e.g. procedures for comparing repertory grids; Watson, 1970a,b) and a host of other techniques. The general aim of these procedures is to identify relevant aspects of the functioning of construct systems and to display these in an intelligible form to the individual. Merely displaying the functional outcomes of his construing does not guarantee that the individual will acquire greater understanding of his constructional outlook. The objective of the final phase of cognitive mirroring is to encourage active elaboration of superordinate construing by requiring the individual to furnish explanations for the outcomes he has observed. The effect of this procedure is to promote superordinate circumspection regarding the fate and the potential of his interpersonal construing. Explaining his observations directs his attention to the needs underlying particular patterns of construing and enables the individual to envisage the consequences of construing in different ways.

In summary, we defined social competence as the control and articulation of circumspection and preemption in accordance with the demands of social episodes. This control requires the individual to bring to bear superordinate constructs for appraising situational exigencies and the functional capacity of his subordinate constructs to meet those exigencies. From this definition a rationale for enhancing superordinate control was derived which centred on the acquisition of skill in discriminating constructional behaviours and their functional outcomes. Finally, the three operational phases of the cognitive mirroring paradigm were proposed as a general scheme for implementing this rationale. As a final note, we might observe that although the rationale we propose is speculative and clearly demands systematic research, it does not depart too widely from the practice of personal construct psychotherapy. Rather, it focuses attention to a particular facet of personal construing and systematises what might otherwise be a haphazard process.

References

Alexander, C. N. and Lauderdale, P. (1977). *Sociometry* **40**, 225–233.

Anderson, N. H. and Jacobson, A. (1965). *J. Personal. Soc. Psychol.* **2**, 531–539.

Argyle, M. (1972). "The Psychology of Interpersonal Behaviour". Penguin Books, Harmondsworth.

Argyle, M. (1976). *In* "Personality" (Ed. R. Harré), pp. 145–188. Basil Blackwell, Oxford.

Augstein, E. S. and Thomas, L. F. (1975). Paper presented to Annual Conference of British Psychological Society, University of Nottingham.

Bandura, A. (1974). *Am. Psychol.* **29,** 859–869.

Bannister, D. (1975). *In* "Issues and Approaches in The Psychological Therapies" (Ed. D. Bannister), pp. 127–146. Wiley, Chichester.

Berger, P. and Kellner, H. (1975). *In* "Life as Theater:1a Dramaturgical Source-book" (Eds D. Brissett and C. Edgley), pp. 219–233. Aldine, Chicago.

Bowers, K. S. (1973). *Psychol. Rev.* **80**, 307–336.

Bruner, J. S. and Postman, L. J. (1949). *J. Pers.* **18**, 206–223.

Bruner, J. S. and Tagiuri, R. (1954). *In* "Handbook of Social Psychology" (Ed. G. Lindzey), Vol. II. Addison Wesley, Cambridge, Mass.

Chomsky, N. (1957). "Syntactic Structures". Mouton, S'Gravenhage, Netherlands.

Clarke, D. D. (1975). *Br. J. Soc. Clinic. Psychol.* **14**, 333–339.

Clarke, D. D. (1977). *In* "Social Rules and Social Behaviour" (Ed. P. Collett), pp. 42–69. Basil Blackwell, Oxford.

Fransella, F. and Bannister, D. (1977). "A Manual for Repertory Grid Technique". Academic Press, London and New York.

Goffman, E. (1972). *In* "Interaction Ritual", pp. 113–136. Penguin Books, Harmondsworth.

Gonos, G. (1977). *Am. Sociol. Rev.* **42**, 854–867.

Holding, D. H. (1965). "Principles of Training". Pergamon, Oxford.

Holland, R. (1977). "Self and Social Context". Macmillan, London.

Kanouse, D. E. (1972). *In* "Attribution: Perceiving the Causes of Behaviour" (Eds E. E. Jones, D. E. Kanouse, H. H. Kelley, R. E. Nisbett, S. Valins and B. Weiner), pp. 121–135. General Learning Press, New Jersey.

Kaswan, J. and Love, L. R. (1969). *In* "Studies in Self-cognition: Techniques of video-tape self-observation in the behavioural sciences" (Ed. R. H. Geertsma). Williams and Wilkins, Baltimore.

Kelley, H. H. (1972). *In* "Attribution: Perceiving the causes of behaviour" (Eds E. E. Jones, D. E. Kanouse, H. H. Kelley, R. E. Nisbett, S. Valins and B. Weiner), pp. 1–26. General Learning Press, New Jersey.

Kelly, G. A. (1955). "The Psychology of Personal Constructs", Vol. I. Norton, New York.

Kent, G. G., Davis, J. D. and Shapiro, D. A. (1978). *J. Personal. Soc. Psychol.* **36**, 13–22.

McCall, G. J. and Simmons, J. L. (1966). "Identities and Interactions". Collier Macmillan, New York.

McCoy, M. M. (1977). *In* "New Perspectives in Personal Construct Theory" (Ed. D. Bannister), pp. 93–124. Academic Press, London and New York.

McHugh, P. (1968). "Defining the Situation". Bobs-Merrill, Indianapolis.

Meichenbaum, D. (1976). *In* "Behavioural Approaches to Therapy" (Eds J. T. Spence, R. C. Carson and J. W. Thibaut), pp. 275–294. General Learning Press, New Jersey.

Mischel, T. (1964). *Psychol. Rev.* **71**, 180–192.

Mischel, W. (1973). *Psychol. Rev.* **80**, 252–283.

Orvis, B. R., Kelley, H. H. and Butler, D. (1976). *In* "New Directions in Attributional Research" (Eds J. H. Harvey, W. J. Ickes and R. G. Kidd), Vol. I, pp. 353–386. Lawrence Erlbaum, New Jersey.

Popper, K. R. (1977). *In* "The Self and its Brain" (Eds K. R. Popper and J. C. Eccles). Springer International, Berlin.

Price, R. H. and Bouffard, D. L. (1974). *J. Personal. Soc. Psychol.* **30**, 579–586.

Radley, A. (1977). *In* "New Perspectives in Personal Construct Theory" (Ed. D. Bannister), pp. 221–249. Academic Press, London and New York.

Robinson, P. (1977). *In* "Social Rules and Social Behaviour" (Ed. P. Collett), pp. 70–87. Basil Blackwell, Oxford.

Rogers, C. (1958). *Am. Psychol.* **13**, 142–149.

Rycroft, C. (1972). "A Critical Dictionary of Psychoanalysis". Penguin Books, Harmondsworth.

Searle, J. (1970). "Speech Acts". Cambridge University Press, Cambridge.

Secord, P. F. and Backman, C. W. (1965). *In* "Progress in Experimental Personality Research" (Ed. B. Maher), pp. 91–123. Academic Press, New York and London.

Shapiro, D. A. (1976a). *Br. J. Soc. Clin. Psychol.* **15**, 213–215.

Shapiro, D. A. (1976b). *Br. J. Soc. Clin. Psychol.* **15**, 353–356.

Snyder, M. and Swann, W. B. (1977). *J. Exp. Soc. Psychol.* **14**, 148–162.

Thomas, L. F. and Augstein, E. S. (1974). Paper presented to Congress of International Reading Association, Vienna.

Thomas, L. F., Harri-Augstein, E. S. and Farnes, N. C. (1977). Unpublished manuscript.

Trower, P., Bryant, B. and Argyle, M. (1978). "Social Skills and Mental Health". Methuen, London.

Waele, U.-P. de and Harré, R. (1976). *In* "Personality" (Ed. R. Harré), pp. 189–246. Basil Blackwell, Oxford.

Watson, J. P. (1970a). *Br. J. Psychiat.* **117**, 309–318.

Watson, J. P. (1970b). *Br. J. Psychiat.* **117**, 319–321.

Weinstein, E. A. (1971). *In* "Handbook of Socialisation Theory and Research" (Ed. D. A. Goslin), pp. 753–775. Rand McNally, Chicago.

Weinstein, E. A. and Deutschberger, P. (1964). *Social Forces* **42**, 451–456.

Weinstein, E. A. and Deutschberger, P. (1972). *In* "Symbolic Interaction: A Reader in Social Psychology" (Eds J. G. Manis and B. Meltzer), pp. 327–336. Allyn and Bacon, Boston.

White, R. W. (1959). *Psychol. Rev.* **66**, 297–332.

Wish, M. and Kaplan, S. J. (1977). *Sociometry* **40**, 234–246.

Young, G. C. D. (1977). Paper presented to Second International Congress on Personal Construct Theory, Oxford.

Reprimand: The Construing
of the Rule Violator's
Construct System

James C. Mancuso

Introduction

Few of the essayists, theorists and investigators who have written about rule
following have worked outside the mechanistic paradigm which guided the
thought of Hobbs, Hume, Bentham and J. S. Mill. In the system used by
these influential utilitarians a reprimand would act as a causal preventative.
Their work is based on an implicit assumption that pain and pleasure are
direct causal events which steer the course of behavior. An effective
reprimand withholds or delivers, or otherwise promises to regulate, a pleasure or a pain that would counteract the energic force of the pleasure or the
pain that was produced by engaging in the unwanted conduct.

In the 1950s prestigious, mechanistically oriented investigators (Bandura
and Walters, 1959; Glueck and Glueck, 1950; Sears et al., 1957; Whiting
and Child, 1953) wrote about punishment and reward as efficient causes of
rule following. Studies of socialization within this formulation sought out the
parameters of the hereditary determinants of response to punishment, the
intensity of reward/punishment, the timing of application of reward/
punishment, the neurological centers of pain and pleasure, and so forth
(Aronfreed and Reber, 1965; Eysenck, 1964; Parke, 1969; Parke and
Walters, 1967; Solomon et al., 1953).

In the ambience of this period a student of socialization processes could
attribute little significance to the proposition that, "to the extent that one
person construes the construction processes of another, he may play a role in
a social process involving the other person" (Kelly, 1955, p. 95). The basic
assumptions of the mechanistic paradigm, in the first place, would have
provided little base from which to consider the cognitive systems of either

the transgressor or the reprimander. Further, the conceptions of causality that were held in esteem by the mechanists would have granted little credence to the possibility that the ways in which the transgressor and the reprimander might construe reprimand's functions would, in fact, determine the outcomes of the reprimand situation. Thus, though Piaget (1932) had already published evidence that persons at different developmental levels do construe reprimand situations from very diverse perspectives, there was little attention to the possibility that a reprimander's effectiveness in enacting his role would be related to his ability to construe the transgressor's cognitions relative to the reprimand situation.

Currently, a major reorientation of perspectives in psychological science has allowed consideration of alternative ways to conceptualize the processes involved in rule breaking and reprimand. Attribution of causality, for example, has become a related topic of study (Snyder, 1976; Wortman, 1976), and investigators have begun to question the utility of concepts which define direct, actual causes of behavior. Following these changes, there now exists a sufficient foundation to begin building a theory of reprimand which incorporates explanation of the relationships between reprimand outcome and variables such as the following: (a) the conceptualization of *rule* that is held by the transgressor and the reprimander; (b) the conceptualization of motives to transgress that is held by the transgressor and the reprimander; (c) the participants' causal attributions to varied reprimand; and (d) the reprimander's skill in varying reprimand relative to the transgressor's construction system. In short, a contextualist paradigm might better replace the mechanist paradigm which has guided thought about reprimand and rule following.

FOREWORD

The following discussion will contain a series of conceptualizations that should be useful in developing a contextualist substitution for the flagging mechanistic paradigm that has been the dominant guide to discussions of transgression and reprimand. The use of the terms *mechanistic* and *contextualist* reflects reliance on Pepper's (1942) important analysis of metaphysical systems. In other publications (Jenkins, 1974; Mancuso, 1977; Sarbin, 1977) it has been argued that Pepper's analysis may be applied to explain the paradigm shift that has been taking place in behavior science. The increasing interest in Kelly's (1955) theory of personal constructs is regarded as a reflection of the shift to a contextualist paradigm.

Here it is proposed that Kelly's theory may now be taken as a suitable guide to the study of reprimand. Specifically, this discourse will develop the general proposition that a transgressor will comply with a reprimand when the reprimand situation provides a choice by which the transgressor can anticipate the greater possibility for extending and defining his construing system (Kelly, 1955, p. 64, The Choice Corollary). This proposition is based on the presumption that a *rule* is to be regarded as only one of many alternative constructions of an event. *Reprimand* always contains a dialectic configuration, offering or implying two theses and their contradictions (Kelly, 1955, p. 59, The Dichotomy Corollary). The theses of the reprimand may be either *tangential* to or *relevant* to the specific construction of the transgressive event. Most adult reprimanders, we propose, implicitly "know" that if they would successfully play the role of reprimander they must construe the transgressor's system and "feed in" a dialectic configuration which has appropriate relevance to the range of convenience of the transgressor's system. Thus, when they construe the transgressor as having available the appropriate constructions, they will advocate, and use, relevant reprimand. When they sense that relevant reprimand will not provide the transgressor with an appropriate dialectic they will take recourse to irrelevant reprimand, expecting thereby to unbalance the transgressor. Commonly used forms of *retributive* reprimand, in that the transgressor is asked to subsume the transgression under constructs like *body comfort–body discomfort* or *restraint–freedom*, are taken as examples of irrelevant reprimand.

A Personal Construct Approach to Transgression and Reprimand

One could begin an exploration of rules and reprimand by asking, "What are the causes of rule following?" To the personal construct theorist, who works from a contextualist rather than a mechanist world view, there would be no possibility of answering the above question. A more suitable question would be, "What is the context within which a person accepts another person's construction of an event?" As a part of the reply to the question one would refer to Kelly's (1955) Choice Corollary, "A person chooses for himself that alternative in a dichotomized construct through which he anticipates the greater possibility for extension and definition of his construction system" (p. 64). Reworked so that it becomes a response specific to the above-stated question about reprimand acceptance, the Choice Corollary would read as follows: *A person will accept a reprimand* (another person's construct of an event) *if he anticipates that doing so provides possibilities for extending and defining his existing systems*.

Consider the following as a background for developing a constructivist view of reprimand effectiveness.

A person engages in an unwanted behavior. Obviously, his behavior is the experiment on the validity of his "reference signal", where the term "reference signal" is Power's (1973) name for the analogue of that which a personal construct theorist would call a *construction*. Other theorists might use the term *schema* (Rumelhart and Ortony, 1977). Thus, when a person behaves, he is "trying on" his construction. All behavior, wanted or unwanted, reflects the person's effort to control his perceptions, so to speak. Persons seek to anticipate events. They predict that the sensory input resulting from the situation as changed by the behavior will match the construction (the schema or the reference signal) that guided the action.

Now we begin to see why one speaks of contextualism. The explanation of a reprimand situation must describe a continuously flowing context. In that context one includes, at least, (a) the sensory input generating the actors' constructions, (b) the available generic and specific constructions, (c) the motor output that is a part of the construction, and (d) the sensory feedback associated with the altered environment, which acts as "information" that is absorbed by the construction.

It is now appropriate to introduce another main strand of the context relative to those constructions of events which are called rules. In a reprimand situation there are two or more actors each of whom generates his own constructions. As persons, all the actors seek to anticipate events. The very fact that someone construes an actor as a "rule violator" indicates that the judge (and potential reprimander) has observed a person who behaves in ways which invalidate the constructions which the potential reprimander would apply in that event.

The Sociality Corollary provides the basis for the ensuing emplotment: *To the extent that one person construes the construction processes of another, he may play a role in a social process involving the other person* (Kelly, 1955, p. 95).

REPRIMAND AND KELLY'S SOCIALITY COROLLARY

The person who would play the role of the reprimander, then, attempts to validate his rule—his construction of the event to which the rule applies. Eventually, the reprimander must have the rule violator endorse the construction which he *should have* applied to the situation. To get validation the observer takes the role of reprimander. His reprimanding action may take many forms, but like the behavior of any person in any situation, the reprimander's behavior is designed to create, eventually, a sensory feedback which matches the construction that he has created for the event. He tries to create a predicted plot.

To do this successfully, he must construe and then build into his plan the construction processes of the rule violator. Thereupon, depending on his construction of the situation, he may produce any of a number of diverse reprimand strategies; any of which might be effective relative to the transgressor's system.

He might say,

"Little boys who love their mommies don't do things like that;" or
"Good little boys don't do things like that," or
"If you really want me to be nice to you, you wouldn't do things like that," or
"We draw and quarter little boys who do things like that," or
"If you do that again, I'll whale the daylights out of you," or
"You could have been more careful with that, so that next time you were there they would trust you to do it properly," and so on.

Now the rule violator would have an opportunity to respond, and that makes another scene in the drama; because his possible constructions of the reprimander will have a great deal to do with the flowing context. For our purposes, we can stop the action here, and ask about the reprimander's conduct and try to relate it to our question, "Under what conditions does a person accept another person's constructions of an event?" We also want to look at the claim that the question is best answered within the framework of Kelly's Choice Corollary.

Consider the first example of the reprimand. What is happening, from the perspective shown here? The reprimander says "Little boys who love their mommies don't do things like that". How would this conduct possibly bring about validation of the reprimander's construction? The action could be interpreted as follows.

The reprimander construes the construction processes of the violator. He knows, implicitly, Kelly's Choice Corollary. Thus, he frames an input that tells the violator:

You construe yourself as a person who loves his mommy. But, in the transgression-related situation you applied an inappropriate construction to guide your behavior. Now, take your choice! Which choice will most efficiently extend and elaborate your existing system. Do you choose to be construed as a mommy-lover? Or, do you choose to continue to perceive the situation in the way which led to your transgression? To validate both constructions would produce a contradiction within your own constructions.

(i) The structure of a reprimand

Each of the illustrative reprimands embodies the same general structure. Each contains a dialectic configuration offering or implying two sets of theses, along with contradictions of those theses. (1) Good boys don't do that. (2) Bad boys do, indeed, do that. Which extends the transgressor's system? To believe that he is a *good* boy or to believe the implied contrast, that he is a *bad* boy? If he chooses to continue the act he will be expected to accept the category *bad* as a self descriptor. He may, the reprimander tells him, construe himself as *good* only if he desists from the act. The reprimander's success depends on which of these constructions the transgressor, in this situation, can choose as the best definition and extension of his construct system.

The dimension tangential–relevant is particularly important in considering reprimand from a personal construct perspective. Reconsider the list of reprimands shown above. Think of a child who has inadvertently spilt his glass of milk at the dinner table. His inapporpriate construing of the action of reaching for the mashed potatoes results in the spilt milk. To talk about the relationship of this action to his love of his mother is to raise a somewhat remote construction. Any discussion of the very superordinate bad–good construct raises a very confusing construct, particularly for a child. The child's subsuming of his self under this construct is hardly relevant to spilling milk. Certainly, drawing and quartering has very little to do with building a useful construction of reaching across the dinner table. To speak about care, caution, observing the location of one's elbows, the precariousness of food containers, etc., would be quite relevant. A demonstration of why spilling would happen could be very directly related to promoting reconstruing of the situation itself. A discussion of why carefulness is prized would also be useful. Thus, though the distinctions are difficult to make and to maintain, one could profitably think of reprimand activity as being *construct relevant* and *construct irrelevant*.

Another way of seeing the idea of relevant and tangential is to think of a coercive behavior change strategy in contrast to a persuasive behavior change strategy. Some writers (Dienstbier *et al.*, 1975; Hoffman and Saltzstein, 1967) invoke a related dichotomous category, using terms like punishment–explanation, or power assertion–induction. The punishment strategies would be categorized at the irrelevant end of the irrelevant–relevant construct for categorizing reprimands. The state of one's pain receptors, for example, has little to do with the placement of one's elbows at the dinner table. The use of punishment informs the transgressor that the rule violation will produce pain stimuli, which, like many other kinds of irrelevant reprimand (for example, restriction of freedom, removal of positively valued objects, disfigurement) proves to be a disruption of core constructions applied to self. Thus, coercive reprimands do provide the transgressor with alternative constructions of the rule-related event. When he chooses to apply these kinds of constructions, however, he extends his construings of self state to subordinate rule violation. If the rule-related behavior becomes associated with his self-defining schema, he will thereupon anticipate relative to the rule within the same constructions by which he anticipates self-related events. Thus, he has extended and more precisely defined his construction system, but the extension subordinates the rule-related event to constructs which are tangential to the situation.

(ii) Is restitutive reprimand relevant?

Discussions of reprimand often develop a category called *restitutive* reprimand. In this kind of reprimand the transgressor is asked to rectify his wrong-doing by compensating the victim of his transgression. Can we fit the proposed category, tangential–relevant, to this category of reprimand? In many ways restitutive reprimand conveys the "whys" of the desired construction. Restitution can give the transgressor a vivid example of the consequences which his act has to others. In these ways, restitutive reprimand can evoke a relevant reconstruction of the event, in that the restitution can generate reconstruction relative to constructs like social distrust–trust, competitiveness–cooperativeness, and so on. The development of sympathetic distress and altruism, through the use of inductive reprimand, as described by Saltzstein (1976) and Hoffman (1976), would be attributed to this kind of reconstruction. However, if the transgressor were to construe the rule-related event entirely in terms of his ability to provide the restitution, then there would be a question about whether restitution is described by the relevant pole of the tangential–relevant construct as it is applied to reprimand.

(iii) Motives and relevance

Behavior scientists have generally conceptualized punishment as a direct causal stimulation. Pain stimulation has been regarded as a counter-energy to the energy which induces rule violation. The formulations in this chapter require the use of an entirely different conception of what has been called punishment. It is here proposed that thinking on the issues concerning reprimand will advance by adopting another view of motive. The suggested formulation grows out of Kelly's (1955) explanation of motives, as elaborated by some of the current thinking on attention and activation (Mancuso, 1977). Basically, it is argued, persons are activated toward reconceptualization and associated action at points where there is a discrepancy between available cognitive organization and sensory input.

An analysis of what is usually called punishment shows that the created condition invariably involves a presentation of stimuli which are difficult to intigrate with the transgressor's available constructions. When the transgressor avoids rule violation in order to avoid punishment, he is not seen as a person being pushed away from temptation by a counter energy. Rather, he is taken to be a person seeking to continue to anticipate events successfully by the continued application of his currently available constructions.

REVIEW

The major points are summarized as follows. We wish to understand those events which are ordinarily discussed as reprimand. Firstly, it is proposed that the main question should be restated so that one talks about a transgressor accepting a rule-giver's constructions of an event. Rules represent prescriptions for construing events. Secondly, we offer the proposition that a person will accept reprimand (another person's construction of an event) if he anticipates that doing so provides possibilities for extending and defining his existing construct systems. Kelly's Choice Corollary goes into full operation in a reprimand situation. Thirdly, reprimands invariably reveal the reprimander's understanding that he must show the transgressor that continuing the transgression will lead to a constriction and an invalidation of various aspects of the transgressor's existing system. To play the role of reprimander, one must construe the construction processes of the transgressor. Further, the construct tangential–relevant will be of considerable value in developing a personal construct treatment of reprimand. Finally, punishment; that is, tangential reprimand, is interpreted as a special case of stimulation that is not readily incorporated into the cognizer's construct system.

Related Research Programs

When one takes a personal construct approach to rule following and reprimand one will need to create data very different to those used to explicate the relationships within mechanistic explanations of reprimand. The constructivist, obviously, looks for data about people's constructions of causal influences relative to behavior. He can even entertain the possibility that the belief in "punishment" as a cause represents one possible causal attribution. His interest in this attribution would center on understanding of the causal functions of the attribution, rather than centering on the actual causal function of punishment. He would be interested, for example, in what happens when punishment is used to reprimand a transgressor who believes that punishment is a cause. In fact, the constructivist would theorize that people's beliefs about reprimand would, in themselves, figure causally into any reprimand situation. Overall, he would eventually want to explore the relationships between attributions about reprimand and the outcomes of a reprimand situation. The constructivist would see value in studying the relationships between a reprimander's causal attributions, the types of reprimands he uses, and the outcomes of reprimands in varied transgression situations. If we extend Kelly's Sociality Corollary to its limits, we would expect the successful reprimander to have developed a full repertoire of reprimand related constructs. Having achieved skill in construing reprimand he may play his role through being better able to construe the constructs by which the transgressor interprets and anticipates reprimand's functions.

The study by Bugental *et al*. (1977) illustrates the general trend of studies (Baron *et al*., 1974; Sherman, 1973) which explore the relationships between outcomes of behavior change strategy and the causal schemata of the target. Bugental *et al.* studied hyperactive boys. They used two motivating treatments. One half of the boys were provided with direct reinforcement for appropriate and effective task involvement. This treatment follows from mechanist principles of reinforcement as direct cause. The second half of the boys were subjected to an adaptation of the Meichenbaum and Goodman (1971) verbal mediation procedures. Essentially, the boys modelled overt self-controlling statements, and then were asked to use such statements covertly. By using video-taping of the child, asking him to report his covert speech, and so on, the child was coached to direct and evaluate his own performance. The motive principles assumed to work in this treatment are not clearly explicated.

One half of each of the two treatment groups (self control and direct reinforcement) was composed of boys who had been assessed to make internal control attributions. The other half of each treatment group was made up of boys who showed the use of external control attributions. Bugental *et al.* conclude,

> As predicted, attributions of causality were associated with differential effectiveness of the two intervention strategies. Behavior change was greater when the child's causal attributions matched the implicit attributional emphasis of the intervention. (p. 881)

This study, like other work which indicates that a person's expectations figure causally into the behavior change context (Kazdin and Wilcoxon, 1976), highlights the general issue of the role of expectation and anticipation in behavior change sequences. Specifically, one is encouraged to think about how expectation about reprimand might significantly influence reprimand outcomes. A psychologist who considers the applications of his discipline would immediately think about a reprimander's understandings of his target's expectations. Do different reprimanders differ in their understandings of such expectations? How do these understandings relate to success in playing the role of reprimander?

REPRIMANDER'S AND CHILDREN'S ATTRIBUTIONS

It would follow from the Bugental *et al.* study that a reprimander seeking to play a successful role in the reprimand process would consider the kinds of differing causal attributions made by children of varied developmental level. As noted, Piaget (1932) provided early evidence that children of different ages perceive reprimand differently.

Mancuso and Allen (1976) took a developmental perspective in their study of children's perceptions of reprimand's functions. These investigators studied children at the kindergarten, the third grade, and the sixth grade levels to record their judgments of the consequences of a transgressor exposed to three different conditions of reprimand. All the children watched a boy engage in the same transgression; and then observed the boy exposed to either no reprimand, coercive reprimand (tangential), or explanatory reprimand (relevant). Following the observations of the video-taped sequences the children responded to a global rating scale and a moral behavior prediction test developed for use by Morrison (Morrison, 1973, 1975; Mancuso *et al*., 1978). Children at different ages showed significantly different judgments of the persons in the different treatment conditions. The kindergarteners judged a reprimanded transgressor to be more bad than a non-reprimanded transgressor. They judged the transgressor as strongly negative and "unsocialized" regardless of how he had been reprimanded. Third grade children clearly differentiated the transgressor on the basis of the kind of reprimand he received. The coercively reprimanded transgressor was perceived to be more bad than was the non-reprimanded transgressor, whereas third graders judged the transgressor given the explanatory reprimand to be considerably more good than the non-reprimanded rule-breaker. Sixth graders showed yet another kind of perspective on transgression and reprimand. Reprimanded transgressors were judged to be more positive than was the non-reprimanded transgressor, and this was true regardless of the type of reprimand that had been administered.

Overall these findings can be interpreted as follows. The youngest children do not include the idea of behavioral change in their thinking about reprimand. In their realist world a reprimand serves only to balance the scales of justice, and thus, the person receiving the authority's reprimand has been labeled as bad, so that all the world may know of his evil. Third graders seem to continue to hold this same view of the purposes of coercive reprimand. When, however, they see the reprimander aim his reprimand at the transgressor's relevant constructions, they perceive the transgressor as more positive. (At this point one can only speculate on the nature of the cognitive processes which influence this judgment.) Apparently sixth graders think of both explanatory and coercive reprimand as having some kind of causal influence in inducing rule following in a transgressor. They see coercion as being associated with behavior change, but do not see it as a necessary condition. To sixth graders, explanatory reprimand—at least under the circumstances portrayed in these incidents—is causally related to rule following as effectively as is coercive reprimand.

Aldrich and Mancuso (1976) studied the matter of how children look upon reprimanded transgressors who, in turn, respond differentially to reprimand. The subjects watched a filmed portrayal of a child who had created accidental damage and thereupon was reprimanded by his mother.

The reprimand was judged to be an explanatory reprimand. Following the reprimand the transgressor was shown responding to the mother's verbal statements. In one condition he offered no response. In other conditions (1) he openly and honestly disagreed with his mother's assessment of the situation, or (2) he openly belittled his mother's reprimand, or (3) he openly accepted the reprimand, but upon his mother leaving the room he verbalized his annoyance, complaining that he had not been at fault in the transgression, or (4) he simply indicated that he would try to follow the mother's prescriptions.

Participants in the study then reflected their perception of the transgressor by responding to the Global Rating Scale (GRS) and the Moral Behavior Prediction Test (MBPT). Hypotheses were framed from two general assumptions, as follows: (1) Children in early stages of cognitive development—first graders—would not vary their negative judgments of an accidental transgressor in ways which would show that they were influenced by variations in response to reprimand. (2) Children in later stages of cognitive development—sixth graders—would judge a transgressor more positively if he responded to reprimand in ways which showed willingness to accept the reprimander's conception of the transgression event.

In this study the first graders, like the kindergarteners in the Mancuso and Allen study, indicated that they expected continuation of transgression from the transgressor who had been reprimanded. They did not, however, extend this view to the child who openly accepted the mother's reprimand. Apparently, even these young children regard open agreement as an indication of personal change. Sixth graders varied their judgments to reflect the variations in the transgressor's response to reprimand. Interestingly, when the child made *no response* to the reprimand given after this apparent accidental transgression, the sixth graders judged him to be more negative than was the child in the conditions where there was open response to reprimand. (Perhaps the children took no response to mean that the transgressor would not actively consider the reprimander's verbalized constructions of the transgression situation.) These older children indicated quite positive evaluations of the transgressor who responded to the mother's reprimand in ways that directly verbalized a willingness to consider (not necessarily accept) the mother's constructions of the events under consideration (open acceptance, open expression of his honest disagreement, and covert rejection), but showed a negative perception of the child who had responded by openly belittling the reprimand. The positive evaluation of the transgressor in the covert rejection situation ran counter to the hypothesis of the study, for it was expected that the observers would apply the view that the covert rejection represented a duplicity aimed at deceiving the reprimander. Apparently, however, 12-year-old children focus more on the transgressor

having avoided a direct invalidation of the mother's verbalized constructions, even though it was clear that he did not seriously try to integrate his
mother's construction of the event.

In other reports of continued study of perceptions of reprimand effectiveness, Handin and Mancuso (1978), and Mancuso and Handin (1978), and
Mancuso and Eimer (1978) present date which convey something about
how professional child care workers and school of education students construe varied reprimands. In these studies the participants observed
transgression-reprimand scenarios like those used in the Mancuso and Allen
(1976) studies, with a third type of reprimand, restitutive reprimand, being
portrayed as another variation.

On the basis of clinical observations in child care settings Mancuso and
Handin had developed the hypothesis that child care workers characteristically use implicit personality theories, relative to reprimand attributions, in
which retributive reprimand would align with the *bad* pole of a generalized
bad–good construct. Clinical experience also promoted the investigators to
believe that those workers who were most effective in their work with
children avoided the constant confrontation episodes that were generated
by workers judged to be less effective. Avoiding confrontation, it was
concluded, depended on the fact that effective workers, rather than being
guided by a mechanistic implicit personality theory were guided by a constructivist implicit personality theory. Rather than seeing their own reprimander's role as a matter of applying appropriate positive and negative
reinforcers, it was assumed that the effective workers' reprimands were
guided by their efforts to produce relevant invalidations which the transgressor could successfully integrate into his intact construct system. Thus the
effective workers would not conclude that every unwanted act would require
the creating of a negative, non-integrable state in the child. The children
under the care of the workers studied here were quite adept at retaliating at
the persons who were responsible for their aroused state; and such retaliat-
ory behavior, itself being unwanted, would induce some workers to apply
even more arousing stimulation. In this way, numerous confrontation
episodes were generated.

From this set of assumptions, it was predicted that most child care workers
would endorse explanatory and restitutive reprimands, whereas they would
show disapproval of retributive reprimands. Furthermore, it was predicted
that more effective child care workers would evaluate explanatory
reprimand more positively than would the less effective child care workers.

Overall, the predictions which guided the Mancuso-Handin work were
supported by the data. As in any investigation, however, one must introduce
a series of qualifications. In the first place, it appears as if the worker's
evaluations of reprimands are not subsumed directly to their *ineffective–*

effective construct. Instead, a *severity–leniency* construct appears to directly superordinate the reprimand type. One might believe that their *severity–leniency* construct would plot into the *ineffective–effective* hierarchy, but this does not seem to be the case. Instead, the *severity–leniency* construct appears to plot into a hierarchy that includes a *socially disapproved–socially approved* construct. And, of course, the *severity* pole, represented by retributive reprimands, aligns with the *socially disapproved* pole. The effectiveness construct appears to be embodied, statistically, in a separate discriminant function, which, incidentally, accounts for little of the variance in the differentiation of the perceived attributes of reprimand. In other words, these workers appear to be quite concerned about attributes of reprimand which have little to do with the reprimand's immediate effectiveness in altering the unwanted behavior.

To these child care workers and prospective teachers the restitutive reprimand is judged to be the most desirable reprimand technique. About 75% of all participants see restitution as the most proper and as the best teaching method of the three reprimand techniques. The retributive reprimand, seen as the most severe reprimand, was unanimously rejected by the participants of these studies; and 75% perceived it to be the least proper of the three methods. About 30% of the participants see explanation as the worst reprimand method and as least proper; whereas another 30% see explanation as the best teaching method and as the method most similar to their own approach.

The findings regarding the hypothesized relationships between worker effectiveness and personal construings of reprimand are tempered by the overall strong endorsement of restitutive reprimand. Nevertheless, when we find a participant judging explanation to be the desirable reprimand technique, or stating that explanation is like his own approach, we would also find that in about half the cases this person would be rated as highly effective by his co-workers. This simply is not the case for the lower rated workers. A very small percentage (about 15%) of lower peer-rated workers advocate explanatory reprimand.

Despite the equivocation that is introduced into the conclusions, these findings about worker effectiveness and choice of reprimand are taken as very meaningful results. The measure of worker effectiveness was obtained by having participants give to persons of their choice a questionnaire which was returned anonymously to the investigators. The chosen peers then rated the participants on ten scale items. A rater could not have predicted that a particular bias in his ratings would relate one or another way with the participant's ratings of the reprimand techniques. It is difficult, then, to believe that an extraneous biasing factor produced the observed results. Even if the raters had been biased by their own feelings toward the participants, one would want to explain why a worker who was well-liked would tend to be the same worker who endorsed explanation. Indeed, perhaps a person who used explanatory reprimand, built from evaluation of the other person's relevant constructions, would generally be more successful in his interpersonal interactions; so that his worker peers would think positively of him and would bring this positive perception into ratings of his effectiveness.

Some needed information

These first studies point out some directions to follow when exploring the ways in which reprimanders construe the reprimand situation. To explicate reprimand from a personal construct perspective one would want to clarify the finding that it is the judged-effective worker who is most likely to endorse the explanatory reprimand. We would deduce that his peers perceive that his reprimands, whether they are directed to his charges or to his peers, are gauged to produce an arousal level that is most likely to allow the transgressor to make a relevant cognitive reorganization of the rule-related event. Conversely, his reprimands do not create an excessive arousal level which encourages the transgressor to attend to escaping the arousal, which is itself tangential; nor does he introduce other tangential invalidations which can be evaded only through compliance. There needs to be, of course, validation of our constructions relative to the judged-effective worker and his reprimand techniques.

These studies also allowed a focus on another set of considerations which a successful reprimander would take into account as he construes the transgressor's system. The subjects in this study clearly expressed the need to take into account the transgressor's view of his relationship to the reprimander. We predict that the salient *severe–lenient* dimension will be shown to acquire its salience from consideration about the relationship between *severity–leniency* and the *negative–positive* character of the relationship between the transgressor and the reprimander. We would deduce that successful reprimanders implicitly know that severe reprimands from a person who is held in positive esteem would lower the esteem in which the reprimander is held. In this way, a severe reprimand from a positively regarded person would be less likely to bring about positive results in terms of long-term socialization efforts. On the other hand, people might expect that in an impersonal situation a severe reprimand is justified.

Whatever specific questions one may address within this approach to reprimand one may be sure that subjects do not judge reprimand effectiveness in terms of direct blocking of unwanted response and direct evocation and reinforcement of wanted responses. Even these simple studies show that adults and school-aged children employ complex constructions of the causal aspects of reprimand. Determinations of causal effects are made within an extended context in which the transgressor's total construct system is taken into account.

Conceptions of Causality and Reprimand

The behavior sciences have produced few satisfying clarifications of causality. The psychological literature on causality and reprimand, in fact, reveals little other than the lack of agreement that may pervade an area of study even after thousands of years of debate. It is easy to say that the main efforts of behavior scientists have been directed toward verifying the ancient, commonly held naive theories of "punishment". By applying the mechanist's paradigm, punishment has become the "aversive stimulation" which, in essence, stands in as the counter-energy to the "habit strength" or the "impulse" which supposedly provided the initial energy for the emission of the unwanted conduct. Despite recent systematic study a modern reprimander, working from the foregoing paradigm, would have no convincing advantage were he required to debate the topic of punishment with a resurrected governor of Roman Britain. The causal properties of aversive stimuli remain poorly defined, and behavioral scientists, even when they propose the validity of conceptualizing punishment as cause, are reluctant to advocate the wholehearted implementation of practices based on principles which are assumed to define the mechanistic causal relationships. Since studies have reached this kind of confused state, we suggest that investigators could profit from framing their work within another paradigm. Specifically, a contextualist paradigm, exemplified by Kelly's theory of personal constructs, might usefully explain the causal aspects of reprimand.

PUNISHMENT AS CAUSE

An investigator who tries to explicate the causal properties of punishment would be tempted to use the assumptive base provided by a mechanist paradigm. In this formulation punishment is treated, mechanistically, as the counter-energy which is applied *to cause* the disruption of the unwanted act.

Upon inquiry about the specific property of causal punishing stimuli, one meets some equivocation. Those who discuss punishment have been careful to point out that punishment is not necessarily equivalent to aversive stimulation (Johnson, 1972; Walters and Grusec, 1977). Instead, it is said, one best defines punishment as a stimulus that produces "a reduction in the future probability of the punished response" (Azrin and Holz, 1966, p. 382). But, which stimulus, of many thousands of possible sensory inputs that a reprimander might create, should be selected as the most effective input to deliver to a person who has performed an unwanted act? As Maurer (1974) has noted, a warm embrace will reduce the probability of the recurrence of weeping! If one agrees with Johnston (1974) that "By definition it is incorrect to specify a stimulus as punishment before that reduction in response rate has occurred" (p. 1040), then a reprimander must approach any reprimand situation with a willingness to select from an assortment of possible behaviors one random act, which can earn its status as punishment only after it has produced a response rate reduction.

To add to the confusion, commentators seem unable to resist the propensity to revert to the same kinds of implicit theory that guided Roman governors. Even an astute commentator can, as does Johnston, revert to the ancient maxim that more punishment, whatever it is, is better. Johnston included in his "list of methodological rules for maximizing the effectiveness of punishment procedures" the principle that "the initial intensity of the punishing stimulus should be as great as possible and continued intensities should also be at the highest reasonable levels" (p. 1034). Following these assumptions one may at least expect that a "stronger counter-force" will more effectively reduce re-occurrence of the unwanted response. Thus, if one chose, by chance, to use a branding iron as the source of the punishing stimuli, one would know, at least, that it should be white hot, and it should be kept white hot as it is applied; unless, of course, one is constrained by an inappropriate interpretation of Johnston's term "reasonable". Then the reprimander might conclude that "the highest reasonable" heat would be something less than white hot.

One suspects that the behavioral scientist, like the future educators and child care workers in the Mancuso-Handin-Eimer studies, would be constrained from offering unequivocal endorsement to a strict mechanistic view of reprimand. Our daily observations provide a constant stream of data to support an implicit personality theory within which we cannot incorporate a straightforward mechanistic view of reprimand. Mechanistic principles function well in the laboratory, where the investigator follows a view of science that forces him to search out nicely quantifiable variables to which he can attribute causality. In real life (and frequently in the laboratory) one must recognize that the transgressor's cognizing system is as much a "cause" (Bugental et al., 1977; Page, 1972) as the "reinforcement" offered by the investigator. Even the most convinced mechanist would hesitate to use electric shock as a means of reducing "out of seat behavior" in the three-year-old who is being introduced to the pleasures of sharing the family's dinner time. There would need to be some evidence that the child could construe his behaviors within the construct *out of seat behavior!* His constructions, then, are judged to have some relationship to the causal effectiveness of the reprimand.

What is caused?

It is perhaps trivial to observe that one need not look at causality from the mechanistic perspective, which Rychlak (1976) calls a "tracking approach" to science. Rather than focusing on predictions of the trajectory of discrete responses one may take the total context as the basic unit of study. One may then adapt the position that *contexts are determined*.

Specifically, the relationships between strands in the context are determined. Even more specifically, one predicts that any change in the relationship of one strand to other strands will cause counter reactions that will tend to preserve the original relationships. But, as Piaget notes when he describes the accommodation of a cognitive organization, the original relationships will never be totally achieved, so that novel reorganization is expected as a given. "The ineradicable contextualist categories may thus be said to be change and novelty" (Pepper, 1942, p. 235). Contexts flow, they are not to be conceptualized as discrete, unique events. This point is expanded by Neisser, who revised the model of cognition he (Neisser, 1967) had previously developed. In the first work perception had been treated as a static, temporally discrete affair. Neisser has subsequently advocated the perspective reflected in the following quotations:

> Not only reading, but also listening, feeling, and looking are skillful activities that occur over time. All of them depend on preexisting structure, here called schemata, which direct perceptual activity and are modified as it occurs. (Neisser, 1976, p. 14)
> At each moment the perceiver is constructing anticipations of certain kinds of information, that enable him to accept it as it becomes available. (p. 20)

To the contextualist psychologist the world is a flow of contexts—what a person "sees" in that flow moves out of what he "saw" in the immediately preceding event. In Kelly's (1955) system all of a person's processes are channelized by what he "saw" as the probable outcome of the event, and a person chooses to "see" events in ways that anticipate greater extension and definition of his existing system. To Niesser (1976) the flow of contexts involve schemata which direct the cognitive flow, as well as modify the input. There can be nothing that "suddenly appears" in that context—because the context must include the construction system by which one "looks", and nothing can suddenly jump into that constructive system. There can be slight alterations in the content of the system, and relationships may change—for example, what was subordinate can become superordinate, and conversely. Relationships change. The place to which they change is determined by what is already there. The flowing of the strands and the way that they converge and relate to each other will also determine the emerging relationships—but systemic reorganization follows, because those changed relationships will change other relationships.

If one holds this kind of view there is little value in talking about a cause and effect relationship as a truth, or in trying to state truths entirely in cause and effect terms. If change is constant, and if analysis is a matter of ferreting out the strands and their relationships, there is little value in pushing toward specifications of the *causes* of the ever changing context. The task is to describe contexts and the shifting of relationships in the flow of contexts.

In Kelly's (1955) theory of personal constructs this kind of causal scheme is expressed by the Fundamental Postulate, as supplemented by the Choice Corollary. The Fundamental Postulate echoes Pepper's dictum that change is a given in a contextualist perspective: "A person's processes are psychologically channelized by the ways in which he anticipates events" (p. 46). The Fundamental Postulate holds that the person, as a constantly moving process, is systematically directed. Anticipation guides the flow of the process. In a treatise which links Kelly's Fundamental Postulate to current work on attention and novelty, Mancuso (1977) concludes that, "A person's processes—his conduct—are directed toward those events which are incongruent with the internalized structures against which information has been monitored" (p. 65). In this way, anticipation is viewed in terms of a foreward projection of internalized structures. Powers (1973) uses a similar conceptualization to discuss the relationship between internal structures and action.

> If there are no effects in the environment tending to drive the controlled quantity away from the reference condition, there will be no change in the organism's pattern of behavior. Any disturbance, however, will call for an action which opposes the effects of the disturbance on the controlled quantity. (p. 48)

Note that in Powers' formulation *disturbances* are incongruities between feedback (sensory input) and the reference condition. The *reference condition* refers to "a *perceptual* condition—the perceived state of affairs, naturally from the subject's point of view and not the experimenter's, that calls for no change" (p. 46). To interchange terms, one could say that "a person's processes are psychologically channelized by the ways in which he acts to oppose the disturbances on the controlled quality". Or, if the reference condition capably anticipates, that is, fits, the sensory input there will be no action. At this point another set of stimuli which requires integration will be brought on to "central processor", and the flow of the context continues.

If the relationships in the psychological context remain out of phase, a new construction must be built by rearranging other constructs that are available in the person's memory store. A rearranged construction will emerge as a part of the total psychological context. The new construction will be constrained by a kind of economic demand. The new reference signal will be that which produces least disequilibration in the system.

It is assumed that the choice of a new reference signal will be limited to those that allow for "the greater possibility for extension and definition of [the person's] system" (Kelly, 1955, p. 64). The limits on change within a system, that is, the alternative reference signals that can be applied in a context, are established by the person's cognitive system, which is an integral strand in the total context.

Most importantly, this contextualist view of change and cause would be violated if one were to claim that the person's new reference signal or the actions associated with that reference signal are caused events. These strands of the context could be only artificially "lifted" from the context. *Changed relationships have been caused.* Relationships between the motor acts, the cognitive organizations, the sensory inputs, and so on, have changed. All of these strands had already existed in the context.

A simple illustration might be useful to concretize these abstractions. In a study intended to demonstrate constructivism in the processing of stimulus input, Paris (1975) read to children a story about a girl who was trying to devise a carrying box for a creature she had discovered near her house. The text says that the little girl "found eight sheets of yellow paper. She cut up the paper into little pieces, and put them in the bottom of the box" (p. 233). Almost every listener builds a construction which involves the girl holding a pair of scissors, cutting the paper, and putting the pieces into the box. One must conclude that the sensory input is held in short-term memory, that there is a search of the listener's memory for generic constructions which allow an incorporating of the specific input, that the schema "cuts with scissors" is a part of an act schema involving paper, that the schemata are "tried on" the data, and that the "fit" is precise enough to allow the context to flow forward. No arousal is generated, and no rearrangements of the person's construction system are required.

A small experiment is easily conducted by a lecturer who is explicating the above explanation. The story is read to the listener. After reading the phrases "she cut up the paper into little pieces, and put them in the bottom of the box", the reader pauses then says "she put away the meat cleaver . . ." Inevitably the listener will laugh. We may be sure that the laugh follows the resolution of the arousal generated by the requirement that one reconstrue a meat cleaver as an appropriate instrument for use as a paper cutter, especially by little girls. The arousal caused a change in the relationships between the schematizations applicable to the many elements of the context. No new strand need be introduced into the context. All were already available.

Reprimand Effectiveness Reconsidered

Every type of reprimand can have the effect of producing an incongruity between anticipatory constructions and the environmental feedback that registers on the sensory systems. Thus, violent reprimands, though tangential to construing the rule-related event, can invalidate the person's core self-defining constructions. The person's counter reactions toward restoring the original relationships in the context might generate a script in which compliance is enacted. Body pain, for example, is not an anticipated sensory input for most people. In contexts where a predictable state of affairs is restored by complying to avoid body pain an investigator could conclude that aversive stimulation counteracts the forces which maintain unwanted behavior. But an aspiring reprimander would be advised to avoid the belief that his reprimand is connected to the transgressor's action in a straight line causal sequence.

On occasion, a reprimanded transgressor can build anticipatory schemata which include a sub-schema in which his pain producing resources are superior to those of the reprimander. The transgressor could also be one of those "mentally ill' persons in whose construct system *pain* aligns with *good*. Such cases of "hyper-aggressiveness" and "masochism" should encourage abandonment of mechanistic causality conceptions in reprimand explanation. Again, they illustrate that effectiveness can best be attributed to a reprimand by considering the context that includes the transgressor's construction of the reprimand, his self role definition, and his construction of his relationship to the reprimander.

The thesis of this chapter is based on the assumptions that the successful reprimander (a) takes into account the strands of the existing transgression context, particularly the transgressor's construct system; and (b) implicitly knows that his reprimand will succeed only if it brings about that level of contextual disequilibrium which allows a shifting of contextual relationships. In short, we are tacitly accepting the assumption that persons, in their everyday work as practising psychologists, implicitly use a conception of causality that had been advocated by Jung (1960) who was very critical of the causal conception embedded in Freud's mechanistic theory of behavior. People carry out their reprimand activity from a contextualist perspective, using the kinds of causal conceptions that are compatible with contextualist paradigms.

Suitable studies should show that reprimanders implicitly calculate the "fit" of their communication and the transgressor's cognitive systems. An appropriate reprimand would allow the transgressor to evolve a hypothesis that promises to extend his personal construct system by adopting the construction offered by the reprimander. These propositions, in effect, echo

Kelly's (1955) Sociality Corollary, in that they reflect the proposition that to the extent that a reprimander "construes the construction processes of another (the transgressor), he may play a role in the social process involving the other person" (p. 95). In short, *the reprimander manipulates the motivational conditions of the situation by manipulating his communication relevant to the transgressor's cognitive system*. If the reprimander has an understanding of the transgressor's construction of the event—the "rule" which led to the transgression—and if he has an understanding of the relationships of that "rule" to other aspects of the subject's cognitive organization, he can construct a reprimand that will promise to bring about a desired rearrangement of the transgressor's organizations relative to that rule. Under these circumstances the transgressor is expected, in effect, to adopt the new "rule", that is, the reprimander's construction of the event, and this rearrangement of the rule-relevant construction should terminate the disequilibrium which the reprimander had introduced. When the reprimander's construing of the transgressor's system informs him that a violent reprimand will bring about the needed rearrangement it is probable that violent reprimand will succeed. In another context, where the transgressor has developed a particular kind of construct system, the reprimander might effectively play a role relative to that transgressor's system by using an explanatory reprimand.

A reconsideration of reprimand, using a contextualist paradigm, could divert behavioral scientists away from a search for specific effective reprimand techniques. Any number of techniques would be effective, so long as they serve to provide the transgressor with a mode of construing events which would allow for appropriate extension and definition of his construction system. At best, investigators might search out effective reprimanders, that is, persons who are implicitly aware of Kelly's Sociality and Choice Corollaries.

References

Aldrich, C. C. and Mancuso, J. C. (1976). *Percept. Mot. Skills* **43**, 1071–1082.

Aronfreed, J. and Reber, A. (1965). *J. Personal. Soc. Psychol.* **1**, 3–16.

Azrin, N. H. and Holz, W. C. (1966). *In* "Operant Behavior" (Ed. W. K. Honig), pp. 380–447. Appleton-Century-Crofts, New York.

Bandura, A. and Walters, R. H. (1963). "Social Learning and Personality Development". Holt, Rinehart and Winston, New York.

Baron, R. M., Cowan, G., Ganz, R. L. and McDonald, M. (1974). *J. Personal. Soc. Psychol.* **30**, 285–292.

Bugental, D. B., Whalen, C. K. and Henker, B. (1977). *Child. Develop.* **48**, 874–884.

Dienstbier, R. A., Hillman, D., Lehnhoff, J., Hillman, J. and Valkenaar, M. C. (1975). *Psychol. Rev.* **82**, 299–315.

Eysenck, H. J. (1964). "Crime and Personality". Routledge and Kegan Paul, London.

Glueck, S. and Glueck, E. T. (1950). "Unravelling Juvenile Delinquency". Harvard University Press, Cambridge, Mass.

Handin, K. H. and Mancuso, J. C. (in press). *J. Soc. Psychol.*

Hoffman, M. L. (1976). *In* "Moral Development and Behavior" (Ed. T. Lickona), pp. 124–143. Holt, Rinehart and Winston, New York.

Hoffman, M. L. and Satzstein, H. (1967). *J. Personal. Soc. Psychol.* **5**, 45–57.

Jenkins, J. J. (1974). *Am. Psychol.* **29**, 785–795.

Johnston, J. M. (1972). *Am. Psychol.* **27**, 1033–1054.

Jung, C. G. (1960). *In* "The Collected Works of C. G. Jung" (Eds H. Reed, M. Fordham, G. Adler), Vol. VIII. Pantheon, New York.

Kazdin, A. E. and Wilcoxon, L. A. (1976). *Psychol. Bull.* **83**, 729–578.

Kelly, G. A. (1955). "The Psychology of Personal Constructs". Norton, New York.

Mancuso, J. C. (1977). *In* "Nebraska Symposium on Motivation: Personal Construct Psychology" (Ed. A. W. Landfield), pp. 43–97. University of Nebraska Press, Lincoln.

Mancuso, J. C. and Allen, D. (1976). *Hum. Devel.* **19**, 277–290.

Mancuso, J. C. and Eimer, B. (in press).

Mancuso, J. C. and Handin, K. H. (in press).

Mancuso, J. C., Morrison, J. K. and Aldrich, C. C. (1978). *J. Genet. Psychol.* **132**, 121–136.

Maurer, A. (1974). *Am. Psychol.* **29**, 614–626.

Meichenbaum, D. H. and Goodman, J. (1971). *J. Abnorm. Psychol.* **77**, 115–126.

Morrison, J. K. (1973). Unpublished doctoral dissertation, State University of New York, Albany.

Morrison, J. K. (1975). *In* "Children's Behavior" (Ed. H. C. Lindgren), pp. 15–22. Mayfield, Palo Alto, California.

Neisser, U. (1967). "Cognitive Psychology". Appleton-Century-Crofts, New York.

Neisser, U. (1976). "Cognition and Reality". Freeman, San Francisco.

Paris, S. G. (1975). *In* "Cognitive Theory" (Eds F. Restle, R. Schiffrin, J. Castellan, H. Lindman and D. Pisoni, Vol. I, pp. 227–241. Lawrence Erlbaum Associates, Hillsdale, New Jersey.

Parke, R. D. (1969). *Child Devel.* **40**, 213–235.

Parke, R. D. and Walters, R. (1967). *Monog. Soc. Res. Child Develop.* **32** (1, Serial No. 109).

Pepper, S. C. (1942). "World Hypotheses". University of California Press, Berkeley.

Piaget, J. (1932). "The Moral Judgment of the Child". Kegan Paul, London.

Powers, W. T. (1973). "Behavior: The Control of Perception". Aldine, Chicago.

Rumelhart, D. E. and Ortony, A. (1977). *In* "Schooling and the Acquisition of Knowledge" (Eds R. Anderson and W. Montague), pp. 99–135. Lawrence Erlbaum Associates, Hillsdale, New Jersey.

Rychlak, J. F. (1976). *Personal. Soc. Psychol. Bull.* **2**, 213–228.

Saltzstein, H. D. (1976). *In* "Moral Development and Behavior" (Ed. T. Lickona), pp. 253–265. Holt, Rinehart and Winston, New York.

Sarbin, T. R. (1977). *In* "Nebraska Symposium on Motivation: Personal Construct Psychology" (Ed. A. W. Landfield) pp. 1–41. University of Nebraska Press, Lincoln.

Sears, R. R., Maccoby, E. E. and Levin, H. (1957). "Patterns of Child Rearing". Row, Peterson, Evanston, Illinois.

Sherman, S. J. (1973). *J. Personal. Soc. Psychol.* **26**, 23–29.

Snyder, M. (1976). *In* "New Directions in Attribution Research" (Eds J. H. Harvey, W. J. Ickes, and R. F. Kidd), pp. 53–72. Lawrence Erlbaum Associates, Hillsdale, New Jersey.

Solomon, R. L., Kamin, L. J. and Wynne, L. C. (1953). *J. Abnorm. Soc. Psychol.* **48**, 291–302.

Walters, G. C. and Grusec, J. E. (1977). "Punishment". W. H. Freeman, San Francisco.

Whiting, J. W. and Child, I. L. (1953). "Child Training and Personality". Yale University Press, New Haven, Connecticutt.

Wortman, C. B. (1976). *In* "New Directions in Attribution Research" (Eds J. H. Harvey, W. J. Ickes, and R. F. Kidd), pp. 23–52. Lawrence Erlbaum Associates, Hillsdale, New Jersey.

The Personal and the Interpersonal in Construct Theory: Social and Individual Aspects of Relationships

Steve Duck

It is curious that the area of interpersonal attraction and social relationships is one that has been largely neglected by research workers who adopt a Kellyan perspective. It is "curious" because Kelly himself (partly because of his involvement with psychotherapy and partly because he was very much interested in the issue of the development of "self" and thereby relationships with others) would certainly have thought it a primary issue. Indeed, it is not as if Kelly himself did not have several stimulating insights into the nature of social relationships (e.g. Kelly, 1969a) and although his analysis does need re-evaluating in the light of illuminating work done from other perspectives (Clore, 1977), his general approach can be shown to tie together some interesting themes which have wide-ranging implications (Duck, 1973, 1977a,b). To consider these contributions adequately it is necessary to approach the problem from two angles: first, to consider Kelly's theoretical analysis of the nature of individuality and sociality (including his views about the main ingredients of social dependency); and second to expound some of the theoretical work that has been done by other thinkers on the question of the development of social relationships from first encounter to close friendship.

PCT and the Nature of Individuality in Social Settings

For Kelly (1955) a person's individuality is defined by the system of constructs that he relies upon in order to anticipate events. Persons erect for their convenience in anticipating the replication of events, a system which is uniquely theirs and one which reflects their view of events, their anticipation of the future, their own interpretation of the systems that lie beneath the reality we all somehow experience. In other language (Kelly, 1969b) this means that a person should not be seen as if he were a prisoner of events. Since he can manipulate events, through interpretaion of them, the person can assume reality without having to believe that his life is run by it. Each person is charged with the task of erecting and elaborating a system of interpretation of reality that helps him cope with the unfolding future.

It must be clear, however, that a complete independence from reality or a complete insufficiency of constructive contact with the outside world and the people in it would be strange and unsatisfactory. To deal with events the person needs to have an adequate constructive apparatus, and to deal with other people the person needs not only to be able to construe them adequately but also to share certain construct systems with them so that communication and social life become possible. In this context, "adequate" and "adequately" mean that the system of constructs must have a degree of validity in interpreting the world and its occupants. But how does a person decide whether his system (or part of it) is valid? As noted by Festinger (1954), in another context entirely, individuals can evaluate their opinions and abilities by two means: physical and social. The brittleness of glass can be assessed by the physical agency of a hammer; the individual's athletic prowess can be evaluated by comparison of his own athletic performance with the performance of other, similar persons. More abstract concepts (e.g. the nature of justice; the rightfulness of capital punishment; the attractiveness of that third year student) can, to an extent, be assessed by comparing one's own opinions or reactions with the opinions or reactions of other people. Whilst the choice of person with whom to compare oneself (and, ultimately, the judgement about what the comparison portends) rests with oneself, the validity or acceptability of certain opinions (or constructs) can be established in some degree by such comparisons. There are, however, many degrees and levels of "validity" in this context and they take their significance from the degree or level of concept that is being tested (Duck, 1973). Thus one can ask other people whether they also saw a pink elephant just now ("Is it there?") or whether "these" are "eggs" ("Is this opinion acceptable?")—and a whole range of other things. The answers given by other people will help the individual to decide about the validity of his experience of reality.

As Kelly has often pointed out, however, reality is not static. Things change, events do not repeat themselves exactly, people undergo transformation, individuals develop new breadths of vision. In order to respond to the natural changes in himself and in the outside world, the individual needs to adapt his construct system and to develop his self in various important and unimportant ways. These changes are, crucially, not sudden upheavals where Income Tax collectors, taking to vodka, suddenly turn into playboys and gigolos. Typically they are the minute but continual developments of perspective that we call ageing, experience, growth and the like. They are not brief earthquakes in the self but continual tremors.

Naturally each and every change presents the individual with a new problem of validity: each new perspective has to be tested—and that is what makes the human enterprise both exciting and worth doing. Each act, each change of perspective asks a new question (Kelly, 1970) and requires the testing out and validating of each new answer. Thus the problem of validity is a continual and recurrent one and the unique relationship between individual validation and social relationships becomes especially important. Fortunately, human relationships and the opportunity for validation are also continual and recurrent. Thus, in the normal course of human events the individual is able to engage in continual test and re-evaluation of his changing ways of looking at the world and its contents. Apart from this an essential aspect of relationships is that they themselves are also continually unfolding, developing, moving, dynamic and variable (there are even days when we hate those that we love!).

SOCIAL SETTINGS AND INTERPERSONAL RELATIONS

Clearly a large class of contents of the world consists of people. The implications of living as an individual in a social context are manifold, especially when these parts of the social context keep coming up to one and introducing themselves. The questions that these introductions pose for the individual are manifold and multi-layered: the individual needs to choose appropriate roles for successful social interaction; is occasionally faced with the problem of which role to adopt; and often has to decide between a formal "pure role" interaction and a more intimate or friendly one. What does Kelly say about this?

The nature of the benefits and obligations of social interaction have perhaps received rather narrow attention in Kelly's thinking. The Sociality Corollary of Kelly's (1955) theory is a relatively familiar but also a rather bare statement about social interaction when taken on its own out of the context of Kelly's other work and work by non-Kellyans. It states that "To the extent that one person construes the construction processes of another person, he may play a role in social processes involving that other person". It has been observed, however, that one can construe the construction processes of one's mother-in-law. Furthermore, the fact that one can construe the construction processes of a young child does not adequately account for one's feelings towards a child, and it is also clear that the interaction is somewhat one-sided. Kelly is, however, in a quite subtle way, noting that one's ability to play a role with someone else is limited by (*not* established by) one's understanding of the other person's construction scheme. Thus confidence tricksters rely on the fact that they have a better grasp of the "mark's" constructs than the mark does of theirs. On the other hand, whilst Kelly's view may be a useful one for characterising what occurs in a given interaction, the Sociality Corollary itself describes no mechanisms for choice between different associates: it tells us about the limits on people's ability to function together in an interaction without telling us how they came to be together in the first place nor whether this came about through mutual choice or not. What, in Kelly's view, could be the basis of choice or attraction, on the one hand, and of the decision to become intimate with some people on the other, holding the rest at the distance of formal role interactions? I think that Kelly could have offered one answer to this query by conjoining the Sociality and Commonality Corollaries. The Commonality Corollary states that "To the extent that one person employs a construction of experience which is similar to that employed by another, his processes are psychologically similar to those of the other person". Taking the Commonality and Sociality Corollaries together, one could then argue—Kelly did not—that, since similarity (commonality) of constructs makes them easier to understand, similar individuals will find it easier to understand one another and to play social roles together. They will thus prefer one another's company.

In my view (Duck, 1973, 1977b) a better argument can also be provided without doing violence to Kelly's postulates and corollaries. This argument is based on the ideas outlined by workers in non-Kellyan frameworks (e.g. Byrne, 1971; Clore, 1977) and concerns the notion of validity of constructs that was described earlier. In my view, people prefer others who have similar constructs since this provides the opportunity to validate the constructs concerned. This argument is rather more complicated than that (see below), but that is the basic theme which can be interwoven with several of Kelly's other ideas to produce a coherent and cogent view of the nature of interpersonal relations.

So far, however, the discussion has concerned the ability to enact a social relationship, or the factors which might make someone prefer one person to another. Neither of these is quite the same thing as being attracted to someone else or taking steps to associate with them (for example, one may prefer one person to another as the lesser of two evils without feeling attracted in the true sense). As Kelvin (1977) has rightly pointed out, attraction to someone is self-imposed; that is, people do not attract us against our will but we have to accept or decide that the inducements they offer actually are desirable. Hence two people can come to different conclusions about the attractiveness of the same other person. Also, in deciding to be attracted to someone else the individual begins to make himself vulnerable to that person; when the relationship develops or deepens so the areas and depth of vulnerability increase, as more private areas of one's self are disclosed (Kelvin, 1977); so we need to think hard also about the dynamics of acquaintance. Kelly (1969a) almost arrived at the same point, but from his clinical perspective he chose to emphasise another facet of vulnerability: namely, dependency. Kelly perceptively recognised the important place that dependency plays as an ingredient of interpersonal attraction, liking and more general human relationships. For Kelly, dependency in human relationships was not a blameworthy thing, but rather something to be regarded as an entirely natural ingredient of relationships. He argued (Kelly, 1969a) against the tendency to encourage independence at all costs, since it ultimately, in a thoroughgoing analysis, makes social nonsense to do so. His view was that dependency was no bad thing in human affairs but that society had a wrong view of it and did not do enough to ensure that it was allocated wisely.

Dependency, for Kelly, amounted to a form of security which all people require in different degrees at different times in different forms in different relationships. Naturally Kelly's clinical concerns made him rather more aware of the harmful effects of some of society's views about dependency and may even, to some extent, have provided him with a model for human relationships. Indeed, the ways that therapy proceeds are often a reflection of processes in the outside world of acquainting (disclosure, reassurance of worth, and so on; Duck, 1977b). Most important, however, are the implications that dependency has for sharing in a relationship.

Interesting and useful though such thinking is, and although it clearly identifies an important general ingredient of social relationships, it still tends to focus attention on a general predisposing tendency for people to associate with one another generally—to "be social"—rather than identifying a precipitating cause that induces particular instances of personal liking. In a sense this highlights the difference between sorts of social relationships, some of which come about through a general human interdependency and some of which evolve into particular friendship and close personal relationships. Thus some "relationships" are little more than the random association of two sets of social protoplasm, or the momentary conjunction of two people who serve functions for each other with no depth or permanence to the relationship (shop assistant and customer, telephone operator and caller, for instance). Others are different in implication, depth and permanence (lovers, friends, family, work-team members). These differences in gross type of relationship are defined in terms of, and carry implications for, the sorts of sharing and interdependency upon which the interaction rests. Thus friends are expected to share more than a common interest in a given consumer durable or six digit number. These, however, are resources, goods, concrete items, "things" that can be shared or exchanged (often physically) in interaction. The sort of sharing that I am most interested in at this point is the psychological sharing that creates interdependence.

As argued above, psychotherapy, whilst it has many parallels with the processes occurring in other social settings (Dewhurst and Duck, 1978), is hardly the paradigm for other forms of social interaction. However, between psychotherapy and social relating it could be argued that there are differences of degree but not of kind. In both, the partners reveal things about themselves by degrees, perhaps reluctantly; in both at least one partner attempts to encourage the other by warmth and openness; in both at least one partner tries to meet the other's need for various kinds of help and support; in both a satisfactory form of the relationship proceeds dynamically, by degrees from one level or form of interaction to another; in short, it develops and changes.

A similar point can be made about other types of social relationship: that they differ in degree rather than in kind. Indeed, it has been proposed (Duck, 1973) that social relationships can be defined in part in terms of the kind of sharing that takes place. I do not mean this in terms of the kinds of exchange resource that occur (e.g. information for information; money for love, Foa and Foa, 1971; La Gaipa, 1977) but in terms of the concepts, constructs or dimensions of thought that are shared. For example, to enter into any kind of relationship with anyone, some form of communication needs to be shared, whether it be a common language, a shared system of signs, a communal culture, or an agreed set of ideas and beliefs. The kind of relationship that is implied in each case does, to some extent at any rate, depend on the kinds of things that are shared: for instance, if two people share the same language and cultural assumptions but not the same beliefs then their relationship is likely to be a polite formal one rather than an intimate one. This stimulates the thought that part of the business of changing the nature of a relationship as it develops (e.g. growth in intimacy) is centred upon changing the level of sharing in this special sense. I want to go on to argue that personal relationships are nurtured not only by the sharing of ideas, language and so on, but by sharing of *constructs*, or ways of looking at or reacting to, the world. In this sense, it is possible to regard constructs as a class of entity that differs from "language" or "ideas" or "attitudes" and to see them as a set of cognitive building blocks that can be made into attitudes, ideas or language. Thus to share constructs is to share the things that lie behind attitudes, etc. and thus to share something primary to them. But I wish also to emphasise the implications that this notion has for the interpretation and explanation of the dynamic changes taking place as relationships develop.

It is also possible to see that "constructs" are a large class of heterogeneous items that can itself be subdivided. Thus we can have constructs about things, about events or about people; we can construe people as people, or as people in relation to their environment; or we can construe relations between people in the same environment; and so on. We can construe people in terms of their outward physical appearance, their visible behaviour, their roles or their psychological characteristics. All of these ways of construing people are different levels of construing and all of them can be shared with other individuals. Perhaps at this slightly more sophisticated level we can begin to talk of types of construct sharing as the basis for personal relationships and relationship growth.

Now of course some construct sharing reflects nothing particular about the relationship of the two people concerned. As Kelly (1970) pointed out, man's ability to construct alternative ways of construing events is limited by his feeble wits, his timidity, and his laziness, amongst other things. Although individuals can be individual, they also have some commonalities by virtue of their membership of the human race, a given culture, a particular region, a single street or the same family. These however are, in general terms, not the interesting commonalities (except in so far as the above list implies that these will be a basis for distinguishing families, streets and so on).

It does make quite a difference to how we react to personal construct theory, however, if we start to draw distinctions between different types of constructs and different levels of construct and then go on to say that the sharing of, or the validation of, these construct levels is *functional* for individuals. Without opportunities to test out the validity of different levels of constructs, a person's system would lack its essential validational support and his psychological integrity would be shaken or sapped. As an indication of this possibility, Duck (1975) studied the relationship between adolescents' friendship choices and their personality development and concluded that friendship choice with similar others provided adolescents with an impetus to development: to develop a new style of construing (as occurs in adolescence) is to develop a need for validating it and friendship with a similar other satisfies that need, whilst also introducing the partners to a fuller range of constructs than they presently possess. This argument has also been extended to the interactions of children and their development of adult ways of viewing the world and the social relationships in it (Duck *et al.*, in press). In these special cases, then, the development of personality is related functionally to social interaction just as, in general, in adult interaction sustenance of personality is so related. The personal and the interpersonal thus have close links. When one considers also the dynamic nature of social relationships and the ways in which they grow or change then these links can be seen to be even more powerful and useful to the individuals concerned. Establishing that one is initially similar in outlook to one's partner is a way of providing a good basis for exploring further, finding out more and coming to know him (and possibly, to like him) more deeply.

Before proceeding to develop this argument I should again stress Kelly's implicit point that similarity to another person and knowledge of him are not the same thing. Kelly distinguished between commonality (similarity) and sociality (based on knowledge) and it is clear that cases can be devised where either is greater than the other: thus, one can know more about a child's system than one has in common with it; and can have a large number of similarities with a trickster's system without understanding it sufficiently. Whilst it is knowledge of the other's construct processes that limits our ability to interact with him ("play a role in social processes involving him") it is the similarity and its implied validation for the shared construct system that is the engine of interaction. What is important as the above discussion shows, is to see that this knowledge of the other person and this similarity to him can occur at several different levels (whether simultaneously or not) and that it is the highest level at which it occurs that exposes the limits of the relationship and defines the kind of interaction that can follow.

Social and Personal Relationships

Up until now I have been using the terms "personal relationships" and "social relationships" more or less interchangeably, but enough has now been said to form the basis of a categorical change of usage in the rest of the chapter. Having drawn a distinction between the two in this section, I can then proceed in the next section to discuss several different types of personal relationships. The basis for the major distinction here is in terms of interchangeability of partners: social relationships are those where almost any other human would serve equally well; personal relationships occur where a change in partner means a different relationship altogether. This basic idea will be elaborated below and related to the differing validation functions that different relationships serve for the individual's construct systems. We need therefore to go further into the issues surrounding the functions of relationships and the nature of validity and dependence in order to consider the sense of the distinction being drawn here.

ORIGINS AND FUNCTIONS OF RELATIONSHIPS

There are many causes for relationships that have little direct connection with the fulfilment of some psychological need. Amongst these causes would be things like propinquity or frequency of interaction, which may precipitate relationships; or economic dependence or instructional relationship (teacher/pupil) or common activities (like being members of the same tennis club) and so on. Whilst such things provide opportunities for interaction and predispose people to relationships, they do not provide a sufficient psychological explanation for their final occurrence.

It is a little surprising that even attraction researchers have done little work on the origins of different sorts of relationships and it has only recently become a matter of great interest to attempt distinctions and definitions of different sorts of relationships (Huston, 1974; Levinger, 1974; Duck, 1977a; Huston and Levinger, 1978). Indeed until relatively recently research on interpersonal attraction has been almost exclusively concerned with one specific sort of "relationship"; namely, first encounter with a (bogus) stranger. For these sorts of reason the mammoth task of constructing a taxonomy of relationships tends to have been overlooked and, for example, Maslow's (1953) notion of a hierarchy of needs and its implications for such a taxonomy has not yet received the attention that it deserves. It is also immensely important that people cease regarding relationships as static, fixed phenomena and begin to regard them as fluid, dynamic, and developing things.

Researchers are now agreed, perhaps, that there are at least three gross categories of phenomena under the umbrella of interpersonal attraction. They distinguish *general affiliation* (a seeking out of company, whoever it is, or the general tendency of humans to be sociable); *short-term encounters* (for instance, encounters with strangers) and *developing relations* (particularly courtship and long-term friendship). This gross trichotomy is, however, only one way of slicing the conceptual cake. We could just as well divide the realm of discourse into those relationships where people act truly as themselves, and those where rules, roles and social norms make the consequent interaction rather more formal. (This is difficult ground to tread, given the work of Mead and others who maintain that the distinction is not that simple.) Equally, we could concentrate on a distinction between the ways in which relationships start, the ways they develop and how they are maintained—a set of distinctions that have certain areas of overlap with the other conceptualisations proposed.

Various explanations are offered for man's affiliative tendencies, and to some extent these reflect the fact that the term has two meanings: (i) human social tendencies; (ii) the general sociability levels of individuals. Many of these explanations go back to man's animal origins (Tiger and Fox, 1972) and point out that needs for defence or conjoint activity in hunting food may have been original causes for sociability. Other work (e.g. Mehrabian and Ksionzky, 1974) speaks of a history of reinforcement experiences which has gradually predisposed an individual to expect certain types of thing to happen to him in interactions with others and has thus made him largely affiliative or largely "flightful". More acute causes of affiliation are seen to arise where anxiety or need for self-evaluation are momentarily high (Schachter, 1959). These seem to me to be both useful and unsatisfactory explanations. They usefully identify cases where an individual may feel a surge of affiliation coming upon him, but they do not identify the mainspring of affiliation in Kellyan language or terms compatible with it. Nor do they seem to me to be describing—nor in most cases do they claim to be describing—deep personal relationships in any clearly recognisable form. Clearly, however, they are describing components of relating at some level and I would count such relating as is provoked by these "general tendencies" as "social relationships", i.e. those relationships where the individual relates not to someone specific but to "faceless" others, interchangeable others, others who have no single, personal attractiveness to him as individuals, but a general, diffuse attractiveness simply as members of the human race. These approaches describe circumstances where someone seeks "related-ness" in preference to non-relatedness, or they offer general explanations why man is a social animal. They are not explanations of specific individual selections of associates, still less are they explanations (or even descriptions) of close personal ones.

Other work in interpersonal attraction concerns not the vibrant reciprocity of working personal relations, but the initial attraction of one person to another (often a fictitious other who is experienced only through the mediation of (rigged) written questionnaires or (falsified) tape recording). Explanations of such attraction focus on things like physical attractiveness, reinforcement, similarity, information processing and general approaches to the assembly of information into affective responses. Again, I do not experience the feeling of satisfaction that is supposed to suffuse someone hearing a convincing explanation. *Why* is a physical attractiveness attractive? Do people *just* like aesthetically pleasing others or is there more to it? Is physical attractiveness attractive only in reduced stimulus conditions and does it perhaps lose some of its appeal when one has to interact with the physically attractive other? Might physically attractive people be liked for some reason that is not just skin deep (because an attractive personality is presumed, for example)? Are people just pushed and pulled by stimuli like physical attractiveness, or, with Kelly and Kelvin, must we accept that this type of explanation is both circular and simplistic? Whatever explanation one wishes to offer for the attractiveness of such things, however, they are *not* explanations that go to the root functions of relationships. They take a narrow and one-sided view of interpersonal attraction and act as if decisions about relationships are all in the hands of one individual in the pair (i.e. the one reacting to the stimuli that the other displays). We now know that these views are inadequate, and whatever good experimental, practical reasons there may be for adopting such an approach to interpersonal attraction, it remains too narrow to be convincing. One needs to ask the wider question: what functions do these attractive stimuli serve for the individual and what do these functions imply about the nature and structure of personal relationships?

So these explanations of attraction and attractiveness are not—and usually, in fairness, one must admit that they do not claim to be—complete explanations of deep personal relationships, still less explanations of how initial attraction to a stranger gets converted into a deep, involving, evolving, progressive, dynamic, programmatic personal relationship. I shall have more to say about the development of relationships below, so let us look for a moment at the kinds of relationships that do need the kind of explanation that I am seeking. Several can be differentiated *a priori* and split into those that are (like those above) at the reactive end of a continuum from reaction to relationship; others are social relationships of the kind delineated above; and some are personal relationships in the sense that I want to develop here. Whilst doing this I will try to bring the notion of validation back to the front of the argument.

VALIDATION IN RELATIONSHIP

Types of relationship could be proposed by means of several different taxonomies. For example, Foa and Foa (1971) define relationships in terms of the resources that are exchanged during an interaction. They distinguish six resource classes (Love, Services, Goods, Money, Information and Status) which can be conceptualised as differing in concreteness (Goods and Services are highly concrete, Status and Information lowly concrete) and particularism (Love is most particularistic; Money is least particularistic). Various combinations of these resources can be permuted to assess the type of relationship that is implied.

This is undoubtedly one useful way of looking at relationship processes in certain circumstances, but it is clearly rather more concerned with the *conduct* of relationships than with their origins and functions. I would suggest that a typology of functions for relationships can be provided on the basis of the validation that occurs in them. In some relationships the validation occurs without sharing or agreement, in a one-sided way: thus in establishing a power relationship over someone else the individual is able to validate certain aspects of his construct system that relate to his own competence as an individual. Perhaps this is the cause of the frequent cruelties that are inflicted on the weak or conquered: "Look, I am competent, able to deal with the world, after all. I told you so and I'm proving it to us both by doing this to you". This is rather reminiscent of what Kelly had to say about hostility in social relationships and it is important to consider these strongly distorted or "skewed" relationships, just as it is important to explain the functions of negativity in relationships. A Darwinian, for example, may want to argue that the existence of an observable variety of feelings and emotional states is testament to their functional importance to an individual or culture: those are retained and discriminated which protect either a society's efficient working or an individual's psychological integrity. It is in its powers to explain the functions that negativity can serve an individual that testament can be found to the value of Kelly's theory in this area. I believe that Kelly could explain negativity and positivity in relationships in a single explanatory framework—if one imports this idea of validation or elaboration of the construct system as a mainspring of relating.

Kelly had little to say about negativity in general except for one crucial form: hostility. For Kelly, hostility was an attempt to extract evidence from the environment for a form of social prediction that is already recognised to have failed; as when a child throws a temper tantrum to convince the neighbours that its parents have made a horrible mistake (Kelly, 1969c, p. 276). In our terms, this "extracting of evidence" is a form of validation, when all else has failed. Becoming hostile would then, from a Kellyan perspective, be a way of validating parts of the construct system, just as is achieved in liking and positive personal relationships in a different form.

What forms of validation are there, then, and do the two methods that are implied here differ? For Kelly, an individual is continually in search of means of elaborating his construct system and thus in search of better ways of coping with events. Elaboration of the system can take two forms (Duck, 1977b): definition and extension. *Definition* of part of the system occurs either when a person underlines some of his constructs and comes to believe in them in six foot high capitals, as it were (for example, in hostility), or when he is able to add finer and finer discriminations to his existing set (as, for example, happens when someone takes an instructional course in, say, physics and has his existing common sense views of "heat" made a bit more sophisticated). *Extension* of the system occurs when the individual comes to grips with areas of the world and of experience which previously lay outside of the system (as for example, when someone introduces him to aspects of life that are new to him, e.g. ornithology or porcelain collecting). Now, the examples that I have given so far suggest that definition and extension refer mainly to parts of the world that are exterior to the individual. However, it should be clear that a person's self or his attitudes, for example, can also be extended or defined in a similar way. This, I believe, is what happens in social relating; and the "validation" that I have been discussing can be slotted under the headings of definition of the system (where the individual wishes to see if a particular construct is regarded as valid by other people) and extension of the system (where the individual wishes to find out what else that other people know can be subsumed in and accounted for by the system that he presently employs).

Let us take this further. I have remarked during the chapter that relationships are dynamic and developing things, and I will do so again in the next section. It seems to me to be something that is consistent with Kelly's view of the human enterprise and yet something about which he had little to say. Yet here in this notion of elaboration of the construct system lies a fruitful possibility for explaining some of the features of relationship growth. Perhaps development of relationships is characterised by switching between the two methods of elaboration. Perhaps people start relating by seeking out areas where their two construct systems overlap (and therefore offer one another definition) and proceed, if the relationship looks workable, to explore ways in which they will be stimulated by one another (and therefore will help one another to extend their systems). I don't know: this is a guess, but there is some work which is consistent with that idea. McCarthy and Duck (1976) found that, whilst similarity was attractive to pairs of newly encountered strangers, dissimilarity on side issues was found to be attractive by those who had known each other for four to six months.

Thus, it seems to me, Kelly's idea can be made the basis for describing the functions of negativity in relationships as well as liking, whilst also giving some useful insights about development of relationship. Kelly is telling us, I believe, that people develop relationships from a need to elaborate their construct system, as outlined above; but he could also be saying that the course of development of relationships—their growth of intimacy—is prescribed by the ways in which this elaboration takes place. If I am right (Duck, 1973, 1977b) that relationships develop by validating constructs at progressively finer layers of the construct system, then Kelly's approach is a fruitful hypothetical starting point there, too. In order to make this judgement soundly, however, it is necessary to consider other work on the development of relationships in order to see how adequately this Kellyan view could account for the emphases that are found there.

Development of Relationships

So let us stand back from where we have been led by the arguments derived from, and extending, Kelly's (1955) position and look at work by non-Kellyans on the development of relationships. There is not as much of it as one might expect: it is largely a product of thinking in the 1970s and, because it is so recent, remains largely untested in detail. For the most part, work on interpersonal attraction has examined only stationary, non-dynamic interactions (e.g. attraction to strangers) and whilst the principles underlying relationship development may have something in common with those explaining initial attraction, this has yet to be established for sure. This emphasis seems odd given the crucially important observation that people who experience difficulties with relationships are usually complaining of difficulty in developing or sustaining them at a satisfactory level rather than protesting that people do not like them at a superficial stage. In relating clinical work to social psychological research, therefore, more is to be gained from an understanding of developing relationships than of first impressions.

Readers may already know something of the work of Levinger (Levinger and Snoek, 1972; Levinger, 1974; Huesmann and Levinger, 1976) who outlines a three-stage developmental approach to relationship growth. He has identified one level of unrelatedness (Zero Contact, where two people may not even know that each other exists) and three levels of relatedness, one of which is actually a continuum. At Level One (Awareness) each person may know enough about the other person to have formed an attitude or impression of him, but interaction itself has not occurred. At Level Two (Surface Contact) the individuals interact in relatively unimportant ways and are no more than mere acquaintances. At Level Three (Mutuality—this level is a continuum) the relationship ranges from a very basic level of mutuality to a large degree of overlap of attitudes, beliefs, personalities and so on. At this stage the partners regard the relationship as an entity worth preserving and have enough information about each other and enough shared experience to feel that they are truly in a personal relationship. Recent work on this theory has begun to try and identify the ways in which people shift from one level to another and proceed along the continuum in Level Three, but this work is presently acknowledged (Huesmann and Levinger, 1976) to be at a fairly rudimentary stage.

An alternative perspective is provided by Altman (Altman and Taylor, 1973; Altman, 1974; Morton *et al.*, 1976) who has considered relationship growth in terms of an "onion skin model". This analogy describes the layering of personality that Altman sees as relevant to relationship growth and the model discusses various ways in which slices into the "onion" can be achieved during the relationship's endurance. The processes that are envisaged to describe such growth concern different patterns of non-verbal behaviour and relationship definition. Relationships will grow in intimacy as long as the partners share a common definition of the relationship and are able to exchange information and non-verbal indications which support the definition.

Work on the specific type of relationship that is found in courtship has been done by Murstein (1971, 1977) who is concerned to describe and explain the ways in which courtship progress is maintained. He believes that there are essentially three stages to courtship growth: *Stimulus stage* (where such things as physical appearance are influential): *Value stage* (where discovery of shared values is important): and *Role stage* (where a complex set of role-related factors is significant, e.g. whether the partner's beliefs about the role of husband and wife are compatible). This theory is better supported by empirical research than are the above two approaches, but it is, of course, limited (in so far as we know) to courtship. It is arguable whether it can be used as a general theory of relationship growth.

It can be seen that these three examples differ in their level of approach to relationships as well as in their own particular theoretical tenets. What, then, are the common features of these (and other) theories of relationship growth? They focus on stages of relationships that are characterised by attention to specific types of characteristics in the partner or by tendencies to conduct the relationship in a particular way. Interestingly, they do not spend much time analysing the motive force behind the progression of intimacy and it is more often described than explained. Recently Huesmann and Levinger (1976) have cast their model in terms of exchange theory and suggested that it is the anticipation of an improved reward matrix at the next level of interaction that provides the spur for progression in relationship.

Whilst I would accept that changes in the level of intimacy are tentative and have to be negotiated, I think also that three explanations can be offered for the impetus toward such growth: Time; Boredom; Validation. Time explains that the restless progression of human activity will continue, but does not specify the directions which it will take. On its own therefore it predicts that changes will occur but does not show what sort they will be. Boredom suggests that after discussing things once there is no need to do it again and so new areas will be sought. On its own therefore it predicts that changes will be concerned with the topics of the interaction but does not specify how they will alter. Validation provides the key. It predicts, taken with the other two forces, that individuals will steadily attempt to validate more of their construct system. The stages of growth in a relationship can then be identified according to the parts of the system that they tend to elaborate and validate. Thus the early stages may concern constructs about physical appearance whilst later ones concern more psychological construal (Duck, 1977a,b,c). In essence, however, the process is characterised by prediction and guess work: being able, at very early stages, to observe only visible properties of other people one has to deduce, infer, guess about their personality or their construct system. The guesses can be subsequently tested against actuality when one has come to know the partner better and has the relevant information at hand.

In the context of development it is worth noting that this model of growth (more fully described in Duck, 1977a,c) points up an interesting parallel between the development of a relationship between adults (from strangers to friends) and the development of acquainting in children and adolescents. In both cases the natures of the similarities in construal that characterise relationships at different (st)ages demonstrate considerable parallelism (Duck, 1975; Duck *et al.*, 1979). It remains to be seen whether there are many insights to be gained from this observation but it is worth speculating that some of the impetus to development of ideas about social relationships comes from interaction with peers, and interaction with peers is probably based on construct similarity in children, as with adults.

Kelly's notions about individuality and the nature of sociality thus provide plenty of scope and suggestions for those wishing to come to grips with interpersonal attraction research. His approach can be made the starting point for several useful speculations on a variety of issues in the literature. However, Kelly also had something to say about the negative side of relationships and in addition to its useful indications about the growth of relationships, his theory can, I believe, provide some insights into the decline or collapse of relationships also.

Collapse, Breakdown and Negativity in Relationships

Since there is relatively little work on the breakdown of relationships it is not yet agreed by research workers whether collapse of relationships is a simple contrary of intimacy growth or indeed if "collapse" is a satisfactory word to use at all, carrying, as it does, some moral overtones and implications. Of course, relationships break down for lots of reasons, some of them reflecting "inability" or "incompetence" (I use these here as descriptive rather than evaluative terms) and some after deliberate decision. We are concerned with both.

Earlier in this chapter I remarked that negativity in relationships may serve a function for individuals. Given Kelly's insistence on the dichotomous nature of constructs and his emphasis upon what is rejected when something is chosen, one would expect to find similar insistence that negative aspects of an individual's relating help to define in part what his other relationships mean to him and do for him. I have previously argued (Duck, 1977a) that both positive and negative aspects of relationships, both growth and decline in intimacy must be explained in the same kind of framework. People that one likes, I suggest, are liked because they support the construct system of the liker. The same can be said of certain sorts of disliked others: that they attract emotion because they support certain aspects of the construct system—especially those that we love to hate. For example, when a person thinks that the construct "X–Y" is important and X is desirable, someone who is both Y and undesirable will reinforce his belief in the X–Y construct.

In this case, therefore, interaction with the person continues to reaffirm the value of the X–Y construct whereas in hostility (described earlier) the interaction is unnecessary in view of the fact that the person extorts the validation from the environment without needing to interact with others. Equally, in anxiety where, Kelly says, an imminent comprehensive change in core (self-maintenance) constructs is anticipated, the person presumably requires as immediate and firm a definition of self as is possible, such as frenetic, intensive social interaction or hostility could equally provide.

These, however, are special kinds of intercourse with the outside world and would not be classed as "relationships" by everyone. They are, however, precisely those kinds of odd and distorted social interactions whose function needs to be explained, since collapse of a relationship can be explained not only in general terms (e.g. "He *needs* to be rejected") but in terms of a failure to find in the relationship what one is seeking. By this I mean to explain how apparently intimate and successfully established relationships can break down or decline. Again there are clearly many different sources for such decline that are not based solely on the psychological functions of friendship (e.g. moving house, financial ruin, death of a loved one, marriage and subsequent decline of "extramarital" connections). For those that can be identifiably related to a psychological function for relationships, Kelly's approach can be used to supply an explanation (and ultimately a basis for prediction) of collapse. The explanation that I have proffered before (Duck, 1977a) goes like this: relations with specific others are attractive in so far as they (directly) produce or (indirectly) suggest support for the construct system; they develop in intimacy in so far as the partners expect to find more subtle parts of their construct systems validated as the relationship continues; these expectancies are either confirmed or not; where confirmation is strong the relationship will be likewise, and where it is weak or not present at all, the relationship will fail to grow or will actually decline. In a brief study by Duck and Allison (1978) the relationships of a group of second year students were explored. These students had all lived in the same campus residence in first year, had formed likes and dislikes, and had distributed themselves in various ways around the town when they were required to leave university accommodation at the end of first year. Some had gone to live on their own, some had decided to share flats with others from the original group. An exploration of the amounts of construct similarity between each member of the population and all other members revealed that the isolates were significantly less similar to non-isolates in construct terms but, more interestingly, revealed that of the flat-sharers those who subsequently broke up were in key ways significantly less similar to their partners than those who stayed together through second year. The study, whilst provocative, was somewhat incomplete, due to the necessarily small number of subjects, but it is still an instructive basis for further work.

Implications

Several useful pointers about the nature of personal relationships are to be found by conjoining Kelly's insights with the work done by researchers in interpersonal attraction. Now that calls for more sophisticated views of attraction and acquaintance are increasing—and particularly now that there is more demand for study of developing relationships and collapsing ones (Huston and Levinger, 1978)—we need a worked out, sophisticated, human, personal theory of individuality and interpersonal activity. One fruitful place to direct such calls would be towards the personal construct theorists. But there is one problem: Look back to p. 279 and you'll find that this is where we started.

References

Altman, I. (1974). The communication of interpersonal attitudes: an ecological approach. *In* "Foundations of Interpersonal Attraction" (Ed. T. L. Huston). Academic Press, New York and London.

Altman, I. and Taylor, D. A. (1973). "Social Penetration". Holt, Rinehart and Winston, New York.

Byrne, D. (1971). "The Attraction Paradigm". Academic Press, New York and London.

Clore, G. L. (1977). Reinforcement and affect in attraction. *In* "Theory and Practice in Interpersonal Attraction" (Ed. S. W. Duck). Academic Press, London and New York.

Dewhurst, D. and Duck, S. W. (1978). Personal relationships and clinical practice. Paper presented to the Conference on Social Psychology and Clinical Practice, Loughborough, England. March, 1978.

Duck, S. W. (1973). "Personal Relationships and Personal Constructs: A Study of Friendship Formation". Wiley, Chichester.

Duck, S. W. (1975). Personality similarity and friendship choices amongst adolescents. *Eur. J. Soc. Psychol.* (**5**) 70–83.

Duck, S. W. (1977a). "The Study of Acquaintance". Saxon House (Teakfield), London.

Duck, S. W. (1977b). Inquiry, hypothesis and the quest for validation: personal construct systems in the development of acquaintance. *In* "Theory and Practice in Interpersonal Attraction" (Ed. S. W. Duck). Academic Press, London and New York.

Duck, S. W. (1977c). Developing a predictive filter model of friendship formation. Paper to the Annual Conference of the Social Psychology Section of the BPS, September, Durham.

Duck, S. W. and Allison, D. (1978). I liked you but I cannot live with you: a study of lapsed relationships. *Soc. Behav. Pers.* **6**, 43–47.

Duck, S. W., Miell, D. K. and Gaebler, H. C. (in press). Attraction and communication in children's interactions. *In* "Friendship and Childhood Relationships" (Eds H. C. Foot, A. J. Chapman and J. R. Smith). Wiley, Chichester.

Festinger, L. (1954). A theory of social comparison processes. *Hum. Relat.* (**7**) 117–140.

Foa, U. G. and Foa, E. B. (1971). Resource exchange: Toward a structural theory of interpersonal relations. *In* "Studies in Dyadic Communication" (Eds A. W. Siegman and B. Pope). Pergamon Press, New York.

Huesmann, L. R. and Levinger, G. (1976). Incremental exchange theory: A formal model for progression in dyadic social interaction. *In* "Advances in Experimental Social Psychology" (Eds L. Berkowitz and E. H. Walster), Vol. 9. Academic Press, New York and London.

Huston, T. L. (1974). A perspective on interpersonal attraction. *In* "Foundations of Interpersonal Attraction" (Ed. T. L. Huston). Academic Press, London and New York.

Huston, T. L. and Levinger, G. (1978). Interpersonal attraction and relationships. *Ann. Rev. Psychol.* (**29**) 115–156.

Kelly, G. A. (1955). "The Psychology of Personal Constructs". Norton, New York.

Kelly, G. A. (1969a). In whom confide? On whom depend for what? *In* "Clinical Psychology and Personality" (Ed. B. Maher) Wiley: New York.

Kelly, G. A. (1969b). Ontological acceleration. *In* "Clinical Psychology and Personality" (Ed. B. Maher). Wiley, New York.

Kelly, G. A. (1969c). Hostility. *In* "Clinical Psychology and Personality" (Ed. B. Maher). Wiley, New York.

Kelly, G. A. (1970). Behaviour is an experiment. *In* "Perspectives in Personal Construct Theory" (Ed. D. Bannister). Academic Press, London and New York.

Kelvin, P. (1977). Predictability, power and vulnerability in interpersonal attraction. *In* "Theory and Practice in Interpersonal Attraction" (Ed. S. W. Duck). Academic Press, London and New York.

La Gaipa, J. J. (1977). Interpersonal attraction and social exchange. *In* "Theory and Practice in Interpersonal Attraction" (Ed. S. W. Duck). Academic Press, London and New York.

Levinger, G. (1974). A three-level approach to attraction: Toward an understanding of pair relatedness. *In* "Foundations of Interpersonal Attraction" (Ed. T. L. Huston). Academic Press, New York and London.

Levinger, G. and Snoek, J. D. (1972). "Attraction in Relationship: A New Look at Interpersonal Attraction". General Learning Press, Morristown, New Jersey.

McCarthy, B. and Duck, S. W. (1976). Friendship duration and responses to attitudinal agreement-disagreement. *Br. J. Soc. Clin. Psych.* (**15**) 377–386.

Maslow, A. H. (1953). Love in healthy people. *In* "The Meaning of Love" (Ed. A. Montagu). Julian Press, New York.

Mehrabian, A. and Ksionzky, S. (1974). "A Theory of Affiliation". Lexington Books, Lexington.

Morton, T. L., Alexander, J. F. and Altman, I. (1976). Communication and relationship definition. *In* "Explorations in Interpersonal Communication" (Ed. G. R. Miller). Sage, New York.

Murstein, B. I. (1971). A theory of marital choice and its applicability to marriage adjustment. *In* "Theories of Attraction and Love" (Ed. B. I. Murstein). Springer, New York.

Murstein, B. I. (1977). The Stimulus-Value-Role (SVR) Theory of dyadic relationships. *In* "Theory and Practice in Interpersonal Attraction" (Ed. S. W. Duck). Academic Press, London and New York.

Schachter, S. (1959). "The Psychology of Affiliation". Stanford University Press, Stanford.

Tiger, L. and Fox, R. (1972). "The Imperial Animal". Secker and Warburg, London.

Individual Interpersonal Judgements Re-described and Re-evaluated

Mildred McCoy

A personal construct theory (Kelly, 1955) approach to issues of social psychology requires no Procrustean stretch. As a frame of reference it offers two "fitting" major dimensions. Kelly's emphasis on the central concept of role, a predominantly social view of the self involving one's construction of others' construct systems, is one matching dimension. The Sociality Corollary, expressing the processes for significant social interaction, is the other. It has already been recognized that these two interact to provide a foundation for a social psychology (Kelly, 1955, p. 95).

This chapter presents yet another pertinent facet of personal construct theory offering a new approach to a topic in which the social psychologists have a proprietary interest. It is an attempt to relate a model of personal construing to some aspects of the broad field generally called "person perception". The model is derived from an explication of basic principles of construct systems laid down by Kelly but is also based on more recent research on the hierarchical levels of construct networks.

In brief, the model calls for a reversal of the commonly held view of the direction of causality between attribution of evaluative and descriptive aspects in interpersonal judgements. The ubiquitous halo effect and its many reincarnations hold that liking and disliking unduly influence one's judgement of other characteristics of a person. The implications of this view obscure our understanding of the nature of construing and the actual, human experience in judging other people. The presented model insists upon an important distinction. It proposes that people are judged on *descriptive* dimensions which may eventuate in liking or disliking but need not do so. The relationship between descriptive and evaluative judgements in a hierarchical construct network clarifies both the phenomenological experience and the incipient evaluation so often appearing in studies of judgement.

It is not intended to denigrate the many and varied approaches to person perception within social psychology. But as Cohen (1973) has reminded us, the judgement process itself has received scant attention within mainstream person perception studies. For the most part, increasingly sophisticated research has been designed to deal with systematic tendencies in the relationship between the judge and the object judged. That primarily "social" approach has been balanced by the work of "cognitive" psychologists focusing on the decision processes (Kaplan and Schwartz, 1975). The cognitive approach relates to social psychology especially when the concentration is on social judgements such as in Kaplan (1975).

Both cognitive and social psychology have explored the territory of interpersonal judgements. Each discipline seems to have slightly different objects for its own pursuit but there is a great deal of overlap with mutual cross referencing. Both appear to have welcomed the halo effect, not tentatively, as a useful concept, but as an account of reality. It has become an accepted tenet and been held with conviction.

Regardless of how reified the concept may have become, ultimately, the halo effect is the name of a mini-theory which nicely fits various sets of data; data which, quite naturally, have been gathered with a particular focus of attention determining the nature of the observations and their treatment. Applying a personal construct point of view to interpersonal judgements offers a fresh outlook. In this approach, the halo effect loses some of its blinding shine. In a different light we can see some of the difficulties which have been obscured, particularly when it comes to understanding specific interpersonal judgements about significant others.

There are several problems with an uncritical acceptance of the halo effect. For one thing, there has been no basis for predicting when or where the halo effect will work. Also, the operation of the halo effect is limited in a number of specific ways. Further, its usefulness under some circumstances cannot be generalized to the practicular process of one individual construing or judging another without distorting or contorting human experience.

In particular, experience seems to be that we do not always like or dislike everyone we construe. Reliance on an account such as the defence mechanism of *denial* to explain the claim of neutral affect in an interpersonal judgement is a bit of mental contortion. Here, "denial" is an *ad hoc* explanation which explains "nothing" quite literally. On the other hand, distortion is introduced when we try to explore interpersonal judgements in terms other than those natural to the subject, when we force artificial decisions among a set of limited choices or on the basis of restricted information.

This is not the first murmur of dissatisfaction with the popularity and uncritical acceptance of the halo effect (see Peabody, 1967, 1970). Previous efforts to throttle its impact seem to have been hampered by the lack of an alternative model of the judgement process. Presentation of such a model is the main purpose of this chapter. However, in deference to the widespread acceptance of the halo effect and related concepts, an attempt will be made to account for its popularity. Likewise, the empirically demonstrated conditions which contribute to shaping data which appear to fit the halo hypothesis will be briefly reviewed. These point to the unsuitability of applying the concept to typical, individual judgements of others in real life.

Another component of this presentation is a discussion of the meaning of the two adjectives, *evaluative* versus *descriptive* as they apply to interpersonal judgements. This is necessary to clarify the frame of reference created by reliance on the halo effect or an imprecise appreciation of its limits. The distinction provides the basis for taking an alternative position and an important dimension of the model.

The model itself is then presented in the following section. That section also contains an amplification of the model's features and a brief discussion of some practical applications.

Pertinent data from a study of liking and disliking are presented in the final section. This is in order to demonstrate the reasonableness of the hypothesis that interpersonal discriminations are commonly and primarily descriptive rather than evaluative and therefore most usefully so considered by those interested in interpersonal relations. Data include judgements on two sets of constructs. One set was elicited, a condition which most emulates the everyday, ordinary construing of significant others. The other set was supplied, using the popular Bieri group of ten constructs listed in Irwin *et al*. (1967). The later poses an especially severe test of the descriptive construction hypothesis.

The Halo Effect and Related Concepts

The halo effect has been an influential concept in social psychology since Thorndike's use of the term in 1920, although it should be acknowledged that Guildford (1954) attributes the first description of the halo effect to Wells (1907). The halo effect implies that one's judgements of characteristics in a person are unduly influenced by liking or disliking that person. Several versions of nearly the same notion have appeared since 1920 including Newcomb's (1930) *logical error*, Cronbach's (1955) *implicit personality theory* and Hays' (1958) concept of *trait inference*. A difference among these approaches lies in the loci of their effect. Newcomb's logical error explanation points to something in the nature of the traits themselves or at least to their logical connections whereas the others usually attribute the phenomenon of trait intercorrelation to characteristics of the judge or of the style of judgement. This is also true of the cognitive complexity approaches which rely on the explanation power of the first factor as an inverse measure of complexity of the judge and then identify the first factor as evaluative (e.g. Jones, 1954).

Asch's (1946) concept of *trait centrality* is also consistent with the halo effect in that his impression formation research established that either a positive or negative set can be aroused by the inclusion of a single central quality of one or the other bias among a list of other traits. By switching *cold* for *warm* in otherwise similar sets there were extreme reversals in impressions derived from a set which included generosity, shrewdness, happiness, irritability, humor, sociability, popularity, ruthlessness, self-centeredness and imaginativeness. But this "halo effect" did not operate indiscriminately on all adjective traits. There was also a set of qualities not affected by the transition from warm to cold. These were: reliability, importance, physical attractiveness, persistence, seriousness, restraint, strength and honesty. Asch noted that the trend "was decisively limited at certain points". Unfortunately, this limitation has often been overlooked in later work said to be substantiating the halo effect and the overwhelming power and pervasiveness of evaluation.

A reiteration of the debilitating influences which shaped psychological trends in the past half century would include a positivistic bias and the idolization of a nineteenth century natural science model, a premature search for generalizations, a reductionistic heritage, and dogmatic methodism which insisted upon "palpability", distrusted conscious reports and banished subjective experience. All are reflected in the predominance of an undifferentiated acceptance of the halo effect. Consequently, its limitations have generally been overlooked while increasingly widespread support has been garnered for it, either directly or through the proliferation of related concepts.

The limitations which have already been identified but generally ignored begin with Symonds' (1931) analysis. He reported that the halo effect is found particularly in cases where the traits are unclearly defined, difficult to observe, or rarely discussed, especially when they are concerned with interpersonal relationships or moral attitudes. The early finding has been confirmed by Jaspars (1966) who presented data comparing subjects' judgements on self-constructed scales *vs* semantic differential scales. The self-constructed scales were regarded as more meaningful to the subjects than the general, semantic differential scales. He suggests that the use of a set of general rating scales in describing other people may introduce an evaluative factor which is not present in direct rating of perceived differences between persons. The more general the dimensions, the more likely that an evaluative, rather than a descriptive, one will dominate. From his research, Jaspars concluded that the distinctions which are made by subjects in judging other real people are not predominantly evaluative in nature if they use self-constructed scales.

Cohen (1973) was also aware that a significant feature in the occurrence of the halo effect is insufficient information. This can be the result of either stimuli impoverishment, often deliberate on the part of the experimenter, or the failure of the subject-judge to take advantage of potentially available information. The latter, presumably, is the true halo effect in operation. Stimuli impoverishment can be accomplished, for example, by asking for judgements of strangers from photographs or handwriting samples, or asking for descriptions of people-in-general, not any one individual. Quite similar in impact is Koltuv's (1962) finding that asking for ratings of relatively unknown persons leads to a more stereotyped response than ratings of familiar people. Taken together, these limitations indicate the large role played by artefacts of the experimental situation in the ubiquitousness of the halo effect.

Two further artificialities may be contributing to its survival. One is the custom of naming the first or first few factors which emerge from factor analysis or a principal components analysis of a judgement matrix. This factor is often called "an evaluative first factor". Attempts to account for the frequent finding of the "evaluative" first factor usually attribute it either to the judge (frequently in terms of cognitive style), the generality of the judgement dimensions, or the positive and negative qualities of the stimuli being judged. The significant part played by the mental set of the person interpreting and naming the first factor should also be considered. Naming factors is a fine art. Names must be derived through much the same kind of abstraction process as the factor itself. But the process of abstraction in naming is certainly not the same exercise of mathematical objectivity. In fact, subjective intuitions contribute greatly to the creativity required to meet the challenge of integrating a number of high loading elements into a single concept name. Therefore, subjectivity is implicated in the generalizations regarding the evaluative nature of the first factor.

The second artificiality arises from the very nature of the task of abstracting from descriptive dimensions. It is possible that the first factor becomes evaluative by default because the various descriptive dimensions are not related to each other. They may, in fact, have been deliberately chosen to be comprehensive as a set but as orthogonal as possible individually. They would not be expected to show any great correlation with each other or any common descriptive component. At the same time the range of convenience of evaluation is much wider than that of most other abstractions commonly considered significant in interpersonal judgements. There are other abstractions with wide applicability such as "spiritual–material" or "cause–effect" but they do not seem to reflect pertinent discriminations for psychologists interested in interpersonal perceptions.

In summary, although there is evidence of what could be considered an evaluative component in much of human judgement, certain experimental conditions have contributed to the unduly eminent position assigned to evaluation in the interpersonal judgement process. These experimental conditions or artefacts include:

(1) stimuli impoverishment;
(2) providing inadequate information for the kind of judgement task expected of subjects;
(3) requiring use of general and therefore relatively meaningless rating scales;
(4) asking for judgements about relatively meaningless stimuli such as people-in-general or traits apart from persons;
(5) finally, the very task of abstraction of common elements from a set of judgements leaves very little possibility that the descriptive nature of individual judgements would have survived the winnowing process.

The thrust of this criticism is not to deny the reality of evaluation in judgements but to indicate that the role it plays in actual judgements of significant others may have been exaggerated. Particularly, the impression created by the halo effect that evaluation precedes descriptive judgements should be questioned. With an historical perspective we can appreciate the attraction of the halo effect while recognizing that changing emphases in psychology are likely to enhance understanding of the actual process of human judgements.

Recent trends in psychology are towards a more holistic embrace of human complexity and a renewed interest in studies of the individual. This should lead to an increasing awareness of both the limitations of the halo effect and its inapplicability to the attempt to understand individual social-judgement acts. Other perspectives are beginning to be recognized as having greater potential.

"Evaluation" and "Description"

A series of articles initiated by Peabody (1967) reports a direct experimental confrontation of the evaluative *vs* descriptive issue. Peabody challenged overemphasis on evaluation in personality perception and devised a method for separating evaluative from descriptive aspects of trait judgements. His evidence, later corroborated by Felipe (1970), shows that subjects overwhelmingly choose descriptive similarity over evaluative similarity in judgement tasks which permit the choice. This result is consistent with the evidence on artefacts contributing to the halo effect, i.e. much of the research which finds evaluation dominant may inadvertently limit the possibilities.

In what follows, *evaluation* is a particular construing process in which the sorting of objects or events occurs along a dimension of unspecified worth or value. The subjective nature of worth is emphasized and a subjective basis for the discrimination is implied. Evaluative judgements are contrasted with descriptive ones in that the latter discriminate on a basis of identifiable and verifiable features of the event being judged. *Description* is considered objective or factual and rooted in the reality of the event. This use of evaluative *vs* descriptive can be found in a number of places (Osgood *et al.*, 1957, pp. 17, 24, 62ff; and throughout the series: Peabody, 1967; Rosenberg and Olshan, 1970; Felipe, 1970; Peabody, 1970).

Evaluative dimensions are very general and do not inherently specify descriptive subordinate aspects. They include: favorable *vs* unfavorable, desirable *vs* undesirable, good *vs* bad, likable *vs* not likable, valuable *vs* worthless, etc. In the context of interpersonal judgements, evaluation is intended to refer to a core of desirability apart from the specifics which are identified as descriptive features.

Other judgement dimensions such as beautiful *vs* ugly, virtuous *vs* sinful, brilliant *vs* dull, just *vs* unjust, etc. have specific and descriptive meaning components as well as conveying an aspect of desirability or undesirability. They are said to "load heavily" on evaluation following the practice of subjecting interpersonal judgements to a factor analysis or principal components analysis and then identifying the factors by name, one of which almost always is called an evaluative factor. Despite the fact that these dimensions have an evaluatively preferable pole, it is my contention that they refer to an underlying aspect of reality which is more objective, identifiable and verifiable than evaluation dimensions. These dimensions should then be considered descriptive in this discussion.

Descriptive dimensions may embody contrasting evaluative components as the previous examples have, or they may have poles of approximately equal evaluation as for example: serious *vs* gay, fussy *vs* careless, steady *vs* flexible, severe *vs* lax, etc. Likewise, they may have no apparent intrinsic evaluation at all: sunny *vs* shady, wet *vs* dry, left *vs* right, high *vs* low, etc. It is useful to retain Kelly's idea that the poles are only convenient names used in identifying a dimension of judgement, not the actual dimension itself. For example with the so-called serious *vs* gay dimension, is probably "disposition" or "demeanor". This emphasizes that use of the dimension is a construction of a reality event inherently "describable" by a range of constructions. The judgement a person makes is primarily about the event not the construer's *a priori* positive or negative "feelings".

An appreciation of the distinction between evaluation and description which has just been made is essential to much of the discussion which follows. In summary, as used here as well as in other areas of social psychology, evaluative dimensions are general and subjective, and they sort events on the basis of unspecified worth. In contrast, descriptive dimensions, although they are personal constructions, discriminate identifiable, verifiable, objective features rooted in the reality of the event. Whereas previous approaches have stressed the evaluative component inherent in constructs, in this approach the emphasis is on the descriptive component.

The Personal Construct Theory Model of Liking and Disliking

The special feature of this model is that it reverses the commonly held view (in psychology) of the direction of causality between attribution of evaluative and descriptive aspects in interpersonal judgements. Whereas the halo effect maintains that liking or disliking unduly influence one's judgements of other characteristics, this model proposes that people are judged on descriptive dimensions which may eventuate in liking or disliking. Additionally, according to the model, the most personally significant descriptive dimensions tend to be involved in a network of related dimensions which may include a relatively superordinate construction such as like *vs* dislike. However, the tendency to include evaluation is limited. Variations in it are both individual and cultural.

Personal construct theory contributes to an understanding of the relations among constructs in a hierarchical system. The relation established by a construct system over its subordinate elements is deterministic. The construct structures we erect rule us. However, freedom characterizes the independence of construction from reality. Subordinate constructions do not determine superordinate ones. Events do not demand some particular construction, although there are limits to the set of possibilities if we wish the constructions to serve a practical purpose.

Kelly says,

> determinism characterizes the control that a construct exercises over its subordinate elements, freedom characterizes its independence of those elements. Determinism and freedom are then inseparable, for that which determines another is, by the same token, free of the other. (1955, p. 21)

Deterministic control flows from the superordinate to the subordinate, not from reality to its construction. Therefore, reality does not determine that we place an evaluative judgement on an event. We are free to construe evaluatively or not.

The "halo effect" and related approaches create the impression that evaluation is pervasive and both precedes and determines subsequent construction. In so far as evaluation is a superordinate construction, indeed it does determine its elements according to the personal construct theory model. The difficulty lies in the assumed pervasiveness and sequence, in confusing the control of organization with a cause and effect type of determination, and the supposition that we are determined to construe evaluatively and therefore must like or dislike. Beginning with Kelly's assumption of infinite freedom to construe events alternatively, we can form an account of the personal experience which recognizes that liking or disliking are not always salient when we make interpersonal judgements.

Strictly speaking, a superordinate evaluative construct directly sorts its subordinate constructs and not a set of external events. One evaluates other constructions which in turn sort the events in question. Even the stable treasures of history such as gold, precious stones, peace and love have worth only because of some agreed human constructions of them. Not only are such constructions of worth relative, but events which elicit them can be alternatively construed as well.

Liked and disliked do not refer directly to events which are construed (except in the case distinguished below) but rather to one's response, i.e. construction of them. There is no aspect of reality in an event which *per se* is likable or dislikable in the same way that an event can be judged on a subordinate descriptive dimension such as "red" or "wet" or "kind-hearted". That evaluation is subjective rather than objective is generally recognized and accepted in such sayings as "*De gustibus non est disputandem*". Strictly speaking, evaluation is a particularly personal construction, events themselves are neither likable nor not-likable. It is our constructions of events which are evaluated. No thing or event has some aspect of reality which demands an evaluative response and only an evaluative response. It is only one's construction of some aspect of an event which is satisfying or dissatisfying in the ultimate reduction to a fundamental principle of motivation.

In contrast to the superordinate evaluative dimension, descriptive dimensions tend to be subordinate. Therefore the descriptive dimensions do not determine that an event so construed will be evaluatively construed. According to the principle of constructive alternativism, elements do not exert control over the construction of themselves. As a result, an event construed on a descriptive dimension may or may not also be evaluated. This accounts for the familiar experience that liking and disliking are not always salient even though one is construing events or people which are potentially likable or dislikable. This experience is often disregarded by theorists.

It is true that one can "learn" that certain events are regularly present when one construes a construction of them as likable. They can become the immediate occasion of a liking construction in the manner of a short-cut. This model is more fully described elsewhere (McCoy, 1977), but this construction becomes an identification or naming dimension and hence it is of a descriptive type rather than an evaluative one. In other words, learning can eventuate in one's construction of ice cream as "one of the things I have learned I usually like" which is not a superordinate evaluative construction in the sense considered above. It is subordinate and used as a descriptive dimension.

The model has another feature which has not yet been described. This is its ability to predict which descriptive bases will lead to evaluation when it does become salient.

The model predicts that although potentially any construct can be subsumed evaluatively, when it comes to expressing an actual distinction between liked and disliked elements, much of the variance can be accounted for along a single dimensional direction* which is subsumed in the manner described as parallel. (One pole of the dimensional direction is subsumed by a "liked" pole of an evaluative dimension, the other pole is subsumed by a "disliked" pole of an evaluative dimension. It does not matter whether this is one or two evaluative dimensions.)

The dimensional direction which will operate in this manner is the one which is most salient in the context. If the judgement task is one involving other people, then among the set of constructs useful in interpersonal judgements for any one subject will be one major dimensional direction which has acquired the greatest personal meaning. It will be the major discrimination basis and it will be subsumed, on occasion, by evaluative dimensions. The content of this dimensional direction will be idiosyncratic. For example, for one person it could be a set of dimensions closely related to social adeptness, for another a set related to achievement and competence and for a third the major set of axes could relate to social status or familial relationships. The model predicts that whatever this major dimension is, and it can vary widely among people, cultures, etc., it will operate in parallel with an evaluative dimension. Specifically, if for some person social adeptness is the most important dimensional direction, then people judged to be socially skillful will be construable as liked and those judged socially inept will be construable as disliked. Other constructs not associated with the major dimensional direction are less likely to be evaluated.

In short, when viewed in the perspective of evaluation *vs* description, the model has six features:

(1) *Discriminations are ordinarily made on the basis of some feature which is most appropriately regarded as descriptive.* Responses are not intuitively

---

*Recall that constructs are to be regarded as dimensional axes in Kelly's system. The term "dimensional direction" has been used to account for several very closely related dimensions which sort elements in nearly the same manner but are not completely identical. They can be pictured as a set of axes following in the same general direction rather like a bundle of straws.

evaluative, implying that they are based upon no discernible descriptive feature.* Evaluation does not unduly influence descriptive discrimination. Rather, descriptive construction is the basis and context of evaluation.

(2) *A number of constructs may be usefully regarded as directionally aligned dimensions functioning in a similar manner.* This is because constructs are organized within a hierarchical network. It is likely that the constructs united in such a major dimensional direction will be subsumed in a parallel manner by a superordinate evaluation construct. They will function in a manner which approximates an evaluative dimension. This does not mean that they are evaluative, only that they sort elements in a nearly similar manner, just as two roads linking the same cities could function in the same way while maintaining several distinctive features and separate identities.

(3) *Each person's major dimension direction is idiosyncratic.* Similarity of socialization produces some overlap among individuals. Nevertheless, the basis for evaluation is likely to vary among them.

(4) *The evaluative dimension is superordinate.* As such, it sorts subordinate constructs, not direct external events. This feature of the model is necessary to account for the relationship between positive or negative emotion and certain acts of construing not otherwise discussed in this paper. It is also consistent with Kelly's description of the nature of superordinancy. The relationship between superordinate and subordinate constructs may be described appropriately using any of the general diagnostic terms which Kelly offers. These include the possibility that the superordinate evaluative dimension could be a permeable or impermeable, pre-emptive, constellatory, propositional or regnant construct.

(5) *Events can be construed directly, but descriptively, such as "liked events" or "disliked events".* This short-cut through the construct hierarchy arises when we recognize (i.e. construe) certain events as regularly the occasion of an eventual evaluative discrimination.

(6) *The choice of a particular construction from among the suitable set is a function of the context but not determined by it.* Kelly never exactly stated a principle governing choice among constructs in the way in which the Choice Corollary predicts that a person chooses in a dichotomized construct, the alternative, which offers the greater possi-

---

*The relatively rare cases where the basis for evaluation cannot be verbally identified should not be considered evidence in support of a non-descriptive basis for evaluation. There is always the possibility of the involvement of preverbal construction which must be considered as an alternative explanation.

bility for extension and definition of his system. However, applying the principle of the Choice Corollary to this situation, one could predict that a construct would be chosen which offers the possibility for greater meaningfulness. Meaningfulness is not only a function of construct implications but of salience. The relative meaningfulness of evaluation and description for particular individuals in particular situations thus can be considered to determine the use of evaluative constructs. Simply because they are potentially applicable does not indicate they are always employed. This seems to be an area in which the freedom of constructive alternativism is most applicable. One can evaluate if that construction is salient, but one is also free to not evaluate. This notion of freedom seems to be absent from the halo effect and related concepts.

Empirical Applications of the Model

The model predicts that the major dimension of discrimination in the context of interpersonal judgements operates in a manner which is better regarded as descriptive than as evaluative. However, because of the relationships inherent in a cognitive structure network one would expect this descriptive dimension to be highly correlated with a superordinate evaluative discrimination. The usefulness of regarding the first component as primarily descriptive serves several objectives. It enhances understanding of a subject's construction of other important people, of the actual judgement dimensions used for interpersonal discrimination, and aids the development of a meta-dimension system for subsuming an individual's construct system. The model provides an entirely different perspective to that available from nomothetic approaches. If one is focusing on the ways in which people are alike, then the nature of dimensions which function in a common way for many subjects is of greatest use. But if the focus is on the individual, then the differences among them, particularly variations in the content of their construct systems becomes significant. Then the actual nature of the discrimination which has been made rather than the approximate, generalized manner in which it may function is of interest.

In order to demonstrate the reasonableness of the hypothesis that interpersonal discriminations are commonly and primarily descriptive rather than evaluative, pertinent data from a more comprehensive study of liking and disliking reported elsewhere (McCoy, 1977) will be presented. Eight subjects were recruited. Each completed two repertory grids with identical personalized element lists. One grid was based on personally elicited con-

structs and the other on the Bieri *et al*. (1955) set of supplied constructs.*
Both grids were subjected to a principal components analysis using Slater's
INGRID 72 Programme (Slater, 1972). The first principal component was
used as the operational equivalent of each subject's major dimensional
direction. Additionally, subjects were asked to rank order the elements on a
like *vs* dislike construct.

The actual elicited content of each subject's major dimension as determined by the principal component analysis of his repertory grids has been
identified and compared. The comparison of the eight subjects' first principal component content, which is based on the constructs which load heavily
on it, shows the great diversity among individuals. This is particularly true
when the elicited construct grids are the basis for the analysis. But even when
the grids with the provided, common set of constructs are analyzed, the first
principal component varies from individual to individual.

Both sets of highest loading constructs are presented. The deduction that
neither set is evaluative *per se* should be obvious in the light of the distinction
between evaluative and descriptive dimensions which has been offered.

The first principal components for each elicited construct rep grid were
named in fresh terminology. Vocabulary used by the subjects was avoided.
Names were derived from the highest loading constructs. This name and the
meaningfulness of the operational major dimensional direction were validated. Validation consisted of asking subjects to rank order the elements
used in the grid on the "named" dimensions. Spearman rho correlations
calculated between this ranking and the element loadings on the first principal component ranged from 0·84 to 0·94, all significant beyond the 0·01
probability level.

Table I presents the validated names of first principal component. The
constructs with the highest loadings on these first component are presented
in Table II. In their diversity they show that the principal component is
descriptive rather than evaluative *per se*. The dimensions are far from
identical or interchangeable and a great deal would be lost by considering
them all simply "evaluative". The idiosyncracy of the first principal component is the main argument for the usefulness of construing it as descriptive.

The content of the first principal component of the supplied construct rep
grids offers another illustration of the individuality which is associated with
this major judgement dimension. In this situation the subjects all had to

---

*The ten Bieri constructs as listed in Irwin *et al* (1967) are: outgoing *vs* shy, adjusted *vs*
maladjusted, decisive *vs* indecisive, calm *vs* excitable, interested in others *vs* self absorbed,
cheerful *vs* illhumored, responsible *vs* irresponsible, considerate *vs* inconsiderate, independent
vs dependent and interesting *vs* dull. This set of supplied constructs was used because it appears
to be the most popular set of bipolar dimensions in rep grid literature.

TABLE I. *Names of each subject's first principal component.*

Subject no.	Name
01	Traditional culture *vs* Modern Australian viewpoint
02	Someone trying to improve *vs* Someone self-satisfied
03	Hardworking and humane *vs* Lazy or ineffectual boor
04	Comfortable, positive people *vs* Aggressively defensive
05	Rather sorry provincials *vs* Experienced, internationally minded people
06	Intellectually and psychologically active *vs* Stodgy
07	Stable, mature people *vs* Grown-up babies lacking genuine satisfaction
08	Ideal professional (lawyer) *vs* People who are preoccupied with self and not "classy"

work with the same supplied set of ten constructs yet the four which load most heavily on the first component vary from subject to subject particularly in their order of size of loading. No attempt has been made to name this supplied construct grid component so the first component will be presented only in terms of the construct names in decreasing order of their size of loading (see Table III).

The content of the first principal component of the supplied construct rep grids shows far more unanimity than appeared in the elicited construct grids. One dimension, "Considerate *vs* Inconsiderate" was among the four highest loading constructs on the first component on all subjects' grids. Three other constructs appear frequently among the first four. Only three other constructs appear among the first four loadings of any subject. To consider the combination of Considerate, Responsible, Adjusted and Interested-in-others as the major cluster of characteristics which are significant in inter-personal relations would be a rash generalization.

However, the issue under consideration at in this point concerns the idiosyncracy of the first principal component. A better measure than the inspection of the four highest loading constructs can be derived from all the construct loadings on a component. Recall that a principal component is completely defined by its latent root, its construct vector and its element

TABLE II. *Highest loading constructs on the first principal components of the elicited construct grids.*

Subject no.	
01	Sees marriage as role *vs* Sees marriage as sharing Self-centered *vs* Giving Culture-bound *vs* Open to other cultures Victim *vs* Personally responsible
02	Sensitive *vs* Very insensitive Positive *vs* Negative Responsive to advice and comments *vs* Defensive Secure and open *vs* Insecure
03	Competent *vs* Incompetent Understanding *vs* Less understanding I admire *vs* Not admired [a] Diligent *vs* Lackadaisical Sociable *vs* Unsociable
04	Optimists *vs* Pessimists Friendly *vs* Hostile Easy to talk to *vs* Difficult to communicate with Not so sociable *vs* More sociable
05	Local *vs* World view Ugly Americans *vs* Sensitive Immature at times *vs* Not a kid (tough life) Pathetic people *vs* Emotionally well off
06	Explorers of the mind *vs* Non-explorers Understanding of motives *vs* Non-understanding Able, creative, "go" *vs* Lack of "gumption", non-creative Reckless *vs* Cautious
07	Extremely clear-thinking *vs* Confused thinking Self-disciplined *vs* Overly self-indulgent Relative emotional satisfaction *vs* Futile emotional involvement Emotional independence *vs* Emotional parasite
08	Generosity *vs* Selfishness Urbane *vs* Rough-hewn Concerned for others *vs* Self centered Vital *vs* Insipid

[a]This is an evaluative construct. Its definition can be surmized from the use of other constructs with which it correlates highly so four descriptive constructs have been included here.

TABLE III. *Four highest loading constructs on each subject's first principal component, supplied construct rep grid.*

Subject no. 01	Subject no. 02
Considerate	Interested in others
Interested in others	Considerate
Responsible	Responsible
Interesting	Adjusted

Subject no. 03	Subject no. 04
Interesting	Responsible
Adjusted	Adjusted
Responsible	Considerate
Considerate	Cheerful

Subject no. 05	Subject no. 06
Responsible	Considerate
Independent	Cheerful
Considerate	Adjusted
Interested in others	Responsible

Subject no. 07	Subject no. 08
Responsible	Adjusted
Considerate	Interested in others
Interested in others	Interesting
Adjusted	Considerate

vector. Given two of those, the third is derivable from the component, i.e. it is fixed. Since each component has its own and only one latent root, if either an element vector or construct vector is held stable the other is fixed for that component. Therefore, the set of construct vectors provides a basis of comparison of a principal component between subjects since the total set of element vectors has been normalized and the sum of their squares equals 1·0 for every subject. Thus it makes sense to compare and contrast the construct vectors based on a *similar set of constructs* to establish the similarity or difference in the nature of the first component among a set of subjects. With one additional transformation of the data, this has been done. The construct loadings are simply the product of the square root of the latent root and the construct vector. Since the square root of the latent root has always the same value for any one of the components, the loadings are linearly related to their construct vectors. The comparison of loadings has been effected through calculation of a correlation coefficient of the rank order of the size of the loading of each construct on each subject's first principal component of the supplied construct grid. This was done with the INGRID computer program and is reproduced in Table IV.

TABLE IV. *Correlations between subjects' rank order of construct loadings on each first principal component of the supplied construct repertory grids.*

Subject no.	01	02	03	04	05	06	07	08
01	—	0·697*	0·188	0·588	0·321	0·564	0·382	0·127
02		—	0·273	0·794*	0·382	0·842**	0.758*	0·503
03			—	0·321	0·382	0·188	0·309	0·442
04				—	0·382	0·855**	0·636	0·176
05					—	0·212	0·576	0·176
06						—	0·515	0·370
07							—	0·127
08								—

For coefficients of correlation, when d.f. = 7, critical values are indicated:
* = 0·666+ ($p<0·05$), ** = 0·798+ ($p<0·01$), from Guidford (1965).

Although some of the first components which different subjects used for the set of elements were quite similar to others, on the whole the evidence generally supports the idiosyncrasy of the first components, even with the highly restricted set of constructs which was available. Four of the five correlations which were large enough to be considered statistically signific- ant involved only one subject. It is interesting to note that this bilingual subject uses English much less than all the others in the sample and therefore one could speculate that she uses it in a more stereotyped manner. The significant correlations are all with other females in the sample while the correlations with males are relatively lower. Nevertheless, of the 28 com- parisons among the subjects, only five reach statistically significant levels. The general individuality of each subject's first principal component is demonstrated by the lack of functional similarily of the components as demonstrated by a comparison of the rank ordering of the constructs on the first component.

In summary, the demonstration of the idiosyncractic nature of the first components, whether they were derived from elicited construct rep grids or supplied construct rep grids, is intended to support the claim that the major judgement dimensions are descriptive rather than evaluative. They differ from one another precisely because each person attends to different aspects of the elements when making interpersonal judgements. It has been demon- strated that at least eight individuals have eight different major dimensions each consisting of more or less related constructs which serve as their principal basis for significant interpersonal judgements. This supports the proposition that it is more useful to regard people as judging others on a descriptive basis rather than an evaluative one.

There are two possible explanations of this general tendency. One is that descriptive discriminations may be developmentally more advanced. Evaluative judgements may be considered to constitute a mode of judgement which is more self-centered and more primitive, less suited to the complex interpersonal interactions of adult existence. The other reason lies in social demands. Society must manage evaluation so that its smooth functioning is not disrupted. It may be that each generation of parents passes on, more or less consciously, certain prohibitions on the expression of evaluation regarding significant people and teaches the substitution of alternative constructions which are more emotionally neutral, hence less disruptive. As the nature of a descriptive dimension is rooted in external events, it is more communicable. Thus, should it prove to be disruptive, it is more defensible.

Having arrived at the conclusion from the evidence that the nature of the first principal component is primarily descriptive rather than evaluative, it is hoped that confusion will not overtake the reader when the next point is that, despite its descriptive essence, the first principal component may serve as the basis of evaluation should the context suggest it. This is a natural consequence of the personal construct theory view of constructs as being united within hierarchical systems.

The model proposes that constructs which contribute most to the principal component become the elements subsumed by a superordinate evaluative construct, either directly or through subsumption by intermediate, more general, descriptive constructs. In practice, this means that although judgements of people are made on a descriptive basis, evaluation is a matter of construing the descriptive construction. For example, someone whose first principal component is named "Social competence" with constructs such as "Cares about people", "Perceptive", "Accepting", etc. loading heavily, construes people as liked or disliked on the basis of how they are sorted by the social competence constructs. In contrast, another person whose first principal component is named "Achievement oriented" with constructs such as "Serious", "Diligent", "Intelligent", etc. loading most heavily, construes people as liked or disliked on the basis of a descriptive construction of their intelligence, work habits and demeanor.

In order to corroborate this aspect of the model, subjects were asked to rank order all elements except self used in the rep grids on a liked *vs* disliked dimension. A Spearman rho was then calculated for the correlation between this rank order and the order derived from the size of loadings on the first principal component. The prediction based on the model states that this correlation should be high when the constructs of the first component serve as a descriptive basis for evaluation in the subordinate/superordinate construct relationship. The correlations are presented in Table V.

TABLE V. *Correlation between the rank order of elements on an evaluative dimension and the first principal component of both the elicited and supplied construct grids.*

Subject no.	Elicited grid first component	Supplied grid first component
01	0·890	0·776
02	0·936	0·916
03	0·673	0·669
04	0·437(n.s.)	0·506
05	0·789	0·556
06	0·801	0·449(n.s.)
07	0·688	0·723
08	0·814	0·760

Spearman rhos have been corrected for ties where the proportion of ties was large. The critical values of rho when $n = 14$ are 0·456 ($p<0.05$) and 0·645 ($p<0.01$).

The hypothesis is well supported ($p<0.01$ that 14 of 16 r_s would be significant by chance). At the same time, these correlations between the loadings on the first principal component and a liking–disliking rank ordering are lower than the correlations between the loadings on the first component and the rank ordering of the elements on the "named" dimension. This is consistent with the predictions derived from the model and is further evidence of the lack of identity between the first component and an evaluation dimension even though it is possible to predict evaluation fairly successfully with knowledge of the functioning of the first component on a set of elements.

Conclusion

Although social psychology has directed a great deal of attention to systematic tendencies occurring in interpersonal judgements, certain practical applications have been beyond its scope. Information derived from previous approaches associated with the halo effect has limitations which are often overlooked. In attempts to understand the actual judgements of individuals an overemphasis on evaluation can be misleading. The model presented here is an amplification of Kelly's (1955) theory concerning the hierarchical network of personal constructs. It focuses on the descriptive bases of interpersonal judgements and relates these to potential evaluation. This is a reversal of the commonly held view of the direction of causality between the attribution of evaluative and descriptive aspects in interpersonal judgements.

Circumstances such as psychotherapy illustrate the practical importance of the model for it can be used to explicate otherwise unassailable, evaluative judgements. The model provides a framework for therapist and client to consider a relatively objective dimension in relation to the client's total construct system and specific elements while highlighting the very personal basis on which liking and disliking judgements are made. Rather than being boxed in with an evaluative fiat of the sort, "I don't know why I love him . . . I just can't help it", the personal construct theorist using this model has a means for exploring highly evaluative situations in terms of constructions of external reality. Matters of taste are not beyond comprehension and communication.

Additionally, the model provides freedom from the domination of evaluation thought to govern interpersonal perceptions. Feeling neutral, neither liking nor disliking someone, is not only actually, but theoretically, possible. Judgements employing superordinate constructs such as evaluation can be suspended when they are inappropriate. They do not have to be posited and then consigned to the unconscious via a defence mechanism.

References

Asch, S. E. (1946). Forming impressions of personality. *J. Abnorm. Soc. Psychol.* **41**, 258–290.

Bieri, J. (1955). Cognitive complexity–simplicity and predictive behaviour. *J. Abnorm. Soc. Psychol.* **51**, 263–288.

Cohen, R. (1973). "Patterns of Personality Judgement" (Ed. and trans. L. Dirk). Academic Press, New York and London.

Cronbach, L. J. (1955). Processes affecting scores on "understanding of others" and "assumed similarity". *Psychol. Bull.* **52**, 177–193.

Felipe, A. I. (1970). Evaluative versus descriptive consistency in trait inferences. *J. Personal. Soc. Psychol.* **16**, 627–638.

Guildford, J. P. (1954). "Psychometric Methods". McGraw-Hill, New York.

Guildford, J. P. (1965). "Fundamental Statistics in Psychology and Education" (4th edn). McGraw-Hill, New York.

Hays, W. L. (1958). An approach to the study of trait implication and trait similarity. *In* "Person Perception and Interpersonal Behavior" (Eds R. Tagiuri and L. Petrullo). Stanford University Press, Stanford.

Irwin, M., Tripodi, T. and Bieri, J. (1967). Affective stimulus value and cognitive complexity. *J. Personal. Soc. Psychol.* **4**, No. 4, 444–448.

Jaspars, J. M. F. (1966). "On social perception". Ph.D. dissertation, University of Leiden.

Jones, R. E. (1954). "Identification in Terms of Personal Constructs", Microfilm of Ph.D. dissertation, Ohio State University, Columbus, Ohio.

Kaplan, M. F. (1975). Information integration in social judgment: Interaction of judge and informational components. *In* "Human Judgment and Decision Processes" (Eds M. Kaplan and S. Schwartz). Academic Press, New York and London.

Kaplan, M. F. and Schwartz, S. (1975). "Human Judgment and Decision Processes". Academic Press, New York and London.

Kelly, G. A. (1955). "The Psychology of Personal Constructs", Vols I and II. Norton, New York.

Koltuv, B. B. (1962). Some characteristics of intrajudge trait inter-correlations. *Psych. Monographs* **76**, Whole No. 552.

McCoy, M. M. (1977). "Liking and disliking: a personal construct theory exploration". Ph.D. dissertation, University of Hong Kong.

Newcomb, T. M. (1930). Does extraversion-introversion offer a clue for the prognosis and treatment of problem boys? *Mental Hygiene* **14**, 919–925.

Osgood, C. E., Suci, G. J. and Tannenbaum, P. H. (1957). "The Measurement of Meaning". University of Illinois Press, Urbana, Illinois.

Peabody, D. (1967). Trait inferences: evaluative and descriptive aspects. *J. Personal. Soc. Psychol.* **7**, No. 4, Whole No. 644, 1–18.

Peabody, D. (1970). Evaluative and descriptive aspects in personality perception: a reappraisal. *J. Personal. Soc. Psychol.* **16**, 4, 639–646.

Rosenberg, S. and Olshan, K. (1970). Evaluative and descriptive aspects in personality perception. *J. Personal. Soc. Psychol.* **16**, 4, 619–626.

Slater, P. (1972). "Notes on Ingrid 72". Mimeo from author at Academic Dept. of Psychiatry, Clare House, St. George's Hospital, Blackshaw Road, Tooting, London S.W.17.

Symonds, P. M. (1931). "Diagnosing Personality and Conduct". Appleton, New York.

Teachers and Children: Interpersonal Relations and the Classroom

A. J. Rosie

Personal construct theory is still relatively new to the field of education. The theory's focus of convenience was originally in psychotherapy and to suggest that its range and insights be extended to classroom activity may appear to be more than the theory can cope with. If the mental constructs behind educational theorising are to always include "intelligence", "motivation" and "learning" then it might appear that PCT has little to offer. This chapter is an attempt to re-present the educational concern as primarily a matter of interpersonal relationships and to show that Kelly's work can be a fruitful line of inquiry.

Psychometry and Social Order

The majority of studies in the social psychology of education have had their roots in the psychometric paradigm and psychometry still wields considerable power. It has traditionally been associated with the study of individuals and their abilities with a marked emphasis upon the development of a theory of learning. The terms employed within this paradigm such as "intelligence" and "motivation" have become part of everyday currency and act as indicators of children's progress to teachers, parents and employers. The motivation that the child possesses is seen as a crucial factor since success at schooling is determined by it. The teacher's task becomes one of raising the child's level of motivation so that he or she can achieve his or her full ability potential. Achievement is construed as the mastery of particular bodies of knowledge which can be organised and presented sequentially throughout the child's school career. Teaching as an activity consequently becomes a management task: the management of goals and outcomes.

Support for such a programme has come from the philosophy of education (Peters, 1966). This particular philosophical viewpoint has at least implicitly claimed that it is possible to know something with certainty. Such certainties generate entities of knowledge which become enshrined in school and college curricula and provide a degree of stability. It is possible for the teacher to "know" a particular form of knowledge and to be able to transmit it to his pupils. Such a view of knowledge has been strongly criticised within the educational context (Adelstein, 1972; Hodgkin, 1976) primarily for the fact that learning experiences are robbed of their diversity; interesting learning experiences sometimes lie outside the forms of knowledge and people's common sense apprehensions of new learning experiences are largely ignored.

Perhaps the most crucial weakness in the psychometric approach to social psychology in education has been that it has failed to regard its vocabulary as being in any sense problematic. Terms such as "intelligence" and "ability" are assumed to exist independently of any particular individuals and there has been little attempt to see how individuals can interpret these terms in different ways. Because the personal interpretation of the individual has been largely ignored the social psychology of education has remained outside the classroom; it has not examined the ways in which teachers and pupils interact. In criticising Hargreaves' (1967) study of friendship groups Delamont and Hamilton (1976) point out that pupils may interact together even when they are not members of the same friendship groups and indeed the composition of such groups may change from minute to minute. Thus a new approach to the study of teacher–pupil relations is required, which will do justice to individuals' interpretive procedures.

Fresh Alternatives

The criticisms of the psychometric social order paradigm have come largely from sociologists (Esland, 1971; Stubbs and Delamont, 1976) and the attack has developed from a phenomenological frame of reference. The phenomenological stance not only views children as active meaning makers but sees the terms employed by theorists and teachers as problematic. "Intelligence" and "motivation" are no longer regarded as convenient reifications and the terms of the debate have shifted from the content of learning as an objective fact to the ways in which learning is accomplished. Pupil–teacher strategies for interpreting knowledge become the centre of concern (Barnes, 1976; Barnes and Todd, 1977) and the child's various knowledge structures become susceptible to exploration.

The phenomenological alternative has been articulated independently of educational concerns but the overriding feature has been the study of everyday life. The analyses carried out by Garfinkel (1967) and Cicourel (1973) have been extremely subtle but they have been limited. The explication of a sample of talk becomes a lengthy procedure and no framework has yet been devised within the phenomenological camp which can allow the researcher to examine long samples of talk. The methods employed are essentially descriptive and although they explore the surface features of talk in considerable detail they lack a detailed explanation of why people say and do the things that they do.

The challenge which PCT offers is essentially more radical for the viewpoint offered by constructive alternativism attacks the vocabulary employed by educationists at the very roots:

> One of the possibly distressing outcomes of this venture will be the discarding of much of what has been accumulated under the aegis of learning theory, perhaps even the abandonment of the concept of "learning" at least in its present form. (Kelly, 1955, p. 37)

The thrust of PCT is towards the experiential and the potency of the theory lies in its descriptive and explanatory power. The claim of constructive alternativism is that our certainty in the state of the world is open to revision. We are asked to accept that all our present interpretations of the universe are subject to replacement. Certainly this is not an easy claim to live with for it seems to point towards a never ending roundabout of relativism. But what lies behind it is the humanistic claim that we are always experiencing life and that we have never arrived; we are always on the way.

Personal Construct Theory and the School

In developing a descriptive approach to the understanding of talk in schools, Rosie (1976) examined the relationship between the Individuality and Commonality Corollaries for children in their first year at secondary school. The study revealed that it was possible to devise methodological procedures on a small scale which indicated some of the processes at work in group interaction. The study made no attempt to enter into the world of the teachers and the present chapter extends the methods used formerly to a study of teachers. Both studies form part of a long-term investigation into the way in which teachers and pupils interpret each others actions. For both teachers and pupils the school as an institution acts as an initiator and creator of specific patterns of construing and methods need to be devised which will illuminate the ways in which institutions form individuals' world views.

The school where the two investigations took place was a large mixed comprehensive school in an outer London borough. It had been created by the amalgamation of a grammar school and a secondary modern school. The grammar school tradition remained very marked and academic success was highly prized. I had taught English at the school since 1975 and so knew both staff and pupils well. I taught the children reported below and had gained their confidence sufficiently for them to discuss other members of their class without any apparent inhibition.

Looking at Others

Garfinkel (1967) had attempted to reveal individuals' tacit assumptions by encouraging participants to write down or to tell the investigator what was happening on a particular occasion and why it was that they spoke or acted in the way they did. By tacit assumptions Garfinkel refers to people's common sense, taken for granted knowledge, and his methods are all directed towards revealing what we all know but take for granted. In personal construct theory terms this could be seen as an attempt to explore those aspects of an individual's construct system which might not be immediately apparent to him. However, an equally suggestive possibility is that what is uncovered is the kind of construing process which may be obvious to the participant but much less obvious to the investigator who is anxious to impose his own constructs upon the participant.

In order to elucidate the construing process amongst children, five girls who knew each other well were invited to hold a conversation on their own with no adult present. No restrictions were placed upon what they could talk about and in fact they discussed Cathy,* another member of the class. The conversation was tape recorded and the children were used to working with the tape recorder. The resulting transcript provided a fascinating glimpse into the way in which these particular children viewed another person of their own age. One brief extract from the transcript was selected and shown to the five girls:

(1) *Susan*: Yes but listen, it depends, because I think she blames it on her size. That's why I think she tries to make up for it and become a bit too . . .

(2) *Carol*: I don't think that's fair. Look, you say she doesn't share things out and she doesn't give you drinks and that.

(3) *Jane*: I don't want her to.

(4) *Carol*: Well, she can't! She can't drink out of containers or anywhere that someone else's mouth's been 'cos she gets blisters.

(5) *Jane*: No it's not only that, she doesn't. It's just 'cos her dad don't let her and she's afraid to admit that, 'cos he won't let her support the Bay City Rollers or nothing.

(6) *Susan*: Well, she can't help that.

(7) *Jane*: Well, he's colour prejudiced. No, it's not her fault really, but it is her fault in a way because she's old enough now to understand.

(8) *Carol*: I don't think . . . well, she gets away with it too much.

*All names are fictitious.

The girls were asked to write down why they thought the speaker said what she did and this inevitably included their own contributions. They were then asked to write down how they felt about the interpretation which they had just offered. Since there was obviously dissension between them as to how they should assess Cathy's behaviour it was felt that this method would highlight both the tacit assumptions which they might hold in common and more particularly their own individual and personal interpretations of each other. The findings fell into two categories: an interpretation referring to Cathy, and an interpretation referring to the speaker in the transcript.

CONSTRUCTS REFERRING TO CATHY

Under this heading were placed those interpretations which compared the utterance offered by the speaker with Cathy's behaviour as it appeared to the speaker. Such construings only accounted for 25% of the available interpretations which indicated that perhaps their construings of Cathy were less important to them than their response to the utterance of whoever was speaking.

In response to Jane's utterance: "No it's not only that, she doesn't. It's just 'cos her dad don't let her and she's afraid to admit that, 'cos he won't let her support the Bay City Rollers or nothing." Sandra wrote: "She does like the Bay City Rollers and her dad should let her support them." Such a background assumption is essentially individualistic and probably reveals more about how Sandra construes parental rights than how Sandra views Cathy. This was entirely characteristic of this particular group of construings. Such commonality as existed was limited to an agreement that Cathy was the topic for discussion and that there were problems which the girls experienced in dealing with her.

It might be expected that when one of the girls was interpreting her own utterance she might reveal rather more of how she felt about Cathy. Jane in response to her own utterance above wrote, "I think I said that to spite Cathy. It might not be her dad at all." The reasons for "spiting Cathy" are clearly personal to Jane but such an interpretation provided an interesting clue to understanding how the group saw itself. If Jane is a person who is regarded as particularly forceful and dominant then her desire to spite Cathy might well be concerned with her desire to lead the conversation.

CONSTRUCTS REFERRING TO THE SPEAKER

The majority of the tacit assumptions uncovered (75%) were directed towards whoever was the speaker at the time. If Jane was speaking then Susan and Sandra were on the whole more likely to interpret Jane's utterance in the light of their own interpretation of Jane. In response to Jane's utterance quoted above Susan said, "Jane was annoyed at people sticking up for Cathy. She definitely thinks Cathy is a snob." Similarly in response to Susan's "Well she can't help that" we find the following responses:

Jane: "Susan was sticking up for Cathy when she said that."
Theresa: "I think Susan said that because she feels sorry for Cathy."

This suggests that the children were particularly alert to the construings of each other and that there was a distinct lack of commonality. Such commonality as existed is best described by what Kelly called "temporary commonality" whereby for the purpose of maintaining the conversation the girls are prepared to agree that "it is possible to accept that you don't like Cathy on a temporary basis so that we can begin to describe her as we each see fit". There is thus a delicate balancing act whereby utterances are construed in terms of feelings about the speaker while the fact that Cathy is the focus of the conversation can never be forgotten.

Although the girls construed Cathy in highly individual ways they also appeared to assume that the others would accept their construings. The method revealed something of the network of implications for each child's construct system. The further the network was pursued the more "individual" the child became (D. Bannister, 1976, personal communication). The limitations of such individuality are insufficiently explored in everyday life and a commonality is assumed. In this case Cathy as the centre for discussion provided the commonality but in fact the construing processes were far more individual than might at first appear.

Group Interaction

At this stage the analysis had not revealed anything about the ways in which the girls saw each other's role in the conversation. As their English teacher I felt that I could predict who in the group would command the most attention but a method had to be devised which would avoid any imputation of meaning on my part as researcher. It was felt that since the topic of conversation was "Cathy" the girls would be likely to view Cathy in relation to other members of the class and this would indicate whether she was like or unlike other class members. In order to explore this more fully all the girls completed individual repertory grids with members of the class, including all speakers in the transcript, as elements. The analysis is described in detail in Rosie (1976) but a very clear finding was that all the group members without exception saw Cathy as being distinctly unlike Sandra and Jane. These two were construed as similar in many ways but this similarity was highlighted by their difference to Cathy. Jane's picture of the group shows this very clearly (Fig. 1).

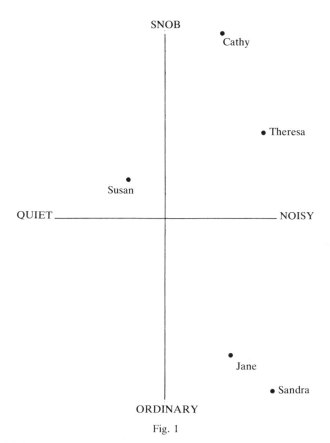

Fig. 1

All the girls located Jane and Sandra in similar ways and they also saw Susan and Cathy as being alike in some respects. Thus the allegiances and hostilities which develop during a conversation are to a large extent the outcome of the way in which the children view particular groupings. If Jane and Sandra can dominate the conversation (they accounted for 68% of all utterances) then Cathy is bound to be seen in negative terms and Susan is likely to be construed negatively. Their written evaluations of Susan's utterances indicated this: "Susan's a bit soft." "I think Susan said that because she is very like Cathy in her ways." "Susan sticks up for Cathy."

Although this particular study had highlighted the importance of the Individuality Corollary and had indicated that commonality might be more of a surface feature of conversation than one might at first suppose it had not explored the full implications of the Commonality Corollary and it had revealed little about the importance of sociality.

Teachers Talk about Each Other

The study reported below was concerned primarily with investigating the Commonality and Sociality Corollaries as they arose in an institution such as a school. The school which was studied remained the same as the one in the earlier research but this time the focus of concern was the teachers. To study construing processes across the entire staff was impractical so one subject department, the English Department, became the topic for investigation. The head of the department had just completed his first year at the school and both he and the second in charge of the department (myself) espoused theories of English teaching which were at variance with much of the department's practice. The rifts which were taking place were a matter of concern to all and changes in departmental policy appeared imminent.

The method employed in the investigation consisted largely of semi-structured interviews. Three teachers in the English Department were studied in detail. The Head of Department was selected because so much of the informal conversation in the school staffroom was concerned with his policies. The other two teachers were openly critical of the Head of Department and were deeply concerned with the changes that they felt they might have to face. Constructs were elicited from all three by asking them to compare and contrast other teachers including members of the English Department. However, the elements presented were not confined to teachers but also included identities such as "You as you see yourself in five years time", "You as a teacher three years ago", "You as a bad teacher". But in order to bring out the allegiances and hostilities that were developing all the constructs elicited were compared with what the teachers said in the interviews. They were asked to comment upon the constructs elicited and were allowed to elaborate them in any way they chose.

THE TEACHERS

Jeff

Jeff was the new Head of Department. Aged 32, he had taught in a number of schools and was keen to develop mixed ability teaching and a language policy as it was envisaged in the Bullock Report (1975).

Stephen

Stephen was in charge of many of the internal examinations and some of the public examinations. Aged 47, he had taught at the school for ten years having taught in a variety of other schools.

Jean

Jean was in charge of Drama teaching. Aged 33, she had taught at the school for four years after training as a mature student. This was the only school in which she had taught.

The school had begun to re-examine its curriculum and all teachers in the school had completed a questionnaire on the reasons why pupils did not always succeed at school. Although the questionnaire formed no part of the present research it did provide a list of dimensions which teachers at the school felt to be desirable if good teaching was to take place. The list of dimensions were regarded as the public dimensions which the school as an institution sanctioned but it was felt that teachers might construe such dimensions in individual ways. The list was presented to the three teachers for their comments. Stephen and Jean expressed complete agreement with the dimensions:

Being quiet and orderly
Not interrupting the teacher when he or she is speaking
Wearing school uniform
Doing homework
Paying attention in class
Keeping up with the work
Learning to work on your own

Jeff agreed that these dimensions were important but felt that features such as teacher–pupil relationships and promoting conversation in class were equally important. It is noticeable that the list of dimensions falls into the psychometric social order paradigm and the differences between Jeff and the other two teachers was in part due to the different paradigms informing their classroom strategies. The dimensions were rendered into construct form in the interviews by eliciting the contrast poles. In order to discover how the three English teachers interpreted these dimensions in their own personal terms a reverse operation was performed: the contrast pole was treated as the emergent pole and they were asked to state the new implicit pole. This implicit pole would be their own personal interpretation of the official school dimension (see Table I).

It is clear from the table that Jeff's position is very different from that of Stephen and Jean and this was no doubt due to his experience of alternative methods of teaching and different theoretical paradigms. It is important to remember that the personal construings are not equivalent to the verbal labels. Nevertheless, it is clear that on some dimensions Stephen and Jean share commonality. For Stephen and Jean "paying attention in class"

TABLE I

STEPHEN

School's official construct	Personal version of the official construct
Being quiet and orderly	Doing as you are told
Not interrupting the teacher	Being courteous
Wearing school uniform	Conforming to standards
Doing homework	Doing as you are told
Paying attention in class	Getting on with the work
Keeping up with the work	Capable of doing the work
Learning to work on your own	Working on your own

JEAN

School's official construct	Personal version of the official construct
Being quiet and orderly	Being well behaved
Not interrupting the teacher	Being well behaved
Wearing school uniform	Not seeking to draw attention to yourself
Doing homework	Remembering instructions
Paying attention in class	Getting on with the work
Keeping up with the work	Able to do the work without trouble
Learning to work on your own	Becoming independent

JEFF

School's official construct	Personal version of the official construct
Being quiet and orderly	Creating conditions for learning
Not interrupting the teacher	Being interested in the lesson
Wearing school uniform	Accepting school rules
Doing homework	Doing as you are told
Paying attention in class	Feel it necessary to listen to the teacher
Keeping up with the work	Finding the work interesting
Learning to work on your own	Discovering that teachers don't know everything

appeared to mean the same thing. For both these teachers "being well behaved" was an important dimension of pupil activity although it seems to carry different implications for them. This is set into greater relief if their own personal construct systems are compared (see Table II).

For Jean "behaving well" is an important construct and this was seen in her attitude to what constituted a good lesson. She said, "If they can't behave in class they won't learn." Similarly "imposing order" was an important construct for Stephen and governed his approach to how well he thought he was progressing with a class. Thus there is a commonality of construing here. For both teachers children "working quietly" and "following teacher instructions" are similarly construed.

Jean described her role as teacher in these terms:

> I expect children to be polite and I think I know more than they do. If I don't there's not much point in my being there. Of course kids are naughty but they can all be well behaved if it suits them.

Stephen described his position as:

> I insist on order in the classroom, and I won't have children disobeying me. They must learn that I'm in authority. They try it on and it's true sometimes I take no notice; that's when they're rude in the street. You expect them to try it on but if they're rude in the class or don't get on with the work I tell them off. I put them in their place.

There appears to be a commonality here but the superordinate constructs differ. For Stephen "status confers duties and powers" controlled a good

TABLE II

STEPHEN

Responsibility – Not having a job to do
Not being dictated to – Giving in under pressure
Teaching has status – Lack of status
Children need to be told what to do – Lack of order

JEAN

Being cared about – Being neglected
Working hard – Being lazy
Behaving well – Being unpleasant
Being an individual – Being one of the crowd

---

deal of his activity whereas for Jean "caring about people" was a superordinate construct in that a good deal of her behaviour appeared to be construed in terms of whether or not Jeff was showing care and support to her.

The commonality that exists here must not be taken too literally; it is a surface commonality similar to that found amongst the children in the earlier study. Such commonality allows the participants to get on with the business of teaching as a daily routine in terms which the other understands. What appears to be a superordinate construct for Stephen and Jean within their different construct systems may be better seen as an example of "comprehensive construing". Kelly defined this:

> Comprehensive constructs are those which subsume a relatively wide variety of events. They are not necessarily highly regnant or superordinate constructs for the events which they subsume may all be relatively low on the superordinate–subordinate scale. (Kelly, 1955, p. 477)

For Stephen and Jean "good behaviour" is a comprehensive construct which subsumes a wide range of teacher–pupil situations and indeed teacher to teacher contacts. It is this comprehensiveness which leads to the commonality. At the level of superordinate constructs Stephen and Jean's individual construct systems differ but at the lower level of regulation of classroom life the comprehensive construing provides a common approach.

Fixing Commonality

The personal construings of the institutional dimensions for Stephen and Jean help to fix the "psychological space" in which such dimensions can operate. They act as implications for the institutional construct and as such are personal implications. It is a dialectical process in that it is from such personal construings that the institutional dimensions can achieve the objective status they possess. Karst and Groutt (1977) develop the notion of a "one-sided commonality" whereby there may be an overlap on one construct pole but not on the other which produces a surface commonality effect. In addition to this there is the need to explore a "multi-faceted commonality". For commonality to exist requires not only a similarity of construing but also a similarity of construct type. If two people agree that "it is important to treat people as individuals" they share commonality. But if one of them is construing pre-emptively, perhaps in response to a threat or challenge, then the implications that the construct has for him are curtailed. If his fellow construer is in a position where he can construe propositionally then not only will the implications of his construct be available because there is that extra degree of openness, but the construing will be different to that of the pre-emptive construer. The verbal label may remain the same but the actual process of construing will differ and hence the apparent commonality at that particular time will be a surface feature.

To the extent that Stephen and Jean both construe in an apparently pre-emptive manner then such commonality as exists is likely to be more than a surface feature. From different construct positions they both move towards a common view:

> *Stephen*: Jeff just sends me bits of paper—he doesn't talk to us unless you're in favour and of course I'm old fashioned.
> *Jean*: We are never told anything and there seems to be no clear direction. Jeff is far too indecisive and you are lucky if you can find him. I suppose that depends on whether you're in favour.

Both Stephen and Jean regard themselves as being "out of favour" and investigation revealed that they construed this in a pre-emptive manner. For instance both felt that any attempt by Jeff to see their work was a fault finding exercise and they appeared to disbelieve his explanation that it was an attempt to see how all members of the department approached English teaching. To this extent there was a real commonality of construing between them and it appeared to be more than a surface feature since they were both contemplating the same action:

> *Stephen*: Well, I will probably leave when my wife finishes the course she is doing. I need the money and I've been a Head of Department before and I've done all the work.
> *Jean*: I think I will leave. I wish I had stuck to my guns before when I handed in my notice. No one seems to spend time on people here and there's no caring. It's the little things that matter.

Both teachers reveal commonality in that they see themselves as "out of favour" and about to take similar lines of action. But the conversation shows that in each case certain superordinate constructs which are individual are controlling the feeling of being out of favour. For Jean it is her construct of "Being cared about" and for Stephen it is his construct of "I can handle responsibility and know what I'm doing". Once again following through the network of implications for an individual's construing it is found that he or she becomes more "individual" although at the level of everyday interaction the implications each construct holds for a person are rarely followed through and only a systematic investigation reveals them.

It would be inaccurate to suggest that commonality necessarily requires a similarity of construing type. It is possible for one person to construe pre-emptively and for another to construe propositionally and for there still to be a level of commonality. But such a situation requires that the propositional construer recognise the fixity of his pre-emptive partner. This is illustrated by Stephen and Jeff.

Stephen: Now last January when we were organising the C.S.E. orals I liked the way Jeff asked me to organise that. It was clearly laid down and it was sensible. If children didn't turn up they'd had it and they all turned up.
Jeff: The C.S.E. orals had to be organised in a more systematic way. I wanted the children to have a definite list of times for turning up. I would have made sure that they took the oral if they had forgotten but the problem didn't arise. Stephen was happy. I don't think it's the only way of doing it but it served its purpose.

Jeff accepts that Stephen's approach was a possibility in this situation and they appear to construe "organising children for an examination" in a similar manner. Jeff has accepted the pre-emptive nature of Stephen's construing and by accepting its pre-emptive nature is able to present this commonality. However, for Jeff who construes in a more propositional manner Stephen's approach was one amongst a range of possibilities and the approach adopted was one that was generally acceptable. Thus commonality was only achieved (and as a surface feature) when the propositional construer accepted the pre-emptive construer's approach as a possibility amongst a set of available alternatives.

Sociality

The playing of a role in a social process to the extent that a person is able to construe the construction of the person he is relating to (Kelly, 1955, p. 95) is demonstrated from these conversations. The people involved are not required to construe each other very accurately for such role playing to be a success. Indeed it is when apparent failures occur that the process is most wide open to inspection. Both Stephen and Jean had to make decisions concerning Jeff and they had had a year to come to know him.

Stephen: I don't see how Jeff and I can get on. He believes in mixed ability but of course it doesn't work. I don't agree with his ideas. To be honest with you they aren't liked by parents or teachers in junior schools. Take this new business of not marking every mistake and not giving a numerical mark for younger children. It annoys me. I'm sorry. It goes against everything I believe in.
Jean: I don't like the way the department is going. We are never told anything and there seems to be no clear direction. Also we seem to be doing away with things like course books. Well, it's not very good for an English Department. Jeff is far too trendy.

These extracts reveal how both teachers construe Jeff's constructions of English teaching but they do so in different ways. Stephen's approach will be analysed below as an example of hostility but it is clear that his handling of Jeff's construction system is handled pre-emptively. "He believes in mixed ability but of course it doesn't work" is a case in point and acts as the means for the rejection of all new ideas. Since the majority of the staff at the school were also opposed to mixed ability teaching there was considerable institutional support for Stephen's view. However, the possibilities of joint action in harmony are very limited for Stephen and Jeff. The pre-emptive rejection has led to a denial of any commonality but has allowed what might be called a negative sociality to emerge.

Jean's approach might be seen as more constellatory in nature; "not being told things," "lacking direction", and "condemnation of certain materials" are constellatory with either "bad teaching" or "poor leadership". However, the sociality is again of a negative nature for a construing such as "not being told things" is pre-emptive in direction.

It is interesting to compare these constructions of Jeff with the latter's construction of Stephen and Jean.

> *Jeff*: I expect they think I'm remote and that I don't tell them what to do. Well, that's deliberate because I wanted them to try to change the way they went about things without my laying down the law. But it looks as though I shall have to. They are not used to taking responsibility; it's always someone else's job. I know there's a rift between Stephen, Jean and myself. For Stephen I think the fact that he is the oldest person in the department and has always believed in rules has formed his outlook. He is not sympathetic to the needs of children. With him, it's all status—that's very important to him. He works hard according to his lights but it's lists and rules, no thinking. Of course you can run things on Stephen's lines and it would do very well in some ways. It would be clear but it would be limited and there are other possibilities which are just as efficient administratively but they involve more work.
>
> I think Jean needs help. She is obviously under strain but she doesn't respond too well. I don't think her problems are necessarily school based but she is beginning to cause trouble.

Jeff enters into Stephen's constructions to the extent that he identifies status and order as crucial outlooks for him. He is accurate in that they are an important part of Stephen's system. This is a more positive form of sociality in that Stephen's construing is seen as a possibility. In this case commonality has potentiated sociality in that, as described above, accepting Stephen's pre-emptive constructions allows work to proceed and allows a relationship to develop.

It was important to see if this had occurred at all with Jean and so she was asked to compare her present feelings with the way she felt earlier in the year.

> *Jean*: At first I thought he was a welcome change. He was interested in Drama and he wanted to do things. But then we got nowhere. He never remembered what it was like for me to teach eight periods of Drama a day. Then he delayed the timetables.

This shows that initially there had been a more positive sharing of each others construction systems but that what for Jean was a core construct "Being cared about" was challenged. From then all Jeff's negative actions were subsumed under the neglect end of her "Being cared about" construct.

The positive approach was seen to exist in terms of the commonality of "Being interested in Drama" but her later construings included "He doesn't take an interest in what it's like to teach drama". Negative sociality could of course exist without any commonality but the construings would be largely pre-emptive in nature. For a more positive approach a greater degree of propositionality is required.

Hostility as Pre-emption

In terms of personal construct theory the rift between Stephen and Jeff can be seen as a case of hostility. Kelly defined hostility as "the continued effort to extort validational evidence in favour of a type of social prediction which has already been recognized as a failure" (Kelly, 1955, p. 510).

Stephen's attempt to amass evidence that a new approach is a failure, "mixed ability does not work, not marking every mistake is bad", represent a considerable effort on his part to discredit a new programme. This can be studied as an example of psychotherapy but it is also revealing to see it in educationist terms. The bets and predictions Stephen has made belong very closely to the psychometric, order maintenance paradigm whereas the challenge Jeff offers him comes from the phenomenological paradigm.

Stephen's hostility can be seen in his attempts to show that his paradigm is correct and in terms of the institutional support he can receive from this particular school he will be successful. In his case the order maintenance paradigm provides part of his core role structure so the attack on it is crucial. He must discredit the Head of Department if he is to maintain his core constructs. Validating evidence for his perspective is culled from teacher folklore on mixed ability and teaching methods and the support is very real. But the actual articulation of his position requires him to construe pre-emptively but in fact this is a change for him.

> *Stephen*: Eight years ago I was a very different person. I was very touchy and would fly off the handle at the smallest thing. I was terrible sometimes with classes. I was always going on about my status. Getting married made a big difference to me. I'm more easy going now. I'm better with children and I can think of new ideas. Of course you have to change and I expect that from Jeff but the last few months have shown that not all the changes are good.

The challenge to Stephen, as he sees it, is that he must take up residence at the outer end of his personal constructs. He must endorse a diminution of standards, accept chaos, and lose status as he sees it. To avoid this he acts in a hostile manner. But the real challenge for him is not just on the personal level but in terms of a paradigm shift. The articulation of an alternative paradigm can be a painful process because it can lead to precisely this kind of problem. It is not just a matter of changing bets but of construing new implications. When a paradigm shift is threatened hostility will be one of the responses to be expected. But whereas the phenomenological paradigm operates largely at the theoretical level a personal construct theory approach can specify ways of approaching children in classrooms.

Conclusion

This particular study of children and teachers is essentially exploratory. As such it has attempted to throw some light on the Individuality, Commonality and Sociality Corollaries. The descriptive approach has meant that it is possible to capture the flavour of individuals talking about each other but inevitably there are many other areas to explore. A personal construct theory approach to the psychology of education needs to be developed. At the more general level there is a need to develop further methods for investigating how children interpret their experiences of school and the ways in which teachers construe individual children. Such topics lie outside the scope of the present chapter. However, it would also be illuminating to carry out detailed case studies of individual children and teachers over a period of time. Such a study of children could highlight the ways in which an individual's personal construct system develops whereas a case study of a teacher who is new to a particular school could show how institutional demands and career perspectives are handled.

Nevertheless, the role of personal construct theory is radical in nature. The fact that it plays little part in teacher training programmes bears this out. Traditionalist approaches to the psychology of education consist largely of a study of psychometric procedures operating with a fixed definition of learning theory and a Piagetian model of child activity. While a personal construct theory approach has much in common with Piagetian theory there are also crucial differences (see Salmon, 1970). Perhaps the most significant difference is that afforded by constructive alternativism as a philosophical stance. Despite Kelly's disclaimers against phenomenology there is much to be gained from investigating the work of phenomenologically oriented sociologists of education. Esland (1977) provides a theoretical model but makes no attempt to investigate actual classroom practices. Barnes (1976) does provide a detailed glimpse of classroom procedures and children's learning strategies. But although his analysis indicates how different teacher strategies can control different learning outcomes it does not show precisely how pupil and teacher understandings develop out of their personal views of the world. Although the analysis in this chapter is descriptive it is intended to go beyond the narrative accounts of children and teacher talk. Such narratives require explanation and unless a theoretical model can provide a means of relating classroom narratives to the individual's experience of self as a being in the world they are bound to be inadequately explained. Personal construct theory is an approach which allows the researcher to relate the practice of an individual to his place in a group, in other words to uncover some of the hidden areas which allow a person to consider himself a being who is dealing with a real world. Such an apparently existential claim is really a demand that psychology should take as its focus of convenience the way in which individuals operate within the groups they come into contact with. As such it is an interpersonal inquiry and one which requires a variety of methodological procedures.

Personal construct theory has tended to ignore the role of the institution (Proctor and Parry, 1978) but any study of individuals must make reference to the groups which act as public definers of what is to count as acceptable. Schools, through the institutional dimensions which they generate, provide rules for what is to count as acceptable performance on the part of teachers and pupils. But a social psychology must uncover the ways in which the participants make personal sense of the institution and its demands. The flexibility which PCT offers allows different methods to be adopted which will illuminate such personal understandings and hence lead to more adequate psychological research.

References

Adelstein, D. L. (1972). The philosophy of education or the wit and wisdom of R. S. Peters. *In* "Countercourse" (Ed. T. Paterman). Penguin, Harmondsworth.

Barnes, D. (1976). "From Communication to Curriculum". Penguin, Harmondsworth.

Barnes, D. and Todd, F. (1977). "Communication and Learning in Small Groups". Routledge and Kegan Paul, London.

Cicourel, A. V. (1973). "Cognitive Sociology". Penguin, Harmondsworth.

Delamont, S. and Hamilton, D. (1976). "Classroom research: a critique and a new approach". *In* "Explorations in Classroom Observation" (Eds M. Stubbs and S. Delamont). Wiley, Chichester.

Esland, G. (1971). Teaching and learning as the organization of Knowledge. *In* "Knowledge and Control" (Ed. M. F. D. Young). Collier Macmillan, London.

Esland, G. (1977). "Schooling and Pedagogy". Open University Press.

Garfinkel, H. (1967). "Studies in Ethnomethodology". Prentice Hall, Englewood Cliffs, New Jersey.

Hargreaves, D. H. (1967) "Social Relations in a Secondary School". Routledge and Kegan Paul, London.

Hodgkin, R. A. (1976). "Born Curious: new perspectives in educational theory". Wiley, Chichester.

Karst, T. O. and Groutt, J. W. (1977). Inside mystical heads: shared and personal constructs in a commune with some implications for a personal construct theory social psychology. *In* "New Perspectives in Personal Construct Theory" (Ed. D. Bannister). Academic Press, London and New York.

Kelly, G. A. (1955). "The Psychology of Personal Constructs", Vols I and II. Norton, New York.

Peters, R. S. (1966) "Ethics and Education". George Allen and Unwin, London.

Proctor, H. and Parry, G. (1978). Constraint and freedom; the social origin of personal constructs. *In* "Personal Construct Psychology" (Ed. F. Fransella). Academic Press, London and New York.

Rosie, A. J. (1976). "The role of personal construct theory in understanding classroom talk". Unpublished M.A Dissertation, University of London.

Salmon, P. (1970). A psychology of personal growth. *In* "Perspectives in Personal Construct Theory" (Ed. D. Bannister). Academic Press, London and New York.

Stubbs, M. and Delamont, S. (1976). "Explorations in Classroom Observation". Wiley, Chichester.

Politics and Identity in South Africa

Peter du Preez

In this chapter I ask, and sketch answers to, the following questions:
What is identity?
Why should identity be thought important to a psychology of politics?
How do we account for the emotional quality of political construction of identity?
How is black identity construed by various political groups in South Africa?
How can we construe a political contract?

What is Identity?

Kelly's concept of core constructs makes an important contribution to our theory of identity. He writes: "Core constructs are those which govern a person's maintenance processes—that is, those by which he maintains his identity and existence" (Kelly, 1955, p. 482). Core constructs are contrasted with peripheral constructs which "can be altered without serious modification of core structures" (Kelly, 1955, p. 483). From this, it follows that persons who act from a clear identity can take decisions on important matters and play their part in relation to significant others. Fragmentation, submergence, and looseness of fit are properties of the core system that make it difficult for persons to know where they stand. It also follows that to understand someone else's identity we have to construe his core constructs.

There are several things that can go wrong in this attempt. We may construe a person's identity in terms of peripheral or even irrelevant constructs. That is, we may simply misunderstand him. We may think that his nationality or his race is the key to his identity; whereas he attaches importance to his religion, the fact that he is a good musician, and his loyalty to his family. Many of the constructs making up the person's identity are preverbal, e.g. an optimistic or pessimistic construction of the world may be based on very early experiences, and are difficult to explain in the casual way I have

341

apparently suggested. To discover the origins of such constructs may be a difficult task, both for the persons being construed and for the construer.

Another thing that can go wrong in our attempts to identify people is that we believe that we are doing well when we locate them like butterflies classified under a taxonomy in a grid of "well understood" constructs—and pre-emptive and constellatory constructs at that! The value of locating people in this way is that we can stop wondering what they will do next. They are, as far as we are concerned, objects. Propositional construing poses too many questions. If someone is a worker we know where we are. But if, on the other hand, we acknowledge that his being a worker leaves many other possibilities open, and if our construing him as such is merely provisional (who knows what the implications are? or whether it would be more useful to construe him in other ways?), we have to be prepared for uncertainty. Social systems may be structured so as to allow for propositional construing or to compel pre-emptive and constellatory construing of persons. We see pre-emptive and constellatory construing in the laws and institutions of many societies. A person's race, religion or sex too often determine which other constructs are applied to him.

Construing persons as objects is quite different from trying to construe their constructs. The first allows us to make them play roles which we determine for them; the second allows us to engage with them in an exchange of roles. Kelly refers to the first as "structuralization" and to the second as "construction". In the first process we arrange a person's behaviours directly under our own system. In the second, we attempt to subsume his constructs under our own—to grasp his ways of construing events, although we always rely on our own construing abilities to do so (Kelly, 1955, p. 455). Bannister and Fransella's (1971, p. 146) remarks on construing self-as-an-element versus construing self-as-a-construct may make this clearer. In grid terms, we may treat a person as a self to which constructs (our constructs, when we are identifying him) are applied. The consequence is to allow him to change only to the extent that our construction of him as an element changes. In society we can treat laws as constructs which are applied more or less rigidly to persons (who are occasionally even referred to as elements!—radical elements, lawless elements, etc.) in a more or less constellatory way. This is particularly evident when classes of persons are subject to civil disabilities in terms of the law and are not allowed political action to change the way in which they are construed. On the other hand, we may prefer to treat the person as a system of constructs which can be applied to various elements (such as work, family, law, etc.). It is the old question of whether man was made for the Sabbath or the Sabbath for man. Once we treat a person as a system of constructs (some of them even propositional, perhaps) we introduce the possibility that he may be a system of pathways ("an arrow of desire", in Nietzsche's phrase) rather than an object.

To summarise, identification may be understood as having two dimensions: (i) core/peripheral (or tangential); and (ii) self-as-element/self-as-construct.

I have used the terms "identify" and "self" rather interchangeably because they overlap to a great extent. But this does give rise to some puzzles. One of these is to be found in Kelly's definition of guilt: "Guilt is the awareness of dislodgment of the self from one's core role structure" (Kelly, 1955, p. 533). This suggests that there is an internal perspective yet more central than, or perhaps merely different from, the self. The same sort of puzzle occurs in discussions of multiple personality (McKellar, 1977; Osgood *et al.*, 1954, 1976) and multiple selves (Mair, 1977; Fingarette, 1969).

In literature, dislodged selves have been remarked on by Tristan ("Journal d'un Autre"), Rimbaud ("je suis l'autre"), and Nerval ("je suis l'autre"), all of whom tried to locate themselves in the "other" with whom they co-existed. "Otherness" as Sartre points out in his definition of conscious as a being which "implies a being other than itself" (Sartre, 1957, p. 47) is a permanent condition of persons.

Do we then say that a person has as many identities (and systems of core constructs) as he has selves? This is the view that Goffman seems to advance in "The Presentation of Self in Everyday Life" (1959), when the self is spoken of as a performed character; but by the time we reach "Asylums" (1961), the self can be violated and mortified. "Indeed, it could be agreed that whereas Goffman's first book was about the self and its *presentation*, the subsequent *Asylums* is about the *preservation of self*" (Sandall, 1978, p. 68). In the first book persons provide bodies for a number of dramatic effects; in the second, the self has to be defended and maintained, and we come closer to a theory of a "real self" among other selves.

Luria and Osgood, in their postscripts to the discussion of "Evelyn's" multiple personality, ask, "Is there an underlying 'real' person in cases of multiple personality?" They note that the original Eve—of three faces of fame—herself referred to her real personality; they also note that one personality in the Evelyn case mediated in the inner conversation of two other personalities. They suggest that "even in clinical cases of multiple personality, like those of Eve and Evelyn, it appears that there is a real personality that is aware of all its roles" (Osgood *et al.*, 1976, p. 286). The roles may be dissociated from each other, but can be addressed by the "real" personality.

The suggestion that there is a "real" personality can, taken in combination with Mair's (1977) metaphor of the community of self, yield a solution to the problems of multiplicity and integrity. Let us start with Mair's metaphor. He points out that different selves are often construed in repertory grids— "myself as I am", "myself as I'd like to be", "myself as I was", and concludes, "In this way any one person can be considered as being constituted of numerous alternative, but potential 'selves' " (Mair, 1977, p. 144). What is central is "the person", who can "live" through many "selves", with each or any construct, so to speak, being potentially the centre of an alternative "self" (Mair, 1977, p. 141).

The suggestion by Osgood *et al.* appears to be that one self is more central than the other; the suggestion by Mair appears to be that the person is protean, assuming selves as "guises and forms through and in which the person can participate actively in experiencing and exploring his world from numerous perspectives" (Mair, 1977, p. 141). The former suggestion could be accommodated quite comfortably within the Kellyan notion of "core constructs" which maintain identity. We could speak of a "core self" or "identity" as the self which mediates other selves. This self is the "I" of subjective identity and the "you" of objective identity.

The problem of the multiplicity and unity of personhood is not a recent problem. In theological dispute, the Sabellians maintained that the Trinity was of one essence and that the three persons of God were merely aspects or manifestations of this other essence. The Arians maintained that there were distinct persons. The resolution of this problem was that the three persons co-existed in and with each other (Bettenson, 1947).

If we assume that there are various selves co-existing in the person, and add the assumption that the relation of these to a core self determines the unity or diversity of personhood, we may solve the problems of unity and diversity that have loomed so large in discussion of personhood. Where there is a clearly established core self, the person has a clearly established identity. Various selves may be dissociated from the core self to a greater or lesser extent. Where this dissociation is severe, we encounter what is referred to as "multiple personality".

The ordering and partitioning of selves can be discussed under the Kellyan corollaries of organisation and fragmentation. Selves are construed by the person during the course of his growth. The person is potential self and potential identity: identity is achieved by a resolution of the conflict of different selves. This, of course, is very close to the psychoanalytic account of the introjection of selves as these are construed by the individual in a series of defensive and analytic identifications (e.g. Mussen, 1967).

How does this differ from "acting", from the performance of selves as it is viewed by those who espouse the dramatic model? First, these selves are not merely assumed for a performance. There is, as Sandall remarks, a pretty clear distinction between "acting" and "action" (1978, p. 64). One does not act "as if" one were one's self—in any of its many forms. One *may*; one *can* act "as if". That does not imply that one cannot draw the distinction between "as if" and "real" acting. Mair (1977) invited his clients to try out the community of selves as a metaphor when experimenting to alter their constructions of events. Kelly (1955) proposes an "as if" performance in fixed role therapy. Neither would deny the distinction between being Joe Bloggs and pretending to be Joe Bloggs. The person is invited to try out Joe Bloggs in order to elaborate the implications of his core self.

Let us then look at the various puzzles of identity and self from this new perspective. The person achieves an identity as he creates a system of core constructs which determine his real or superordinate self. This is not always plain sailing. Persons may modify (with great pain) parts of their core self—particularly during adolescence. The most successful accounts of the crisis in the construction of identity appear to have been given by Erikson (1963).

The integrity of the core construct system, through its various transformations, gives the individual a sense of subjective continuity. It also gives him a consistent position from which to view events, to the extent that problems of organisation, permeability, modulation and fragmentation of the core system are managed.

Though the person has a central self, he has other selves at his disposal. He has, as Mair observes, "as many selves" as he has vantage points from which to act (1977, p. 146). We can reverse this and say that the person has as many vantage points from which to act as he has selves. It is always from the point of view of some self that he is able to engage in coherent action. This capacity to act by making use of other selves is not only a source of change; it also enables us to understand how guilt is possible and how the person can construe the dislodgement of his core self from its roles.

When we construe other people, we attempt to construe the self which is acting; an attempt at "deep construing" (as when Osgood *et al.* detected Gina's "real" personality) requires that we construe the person's core self in its relation to the claimed and unclaimed or alienated selves of his personality. This was one of the insights of psychoanalysis.

Why Should Identity be thought Important to a Psychology of Politics?

The shortest answer to this is that politics is concerned with the power to allocate roles to persons of given identity. That is, the roles which blacks, women, children, foreigners, Jews or any other group may play in a society will be limited by political decision.

This assignment of roles can reach through the family into the earliest years of childhood and become part of the core role structure of the person.

Furthermore, since the allocation of roles depends on identification according to common constructs such as race, sex, ethnicity or religion, these common constructs become part of dominated man's hated and depised self.

In many societies, (wo)men are selected for roles according to criteria which may, from a rational point of view, have little to do with their fitness for these roles. On closer examination, we discover that these criteria serve the interests of persons with power. By construing another in such a way that he has to play a certain role in relation to one, he may (a) validate the self that one is—and it is fundamental to Kelly's conception of role that one needs someone else for one's performance; (b) validate the equity of the arrangement by consistently being inferior—in inferior roles; (c) be rendered harmless; (d) do one's work for one; (e) enrich one; (f) serve one's sexual interests; (g) take on all the dangerous and dirty work; etc.

This does not mean that roles are allocated only in what we regard as the state political system. There is a politics of the family, a politics of the school, a politics of the factory, a politics of all institutions in which identity is negotiated by the allocation of roles. But the politics of the state are often seen to be superordinate, and quite correctly so. One cannot immediately alter the regulations of all other systems by capturing power in the state system, but one can go some way. And for this reason, political power is often seen as a big issue by movements of various sorts.

Identity can be imposed by those who construe others from a position of power. There is, firstly, the simple identification of others as elements in the construct system shared by those who have power. This is what Kelly called "structuralisation" and Bannister and Fransella called construing self-as-an-element.

But once identity has been construed *for* a person, he is denied those roles which would invalidate this construction. This is oppression. The oppressed person is one whose identity is construed for him. The basis of this construct may seem arbitrary and irrelevant; but he finds himself confined to roles in which the imposed identity becomes increasingly true of him. We know this of women (e.g. Fransella and Frost, 1977) and of blacks (e.g. Fanon, 1970; Mannoni, 1956; Erikson, 1968). Their core selves are constituted in the roles they must play (though not all of these are determined by the state).

The position of a dominated person is this: his shame is that he is not what he ought to be (who can be "feminine" enough to compete with advertisements?) and his guilt is that he is dislodged from the self he wishes to be (free, independent, an equal among others).

Though some are perfectly lodged in their core roles, many are not. Their deviance becomes the source of future growth.

How is this possible? First, there is the reaction of anger when the person's pathways to growth are blocked. In construct theory, anger may be described as an "awareness of invalidation of constructs leading to hostility" (McCoy, 1977, p. 121). Erikson speaks of the growing child's "vitalising sense of reality" when he realises that his "ego synthesis is a successful variant of a group identity" (Erikson, 1971; p. 49). What if a group identity does not readily permit a "successful variant"? What if it is so deprived that many of the opportunities it offers lead to unsuccessful variants? True, many variants of deprived group identity lead to depression, withdrawal, submission, etc. But every community has contradictions. Children of the deprived go to schools where some of them elaborate selves which are blocked. It is from the invalidation of personal constructs out of which their growing selves are being put together that the most destructive anger is generated.

The next form of deviance arises out of a change of pole. When persons transvalue their negative identity images, they become deviant though they have not changed their construction of wants. They still construe the world by means of the same grid of constructs, but their position in that grid has changed. The transvalued negative image may then be elaborated in action—it may become a positive thing to be a worker, a suffragette, Jewish, or black. Such a shift will occur when the implications of what was previously the negative pole become more attractive than the implications of the position or hitherto adapted pole. For this to happen, the implications must be spelt out and tested (in personal or modelled behavioural experiments) and must promise elaboration of the construct system. Part of this is the work of ideologists; part the work of supportive communities of like-minded persons.

A third way in which deviance becomes the source of growth is when new constructs are created in the dialogue between and within persons. What this requires is essentially the creation of new points of view, utilising selves over which each person disposes. It is from this vantage point that he can examine his core self, and in this scrutiny new possibilities may be discovered. The term "scrutiny" is perhaps too lifeless. Each of these selves, whether "metaphorical" or "real", can be the beginning of an experiment. Whereas the first two forms of deviance (anger and transvaluation of poles) leave the system of constructs intact (at least initially), the third form of deviance leads to change of the system itself.

Identities are often summarised and communicated in widespread myths, each with a core identity and complementary identities. The core identity (pioneer, cowboy, trekker, etc.) tells the person what his group identity really is—by virtue of shared and inherent characteristics. It also tells him what the others are like (the complementary identities) and justifies the relation between the core identity and the others.

At the level of folk culture these myths are very common. We also see them penetrate scholarly histories and many forms of "social science", representing at the symbolic level the actual relations of power and production in society. Political change must be brought about by changing the roles which people play—not merely their representations of these roles. But part of the preparation for change is the changing of myths and the transvaluation of negative constructs. A little real success may make a big impact on a prepared mind. Symbolic and actual change feed on each other. To end shame, the other person's construction of one's self has to be rejected; to end guilt, the person has to be what he is; that is, the other person has to be stopped from determining one's identity.

We shall see the implications of this a little later.

How do we Account for the Emotional Quality of Political Construction of Identity?

Emotion, in personal construct theory, is "a state of awareness of some fate of the construct system" (McCoy, 1977, p. 99). We have seen above that guilt and shame are present in the relations between dominating and dominated people. It is clear that many other emotions—threat, anxiety, anger, love, happiness—can be present in political struggle, because politics is about the fate of construct systems, especially those common construct systems which take the form of ideology.

People build up more or less stable ways of construing political relations. Some of these constructs are peripheral, others are deeply connected with the person's identity. The emotion experienced under change would depend on the way in which these constructs function. What is to some an uncertain or doubtful situation will be to others threatening and frightening. Some may be anxious and others more interested than anxious as the question of the goodness of fit of their constructs arises.

We can advance the general proposition that people seek to maintain their core structure and that to the extent that the existing political relations are necessary to this, they will experience threat and fear when change appears to be irresistible, and anger leading to hostility when resistance appears possible. There is a general axiom in information theory that information destroys meaning, where meaning refers to stable pattern and predictability (Moles, 1968). The meaning of core constructs which are constellatory, pre-emptive, and impermeable will be easily disturbed by information, will be well defended by censorship, banning of dissident voices, formalism, and exclusion of contradiction from the public media. These are the political equivalents of intra-psychic defence mechanism.

How is Black Identity Construed by Various Political Groups in South Africa?

White identity was, till the 1960s, the pivot of political identity in South Africa. All others were non-white (or non-European). Since the retreat of colonial powers, black has become the pivot of identity construction. All other identities are construed relative to it, in a series of oppositions or in an attempt to transcend these oppositions. The main oppositions are, obviously, white/black, coloured/black, and (coloured) black/black. The attempt to transcend this opposition, at a superficial level which has not permeated the community, unites all these identities as South African. But there is no core South African identity to which the various groups can be assimilated at a grass roots level. An opposition which would transcend the internal division would have to take the form of South African/Nigerian, American, British, etc.; but black and white South Africans would not form a natural group identity which could be contrasted with Nigerians and Kenyans, etc.

Since black identity is the pivot of South African identity, I shall be examining various construals of black. In doing so, I shall recall a number of themes from previous discussion.

(a) Politics is about the allocation of roles to persons of given identity. The different allocation of roles to blacks and whites in South Africa will be taken as given, and not examined in this chapter.

(b) The "given identity" to which we are referring here is determined by what Kelly referred to as "structuralisation". Power politics is about who may subsume whose identity as an element in the determination of roles.

(c) Since social constructs are validated in social interaction, "structuralisation" may lead to the structuring of a dominated person's self.

(d) Deviance is possible since "structuralisation" can never be complete. There are always "deviant" forms of sociality in which persons validate the nuclei of deviant selves. External deviance and internal deviance reinforce each other, as the person gains different vantage points from which to construe himself and others. Since sociality is always reflexive, persons construe us as we construe them; they construe our construction of their roles and from the vantage point of "deviant" selves may reject the structuralized self, the self as element.

(e) Rejection of the "structuralised" self (the "culturally consolidated self" in Erikson's term), the self which becomes what it does within the grid of shared constructs of the dominant ideology, occurs when other selves are articulated. These implications have to be spelt out in action and words (the person has to know that another self is possible and see what it is like) and have to offer greater possibilities of elaborations of the core self than the "structuralised" self does. Here, we can use Fransella's treatment of stuttering to understand the process by which the person is "cured" of his stereotypes and enabled to see the implications of a preferred self.

When I examine a white construction of black I shall be looking at the way in which a particular group of whites subsumes black identity as an element. I shall be looking at the hostility which results when this construction of black fails. The way in which black identity is construed is an integral part of the construction of white identity. Whites can be what they are because they construe themselves as superior to black.

What I shall be doing here is to look at the ways in which white Nationalist politicians in Parliament, members of the Coloured Persons' Representative Council, and black spokesmen construe black identity. The first construal—that of the whites—is hostile. They are, or so they felt when this investigation was being done, largely in control of events. Attempts to question their construction of events lead to anger and hostility in the form of a flood of bannings, arrests, and detentions occasionally followed by trial. Hostility here has the specific meaning of repeated attempts to validate a social prediction which has already proved itself a failure (Kelly, 1955, p. 510). Many social predictions failed and aroused anger and hostility: among them, that blacks would come to accept separate development, if not apartheid; that the world would accept apartheid; and that everybody could be kept in separate social compartments.

The second construal of black identity is from a marginal position and may be described as anxious. Members of the Coloured Persons' Representative Council have been asking themselves: are we black? or coloured? or neither? The scope and goodness of fit of being black is construed especially in relation to political power.

What are the implications of being black rather than coloured? To be coloured is an old, familiar thing. Will being black enable one to elaborate a preferred self? What is needed is an ideology—and a series of joint projects in which this ideology is tested—to elaborate the "black self" of coloured persons! It is still a mask, a "performed character" for many. One joint project was the spread of the Soweto riots among coloureds of the Western Cape. Another is participation of some coloured leaders in black movements.

In describing this construal of black identity we are drawing on the themes of deviance from structuralised identity by the elaboration of a preferred self. But the elaboration is conscious: the goodness of fit of the elaborated self to the events of South African and world politics must be tested.

Finally, the construal of black identity from the point of view of black movements is examined, as they aggressively construe the implications of being black. Ideological work has been done on the nature of black identity (from Aimé Césaire's nostalgic "negritude" to black theology and black consciousness movements) and these constructions have been validated in African politics on the entire continent. I use the term "validated" in a sweeping manner, to refer to the ill-defined and emerging possibilities of blackness in Africa, not to suggest any definite or coherent programme, but to indicate that there are, now, many ways of being black and self-respecting, black and politically effective, black and culturally active, etc.

I shall now turn to the details of these three construals.

A WHITE CONSTRUCTION OF BLACK

One may attempt to determine identity by naming people. Sometimes this is a right—a "social fact" which no one questions—as when parents name their children, and politically dominant groups name those they dominate. All colonial powers have named the people they rule (natives, kaffirs, bantu, naturelle, niggers, etc.).

An example of the importance attached to naming as a means of controlling identity is to be found in the following debate in the House of Assembly in South Africa in 1958, in which Dr Verwoerd (then Prime Minister) asserted that those who used the term "African" for blacks "want to impress the world that Africa is not the home of the white man or of other peoples" and that "they want to hurt the Afrikaner. They know that the English word 'African' can only be translated if it has to be translated, by something like 'Afrikane'—that only the 'r' of 'Afrikaner' falls away" (Debates, 1958, p. 4052). There must be no confusion of African and Afrikaner, black and white, those who rule and those who are ruled. One of the speakers in the same debate referred to the power of names to transform people.

> I have been right throughout Africa and if up in the North one calls a Swahili an African he will become a Mau Mau . . . the word "African" today is merely a propaganda word which has come into use under Communist influence. (Debates, 1958, p. 799)

Another member attacked those who were pressing for the introduction of the name "African" (to replace "Native"):

> If there is one reason why these honourable members should no longer be in this House, it is the fact that they are trying to entrench this word in the dictionaries of South Africa. (Debates, 1958, p. 4070)

The naming exercise was carried out without consulting those who were being named. "Native" became "Bantu". A recent sign of a change in construction has been the renaming of the Department of Bantu Administration and Development as a result of pressure from black Homeland leaders: it has become the Department of Plural Relations and Development. A further sign of change is the substitution of the word "black" for "bantu" throughout legislative canon at the request of black leaders. (*Cape Times*, 10 June, 1978).

When we examine the debates of the House of Assembly in South Africa from 1948 to 1968, we discover that certain constructs are very generally applied to blacks by white Nationalists. These constructs are superior/ inferior, traditional/modern, natural/estranged. Furthermore, each of these constructs has a pole with a relatively positive value and a pole with a relatively negative value. Traditional blacks are more highly praised than modern ones; and natural blacks are more highly praised than estranged blacks. Natural blacks stick to their group and work for their people; estranged blacks try to penetrate white society and ignore the boundaries. Representative figures are:

Tribesman (traditional and natural)

Modern Homeland leader (modern and natural)

Agitator (modern and estranged)

The most highly valued figure is the tribesman; then we have the Homeland leader (teacher, office worker, etc.); and finally, the agitator is most disliked, since he threatens the boundaries between white and black (see Leach, (1977) on the breaking of boundaries).

How can one extract widely shared constructs from the flow of debate? The method I have chosen is to try to find *clear cases*. That is, I searched for statements which seem to be typical and which are not contradicted by other members of the party. This is rather like the way in which sociolinguists search for clear cases when constructing linguistic arguments.

Let us examine one or two examples to see how this is done.

> Once the detribalised and westernised Native returns for a while to his own country and his own people, he soon realises what he really is. (Debates, 1958, p. 2431)

This statement, read in context, may be seen to contrast traditional versus modern "Natives" and natural versus estranged "Natives". We also discover that the speaker prefers natural, traditional "Natives" to their contrasts. Incidentally, this preference extends also to traditional, natural white figures (the "trekker" and the "boer").

Another example:

> One of the worst crimes we as whites have committed against the Native in South Africa is that we have spoonfed him. (Debates, 1958, p. 3987)

What clearly emerges here—this hardly needs comment—is the construct of white superiority. What also emerges, in context, is a rejection of "estranged people who try to encourage ideas of equality". This is even clearer in the construct between natural blacks on the farms and estranged city blacks in the following:

Natives on the farms are the most fortunate natives in the whole country . . . we know their mentality and what is good for them [whereas city Natives] imagine they are white people. (Debates, 1948, p. 1403)

And, finally, this rejection of estrangement:

According to my reading of the signs of the times, the public will insist within a period of ten years that a criminal charge be brought against any person in South Africa who dares to advocate anything in conflict with the maintenance of the colour bar. (Debates, 1968, p. 148)

Kelly's Sociality Corollary helps us to understand why people make such an identity attribution: to the extent that we can construe another's psychological processes, we can play a social role in relation to him. When, on the other hand, the role is already fixed (that of dominating and exploiting him), the corollary is that we construe his psychological processes so as to fit *him* for the role which has been allotted to him. Furthermore, dominated men frequently acquire the constructs that are attributed to them, not simply because they are attributed to them, but even more because they have to construe the role they are playing every day of their lives.

A note on the limitations of these findings is in order. A question might be put: Do you suppose that the three constructs you have detected (superior/inferior; traditional/modern; natural/estranged) exhaustively characterise the ways in which members of the National Party construe blacks? The answer must be, no. What were detected were merely constructs with a high degree of commonality. A second question which might be put is: How do you know that there is a high degree of commonality to these constructs? There are two arguments here. The first is that these constructs are used with great frequency. Any reading of the statements by members of the National Party on blacks will show that they occur with great frequency. Any examination of National Party policies—certainly between 1948 and 1968—will show that many attempts were made to assert the superiority of whites relative to blacks (in skill, intellect, and civilisation). It would be strange if this were not so. White superiority to blacks was the prevailing ideology of western European powers for most of the first half of the twentieth century. Furthermore, National Party policies were aimed at keeping blacks "traditional" and "separate" (to prevent estrangement and mixing with whites). Measures range from the use of "traditional" systems of law and government to the prevention of mixed marriages by law.

There is also a negative test. Is there any evidence that any white Nationalist Party members supported black superiority (or equality), black modernisation, or black estrangement (by mixing populations)? Thus, not only an accumulation of positive instances, but also the absence of negatives, demonstrates the commonality of the constructs detected in this analysis.

Since 1968 there have been a number of important changes. An examination of parliamentary debates in 1978 shows that the construct of white superiority to blacks has all but vanished. What is important now, is the construct of differentiation, which means that the political relations between whites and blacks are construed in the framework of *nationalism* rather than within the framework of *racial* differences. This is not entirely novel nor is it consistently worked through. Furthermore, critics may point out that the doctrine of separate development, or plural development, or differentiation, serves the functions of the old construct of white superiority. At the political level, this is perfectly true. But at the psychological level, there is a difference between a relationship construed in terms of national differences and a relationship construed in terms of racial differences. The latter construction, by breaking away from biological or innate differences, enables elaborations which are not possible while differences are construed in terms of race.

One can see in tracing the history of the National Party over the last twenty years the progressive emergence of the construct of national differences and the progressive replacement by it of the construct of racial differences. This does not imply that racial differences are no longer important, nor does it imply that construct systems are consistent. Fragmentation is an important property of most construct systems, and certainly an important property of the construction of reality in a very complicated situation.

A MARGINAL CONSTRUCTION OF BLACK

The debates of the Coloured Persons' Representative Council in 1975 and 1976 were analysed to investigate an anxious construction of black identity—in particular, the self-assignment of black identity. The question was: Are we (coloureds) black? Does the construct fit? What are the implications of asserting black identity?

The particular context (both as an implication and as a superordinate construction) which was very much to the fore was *power*. There are black power (potential) and white power (present fact). What does choosing blackness or colouredness or anything else mean in these contexts?

When there are sharp power conflicts, particular dichotomies may subsume all other distinctions, and we get pairs such as worker/bourgeois, Catholic/Protestant, English/Afrikaans, or white/black. Each of these identifications commits the person so identified to a side in the power conflict. For many people, assignment is nearly automatic by virtue of their social characteristics, though even where such assignments appear to be clearest, doubt is often experienced. However, as conflict intensifies, the dividing social characteristics which symbolise disputed power, determine identity to a greater and greater extent.

The element of choice, or doubt, appears to be greatest in a group with intermediate characteristics in the power struggle. In South Africa, groups such as the coloured and Indian people are in a position of some uncertainty in the black/white power struggle, and it is interesting to examine identity self-assignments as these relate to support for different power structures. Precisely because choice appears to be more significant, the relation between affirmation of identity and support for a given power structure will be clearer than it would be where identity is "bestowed".

The freedom of choice of the coloured people may be an illusion. At the moment when they are being offered new conditions and opportunities by the white Government (with the corollary that they remain "coloured"), black power is increasing on every border. This is a dilemma. Choosing between "black" and "coloured" identity implies support for a definite power structure. Since the coloured people make up less than 10% of the total South African population, there is no prospect of their dominating the State on their own, and converting "coloured" identity into a symbol of authority.

The Debates of the Coloured Persons' Representative Council (CPRC) in South Africa selected for analysis were drawn from a period when choice of identity was a particular problem, since it spanned the Soweto insurrection of June 16, 1976. This insurrection, once started, spread to all major centres of South Africa. Black identity was asserted by many coloured people, especially the young. Coloured students were among the first to conflict with the police in the Western Cape area, on 4 August, 1976. During this period, the relationship between political identity and power was particularly clear to many. The dilemma remained. Should representatives of the coloured people in the CPRC support a change in power and identify themselves as black, or should they retain their coloured identity in a system which offered them some advantages relative to Africans?

In the Debates of the CPRC the constructs of power and identity are occasionally linked. It is these links that are of interest, since roles are allotted to persons with given identities by those who control power. Accepting a system of power depends upon a calculation of interests, upon identity as it has been consolidated in cultural exchanges, and upon an attempt "to gain conscious control of the processes of species self-creation, both technical and cultural" (Sullivan, 1975, p. 90), in the interests of a vision of human dignity.

The first question which faces members of the CPRC is the implication of the name of the Council. Does participation imply that they accept their identification as "coloured"? Or are they "so-called" coloured? Are they black? The dilemma is that accepting a name embodied in the legislation of the dominant white group is tantamount to accepting white separatist ideology. The rejection of separate categories is also seen in the following exchange between Mr Africa (aptly named!) and Mr Adam. Mr Africa is quoting census statistics:

> *Africa*: . . . there will be a coloured population of six million in South Africa.
> *Adams*: How many White souls?
> *Africa*: Six million Whites as well.
> *Adams*: How many Africans?
> *Africa*: 24 million Africans.
> *Adams*: And Indians?
> *Africa*: I am . . .
> *Adams*: Now this is the idea you are propagating: Coloured, Indian, African, White . . . (Debates, 1975, p. 224)

The second question which all members of the CPRC face is: Why are we here? Can the CPRC be taken seriously? Is participation an act of treachery? Is participation a denial of the universalist claim that most participants make? Rayne Kruger is his "Good-bye Dolly Gray" makes this observation:

> The anquished decision of people under enemy occupation is a recurring theme among tragedies of war. Aside from the rank opportunist or award, one man sees "collaboration" as his highest duty towards his own people as sincerely as another believes in dogged opposition at any cost. The fact remains that "collaboration" enjoys little esteem. (Kruger, 1959, p. 456)

He is commenting on the Boers who decided to collaborate with the British towards the end of the Boer War of 1899–1902 and those who decided to go on to the bitter end, refusing to bend. The coloured people are in the position of a vanquished population, subject to laws in which they have no say. Should they collaborate, given an opportunity and the promise of further advancement? Here is one point of view:

> Mr Chairman, any politician who sees the oppressor giving him a platform to organise against him, and refuses to use it, must have his head examined. (Debates, 1975, p. 147)

The other point of view surfaces when the institution is mocked as in the following exchanges (translated where marked by an asterisk):

> *Bergins*: Perhaps the Labourites will become an effective party, then. *
> *Kleinsmidt*: Wake up from your dream world, man, you are dreaming.
> *Africa*: Who's talking in the "kitchen"? *
> $\qquad\qquad\qquad\qquad\qquad\qquad\qquad$ (Debates, 1975, p. 173)
> *Fortuin*: It was always the same old tune: Ja baas, ja baas. And what the baas said, went. *
> *An Honourable member*: And who is saying, "ja baas" now? *
> *Pietersen*: You say "ja baas" very prettily. *
> $\qquad\qquad\qquad\qquad\qquad\qquad\qquad$ (Debates, 1975, pp. 128 –129)
> (the "ja baas" theme occurs several times—1975, pp. 113, 117)
> *Bergins*: It was a real pleasure for me to do that for my people . . .

Adams: Everything else, Bill you gave away, because your lord and master said: Hotnot, you will execute my command. *

(Debates, 1975, p. 61)

Bergins: Are we still in 1948 or in 1950, or are we going towards the end of the seventy decade?
Adams: You are still in the Great Trek era, Hotnot.

(Debates, 1975, p. 192)

The decision to participate in the CPRC requires a resolution of the relation of identity and power. What system of power is acceptable and what set of identities is implied by that system?

The anxiety and guilt of the speakers is shown by the fact that virtually every speaker questioned the implications of being in the Representative Council. For most, the question of the goodness of fit of their constructions of identity and participation was a serious issue; for many, the dislodgement of self from core role structures (defiance, rejection of white domination) was equally serious. The problem of goodness of fit comes up in statements such as the following:

> All of us, the so-called Coloured people have the right to be here, the so-called black people of Africa, the so-called white people, we all have a right to be here. (Debates, 1975, p. 22)

Dislodgement of the self from core role structures comes up clearly in mockery of the CPRC as a "kitchen" and of the participants as "Hotnots". When we turn to identity self-assignments explicity made by 50 speakers in 1975 and 1976, we find a minority who describe themselves as "Coloured" (9). There is, as we would expect in a marginal group, a scatter of self identifications: 14 claim a common identity for all South Africans; and relatively few identify themselves black (7). The remaining 20 rejected identification as black, white, or coloured, but did not indicate what they accepted. Presumably, many favoured a common South African identity.

The results of 1975 and 1976 may be pooled since there was no significant difference between the two. The first characteristic of identity statements is therefore that there is no unanimity. This is only to be expected, as we have said before, in a marginal group.

We now turn to the way in which acceptance of the given power structure and a corresponding identity imply each other. It is not possible, in the present study, to decide which is superordinate. Is acceptable identity decided in the context of a construal of power structure? Or is acceptable power structure decided in the context of a construct of identity? I suspect that power is the context in terms of which identity is elaborated and chosen, but cannot offer firm evidence.

Again, pooling the results of 1975 and 1976, it was found that those who accepted white domination or a coloured/white coalition also identified themselves as coloured (three speakers); those who rejected white domination and those who accepted equality asserted a common South African non-racial identity (11 speakers); and of the two who accept black domination, one identifies himself as black and the other is not clear (two speakers).

Only 14 speakers out of a total of 50 speakers (27 in 1975 and 23 in 1976) were explicit enough about the link between power and identity to be coded. This is to be expected of people in a highly exposed situation which is fraught with anxiety. Will black domination be preferable to white domination? Would speakers be accepted as blacks? These are questions it is not possible to answer: life has to be lived forward and understood backward, as Kierkegaard says somewhere.

Changes in explicit self-identification of some members of the CPRC may follow the closer involvement of the Labour Party with Inkhatha, the Black Cultural Freedom Movement, since the twelfth annual congress of the Labour Party in 1977.

A BLACK CONSTRUCTION OF BLACK

What has been observed, since the decolonisation of Ghana and other African territories, is an increase in the aggressive construal of "black", where aggression refers to "the active elaboration of one's construct system" (Bannister and Fransella, 1971, p. 121). This active elaboration has been validated by political and cultural success—it is not simply "ideas" that are validated, but constructs, or practices.

What was the state of dominated man till recently? "The strongest ally of the oppressor is the mind of the oppressed" (Boesak, 1976, p. 48). This statement sums up the situation well. This is one of the main themes in the seminal writings of Fanon (1970) and Mannoni (1956). Erikson (1968, p. 503) refers to the self-hate which is induced by "negative images cruelly imposed" on minorities (and this includes all dominated men) and sees hope in the creation of a more inclusive identity which "supersedes the struggle of the old—positive and negative—images and roles" (1968, p. 505). Here the theme of the aggressive elaboration of self and its core constructs is touched upon.

What we characteristically observe in people who have been construed in a negative way and who have been forced to validate this negative construal (by taking menial jobs, by public slights, political powerlessness, being "named" bantu, native, kaffir, nigger, etc., by being educated separately, by military defeat, and so forth) is that this construal is difficult to resist while there are not opportunities for alternative self-construal. The validation of a new, positive construal of the self depends, not simply on words, but on actions. The existentialist axiom that existence precedes essence can be taken to mean that core constructs have to be validated in action.

A first attempt at choosing a self which is not negative is almost always violent. It is often remarked, in the initial stages of the transformation of identity, that violence is "irrationally" directed against the property and persons of those closest to the rebels. Churches, schools, libraries, clinics and shops which "serve" the "negative" selves of the rebels are burnt and looted (as in Soweto). This violence is directed against the old self which belongs to the powerful others anyway. If social action depends on construing the other's processes, then the first act of rebellion is to validate the other's construal of our processes. "To ask blacks to love themselves is to ask them to hate oppression, de-humanisation, and the cultivation of a slave mentality" (Boesak, 1976, p. 28).

Another first step is the rejection of the presence of "liberals" and others who attempt to bridge the differences between self and others, in black liberation movements. This is not peculiar to black movements. It was a feature of the Afrikaner National Party as well, which was, initially, for Afrikaners and only for Afrikaners. The black liberation movements are for blacks; this has been stated by Thula (1978), Biko (1978), Khoapa (1972), and Mangayi (1973), among others. Khoapa expresses it well: "Here, as elsewhere, the devil must be driven out first. It is too soon to love everybody", and "black integration must precede black and white integration" (1972, p. 64).

The alternatives imposed by whites are integration and segregation, and it is this dichotomy which prevents black liberation—which prevents the liberation of any minority. While the minority group is segregated, it is by definition dominated; it seems natural, therefore, to suggest that liberation can be achieved by integration. But integration of what? The integration of men who acquiesce in their own domination, who hate themselves, with men who are dominant, simply prolongs domination. The liberal vision prolongs domination. We have heard of "repressive tolerance"; Mauk Mulder (1977) observes that mixing the powerful and powerless in single groups simply aids the powerful in establishing their superiority. It is for this reason that the path to autonomy, to the power and capacity to elaborate one's construct system in one's own way, must lie in ignoring those who dominate. This seems peculiar. How is it different from segregation? Segregation is imposed by dominant groups to validate their construction of events; ignoring those who dominate is practised by subordinate groups to liberate themselves from the presence of dominant men.

Central to integration and separation is the white man. Blacks must either move towards or away from him. But his presence is not nearly so crucial for those who pursue a course of "liberation". Ideally they do whatever they conceive they must do as if whites did not exist at all. (Khoapa, 1972, p. 62)

Khoapa is very much aware of the "mystification" of universal brotherhood when it is used to oppress. He is also very aware of the social context in which racial conflict can be solved: there must be objective economic and political equality.

Ignoring the oppressor is not enough. One might ignore the world by burying one's head in the sand. Liberation—the extension of the construct system so that integration/segregation is subordinated to the construct of justice/injustice, where justice must be understood in terms of the extension of the Sociality Corollary to include a generalisation of perspectives on the self and others—must be achieved by the formation of groups to achieve equality and resist domination. Individuals must be freed by achieving communal freedom, by altering the social system by which constructs are validated. An ideal social system is a system in which people elaborate each other's construct systems. This can only be achieved when generalisation of perspectives makes justice possible.

In order to achieve integration we must have a sense of common identity—of belonging together. But the first stage of this is a sharpening of separation. The division between black and white will be deepened from both sides. No common identity of dominant and dominated man is possible. Segregation must first become separation—the division of unequal people must become the division of equals. And only then will a common identity be possible (though by no means inevitable). This is the argument of those who oppose nationalism by nationalism or racism by a new kind of racism. Is it at all possible to skip the stage of division and achieve the stage of integration without it? One would hope so. But the history of emerging minority groups does not fill one with optimism. Yet a revolution in which men change their masters while preserving their old constructs is not a very hopeful one, nor can one be sure that the thesis and anthithesis of white and black racism or white and black nationalism will be succeeded by a synthesis in which racism and different nationality is forgotten.

Conclusions: And how can we Construe a Political Construct?

Personal construct theory has a number of assets in analysing political issues. We see how "emotion" is related to "action", since emotions are constructs in transition; we see how revolutions may trap people in the same old dilemmas, when movement is along the same dimension; we see people continue to make bad choices when the alternatives seem worse to them; and we see that behaviour is a matter of personal context—a matter of finding ways of elaborating constructs—rather than a matter of cause and effect. We catch the essential social nature of man in our formulation of the essential problem of politics which is: how do we place a construction on events which will enable more people to define and extend their construction of events?

Perhaps what we need is a social contract corollary to supplement the Sociality Corollary:

> To the extent that a person is able to construe third party perspectives on the roles he and others are playing with respect to each other, he can enter a social contract based on general principles.

What we are saying of the person is that he should do more than construe the processes of another: he should imagine how his and the other persons' psychological processes could be construed from the perspective of a third party.

It would be pleasant to think that such a move would solve our problem; but difficulties soon appear when we try to move to the solution of a concrete problem. Should one cancel a seminar when students are having a strike in support of some generally appealing and morally uplifting issue? Roger Brown tellingly describes the difficulties (Brown and Hernstein, 1975, p. 330).

Still, one might agree that the social contract corollary is a necessary condition for entering into principled (and just) relations, when it is allied with such manoeuvres as an obligation to adopt the "original position" (Rawls, 1971). Perhaps, even more important, it should be allied with the obligation to check one's findings by asking people for their construction of the social contract as well! Necessary conditions do not ensure that one ends up in the right place. They are necessary, but not sufficient.

There is another difficulty. People often "talk good and behave rotten". Why, if they can see what is just, don't they do it? The same populations of American students who attained high levels of moral reasoning (on Kohlberg's tasks) were the populations who were "capable of deceitful conformity, vandalism, and indifference to the life and death problems of strangers". Brown and Hernstein concluded (they were not the first to do so) that talk and act may be governed by different variables. This, in itself, does not add much to popular wisdom. A visit to prison led to an observation which was more to the point.

> What should one say of people who reason at stages 1 and 2 when the realities of the world they live in are also at stages 1 and 2? Have they not abstracted the principles it is intelligent to abstract in this situation? (Brown and Hernstein, 1975, p. 325)

And what do we say of those (students and others) who reason at stages 5 and 6 and behave according to the principles of stages 1 and 2?

The point is that social institutions have to support moral reasoning. People will be as principled as they may be. We have to create the institutions in which reasoning and persuasion are more effective than punishment and killing. Hayek (1978), in a recent treatment of the arbitrariness of parliaments, captures this very well. If parliament is absolute and if the only way to get to parliament is by winning the support of interested groups, then we have systematised corruption. Parliament is not *under* the law; or *under* the social contract. The extent of the problem is clear in situations where interest groups are in sharp conflict, as is often the case in plural societies. Most people will be as good as they can be. The bulk of the research shows both that most adults are capable of high levels of moral reasoning and that they are very often induced to behave immorally in particular situations (Asch, 1952; Milgram, 1974; Zimbardo, 1975). This applies as much to the experimenters as to their "subjects".

As Santayana said of Shelley: "For this world is a lumbering mechanism and not, like love, a plastic dream" (Santayana, 1968, p. 175).

Some Research Problems

Under what conditions does national or ethnic identity become a Nationalist movement? The first refers to shared self-description; the second refers to the translation of these into a search for political autonomy or power. For the identification of an individual there must be an "induplicable accumulation of imprecise determination" (Devereux, 1975, p. 43). This applies equally to a group. The shared determinations of language, country, race, religion, customs, identify that group and can transcend class in Nationalist movements. What are the crises that bring about nationalism?

In this chapter I have referred to the way in which people may be grouped by "structuralisation", when their behaviours are arranged under the public construction system of dominant persons. In this arrangement, they become the negative image of the dominant group: they are classified under the construct poles of the shared constructs of the ruling ideology. There are two ways out of this. They may invert the ideology and become positive where they were negative, or they may seek an elaboration of identity in another construct system altogether. In the first instance, one power movement is replaced by another, its negative image. In the second instance, a new way out is sought (as, for example, other-worldly religions have sought a way out of power conflicts by presenting salvation in another world).

Can we give the sort of account of the development of group political identity that Erikson has given of individual identity? We can discern the outline of a number of stages, ranging from the establishment of the basic ingredients of community (language, modes of sociality) to the response of aggressive nationalism when autonomy is threatened and the struggle for integrity when and if material problems have been solved. This may seem fanciful, but accounts of transition must be given if we are to get beyond static description. We can trace, in the history of countries in which new national identity is being shaped, the first steps in which a language is created and distinctive social features are recognised—often the point of articulation is a moment of confrontation with the new (see Giliomee, 1975, for an account of the early development of Afrikaner self-description)—followed by desperate struggles for autonomy (the American civil war, the Boer wars) and a period of domination in which there is a struggle to achieve integrity.

The great question, in the life and death of a nation, is how to achieve community—a sense of common identity for all its people. The difficulty faced by many countries is that there is no acceptable identity to which all may be assimilated. Turk and Greek, Jew and Arab, Afrikaner and Zulu: What can they have in common? Yet why should they oppose each other?

Though the mere existence of exclusive national identities does not necessarily result in nationalism, in a world where equality is rare, differentials in access to power and to material resources will often occur between ethnic groups. It is then that struggles in which class interests take racist or ethnic forms occur.

How can we ensure that a multiplicity of group identities does not become a politics of identity? This is a problem to be studied by psychologists who hope to see men "loosen their chains" as well as "change their masters" (Kelly, 1962, p. 87).

References

Asch, S. E. (1952). "Social Psychology". Prentice-Hall, Englewood Cliffs, New Jersey.

Bannister, D. and Fransella, F. (1971). "Inquiring Man: The Theory of Personal Constructs". Penguin, Harmondsworth.

Bettenson, H. S. (1947). "Documents of the Christian Church". Oxford University Press, Oxford.

Biko, S. Quoted in "Die Burger", 1978 (20 February). "We exclude whites from our struggle because of the inherent contradiction which arises out of the participation of whites in the process of change" (my translation).

Boesak, A. A. (1976). "Farewell to Innocence: A Social-Clinical Study of Black Theology and Black Power". Ravan Press, Johannesburg.

Brown, R. and Hernstein, R. J. (1975). "Psychology". Methuen, London.

Devereux, G. (1975). *In* "Ethnic Identity: Cultural Continuities and Change" (Eds G. de Vos and Lola Romanucci-Ross), pp. 42–70. Mayfield.

Erikson, E. H. (1963). "Childhood and Society" (2nd edn). Norton, New York.

Erikson, E. H. (1968). *In* "Nonviolent Direct Action" (Eds A. Paul Hare and H. H. Blumberg), pp. 492–512. Corpus Books, Washington and Cleveland.

Erikson, E. H. (1971). "Identity: Youth and Crisis". Faber and Faber, London.

Fanon, F. (1970). "Black Skin White Masks" (translated by C. L. Markman). Paladin, London.

Fingarette, H. (1969). "Self-Deception". Routledge and Kegan Paul, London.

Fransella, F. and Frost, K. (1977). "On Being a Woman". Tavistock, London.

Giliomee, H. (1975). *In* "Identiteit en Verandering" (Ed. H. W. van der Merwe), pp. 17–53. Tafelberg, Cape Town.

Goffman, E. (1959). "The Presentation of Self in Everyday Life". Doubleday, Garden City, New York.

Goffman, E. (1961). "Asylums". Doubleday, Garden City, New York.

Hayek, F. A. (1978). The miscarriage of the democratic ideal. *Encounter,* **50,** 14–17.

Kelly, G. A. (1955). "A Theory of Personality". Norton, New York.

Kelly, G. A. (1962). *In* "Nebraska Symposium on Motivation" (Ed. M. Jones), pp. 83–123. University of Nebraska Press, Lincoln.

Khoapa, B. A. (1972). *In* "Black Viewpoint" (Ed. B. S. Bhiko), pp. 61–67. Spro-Cas, Durban.

Kruger, R. (1959). "Good-bye Dolly Gray". Cassell, London.

Leach, E. (1977). Profanity and context. *New Scientist,* **76,** 136–139.

Mair, J. M. M. (1977). *In* "New Perspectives in Personal Construct Theory" (Ed. D. Bannister), pp. 125–149. Academic Press, London and New York.

Mangayi, N. C. (1973). "Being-Black-in-the-World". Spro-Cas/Ravan, Johannesburg.

Mannoni, O. (1956). "Prospero and Caliban; the Psychology of Colonisation". Methuen, London.

McCoy, M. M. (1977). *In* "New Perspectives in Personal Construct Theory" (Ed. D. Bannister), pp. 93–124. Academic Press, London and New York.

McKellar, P. (1977). Multiple personality. *Psychology Today,* 44–46.

Milgram, S. (1974). "Obedience to Authority". Harper and Row, New York.

Moles, A. (1968). "Information Theory and Esthetic Perception". University of Illinois Press, Urbana.

Mulder, M. (1977). "The Daily Power Game". Martinus Nijhoff, Leiden.

Mussen, P. (1967). *In* "New Directions in Psychology III" (Ed. T. M. Newcombe), pp. 51–110. Holt, Rinehart and Winston, New York.

Osgood, C. and Luria, Z. (1954). A blind analysis of a case of multiple personality using the semantic differential. *J. Abnorm. Soc. Psychol.* **49,** 579–591.

Osgood, C., Luria, Z., Smith, S. and Jeans, R. F. (1976). The three faces of Evelyn: a case report. *J. Abnorm. Psychol.* **85,** 247–286.

Rawls, J. (1971). "A Theory of Justice". Bellknap Press, Cambridge, Mass.

Sandall, R. (1978). On the way to the pig festival. *Encounter* **51,** 63–70.

Santayana, G. (1968). "Selected Critical Writings" (Ed. N. Henfrey), Vol. 1. Cambridge University Press, Cambridge.

Sartre, J-P. (1957). "Being and Nothingness". Methuen, London.

Sullivan, W. M. (1975). Options in modern social theory: Haboneas and Whitehead. *Int. Philosoph. Q.* **XV,** 83–98.

Thula, G. (1978). The process of power sharing. Paper presented to the 48th Annual Congress of the South African Institute of Race Relations.

Zimbardo, P. G. (1975). *In* "Applying Social Psychology" (Eds M. Deutsch and H. A. Hernstein), pp. 33–66. Lawrence Erlbaum, Hillsdale.

Author Index

Page numbers in italics refer to reference lists.

365

Subject Index